Optimizing E-Participation Initiatives Through Social Media

Laura Alcaide-Muñoz
University of Granada, Spain

Francisco José Alcaraz-Quiles
University of Granada, Spain

A volume in the Advances in Wireless
Technologies and Telecommunication
(AWTT) Book Series

Published in the United States of America by
    IGI Global
    Information Science Reference (an imprint of IGI Global)
    701 E. Chocolate Avenue
    Hershey PA, USA 17033
    Tel: 717-533-8845
    Fax: 717-533-8661
    E-mail: cust@igi-global.com
    Web site: http://www.igi-global.com

Library of Congress Cataloging-in-Publication Data

Names: Alcaide Munoz, Laura, 1980- editor. | Alcaraz Quiles, Francisco
    Jose, 1972- editor.
Title: Optimizing E-participation initiatives through social media / Laura
    Alcaide Munoz and Francisco Jose Alcaraz Quiles, editors.
Description: Hershey, PA : Information Science Reference, 2018. | Includes
    bibliographical references.
Identifiers: LCCN 2017040010| ISBN 9781522553267 (hardcover) | ISBN
    9781522553274 (ebook)
Subjects: LCSH: Political participation--Technological innovations. | Social
    media--Political aspects. | Internet in public administration.
Classification: LCC JF799.5 .O75 2018 | DDC 323/.04202854678--dc23 LC record available at
https://lccn.loc.gov/2017040010

This book is published in the IGI Global book series Advances in Wireless Technologies and Telecommunication (AWTT) (ISSN: 2327-3305; eISSN: 2327-3313)

British Cataloguing in Publication Data
A Cataloguing in Publication record for this book is available from the British Library.

All work contributed to this book is new, previously-unpublished material.
The views expressed in this book are those of the authors, but not necessarily of the publisher.

For electronic access to this publication, please contact: eresources@igi-global.com.

Advances in Wireless Technologies and Telecommunication (AWTT) Book Series

ISSN:2327-3305
EISSN:2327-3313

Editor-in-Chief: Xiaoge Xu, Xiamen University Malaysia, Malaysia

MISSION

The wireless computing industry is constantly evolving, redesigning the ways in which individuals share information. Wireless technology and telecommunication remain one of the most important technologies in business organizations. The utilization of these technologies has enhanced business efficiency by enabling dynamic resources in all aspects of society.

The **Advances in Wireless Technologies and Telecommunication Book Series** aims to provide researchers and academic communities with quality research on the concepts and developments in the wireless technology fields. Developers, engineers, students, research strategists, and IT managers will find this series useful to gain insight into next generation wireless technologies and telecommunication.

COVERAGE

- Cellular Networks
- Broadcasting
- Digital Communication
- Global Telecommunications
- Network Management
- Mobile Web Services
- Wireless Technologies
- Radio Communication
- Telecommunications
- Grid Communications

IGI Global is currently accepting manuscripts for publication within this series. To submit a proposal for a volume in this series, please contact our Acquisition Editors at Acquisitions@igi-global.com or visit: http://www.igi-global.com/publish/.

The Advances in Wireless Technologies and Telecommunication (AWTT) Book Series (ISSN 2327-3305) is published by IGI Global, 701 E. Chocolate Avenue, Hershey, PA 17033-1240, USA, www.igi-global.com. This series is composed of titles available for purchase individually; each title is edited to be contextually exclusive from any other title within the series. For pricing and ordering information please visit http://www.igi-global.com/book-series/advances-wireless-technologies-telecommunication/73684. Postmaster: Send all address changes to above address. ©© 2018 IGI Global. All rights, including translation in other languages reserved by the publisher. No part of this series may be reproduced or used in any form or by any means – graphics, electronic, or mechanical, including photocopying, recording, taping, or information and retrieval systems – without written permission from the publisher, except for non commercial, educational use, including classroom teaching purposes. The views expressed in this series are those of the authors, but not necessarily of IGI Global.

Titles in this Series

For a list of additional titles in this series, please visit:
https://www.igi-global.com/book-series/advances-wireless-technologies-telecommunication/73684

Examining Cloud Computing Technologies Through the Internet o Things
Pradeep Tomar (Gautam Buddha University, India) and Gurjit Kaur (Gautam Buddha University, India)
Information Science Reference • ©2018 • 311pp • H/C (ISBN: 9781522534457) • US $215.00

Advanced Mobile Technologies for Secure Transaction Processing Emerging Research ...
Raghvendra Kumar (LNCT Group of Colleges, India) Preeta Sharan (The Oxford College of Engineering, India) and Aruna Devi (Surabhi Software, India)
Information Science Reference • ©2018 • 177pp • H/C (ISBN: 9781522527596) • US $130.00

Examining Developments and Applications of Wearable Devices in Modern Society
Saul Emanuel Delabrida Silva (Federal University of Ouro Preto, Brazil) Ricardo Augusto Rabelo Oliveira (Federal University of Ouro Preto, Brazil) and Antonio Alfredo Ferreira Loureiro (Federal University of Minas Gerais (UFMG), Brazil)
Information Science Reference • ©2018 • 330pp • H/C (ISBN: 9781522532903) • US $195.00

Graph Theoretic Approaches for Analyzing Large-Scale Social Networks
Natarajan Meghanathan (Jackson State University, USA)
Information Science Reference • ©2018 • 355pp • H/C (ISBN: 9781522528142) • US $225.00

Powering the Internet of Things With 5G Networks
Vasuky Mohanan (Universiti Sains Malaysia, Malaysia) Rahmat Budiarto (Albaha University, Saudi Arabia) and Ismat Aldmour (Albaha University, Saudi Arabia)
Information Science Reference • ©2018 • 304pp • H/C (ISBN: 9781522527992) • US $215.00

Routing Protocols and Architectural Solutions for Optimal Wireless Networks and Security
Dharm Singh (Namibia University of Science and Technology, Namibia)
Information Science Reference • ©2017 • 277pp • H/C (ISBN: 9781522523420) • US $205.00

For an entire list of titles in this series, please visit:
https://www.igi-global.com/book-series/advances-wireless-technologies-telecommunication/73684

701 East Chocolate Avenue, Hershey, PA 17033, USA
Tel: 717-533-8845 x100 • Fax: 717-533-8661
E-Mail: cust@igi-global.com • www.igi-global.com

List of Reviewers

Cristina Alcaide-Muñoz, *Public University of Navarre, Spain*
Fatima Alsaif, *Victoria University of Wellington, New Zealand*
Cenay Babaoglu, *Nigde Omer Halisdemir University, Turkey*
Ransome Bawack, *Catholic University of Central Africa, Cameroon*
Juana María del Mar Camacho-Miñano, *Complutense University of Madrid, Spain*
Robert Niewiadomski, *Hunter College – The City University of New York, USA*
Sherwin Ona, *De La Salle University, Philippines*
David Pascual-Ezama, *Complutense University of Madrid, Spain*
Elena Urquía-Grande, *Complutense University of Madrid, Spain*
Brenda Vale, *Victoria University of Wellington, New Zealand*
David Valle-Cruz, *Universidad Autónoma del Estado de México, Mexico*
Farhad Yusifov, *Institute of Information Technology of Azerbaijan National Academy of Sciences, Azerbaijan*

Table of Contents

Section 2
Case Studies of Social Media in Developing Countries

Section 3
Behavior of Social Media Users: Tools, Platforms, and Apps

Detailed Table of Contents

Section 1
Role of Social Media in Citizens' Participation: Trends, Challenges, and Future Research

Chapter 1

>   *Cristina Alcaide-Muñoz, Public University of Navarre, Spain*
>   *Laura Alcaide-Muñoz, University of Granada, Spain*
>   *Francisco José Alcaraz-Quiles, University of Granada, Spain*

Citizens increasingly demand an active role in public affairs and decision-making processes. From a critical standpoint, this chapter consolidates existing knowledge and, in turn, provides a better understanding on how social media tools promote the citizens' engagement and participation. The main aim is to assist researchers in the development of their future analyses, identifying trends of research and the methodology used. In so doing, a systematic literature review has been used to examine social media and e-participation research in journals listed in ISI in the field of public administration and information science and library science during the period 2000-2016. The findings reveal that although research on social media and e-participation has increased in the last year, it remains immature. Therefore, further research is needed in order to understand the true impacts of social media tools and their involvement in e-participation.

Chapter 2

Rasim M. Alguliyev, Institute of Information Technology of Azerbaijan
National Academy of Sciences, Azerbaijan
Farhad F. Yusifov, Institute of Information Technology of Azerbaijan
National Academy of Sciences, Azerbaijan

The rapid development of ICT has a significant impact on the lifestyle of and communication among people. Such impact tendencies alter the human activity as well as government functions and the ways these are implemented. The studies related to Web 2.0, social media, social networks, and their use in the government sector show that the issues such as the formation of social media and important role of the latter in public administration have become a broad research topic. Despite the presence of various approaches of states to social media and social media analytics in international practice, the large impact of social media on public administration is of no doubt. The chapter reviews such issues in the presence of the goal of building mutual communication between government bodies and citizens, the role of social media in building feedback between e-government and citizens, the use of social media in e-government, and the transformation of administrative mechanisms.

Chapter 3

Robert Niewiadomski, Hunter College – The City University of New
York, USA
Dennis Anderson, St. Francis College, USA

The recent rise of populism around the world, often accompanied by nationalism and isolationism, is a trend that presents a serious threat not only to liberal democracies but also to global peace and security. Populist forces have already shown their influence through the British referendum on membership withdrawal from the European Union and the election of Donald J. Trump as the U.S. President in 2016. These two events alone had ripple effects and were felt by the international community. The causes of populism are being currently revisited. It appears that socioeconomic and cultural aspects are key contributors. Even though the persistent existence of populist elements within societies comes from the very core of the democratic experiment, the current trend in social media technologies allowed demagogues to utilize viral deception on a considerable scale. The authors argue that social media technologies could be employed through e-participation to inhibit populism by bolstering civic empowerment, transparency, progressive inclusiveness, fact-based analysis, and informed decision making.

Section 2
Case Studies of Social Media in Developing Countries

Chapter 4

Cenay Babaoglu, Nigde Omer Halisdemir University, Turkey
Elvettin Akman, Suleyman Demirel University, Turkey

By improving ICT within the scope of administration, new terms like e-government, m-government, e-governance, e-participation appeared in the field of public administration. The concept of e-government affects municipalities—closest service units to the citizens—and with this effect developed the term e-municipality. Municipalities in Turkey began to use the new technologies for the delivery of services, and terms like e-participation and e-governance are widening rapidly. This chapter investigates whether Facebook pages are an effective tool for local participation. The social media-citizen relationship that is claimed to be more effective, especially at the local level, has been evaluated through the Facebook pages of the municipalities. This chapter focuses on the role of social media in participatory administration.

Chapter 5

David Valle-Cruz, Universidad Autónoma del Estado de México, Mexico
Rodrigo Sandoval-Almazan, Universidad Autónoma del Estado de
*   México, Mexico*

In this chapter, the authors show two case studies of the use of social media in municipal governments: Lerma, a small municipality with a significant growth, and Metepec, an important municipality of the State of México. The purpose of this chapter is to provide empirical evidence of how social media improves government to citizen relationship and promotes e-participation in municipal governments. The results are based on semi-structured interviews applied to public servants and a survey to evaluate e-government services by citizens. So, the citizen perception is contrasted with public servants' interviews. Citizens consider that electronic procedures and services implemented by their municipalities do not generate value. The efforts of governments should focus on avoiding corruption, making governments transparent, opening data, and properly managing the privacy of information.

This chapter on e-participation in developing countries uses Cameroon as a case study
to demonstrate the realities of practicing Web 2.0 and social media tools to drive
collaborative initiatives between government agencies and citizens in developing
countries. The case study was guided by the incentives for e-participation using social
media technologies, the tools used by a government to drive such initiatives, the level
of participation from citizens, and the challenges and risks faced in implementing
these technologies. A study of Cameroon's National Social Insurance Fund (NSIF)
confirmed the main incentives of e-participation initiatives in developing countries
and the major challenges they face in implementing them.

Networks for cyberactivism have been developed in Brazil since the end of the 20th
century. This chapter presents results of a three-year research about networks for
digital political participation developed by civil society. The research analyzed 41
networks according to specific analytical categories to deepen the understanding about
their potential to foster citizens' engagement in political initiatives and strengthen
democracy. Several mechanisms that considerably stimulate a culture of political
participation were clearly observed. Possibilities for political acting through those
networks tend to narrow the gap between citizens' claims and government actions but
that is not always the case. There is a lack of synergy between citizens' demands and
strategic planning of public policies and other political outcomes. Some hypotheses
are discussed to understand this context and reflect on the trends and challenges to
digital democracy in the twenty-first century.

Sherwin E. Ona, De La Salle University, Philippines
Ma. Beth S. Concepcion, De La Salle University, Philippines

Open government initiatives around the world have encouraged governments to be more transparent and accessible while its partners have found new venues to further participate and collaborate. However, realities on the ground have begun to show the complexities of openness, raising questions on how these initiatives could be sustained. In the Philippines, most of the open government-open government data (OG-OGD) programs are considered top-down. This means that almost all of the activities are initiated by the national government and are often funded by multilateral agencies such as the World Bank. However, due to the changes in political priorities, the future of these programs remains uncertain. Current experiences further highlight the importance of institutionalization as one of the ingredients to sustain these initiatives; thus, the authors believe that building capacities play an important part in such an endeavor. As such, this chapter presents an initial set of OG-OGD performance competencies for local government executives and their civil society partners.

Section 3
Behavior of Social Media Users: Tools, Platforms, and Apps

Fatimah Alsaif, Victoria University of Wellington, New Zealand
Brenda Vale, Victoria University of Wellington, New Zealand

This chapter examines the effectiveness of using social media as an aid to primary school students participating in the design of their classroom interior layout. It describes two different attempts to do this that achieved varying degrees of success. Where a blog and Facebook page were set up to provide a virtual space for classroom design to happen, and despite teachers' expressed enthusiasm for involving students in the design of their classroom layout, very few participants resulted. However, one school successfully used the virtual space to show the work of the children and this example is described in the chapter. Social media was of more use in a second example where it formed an additional channel of communication between the researcher in the role of architect and the students. However, here it built on face-to-face communication, suggesting social media can aid in participatory design but is not a substitute for the latter.

Chapter 10

Naser Valaei, KEDGE Business School, France
S. R. Nikhashemi, Sultan Qaboos University, Oman
Hwang Ha Jin, Sunway University, Malaysia
Michael M. Dent, Sunway University, Malaysia

The purpose of this chapter is to examine what aspects of task-technology characteristics are most relevant to fit, satisfaction, and continuance intention of using apps in mobile banking transactions. Applying the SEM approach to a sample of 250 Malaysians, the findings of this chapter imply that the task characteristic of transaction-based apps is more relevant than technology characteristics. The results suggest that degree of fit is highly associated with mobile apps user satisfaction. Furthermore, the higher the degree of fit, the higher is the continuance intention to use apps for online transactions. Surprisingly, the findings show that the task characteristics are not relevant to continuous intention to use apps for online transactions.

Foreword

In the last decades, many governments around the world have undertaken numerous efforts in the implementation of Information and Communication Technologies (ICTs), which have played a key role in democratic, political and governance process. These technological advances represent the new alternatives and initiatives to representative democracy and hierarchical governance. Specially, the innovation and development of e-Government favored the participation opportunities between public managers, politicians and citizens.

Nowadays, the citizens demand greater participation in public affairs for which they need to have access to a greater volume of information. Public organizations, in particular Local Governments, are using new platforms, channels and tools via Internet to reach a wider audience and disclose a huge amount of information for a relatively low cost. In this context, social media technologies support interactive participation between policy-makers and citizens in real time, which represents an important strategy for improving trust in local governments. Social media allow the citizens to offer feedback, comments, ideas, knowledge, opinions and experiences about the public services, public policies, social initiatives, health systems and so on. In fact, the politician could perceive social media technologies as an opportunity to communicate with the public, giving citizens a more active advisory role in public affairs.

In this book, the contributions seek to assist researches and academics in the development of their future analyses, identifying trends of research, barriers in the use of social media, and challenges to be undertaken. The chapters including in this books show with case studies (Mexico, Turkey, Cameroon, Malaysia, Brazil, or Philippines) how the use of social media platforms allows government to communicate more efficiently with citizens. This way of acting increases the efficiency and effectiveness in public sector.

The authors highlighted that e-Participation initiatives using Web 2.0 and social media tools provide new opportunities for participation in good governance in developing countries. Although, the authors consider that the success of such initiatives depends on modern and reliable communication networks and the political will of the governments, the achieved findings in these chapters show that platforms that allow meaningful collaboration (*crowdsourcing*), delegation of final decision-making rights to the public, and the implementation of what citizens decide are almost absent.

Finally, this book shows how citizens' benefits of their participation in social media have gone beyond simple social sharing to building reputations and bringing in career opportunities, monetary income or social life. Social media facilities the co-creation of value through active, creative, and social collaboration processes between public managers and citizens in public services. Managers of public organizations think that social media is an opportunity to integrate information and opinions from citizens into the policy making processes, through the sharing of more information, improving transparency and collaboration with the public and finding solutions for solving governmental problems, and improving efficiency in policies and initiatives.

Manuel Pedro Rodríguez-Bolívar
University of Granada, Spain

Manuel Pedro Rodríguez-Bolívar *is Professor at the Department of Accounting and Finance at the University of Granada (Spain). His research interest is focused mainly on e-government, smart cities, information systems, electronic participation and smart governance at local level. He has authored more than 45 papers in different JCR journals, many contributions to national and international conferences, more than 40 book chapters published in leading editorials (Routledge, Kluwer Academic Publishers, Springer, Palgrave, Nova Publishers and IGI Global) and is author of full-length books published in Spain. He is also editor of books in Springer, IGI Global and Palgrave, and he is a member of the Editorial Board of Government Information Quarterly, Co-Editor in Chief of International Journal of Public Administration in the Digital Age and Associate Editor in other leading international journals.*

Preface

The adoption of Information and Communication Technologies (ICTs) in public sector has supposed a change in philosophies in management and organizational in these organizations (Chan and Chow, 2007). This change of organizational structures has allow to undertake a process of modernization and reform, which has also enabled greater information accessibility and transparency (Jaeger and Bertot, 2010), improved public service delivery (Lindgren and Jansson, 2013), and produced greater interaction and citizens' participation in public administration (Zheng et al., 2014).

According to Harder and Jordan (2013), the use of ICTs has been very useful for society to improve democratic models, increasing trust in governments (Bélanger and Carter, 2008) and improving citizen participation in public affairs (Michels, 2017). Also, it has helped governments to introduce electronic administration in public services (Gao and Lee, 2017) increasing organizational flexibility and agility to respond in a dynamic environment (Holgersson and Karlsson, 2014).

In this contest, Social Media is a powerful technological tool that enables citizens to interact and participate in public issues easily. It facilitates the use of not only content, but also audio and video materials. In this sense, citizenry uses ICTs not only for professional issues, but also in social lives, they wish to interact with governments, public managers or politicians. Hence, governments have undertaken great efforts to implement the Social Media in public sphere, but this is not without risks, problems and barriers.

Although, previous research (Picazo-Vela et al., 2016; Mergel and Bretschneider, 2013) has highlighted that implementation and use of Social Media by governments involves many problems, like as updated information, saturation of channels, low participation, lack of training for public servants, inappropriate use and so on, these technological tools, platforms or channels reduce financial difficulties and improve the quality of government services.

In this sense, previous academic literature describes that social media is an effective means for government to improve citizens' trust in government by enhancing their perceptions of government transparency (Warren et al., 2014; Kim and Lee,

2012). Song and Lee (2016) analyzed how the citizenry's use of social media may lead to have trust in governments, public managers and politicians, as well as the access of more information and offer more transparency also influence on trust in government. Consequently, we can affirm that the exploration of the role of Social Media and its influence on e-Participation is an interesting research topic.

Given that the interdisciplinarity and fragmentation of this field of knowledge (Susha and Grönlund, 2014; Medaglia, 2012), the achieved findings in *Chapter 1* can be very useful for novel readers, because they can have a general vision and know the true impact of these tools and their involvement in e-Participation, as well as academics and researchers can be assisted in the evolution, development and direction of future analysis, identifying trends in this research topic and futures challenges.

Similarly, previous research (Rodríguez-Bolívar and Alcaide-Muñoz, 2018; Rodríguez-Bolívar, 2017; Bonsón et al., 2015) has analyzed the role of Social Media in establishing feedback between e-Government (online public services, transparency or participation) and citizens. In this sense, the findings have highlighted that there are not conclusive evidence, and there are many challenges in Social Media that have to be undertaken by public managers (Weller, 2015). For that reason, Chapter 2 analyzes the implementation "long-term" and construction mutual of communication between public managers and citizens and the use of social media in e-Government and the transformation of administrative mechanisms.

In addition, the recent rise of populism around the world is a trend that presents a serious threat not only to liberal democracies but also global peace and security (Engresser et al., 2017). The authors of the Chapter 3 highlighted how the social media has been used in two international events, Brexit referendum and election of Donald J. Trump as the U.S. President in 2016, and these social media technologies could be employed through e-Participation to inhibit populism by bolstering civic empowerment, transparency, progressive inclusiveness, fact-based analysis, and informed decision-making. In order to promote such a process, creating nonpartisan e-Participation platforms is essential. These platforms would support a collective voice by engaging communities into a deliberative, fact-based, rational, and transparent decision-making process.

On the other hand, the new technological advances make faster, easier and lower cost act and transactions possible. New developments affect to interaction between governments and citizens (Linders 2012). The innovation of public administrations, and the implementations of new technological tools favors transparency, accountability, access to information, more effective and efficient institutions, and more participation to citizens in public issues (Sandoval-Almazan and Gil-García, 2014; Osborne and Strokosch, 2013; Damanpour and Scheneider, 2008). Transferring duties and services to e-channels is being a useful instrument in this process, in special in developing countries (Rodríguez-Bolívar et al., 2016; Alcaide-Muñoz and Rodríguez-Bolívar, 2018).

Thus, the Chapter 4 analyzed how the new technologies for the delivery of services, and the terms like e-Participation and e-Governance are widening rapidly in Turkey municipalities. This study examined whether Facebook pages are an effective tools for local participation, given that previous studies (Bonsón et al., 2015; Ellison and Hardey, 2014) have highlighted that the Social Media citizen relationship is more effective, especially at the local level. The authors aimed to show what kind of a communication channel preferred by municipalities.

Similarly, México municipalities have undertaken a lot of great effort to offer more transparency and participative channels and tools (Sandoval-Almanzan et al., 2011). In the Chapter 5, the authors show how the Social Media has represented an emergent technology that has changes Government to Citizen improving efficiency in communication in México City (Valle-Cruz et al., 2016), since citizen has used this kind of technologies to make information request and complaints.

Also, Cameroon is a country that has a great technological infrastructure potential, but it still performs very poorly in e-Participation and e-Government development (UNDESA, 2016). Chapter 6 shows e-Participation in the case of the National Social Insurance Fund (NSIF) of Cameroon to exemplify the major characteristics, opportunities and challenges face by e-Participation initiatives implemented in developing countries.

In addition, Chapter 7 present the results of a three year research about network for digital political participation developed by civil society in Brazil. For this, the authors analyzed 41 networks to deepen the understanding about their potential to foster citizens´ engagement in political initiatives and strengthen democracy. However, the findings show lack of synergy between citizens´ demands and strategic planning of public policies and other political outcomes.

In this context, open government initiatives have encouraged governments to be more transparent and accessible while its partners have found new venues to further participate and collaborate (Wijnhove et al., 2015). Chapter 8 presents the case of study in Philippines, the authors shows that most of the open government-open government data programs are considered top-down. This means that almost all of the activities are initiated by the national government and are often funded by multilateral agencies such as the World Bank. However, due to the changes in political priorities, the future of these programs remains uncertain.

On the other hand, the initiatives of Social Media do not only used in governments, they also used in primary school to students, parents and teachers participate in the design of their classroom interior layout. Chapter 9 shows how blog and Facebook page were set up to provide a virtual space for classroom design to happen, and despite teachers' expressed enthusiasm for involving students in the design of their classroom layout, very few participant resulted. Finally, Chapter 10 examines what aspects of task-technology characteristics are most relevant to fit, satisfaction, and continuance intention of using apps in mobile banking transactions.

As conclusions, in the sphere of public administration, the adoption of e-government and the development of e-Participation have a large influence in the improvement of public administration. In general, there are many benefits of social networks consists of increasing citizen's trust on the government and to improving the face of government. But there are risks.

There are different forms of implementation and development of e-Participation and social media in developing countries. In general, the provision of a stable and reliable net of ITC is the most measure demanded. But, every country has its own idiosyncratic environment.

Finally, the use of social media tolls in classroom and the use of apps in banking transactions favor the participation of students, and conduce to a continuance intention of using banking apps.

Laura Alcaide-Muñoz
University of Granada, Spain

Francisco José Alcaraz-Quiles
University of Granada, Spain

REFERENCES

Alcaide-Muñoz, L., & Rodríguez-Bolívar, M. P. (Eds.). (2018). International e-Government Development: Policy, Implementation and Best Practices. Palgrave McMillan. doi:10.1007/978-3-319-63284-1

Bélanger, F., & Carter, L. (2008). Trust and risk in e-Government adoption. *The Journal of Strategic Information Systems*, *17*(2), 165–176. doi:10.1016/j.jsis.2007.12.002

Bonsón, E., Royo, S., & Ratkai, M. (2015). Citizens' engagement on local governments' Facebook sites. An empirical analysis: The impact of different media and content types in Western Europe. *Government Information Quarterly*, *32*(1), 57–62. doi:10.1016/j.giq.2014.11.001

Chan, H. S., & Chow, K. W. (2007). Public Management Policy and Practice in Western China: Metapolicy, Tacit Knowledge, and implications for Management Innovation Transfer. *American Review of Public Administration*, *37*(4), 479–497. doi:10.1177/0275074006297552

Damanpour, F., & Schneider, M. (2008). Characteristics of Innovation and Innovation Adoption in Public Organizations: Assessing the Role of Managers. *Journal of Public Administration: Research and Theory*, *19*(3), 495–522. doi:10.1093/jopart/mun021

Ellison, N., & Hardey, M. (2014). Social Media and Local Government: Citizenship, Consumption and Democracy. *Local Government Studies*, *40*(1), 21–40. doi:10.1 080/03003930.2013.799066

Engresser, S., Ernst, N., Esser, F., & Büchel, F. (2017). Populism and social media: how politicians spread a fragmented ideology. *Information, Communication & Society, 20*, 1109-1126.

Gao, X., & Lee, J. (2017). E-government services and social media adoption: Experience of small local governments in Nebraska state. *Government Information Quarterly*, *34*(4), 627–634. doi:10.1016/j.giq.2017.09.005

Harder, C. T., & Jordan, M. M. (2013). The transparency of county websites: A content analysis. *Public Administration Quarterly*, *37*(1), 103–128.

Holgersson, J., & Karlsson, F. (2014). Public e-service development: Understanding citizens' conditions for participation. *Government Information Quarterly*, *31*(3), 396–410. doi:10.1016/j.giq.2014.02.006

Jaeger, P. T., & Bertot, J. C. (2010). Transparency and technological change: Ensuring equal and sustained public access to government information. *Government Information Quarterly*, *27*(4), 371–376. doi:10.1016/j.giq.2010.05.003

Kim, S., & Lee, J. (2012). E-Participation, Transparency and Trust in Local Government. *Public Administration Review*, *72*(6), 819–828. doi:10.1111/j.1540-6210.2012.02593.x

Linders, D. (2012). From e-Government to we-Government: Defining a typology for citizen coproduction in the age of social media. *Government Information Quarterly*, *29*(4), 446–464. doi:10.1016/j.giq.2012.06.003

Lindgren, I., & Jansson, G. (2013). Electronic services in the public sector: A conceptual framework. *Government Information Quarterly*, *30*(2), 163–172. doi:10.1016/j.giq.2012.10.005

Medaglia, R. (2012). eParticiatpion research: Moving characterization forward (2006-2011). *Government Information Quarterly*, *29*(3), 346–360. doi:10.1016/j. giq.2012.02.010

Mergel, I., & Bretschneider, S. I. (2013). A three-stage adoption process for social media use in government. *Public Administration Review, 73*(3), 390–400. doi:10.1111/puar.12021

Michels, A. (2017). Participation in citizens' summits and public engagement. *International Review of Administrative Sciences.* doi:10.1177/0020852317691117

Osborne, S. P., & Strokosch, K. (2013). It takes two to Tango? Understanding the Co-production of Public Services by Integrating the Services Management and Public Administration Perspectives. *British Journal of Management, 24*(S1), S31–S47. doi:10.1111/1467-8551.12010

Picazo-Vela, S., Fernandez-Haddad, M., & Luna-Reyes, L. F. (2016). Opening the black box: Developing strategies to use social media in government. *Government Information Quarterly, 33*(4), 693–704. doi:10.1016/j.giq.2016.08.004

Rodríguez-Bolívar, M. P. (2017). Governance Models for the Delivery of Public Services through the Web 2.0 Technologies. A Political View in Large Spanish Municipalities. *Social Science Computer Review, 35*(2), 203–225. doi:10.1177/0894439315609919

Rodríguez-Bolívar, M. P., & Alcaide-Muñoz, L. (2018). Political Ideology and Municipal Size as Incentives for the Implementation and Governance Model of Web 2.0 in Providing Public Services. *International Journal of Public Administration in the Digital Age, 5*(1), 36–62. doi:10.4018/IJPADA.2018010103

Rodríguez-Bolívar, M. P., Alcaide-Muñoz, L., & López-Hernández, A. M. (2016). Scientometric Study of the Progress and Development of e-Government Research During the Period 2000-2012. *Information Technology for Development, 22*(1), 36–74. doi:10.1080/02681102.2014.927340

Sandoval-Almazan, R., & Gil-Garcia, J. R. (2014). Towards cyberactivism 2.0? Understanding the use of social media and other information technologies for political activism and social movements. *Government Information Quarterly, 31*(3), 365–378. doi:10.1016/j.giq.2013.10.016

Sandoval-Almazan, R., Gil-Garcia, J. R., Luna-Reyes, L. F., & Diaz-Murillo, D. E. L. G. (2011). The use of Web 2.0 on Mexican State Websites: A Three-Year Assessment. *Electronic Journal of E-Government, 9*(2), 107–121.

Song, C., & Lee, J. (2016). Citizens' Use of Social Media in Government, Perceived Transparency, and Trust in Government. *Public Performance & Management Review, 39*(2), 430–453. doi:10.1080/15309576.2015.1108798

Susha, I., & Grönlund, A. (2014). 'Context clues for the stall of the Citizens' Initiative: Lessons for opening up e-participation development practice. *Government Information Quarterly*, *31*(3), 454–465. doi:10.1016/j.giq.2014.02.005

UNDESA. (2016). *United Nations E-Government Survey 2016: E-Government in support of sustainable development*. Retrieved from https://publicadministration. un.org/egovkb/Portals/egovkb/Documents/un/2016-Survey/Executive%20Summary. pdf

Valle-Cruz, D., Sandoval-Almazan, R., & Gil-Garcia, J. R. (2016). Citizens' perceptions of the impact of information technology use on transparency, efficiency and corruption in local governments. *Information Polity*, *21*(3), 1–14. doi:10.3233/ IP-160393

Warren, A. M., Sulaiman, A., & Jaafar, N. I. (2014). Social media effects on fostering online civic engagement and building citizen trust and trust in institutions. *Government Information Quarterly*, *31*(2), 291–301. doi:10.1016/j.giq.2013.11.007

Weller, K. (2015). Accepting the challenges of social media research. *Online Information Review*, *39*(3), 281–289. doi:10.1108/OIR-03-2015-0069

Wijnhoven, F., Ehrenhard, M., & Kuhn, J. (2015). Open government objectives and participation innovations. *Government Information Quarterly*, *32*(1), 30–42. doi:10.1016/j.giq.2014.10.002

Zheng, Y., Schachter, H. L., & Holzer, M. (2014). The impact of government form on e-participation: A study of New Jersey municipalities. *Government Information Quarterly*, *31*(4), 653–659. doi:10.1016/j.giq.2014.06.004

Acknowledgment

The editors would like to acknowledge the help of all the people involved in this project and, more specifically, to the authors and reviewers that took part in the review process. Without their support, this book would not have become a reality.

First, the editors would like to thank each one of the authors for their contributions. Our sincere gratitude goes to the chapter's authors who contributed their time and expertise to this book.

Second, the editors wish to acknowledge the valuable contributions of the reviewers regarding the improvement of quality, coherence, and content presentation of chapters. Most of the authors also served as referees; we highly appreciate their double task.

Laura Alcaide-Muñoz
University of Granada, Spain

Francisco José Alcaraz-Quiles
University of Granada, Spain

Section 1
Role of Social Media in Citizens' Participation:
Trends, Challenges, and Future Research

Chapter 1
Social Media and E-Participation Research:
Trends, Accomplishments, Gaps, and Opportunities for Future Research

Cristina Alcaide-Muñoz
Public University of Navarre, Spain

Laura Alcaide-Muñoz
University of Granada, Spain

Francisco José Alcaraz-Quiles
University of Granada, Spain

ABSTRACT

Citizens increasingly demand an active role in public affairs and decision-making processes. From a critical standpoint, this chapter consolidates existing knowledge and, in turn, provides a better understanding on how social media tools promote the citizens' engagement and participation. The main aim is to assist researchers in the development of their future analyses, identifying trends of research and the methodology used. In so doing, a systematic literature review has been used to examine social media and e-participation research in journals listed in ISI in the field of public administration and information science and library science during the period 2000-2016. The findings reveal that although research on social media and e-participation has increased in the last year, it remains immature. Therefore, further research is needed in order to understand the true impacts of social media tools and their involvement in e-participation.

DOI: 10.4018/978-1-5225-5326-7.ch001

INTRODUCTION

The development of Information and Communication Technologies (ICT) has impacted every aspect of our society, including the way governments interact with citizens. So, the relationship between citizens and governments has changed, and e-government represented the new alternative to representative democracy and hierarchical governance (Hooghe et al., 2010; Nam et al., 2012). The implementation and development of e-Government have produced direct effects on the policy-making process, extending and promoting its participatory opportunities to average citizens (Jho & Song, 2015).

Therefore, citizens demand greater participation in public affairs and, new technological advances promotes their engagement by sharing more information and favour the interaction among politicians, public managers and citizenry (Ganapati & Reddick, 2014). Besides, the new technological platforms and the ease of use of the apps allow the citizens to be involved in shaping services integrated systems, given that they could offer feedback, comments, ideas and experiences about the public services, which increase the efficiency and effectiveness in public sector (Hu et al., 2014; Meijer & Thaens, 2013).

Moreover, the development of Web 2.0 tools has been a crucial influence in the transformation of an Internet from a passive one-way communication, into an interactive two-way communication system (Wirtz et al., 2016; Mergel, 2016). In this sense, social media is considered to be a part of the Web 2.0 revolution which is characterized by user-generated contents, online interactions, and content sharing in a social environment. It is belonged by a set of online tools such as Facebook, Twitter, Blogs, Wikis, and YouTube (Merchant, 2012) introducing substantial and pervasive changes to communication and information sharing between organizations and citizens (Kietzmann et al., 2011).

Furthermore, social media supports interactive participation among public managers, policy-makers and citizens in real time, which represents an important strategy for improving trust in government (Picazo-Vela et al., 2012; Stamati et al., 2015). So, governments have adopted platforms, applications, channels and tools to promote an informed citizens and favour their engagement in make decision process, trying to achieve an increase public confidence in government (Kim & Lee, 2012), monitoring the behavior of public managers and politicians (Hui & Hayllar, 2010), and promoting the democratic process by offering debate and discussion on important issues of public concern. In other words, social media provides the channel to integrate information and opinions from citizens into the policy making, increasing transparency and collaboration with the public to reach decisions or solutions for government problems (Mergel, 2013).

Taking into account these findings, previous studies have highlighted that e-participation is a field of knowledge interdisciplinary and fragmented, and it is not possible that the scholars and academics have a clear idea about the state of art of this research topic (Susha & Grönlund, 2014; Medaglia, 2012). Regarding social media, there are bibiometric studies and literature reviews that offer a general perspective or limited scope (Moon et al., 2015; Weller, 2015; Boulianne, 2015; Wang et al., 2016). Similarly, Alcaide-Muñoz et al., (2017) achieved that the social media and how these tools promote the citizens' engagement is a motor theme, which has increased its publication in the last five years.

Given the great heterogeneity in the literature devoted to social media and its use in e-Participation, and the absence of a broad bibliographical overview of this research topics in the interdisciplinary fields of "*Information Science and Library Science*", and "*Public Administration*", we believe that it is necessary to analyze the main contributions made in order to lay a solid foundation for future research in the field of social media and how they promote and favour the participation of citizenry.

Therefore, to fill this gap, the objective of this chapter is to assist academics in the evolution, development and direction of future analysis, by identifying trends in research topics and challenges to face. In addition, this will identify research gaps and possibilities for improvement in social media and its use in citizens' e-Participation. To this end, the chapter adapts several bibliometric approaches to analyzed papers published at the leading international journals listed in the SSCI index in the fields of "*Information Science and Library Science*" and "*Public Participation*" since for the year 2000 to 2016.

This chapter is organized as follows. The next section presents the research topic in two ways: addressing the utility of systematic literature review and setting out research questions. Section 3 describes the sample selection process and analytical methodology used. After that, the findings obtained from this approach are described. Finally, this chapter closes with discussion and final remarks, highlighting future trends in this area.

UTILITY OF SYSTEMATIC LITERATURE REVIEW AND RESEARCH QUESTIONS

In the previous academic literature, we can find scholars and researchers that carried on a systematic literature review (Alcaide-Muñoz & Gutierrez-Guiterrez, 2017; Tranfield et al., 2003). This kind of review could play a fundamental role in creating and building bodies of knowledge and information policy and practice (Colicchia & Strozzi, 2012). In this way, the academics and researchers can identify the historical roots of a determined field of study, the prospect for future research, and the trends in specific research topic or field of knowledge (Sidorova et al., 2008).

In this regard, Alcaide-Muñoz et al., (2017) consider that the contribution of this kind of studies is very important because they serve not only as a synopsis of existing research, but also as an identification of emerging trends, gaps, and areas for future studies, offering a descriptive state of the art in field of knowledge. Thus, in the field of e-Government, we can find many studies that used bibliometric and scientometric methodologies (Snead & Wright, 2014; Joseph, 2013; Rodríguez-Bolívar et al., 2012). These studies have analyzed the limitations of previous research in the e-Government's field, also have identified publication outlet, methodological approach, the motor research topics, the prolific authors who published the most article in each research topic in this field of study (Rodríguez-Bolívar et al., 2016; Alcaide-Muñoz & Rodríguez-Bolívar, 2015; Alcaide-Muñoz et al., 2014; Scholl, 2014).

In the case of e-Participation, Medaglia (2012) considers that this research field has experimented continued growth, stimulated by increasing attention by both practitioners and academics/researchers. Thus, we can find a field of knowledge interdisciplinary and fragmented (Susha & Grönlund, 2014), which makes it difficult to obtain a single point to access to this research topic, due to a large extent the diversity of research disciplines involved. So, a systematic review is needed in fields of knowledge where contributions are varied and interdisciplinary.

On the other hand, there are a few existing reviews of research focusing on social media with a general perspective or either of limited scope (Wang et al., 2016; Moon et al., 2015; Weller, 2015; Boulianne, 2015). They provide an overview of the key challenges in social media research and some current initiatives in addressing them. Conversely, Zheng and Medaglia (2017) showed a comprehensive review of government social media literature. They offer information about contextual factors that favour the use of social media, user characteristics, user behaviour, and strategic management used by public managers and politicians. Their achieved conclusions are very useful because mapping knowledge will enable public managers to draw on the research findings to improve practices and offer better services.

Although, there is literature review on government social media, we think that there is a currently a lack of comprehensive efforts to map and systematize research on how social media improve of citizens' e-Participation in public affairs. In this sense, we try to provide a critical outlook in this research topic and a common ground, to improve our understanding of social media and its influence on e-Participation evolution and of possibilities for future research. Therefore, it is of critical importance to explore its intellectual core in order to understand the construction of theoretical support underpinning the question of this contribution, by analyzing the cumulative body of knowledge (Alcaide-Muñoz et al., 2017). Taking into account that the majority of published research in e-Participation and social media corresponds to the fields of *Public Administration* and *Information Science & Library Science* (Zheng & Medaglia, 2017; Rodríguez-Bolívar et al., 2016), our first research question is the following:

- **RQ1:** How many articles about social media promoting e-Participation have been published in JCR journals in this field of Public Administration and Information Science & Library Science? Which journals publish such papers most frequently?

According to Rodríguez-Bolívar et al. (2016), it could be of interest to determine whether the research aim influences the methodology used to analyze the subject. Previous studies in e-Government (Rodríguez-Bolívar et al., 2010, 2012) affirm that the used of qualitative methodologies is signs of a research field in constant evolution that has not yet reached a stage of maturity. We want to test if in social media have the same evolution that e-Government, or the evolution is different, and hence we could determine what the possible reasons may be. So, the following research question is derived:

- **RQ2:** What research methodologies are employed in analyzing e-participation related to social media?

There are empirical studies that have highlighted that social media favours citizens' passive role and interaction with governments, as they have the opportunity of publishing their own point of view on the information provided by them (Guillamón et al., 2016; Bonsón et al., 2015). Given that social media provides a space to public managers, politicians and citizens to interact and collaborate, enabling thereby information, ideas on planning, public events, and so on, which makes citizens better informed, favouring citizen empowerment and interaction with governments (Luna-Reyes et al., 2016; Stamati, et al., 2015). So, we wonder the following research question:

- **RQ3:** What social media is most commonly analyzed by scholars and academics? Is there any social media that has stopped being analyzed? Have researchers begun to paid attention to other social media in recent years?

In addition, social media tools have the potential to connect citizen directly to public managers and policy-makers in real time (Mergel, 2016). Governments use social media as a public affairs communication medium to increase transparency by sharing more information (Bonsón et al., 2015). In this way, social media favours the participation of citizens in policy making, offering ideas and expertise –crowdsourcing–, which improves thereby the quality of governmental decision and policy making (Lev-On & Steinfeld, 2015). The implementation of these initiatives and experiences could be useful for countries with limited resources, so the following research question is derived:

- **RQ4:** What are the main analyzed countries that are of interest concerning this research topic?

Finally, despite the advantages of using social media in the context of the public sector, as its use favours participation, transparency, trust in government, and so on (Mergel, 2016; Porumbescu, 2016; Stamati et al., 2015), previous studies (Luna-Reyes et al., 2016; Bertot et al., 2012; Ferro & Molinari, 2010) have highlighted that the adoption of social media can lead to several disadvantages. Taking into account these findings, we propose the following research question:

- **RQ5:** What are the main advantages and benefits in using social media by governments? What are the main problems in adoption of social media that public managers and governments have to face? What could be the possible solutions?

To address these research questions, we conducted a systematic literature review of articles published in the JCR-listed international journals in the areas of *Public Administration* and *Information Science & Library Science*, as described in the research strategy section.

RESEARCH STRATEGY

In order to achieve the aim of this study, we have carried on a systematic literature review (DeVaujany et al., 2014; Tranfield et al., 2003). It differs from the traditional narrative reviews by being more systematics and explicit in the selection of the research, and by developing rigorous and reproducible methods of evaluations (Denver & Tranfield, 2009). This type of methodology follows three phases; the first one is the identification of research questions, taking into accounting the previous research and findings (Delbufalo, 2012). This step is very important in order to avoid issues of publication bias during the article selection process (Wolfswinkel et al., 2013).

In the second phase, we carried out a *search in the database*. In this regard, this study is focused on analysing publication in *Social Science Citation Index* (SSCI) journals, in the view that they constitute a resource that is often used by academics as a source of new knowledge and as a medium for its disclosure (Nord & Nord, 1995), and at the same time, as an indicator of scientific productivity (Legge & Devore, 1987). Also, we have excluded symposia, summaries of communications, letters to the editor, practitioners' articles and book reviews, because the articles and their citation-based measure are taken as reference to determine the significance and performance of scientific journals (Alcaide-Muñoz & Rodríguez-Bolívar, 2015). However, we did take into account articles included in special issues of journals, considering that these reflect a greater interest in the study of a particular issue and in the need to examine it further (Rodríguez-Bolívar et al., 2010).

Then, we select the electronic database and estimate the keywords. In this sense, we collected journals from the SSCI complied by the *Institute for Scientific Information* (ISI) from the beginning 2000 (Rodríguez-Bolívar et al., 2016). As argued by other authors (Newbert, 2007), it was deemed that by restricting the search to peer-reviewed journals, the quality control of search results can be enhanced due to the rigorous process to which articles published in such journals are subject prior to publication.

In order to perform such research, the authors carried out a systematic review for which, we have used keywords related to social media and e-Participation, and we have exclude listed journals of marginal importance that is, those with an impact factor lower than 0.25 or fewer than 50 total citations for the impact factor 2016 (Rodríguez-Bolívar et al., 2016; Alcaide-Muñoz & Rodríguez-Bolívar, 2015). The main reason is that the ISI citation databases 'collectively index more than 8,000 high quality, peer-reviewed journals, cover-to-cover, providing users with complete bibliographic data, full-length author abstract, and cited reference from the wold's most influential research' (Newbert, 2007), which assures high quality and comprehensive search results.

Finally, in the third phase, we establish the *inclusion-exclusion criteria of articles*. Regarding the selection of articles, we have reviewed all journals and articles that met the exclusion-inclusion criteria described above, so we avoid the possible exclusion of articles published in multidisciplinary journals with general descriptions. The title and the abstract, the keywords (Hartley & Kostoff, 2003) and the introduction of the articles to analyze the objective were relevant factors in this process. Although, when the application of these discrimination criteria was not enough, we have read the entire articles. To ensure the greatest objectivity, the authors carried out this comprehensive selection procedure individually, cataloguing each article. After that, the authors met on several occasions to discuss the results, and to reach an agreement where discrepancies arose. In consequence, our sample is composed of 91 articles published in 68 journals listed in ISI of Knowledge in the field of "*Information Science and Library Science*" and "*Public Administration*", during the period of 2000-2016-see Table 1.

Finally, we have created a data base with the following information: the year of publication, the journal title, the main subject dealt, the social networks and the countries analyzed, and the principal methodology used. In case the articles analyzed multiple research topics and/or used multiple methods, the authors focused on the main research item and methodology used in order to avoid double counting. Finally, with the intention of offering knowledge about the evolution and implementation of social media in governments to improve the citizens' e-participation, each author analyzed the papers in order to highlight the advantages, solutions and challenges faced by citizens and public managers/politician makers.

DESCRIPTIVE FINDINGS

- **RQ1:** How many research articles about social media promoting e-participation have been published in JCR journals in the fields of public administration and of information science & library science? Which journals publish such papers most frequently? and RQ2: What research methodologies are employed in analyzing e-Participation related to social media?

Since 2000, there has been a gradual increase in the numbers of studies published in international journals analyzing the experiences and initiatives of e-Government (Rodríguez-Bolívar et al., 2016; Alcaide-Muñoz et al., 2014; Alcaide-Muñoz & Garde-Sánchez, 2014). However, despite the increasing use of social media tools in public administration from their successful role in Barack Obama's presidential campaign in 2008 (Mergel, 2016), little attention has been paid to exploring how social media tools promote bidirectional interaction between citizen and governmental entities (e-participation). In fact, the articles published on this topic in journals of *Public Administration* and of *Information Science & Library Science* amount to only 91 (see Table 1). In this sense, most articles were published in *Information Science & Library & Science* (72.53%), whereas the rest of them are in *Public Administration* journals (27.47%). Regarding *Information Science & Library Science* journals, as shown in Table 1, most of these articles are published in a single journal, called *Government Information Quarterly* (53.03%), which is followed at a considerable distance by others such as *Online Information Review, Social Science Computer Review, Information Technology for Development, Information Development, Telematics & Informatics, Telecommunications Policy, Aslib Proceedings, The Information Society, International Journal of Geographical Information Science, Information Systems Research, Aslib Journal of Information Management, Information Technology & People* and *Journal Computer-Mediated Communication*. Nevertheless, in the case of *Public Administration* journals, we can observe in Table 1 that the interest to publish

Table 1. ISI Journals (2000-2016) that published articles about how social media promotes the citizens' participation

Position	Abbreviated Journal Name	Impact Factor 2016	E-Participation and Social Media Articles
PUBLIC ADMINISTRATION JOURNALS			
1	J PUBL ADM RES THEOR	3.624	-
2	PUBLIC ADMIN REV	3.473	-
3	J POLICY ANAL MANAG	3.415	-
5	PUBLIC ADMIN	2.959	-
8	GOVERNANCE	2.603	1
9	PUBLIC MANAG REV	2.293	5
10	POLICY STUD J	2.153	-
11	POLICY AND POLITICS	1.939	1
12	J PUBLIC POLICY	1.778	-
13	ENVIRON PLANN C	1.771	-
14	POLICY SCI	1.750	-
15	INT PUBLIC MANAG J	1.723	-
16	J EUR SOCIAL POLICY	1.593	-
19	PUBLIC POLICY ADM	1.529	-
21	J SOC POLICY	1.458	-
22	AM REV PUBLIC ADM	1.438	1
23	INT REV ADM SCI	1.350	2
24	J ACCOUNT PUBLIC POL	1.333	-
27	PUBLIC MONEY MANAGE	1.133	1
28	POLICY SOC	1.115	-
29	ADMIN SOC	1.092	2
30	AUST J PUBLIC ADMIN	1.072	1
31	J COMP POLICY ANAL	1.017	-
33	LOCAL GOV STUD	0.930	4
35	PUBLIC ADMIN DEVELOP	0.860	-
36	PUBLIC PERFROM MANAG	0.812	1
37	LEX LOCALIS	0.714	1
38	CAN PUBLIC POL	0.679	-
39	POLICY STUD-UK	0.609	1
42	TRANSYLV REV ADM SCI	0.456	1
43	CAN PUBLIC ADMIN	0.333	1
44	GESTION Y POLITICA PUBLICA	0.324	2
TOTAL ARTICLES IN PUBLIC ADMINISTRATION			25 (27.47%)

continued on following page

Table 1. Continued

Position	Abbreviated Journal Name	Impact Factor 2016	E-Participation and Social Media Articles
INFORMATION SCIENCE AND LIBRARY SCIENCE JOURNALS			
1	MIS QUART	7.268	-
2	J INF TECHNOL	6.953	-
3	INFORM SYST J	4.122	-
4	J COMPUT-MEDIAT COMM	4.113	1
5	GOV INFORM Q	4.090	35
6	INT J INFORM MANAGE	3.872	-
8	J STRATEGIC INF SYST	3.486	-
9	INT J C-SUP COLLAB LEARN	3.469	-
10	TELEMAT INFORM	3.398	3
11	INFORM & MANAG	3.317	-
12	J INFORMETRICS	2.920	-
13	EUR J INFORM SYST	2.819	-
14	INFORM SYST RES	2.763	1
15	INT J GEOGRAP INFOR SCI	2.502	-
16	INFORM PROCESS MANAG	2.391	-
17	J MANAGE INFORM SYST	2.356	-
18	J ASSOC INFOR SCI TECH	2.322	-
20	SOC SCI COMPUT REV	2.293	5
21	SCIENTOMETRICS	2.147	-
22	J ASSOC INF SYST	2.109	-
23	INFORM ORGAN - UK	2.083	1
26	MIS Q EXEC	1.741	-
27	INFORM DEV	1.691	3
30	INFORM SOC	1.558	1
31	ONLINE INFORM REV	1.534	6
32	TELECOMMUN POLICY	1.526	2
34	ASLIB J INF MAN	1.514	3
36	J INF SCI	1.372	-
37	INFORM TECHNOL PEOPL	1.339	1
38	INFORM TECHNOL DEV	1.333	4
43	J GLOB INF TECH MANAG	1.167	-
44	INFORM TECHNOL MANAG	1.067	-
51	KNOWLEDGE ORG	0.831	-

continued on following page

Table 1. Continued

Position	Abbreviated Journal Name	Impact Factor 2016	E-Participation and Social Media Articles
57	INFORM RES	0.574	-
61	J GLOB INF MANAG	0.517	-
62	SOC SCI INFOR	0.490	-
66	DATA BASE ADV INFORM SYST	0.458	-
TOTAL ARTICLES ON INFORMATION SCIENCE			66 (72.53%)
TOTAL ARTICLES			91

Source – Own elaboration with information from ISI of Knowledge

NOTE: This table shows only those journals that have published articles about social media tools and e-Participation.

this type of research is much more spread out. As said above, even though, 27.47% of these articles are published in this field; only a couple of them appear to be more interested in publishing articles related to social media and e-participation, such as *Public Management Re*view (20.00%) and *Local Government Studies* (16.00%).

On the other hand, as Figure 1 reveals, the first articles on analyzing social media tools and e-participation were published in 2010, whose trend has been increasing over time. In this regard, we can observe that there was a pronounced increase two years after, that is, from 2014 onwards. These results are coherent with the achieved findings in previous study (Alcaide-Muñoz et al., 2017), where it highlighted that researchers have a particular interest in social media as communication channel favouring interactions between citizens and politicians. Therefore, there is a clear preference to understand the benefits of social media tools over e-participation in government context, and this research topic plays a role as motor theme of e-government field of knowledge.

Regarding methodology used in these articles addressing e-participation and social media tools, there is a preference for the use of empirical research methods (87.91%, see Table 2) over non-empirical methods (12.09%). Among the empirical method used, most articles apply quantitative methodologies (62.64%) rather than qualitative methodologies (25.27%). In this sense, the most commonly quantitative tools used are descriptive (40.35%) and analysis regressions (40.35%) such as ordinary least square (OLS), logistic regression (LOGIT), probit model (PROBIT) and general linear model (GML).

On the other hand, although the quantitative methodology is the most frequently employed in both fields, we observe a greater use of non-empirical methods in *Information Science and Library Science* (13.63%) than in *Public Administration* (8%).

Figure 1. Chronological evolution of articles about how social media promotes the citizens' participation
Source: The authors

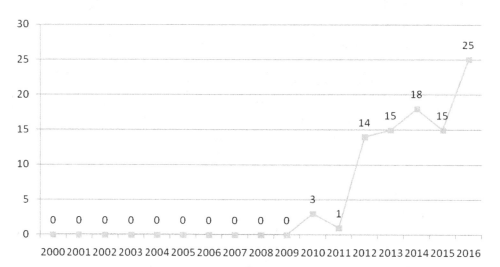

Concerning qualitative methodology, as show in the Table 2, the most frequently qualitative tool applied on these articles is the qualitative evaluation (56.52%) followed by case studies (30.43%). In this sense, we observe a greater preference for the use of qualitative evaluation in Public Administration than in Information Science and Library Science (83.33% and 47.06%, respectively).

From a chronological standpoint, the non-empirical and qualitative methods are predominant, which make sense, since it helps to introduce an emerging topic such as the relationship between social media tools and e-participation. Afterwards, there is an increasing trend towards quantitative methods throughout the four years period and continued to rise in 2014 (see Table 3).

Therefore, although there was originally a trend for the use of non-empirical and qualitative methodologies, its use has gradually been surpassed by quantitative methodologies over time, particularly, from 2014.

- **RQ3**: What social media is most commonly analyzed by scholars and academics? Is there any social media that has stopped being analyzed? Have researchers begun to paid attention to other social media in recent years?

Focusing on the social media tools analyzed in these articles addressing e-participation, there is particular interest in examining social media tools as Facebook and Twitter, followed by Youtube and my-space-see Figure 2. This attention may

Table 2. Methodology used on research how social media promotes the citizens' participation in ISI Journals (2000-2016)

Methodology	Articles	% articles	Art. in P.A.	% P.A.	Art. in I.S and L.S.	% I.S and L.S.
Non-empirical	11	12.09	2	08.00	9	13.63
Qualitative methodology	23	25.27	6	24.00	17	25.74
Case study	7	07.69	1	04.00	6	09.09
Qualitative evaluation	13	14.28	5	20.00	8	12.12
Social networks analysis	1	01.09	-	-	1	01.51
Analytical maps	1	01.09	-	-	1	01.51
Geospatial distributions of analytical results	1	01.09	-	-	1	01.51
Quantitative methodology	57	62.64	17	68.00	40	60.63
SEM	8	08.79	2	08.00	6	09.09
OLS	18	19.78	6	24.00	12	18.18
LOGIT	3	03.29	2	08.00	1	01.51
GML	1	01.09	-		1	01.51
PROBIT	1	01.09	-		1	01.51
Cluster	1	01.09	-		1	01.51
Descriptive analysis	23	25.27	7	28.00	16	24.24
Mult. Reg.	1	01.09	-		1	01.51
ANOVA	1	01.09	-		1	01.51
Total	**91**	**100**	**25**	**100**	**66**	**100**

P.A.: Public Administration; I.S. and L.S.: Information Science and Library Science. Art.: Articles

OLS: Ordinary least square; LOGIT: Logistic regression: PROBIT: Probit model; GML: General linear model; SEM: Structural equations model; Mult. Reg.: Multilevel regression.

Source: Own Elaboration

mainly be linked to the large number of active accounts in both social media tools (adweek.com, 2016); in fact, they are viewed as main social platforms (Hughes et al., 2012; Debatin et al., 2009). However, less attention has been paid to yelp, Snapchat and forums, since as some research studies show, their influence over people's minds and life is negligible compared to Facebook, Twitter or Youtube (Vaterlaus et al., 2016; Moreno et al., 2013; Moore & McElroy, 2012; Cha et al., 2010).

On the other hand, although social media tools such as LinkedIn, Wikipedia, Flickr, My-space and Youtube initially attracted the same attention to be analyzed on e-participation as Facebook and Twitter, there is a decreasing trend over the three last years, as shown in Figure 3. This decrease is the opposite of the trend shown by Twitter, which shows an increasing trend from the beginning. With regard to

Table 3. Methodology used on research about how social media promotes the citizens' participation in ISI Journals per year (2000-2016)

Years	Non-EMP	QUALIT. STD	QUANT. STD	Total	% Non-EMP	% QUAL. STD	% QUANT. STD
2010	2	-	1	3	66.67	-	33.33
2011	-	1	-	1	-	100	-
2012	2	5	7	14	14.29	35.71	50.00
2013	2	7	6	15	13.33	46.67	40.00
2014	2	4	12	18	11.11	22.22	66.67
2015	2	2	11	15	13.33	13.33	73.34
2016	1	4	20	25	4.00	16.00	80.00
Total	**11**	**23**	**57**	**91**	**12.09**	**25.27**	**62.64**

Non-EMP.: Non-empirical methodology; QUALIT. STD.: Qualitative methodology; QUANT. STD.: Quantitative methodology.

Source: Own elaboration

Figure 2. Social media tools used to promote the citizens' participation
Source: Own elaboration

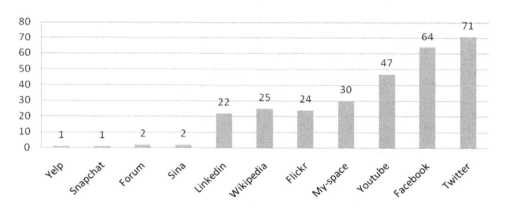

Facebook, its evolution is similar as Twitter's one. Indeed, there is greater attention during 2012 and 2013, but in 2014 there is a decrease which became an increase again in 2015 (see Figure 3).

- **RQ4**: What are the main analyzed countries that are of interest concerning this topic?

Figure 3. Chronological evolution of social media tools used on e-participation
Source: The authors

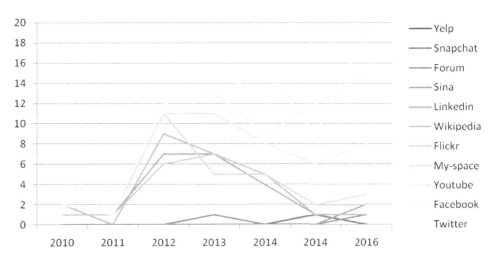

A vast number of research studies focus on analyzing international context (12.09%), since they introduce an emerging topic on how governmental entities adopt social media tools to leverage bidirectional interactions with citizens. In this way, they promote transparency, engagement and participation, including all stakeholders into decision-making processes (Mergel & Bretschneider, 2013). However, as Figure 4 reveals, the main focus is paid upon U.S.A and the members of European Union, leaving developing countries in a second place. Moreover, others seem to get encouraged to examine the influence of social media tools over e-participation on countries such as China and South Korea. In contrast, less attention is paid to less attention has been paid to emerging economies such as the Middle East and North Africa, Arab countries and certain regions of Asia.

CHALLENGES, PROBLEMS AND SOLUTIONS IN THE ADOPTION AND USED OF SOCIAL MEDIA TO FAVOUR THE CITIZENS' PARTICIPATION

- **RQ5**: What are the main advantages and benefits in using social media by governments? What are the main problems in adoption of social media that public managers and governments have to face? What could be the possible solutions?

Figure 4. Countries under study in the articles published on social media and e-participation
M.E. & N.A.: The Middle East and North Africa.
Source: Own elaboration

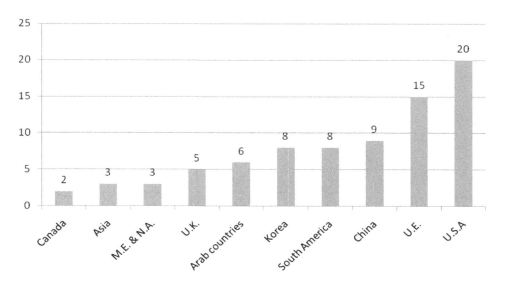

Many governments around the world have carried out great efforts to transform and modernize the public sector. The new technological advances allow governments to ease the public management, delivery of public services and access to more information. In this context, social media is capable of transforming power relationships between citizens and governments to create a more open government (Picazo-Vela et al., 2012, Mergel, 2016). The social networks, such as Facebook and Twitter, facilitate transparency, openness and democratization (Wukich & Mergel, 2016), integrating the citizens in administrative and policy processes –see Table 4. However, there are politicians and policy-makers that have fear to loss the control due to excessive transparency and openness (Guillamón et al., 2016), and to be defenceless against destructive behaviours of the haters.

Nonetheless, previous research (Porumbescu, 2016; Bonsón et al., 2015; Warren et al., 2014) highlighted that social media and Web 2.0 tools increase governmental transparency, which is essential for increasing democratic participation and trust. In this way, the citizenry can be informed about decision making, demanding information and monitoring public managers, and fighting corruption issues (Ellison & Hardey, 2014; Edwards et al., 2013).

The use of these tools allows governments to communicate more efficiently with citizens. Therefore, it is easier to collaborate and participate in policy making with

Table 4. Benefits in the use of social media and challenges that the governments have to face

Benefits in the Use of Social Media	Challenges to Face
1. Government Openness – Facilitate the sharing of government information, which achieve transparency and accountability. Citizenry is better and more informed (Warren et al., 2014; Bonsón et al., 2015; Porumbescu, 2016; Picazo-Vela et al., 2012; Wukich & Mergel, 2016; Merguel, 2016) *2. Democracy and collaboration* – With more information, the citizens are more prepared and motivated to participate and collaborate in public affairs (Edwards et al., 2013; Ellison & Hardey, 2014; Wukich & Mergel, 2016) *3. Human rights* – It promote human rights thanks to a better freedom of information, freedom of speech and accountability. *4. Trust* – A more transparent government in its information and annual statements creates a better image and makes citizens' trust on their public managers and politicians (Porumbescu, 2016; Bonsón et al., 2015; Warren et al., 2014) *5. Corruption* – It is a tool to fight against corruption, given that it is shared more information and the citizens are informed about decision making so they can monitoring the politicians' issues (Edwards et al., 2013; Ellison & Hardey, 2014) *6. Efficient communication* – Governments can communicate faster, efficiency and user friendly with citizens, which causes a greater proximity between organizations and stakeholders (Bonsón et al., 2015). *7. Crowd-sourcing* – The citizens can share their ideas, experiences and possible solutions easier, and co-create better public services (Stamati et al., 2015) *8. Feedback* – Governments can receive information, ideas, experiences, suggestions, complaints (support to community) and so on (Stamati et al., 2015) *9. Knowledge* – Given that the citizens can participate in public affairs, and communicate their suggestions, ideas, complaints and so on, the government can know more about citizens' demands (Bonsón et al., 2015) *10. Image and reputation* – It allows public managers to share images, pictures and events (friendly) which could improve the image about the government. *11. Promoting tourism* – It allows the governments to share pictures, events, concerts, activities and so on, which are celebrate in their municipalities and promote their image outside. *12. Interoperability* – Facilitate create networks between departments inside the government and between other organizations, enabling the transfer of best practices and scale economics (Picazo-Vela, et al., 2012) *13. Costs savings* – Governments can communicate directly with the citizenry at low cost, maximizing resources (efficient and effective) (Stamati et al., 2015) *14. Investment* – Social media are free tools, and their implementation does not require much investment (in economic terms) (Picazo-Vela et al., 2012)	*1. Control* – Politicians and public managers have fear to loss the control due to excessive transparency and openness (Guillamón et al., 2016) *2. Destructive behavior* – In social media there are haters who use their anonymous profiles to adopt destructive behavior. *3. Questions* – The ease of social media use and access to information can lead to a debugging of questions, suggestions and complaints (cannot be distributed) (Luna-Reyes et al., 2016) *4. Updated information* –There are platforms that are no longer used due to lack of information and updated information (Luna-Reyes et al., 2016) *5. Saturation of channels* – Governments often use more than one social network to distribute the same information, and thus, provoke repetition of content in several platforms and dispersion of a message in the different channels (Serrat, 2017). *6. Low participation* – In certain countries the culture by participation is not mark in the citizenship (Sandoval-Almanzan & Gil-García, 2012) *7. Training of public servants* – Lack of training for employees to use this kind of tools, and lack of a citizen-centered culture and open information (Zhao et al., 2012; Park et al., 2015) *8. Inappropriate use* – Public servants and public managers are not qualified to answer customers' inquiries (Zhao et al., 2012) *9. Leadership* – Lack of leadership of public managers, unwillingness to take risk, resistance to change, unplanned decisions and fear of being made redundant (Mergel, 2016) *10. Organizational issues* – Integration of different organizational structures and poor development of knowledge. Also, bureaucratic process for dealing customer needs (Luna-Reyes & Gil-Garcia, 2011) *11. Systems* – Incompatibility of systems which not favouring the interoperability between departments and between organizations. Also, there are systems failures and downtime (Picazo-Vela et al., 2012) *12. Digital divide* – There is a great amount of the citizenry that does not accept this type of technologies, not have opportunities to access this kind of tools (Picazo-Vela et al., 2012) *13. Privacy and security* – Lack of a regulatory framework for the activities related to social media, and freedom of information regulation and practices (Bertot et al., 2012; Picazo-Vela, et al., 2012). *14. Records management* – Vulnerability to attack by hackers and how to store and compile these records. Lack of law, regulations and policies (Bertot et al., 2012; Picazo-Vela, et al., 2012). *15. Resources and budget* – Limited budget to development these initiatives (Kuzma, 2010)

Source: Own elaboration

the collective knowledge, ideas, expectations, and expertise in public services. In this way, crowdsourcing improves thereby the quality of governmental decision and policy making, via collaboration and partnership amongst governments, enterprises and citizens (Stamati et al., 2015). So, governments may provide public services efficient and effective, with a maximization of resources. Nevertheless, according to Sandoval-Almanzan and Gil-García (2012), citizen's collaboration and participation is poor at the local level, so local governments have to identify what initiatives and mechanisms must be promoted in order to foster the interaction among politicians, public managers and citizenry.

However, there are many governments that use different platforms and social networks at the same time, which provoke an increase of questions, suggestions and complaints difficult to manage (Luna-Reyes et al., 2016) –see Table 4. Besides that, many of these networks are no longer used due to outdated information. In other cases, many governments share the same information, which causes repetition of content in several social networks and dispersion of a message in different channels (Serrat, 2017).

On the other hand, social media is a perfect channel to share images, pictures and events with a friendly content, which can improve the image about the government, i.e. they are strategic tools to promote cities and attract tourists (Luna-Reyes et al., 2016). For this, governments need a strategic plan and qualified employees that can reply doubts. In this sense, this is the other risk or challenge governments have to face.

The implementation of social media is not easy, simply attaining a Facebook or Twitter page is not enough, this social media presence should be used in a way that is usually beneficial for stakeholders (Bonsón et al., 2015). These initiatives do not require much investment in economic terms (Picazo-Vela et al., 2012), in the event that governments have implemented a solid technological structure, otherwise, their resources and budget are limited (Kuzma, 2010). Otherwise, this requires adopting a solid organizational structure that favours coordination and evolution of these initiatives (Luna-Reyes & Gil-Garcia, 2011). Also, governments should adopt appropriate technology which allows the compatibility of systems and thus, create networks between organizations, enabling the transfer of best practices and scale economics (Picazo-Vela et al., 2012).

Together with the above, studies show a lack of technical knowledge by employees assigned to IT department, they are not prepared to work in an electronic environment (Park et al., 2015), i.e. public servants and managers have lack of skills, competencies and internal experiences necessary (Zhao et al., 2012). This poor training and knowledge, leads to a lack of vision of the IT department, an inappropriate use of social networks and delay or unsuccessful adoption of social media channels. Therefore, governments often need to hire a community manager.

Besides, public managers do not have clear the benefits of social media and its impact over public management and services (Bonsón et al.,2015) . Politicians and public managers must show a leadership attitude towards their employees, trying to reduce resistance among staff to the use of these tools, and their negative attitude (Mergel, 2016).

Finally, other potential risks in social media implementation are related to security and privacy concerns. As social media includes two-way communication, the risk of inserting bad ware into governments' platforms exists (Bertot et al., 2012; Picazo-Vela, et al., 2012), so the IT people should be prepared to protect government's information technology infrastructure and records management.

CONCLUSION

In this study, we have highlighted that social media research topic is a key theme in the field of e-Government knowledge, which shows a gradual increase in the number of studies published in international journal in the last five years. Also, these results show that there is a preference for a journal in publishing these studies, which pays special attention to understand the benefit of social media tools over e-participation in government context. Unlike the field of e-Government, social media research shows a preference for the use of empirical research methods, which show a sign the early maturity in the theme.

Similarly, these findings show that the main countries under study are U.S.A and the members of European Union; however, less attention seems to be paid into developing countries. When it is perhaps in these countries where there could be more interest in implementing these initiatives to equip them with tools that favour democratization and lead to greater growth in the country (Rodríguez-Bolívar et al., 2015).

In addition, in this chapter we have highlighted that there are many benefits of social networks consists of increasing citizen's trust on the government and to improving the face of government. But there are risks that cloud the potential and advantages of these tools. For example, public managers are aware that the use of social media favours the participation of citizens, but at the same time they fear losing control over information, and facing to the destructive behaviour of haters.

According to Dadashzadeh (2010), the adoption of social media in governmental context requires the configuration of a good strategic plan. In this sense, public managers should identify best channels, tools or platforms to share their information. At the same time, it would be desirable to finance employee training in IT technical skills, reply questions, manage to social network. This set of concerns also stresses the importance of clear guideline for government employees' use of social media

(Picazo-Vela et al., 2012), as well as create or update laws and regulation on privacy and security issues.

Future research can focus on specific projects in developing countries to better understand strategic objectives, gaps in innovation, challenges and risk on the adoption of social media. In addition, international organizations should lead political and social changes in these countries so that their citizenry can freely express their ideas and fight their rights, given that the adoption of technological advances improves economic, democratic and social development of these countries.

In short, future research could analyse strategies and tactics that governments are taking with the use of e-Participation tools. This is, how the use of various platforms is in alignment with the organization's mission (strategy) and how the new online practices can support the organizational mission (tactic) (Mergel, 2012). Therefore, it could be interesting to identify if a "push", "pull" or "networking/mingling" tactic –in terms of Mergel (2013) for social media use- is used by governments and the reasons and factors why they have selected this tactic in their jurisdiction.

REFERENCES

Adweek. (2016). *Here's How Many People Are on Facebook, Instagram, Twitter and Other Big Social Networks*. Retrieved from http://www.adweek.com/digital/heres-how-many-people-are-on-facebook-instagram-twitter-other-big-social-networks/

Alcaide-Muñoz, C., & Gutierrez-Guiterrez, L. J. (2017). Six Sigma and organizational ambidexterity: A systematic review and conceptual framework. *International Journal of Lean Six Sigma*, 8(4), 436–356. doi:10.1108/IJLSS-08-2016-0040

Alcaid-Muñoz, L., & Garde-Sánchez, R. (2014). Implementation of e-Government and reforms in Public Administration in crisis periods: A Scientometric Approach. *International Journal of Public Administration in the Digital Age*, 2(1), 1–23. doi:10.4018/ijpada.2015010101

Alcaide-Muñoz, L., & Rodríguez-Bolívar, M. P. (2015). Understanding e-government Research. *Internet Research*, 25(4), 633–673. doi:10.1108/IntR-12-2013-0259

Alcaide-Muñoz, L., & Rodríguez-Bolívar, M. P. (2015). Understanding e-government Research. *Internet Research*, 25(4), 633–673. doi:10.1108/IntR-12-2013-0259

Alcaide-Muñoz, L., Rodríguez-Bolívar, M. P., Cobo, M. J., & Herrera-Viedma, E. (2017). Analyzing the scientific evolution of e-Government using a science mapping approach. *Government Information Quarterly*, 34(3), 545–555. doi:10.1016/j.giq.2017.05.002

Alcaide-Muñoz, L., Rodríguez-Bolívar, M. P., & Garde-Sánchez, R. (2014). Estudio cienciométrico de la investigación en transparencia informativa, participación ciudadana y prestación de servicios públicos mediante la implementación del e-Gobierno. *Revista de Contabilidad, 17*(2), 130–142. doi:10.1016/j.rcsar.2014.05.001

Bertot, J. C., Jaeger, P. T., & Hansen, D. (2012). The impact of polices on government social media usage: Issues, challenges, and recommendations. *Government Information Quarterly, 29*(1), 30–40. doi:10.1016/j.giq.2011.04.004

Bonsón, E., Royo, S., & Ratkai, M. (2015). Citizens' engagement on local governments' Facebook sites. An empirical analysis: The impact of different media and content types in Western Europe. *Government Information Quarterly, 32*(1), 57–62. doi:10.1016/j.giq.2014.11.001

Boulianne, S. (2015). Social media use and participation: A meta-analysis of current research. *Information Communication and Society, 18*(5), 524–538. doi:10.1080/1369118X.2015.1008542

Cha, M., Haddadi, H., Benevenuto, F., & Gummadi, P. K. (2010). Measuring user influence in twitter: The million follower fallacy. *4th Int'l AAAI Conference on Weblogs and Social Media, 10*(10-17), 30.

Colicchia, C., & Strozzi, F. (2012). Supply chain risk management: A new methodology for a systematic literature review. *Supply Chain Management, 17*(4), 403–418. doi:10.1108/13598541211246558

Dadashzadeh, M. (2010). Social media in government: From eGovernment to eGovernance. *Journal of Business & Economics Research, 8*(11), 81–86. doi:10.19030/jber.v8i11.51

Debatin, B., Lovejoy, J. P., Horn, A. K., & Hughes, B. N. (2009). Facebook and online privacy: Attitudes, behaviors, and unintended consequences. *Journal of Computer-Mediated Communication, 15*(1), 83–108. doi:10.1111/j.1083-6101.2009.01494.x

Delbufalo, E. (2012). Outcomes of inter-organizational trust in supply chain relationships: A systematic literature review and a meta-analysis of the empirical evidence. *Supply Chain Management, 17*(4), 377–402. doi:10.1108/13598541211246549

Denyer, D., & Tranfield, D. (2009). Producing a systematic review. In D. Buchanan & A. Brymand (Eds.), *The Sage Handbook of Organizational Research Methods* (pp. 671–689). London: Sage Publications.

DeVaujany, F. X., Carton, S., Mitev, N., & Romeyer, C. (2014). Applying and theorizing institutions frameworks in ISI research: A systematic analysis from 1999 to 2009. *Information Technology & People*, *27*(3), 280–317. doi:10.1108/ITP-10-2013-0185

Edwards, A., Bekkers, V., & de Kool, D. (2013). Social media monitoring: Responsive governance in the shadow of surveillance? *Government Information Quarterly*, *30*(4), 335–342. doi:10.1016/j.giq.2013.05.024

Ellison, N., & Hardey, M. (2014). Social Media and Local Government: Citizenship, Consumption and Democracy. *Local Government Studies*, *40*(1), 21–40. doi:10.1 080/03003930.2013.799066

Ferro, E. & Molinari, F. (2010). Making sense of Gov 2.0 strategies: "No citizens, no party". *JeDEM-eJournal of eDemocracy and Open Government*, *2*(1), 56-68.

Ganapati, S., & Reddick, C. (2014). The use of ICT for Open Government in U.S. Municipalities. *Public Performance & Management Review*, *37*(3), 365–387. doi:10.2753/PMR1530-9576370302

Guillamón, M. D., Rios, A. M., Gesuele, B., & Metallo, C. (2016). Factors influencing social media use in local governments: The case of Italy and Spain. *Government Information Quarterly*, *33*(3), 460–471. doi:10.1016/j.giq.2016.06.005

Hao, X., Zheng, D., Zeng, Q., & Fan, W. (2016). How to strengthen the social media interactivity of e-government: Evidence from China. *Online Information Review*, *40*(1), 79–96. doi:10.1108/OIR-03-2015-0084

Hartley, J., & Kostoff, R. N. (2003). How useful are key words' in scientific journals? *Journal of Information Science*, *29*(5), 433–438. doi:10.1177/01655515030295008

Hooghe, M., Marien, S., & Quintelier, E. (2010). Inequalities in non-institutionalized forms of political participation: A multi-level analysis of 25 countries. *Political Studies*, *58*(1), 187–213. doi:10.1111/j.1467-9248.2009.00801.x

Hu, G., Pan, W., Lin, H., Kang, K., & Best, M. L. (2014). Study on the Framework of e-Government Services Capability. An empirical investigation. *Social Science Computer Review*, *32*(1), 56–73. doi:10.1177/0894439313501614

Hughes, D. J., Rowe, M., Batey, M., & Lee, A. (2012). A tale of two sites: Twitter vs. Facebook and the personality predictors of social media usage. *Computers in Human Behavior*, *28*(2), 561–569. doi:10.1016/j.chb.2011.11.001

Hui, G., & Hayllar, M. R. (2010). Creating public value in e-Government: A public-private-citizen collaboration framework in Web 2.0. *Australian Journal of Public Administration*, *69*(1), 120–131. doi:10.1111/j.1467-8500.2009.00662.x

Jho, W., & Song, K. J. (2015). Institutional and technological determinants of civil e-Participation: Solo or duet? *Government Information Quarterly*, *32*(4), 488–495. doi:10.1016/j.giq.2015.09.003

Joseph, R. C. (2013). A structured analysis of e-Government studies: Trends and opportunities. *Government Information Quarterly*, *30*(4), 435–440. doi:10.1016/j.giq.2013.05.006

Kietzmann, J. H., Hermkens, K., McCarthy, I. P., & Silvestre, B. S. (2011). Social media? Get serious! Understanding the functional building blocks of social media. *Business Horizons*, *54*(3), 241–251. doi:10.1016/j.bushor.2011.01.005

Kim, S., & Lee, J. (2012). E-Participation, Transparency and Trust in Local Government. *Public Administration Review*, *72*(6), 819–828. doi:10.1111/j.1540-6210.2012.02593.x

Kuzma, J. (2010). Asian government usage of Web 2.0 social media. *European Journal of ePractice*, (9), 1-13.

Legge, J. S. Jr, & Devore, J. (1987). Measuring productivity in US public administration and public affairs programs 1981-1985. *Administration & Society*, *19*(2), 147–156. doi:10.1177/009539978701900201

Lev-On, A., & Steinfeld, N. (2015). Local engagement online: Municipal Facebook pages as hub of interaction. *Government Information Quarterly*, *32*(3), 299–307. doi:10.1016/j.giq.2015.05.007

Luna-Reyes, L. F., & Gil-García, J. R. (2011). Using institutional theory and dynamic simulation to understand complex e-Government phenomena. *Government Information Quarterly*, *28*(2), 329–345. doi:10.1016/j.giq.2010.08.007

Luna-Reyes, L. F., Picazo-Vela, S., & Fernandez-Haddad, M. (2016). Opening the black box: Developing strategies to use social media in government. *Government Information Quarterly*, *33*(4), 693–704. doi:10.1016/j.giq.2016.08.004

Medaglia, R. (2012). eParticiatpion research: Moving characterization forward (2006-2011). *Government Information Quarterly*, *29*(3), 346–360. doi:10.1016/j.giq.2012.02.010

Meijer, A., & Thaens, M. (2013). Social media strategies: Understanding the differences between North American police departments. *Government Information Quarterly*, *30*(4), 343–350. doi:10.1016/j.giq.2013.05.023

Merchant, G. (2012). Unravelling the social network: Theory and research. *Learning, Media and Technology*, *37*(1), 4–19. doi:10.1080/17439884.2011.567992

Mergel, I. (2013). A framework for interpreting social media interactions in the public sector. *Government Information Quarterly*, *30*(4), 327–334. doi:10.1016/j.giq.2013.05.015

Mergel, I. (2016). Social media institutionalization in the US federal government. *Government Information Quarterly*, *33*(1), 142–148. doi:10.1016/j.giq.2015.09.002

Mergel, I., & Bretschneider, S. I. (2013). A three-stage adoption process for social media use in government. *Public Administration Review*, *73*(3), 390–400. doi:10.1111/puar.12021

Moon, K. L., Ngai, E. W. T., & Tao, S. S. C. (2015). Social media research: Theories, constructs, and conceptual framework. *International Journal of Information Management*, *35*(1), 33–44. doi:10.1016/j.ijinfomgt.2014.09.004

Moore, K., & McElroy, J. C. (2012). The influence of personality on Facebook usage, wall postings, and regret. *Computers in Human Behavior*, *28*(1), 267–274. doi:10.1016/j.chb.2011.09.009

Moreno, M. A., Kota, R., Schoohs, S., & Whitehill, J. M. (2013). The Facebook influence model: A concept mapping approach. *Cyberpsychology, Behavior, and Social Networking*, *16*(7), 504–511. doi:10.1089/cyber.2013.0025 PMID:23621717

Nam, T., Pardo, T. A., & Burke, G. B. (2012). e-Government interoperability: Interaction of policy, management, and technology dimensions. *Social Science Computer Review*, *30*(1), 7–23. doi:10.1177/0894439310392184

Newbert, S. L. (2007). Empirical research on the resource-based view of the firm: An assessment and suggestions for future research. *Strategic Management Journal*, *28*(2), 121–146. doi:10.1002/smj.573

Nord, J. H., & Nord, G. D. (1995). MIS research: Journal status assessment and analysis. *Information & Management*, *29*(1), 29–42. doi:10.1016/0378-7206(95)00010-T

Panopoulou, E., Tambouris, E., & Tarabanis, K. (2014). Success factors in designing e-Participation initiatives. *Information and Organization*, *14*(4), 195–213. doi:10.1016/j.infoandorg.2014.08.001

Park, M. J., Dulambazar, T., & Rho, J. J. (2015). The effect of organizational social factors on employee performance and the mediating role of knowledge sharing: Focus on e-Government utilization in Mongolia. *Information Development*, *31*(1), 53–68. doi:10.1177/0266666913494908

Picazo-Vela, S., Gutiérrez-Martínez, I., & Luna-Reyes, L. F. (2012). Understanding risks, benefits, and strategic alternatives of social media applications in the public sector. *Government Information Quarterly*, *29*(4), 504–511.

Porumbescu, G. A. (2016). Linking public sector social media and e-government website use to trust in government. *Government Information Quarterly*, *33*(2), 291–304. doi:10.1016/j.giq.2016.04.006

Rodríguez-Bolívar, M. P., Alcaide-Muñoz, L., & López-Hernández, A. M. (2010). Trends of e-government research: Contextualization and research opportunities. *International Journal of Digital Accounting Research*, *10*, 87–111. doi:10.4192/1577-8517-v10_4

Rodríguez-Bolívar, M. P., Alcaide-Muñoz, L., & López-Hernández, A. M. (2012). Studying e-government: Research methodologies, data compilation techniques and future outlook. *Academia (Caracas)*, *51*, 79–95.

Rodríguez-Bolívar, M. P., Alcaide-Muñoz, L., & López-Hernández, A. M. (2015). Research and experiences in implementing e-Government endeavors in emerging countries: A literature review. In Digital Solution for Contemporary Democracy and Government. IGI Global.

Rodríguez-Bolívar, M. P., Alcaide-Muñoz, L., & López-Hernández, A. M. (2016). Scientometric Study of the Progress and Development of e-Government Research During the Period 2000-2012. *Information Technology for Development*, *22*(1), 36–74. doi:10.1080/02681102.2014.927340

Sabo, O., Rose, J., & Skiftenesflak, L. (2008). The shape of eParticipation: Characterizing an emerging research area. *Government Information Quarterly*, *25*(3), 400–428. doi:10.1016/j.giq.2007.04.007

Sandoval-Almazan, R., & Gil-Garcia, J. R. (2012). Are government internet portals evolving towards more interaction, participation, and collaboration? Revisiting the rhetoric of e-government among municipalities. *Government Information Quarterly*, *29*, 72–S81. doi:10.1016/j.giq.2011.09.004

Scholl, H. J., & Dwivedi, Y. K. (2014). Forums for electronic government scholars: Insight from a 2012/2013 study. *Government Information Quarterly*, *31*(2), 229–242. doi:10.1016/j.giq.2013.10.008

Serrat, O. (2017). Social Media and the Public Sector. In Knowledge Solutions. Springer.

Sidorova, A., Evangelopoulos, N., Valacich, J. S., & Ramakrishnan, T. (2008). Uncovering the intellectual core of the information systems discipline. *Management Information Systems Quarterly*, *32*(3), 467–482. doi:10.2307/25148852

Snead, J. T., & Wright, E. (2014). e-Government research in the United State. *Government Information Quarterly*, *31*(1), 129–136. doi:10.1016/j.giq.2013.07.005

Stamati, T., Papadopoulos, T., & Anagnostopoulos, D. (2015). Social media for openness and accountability in the public sector: Cases in the Greek context. *Government Information Quarterly*, *32*(1), 12–29. doi:10.1016/j.giq.2014.11.004

Susha, I., & Grönlund, A. (2014). 'Context clues for the stall of the Citizens' Initiative: Lessons for opening up e-participation development practice. *Government Information Quarterly*, *31*(3), 454–465. doi:10.1016/j.giq.2014.02.005

Tranfield, D., Denyer, D., & Smart, P. (2003). Towards a Methodology for Developing Evidence-Informed Management Knowledge by Means of Systematic Review. *British Journal of Management*, *14*(3), 207–222. doi:10.1111/1467-8551.00375

Vaterlaus, J. M., Barnett, K., Roche, C., & Young, J. A. (2016). "Snapchat is more personal": An exploratory study on Snapchat behaviors and young adult interpersonal relationships. *Computers in Human Behavior*, *62*, 594–601. doi:10.1016/j.chb.2016.04.029

Wang, C., Medaglia, R., & Saebo, O. (2016). *Learning form e-Government: An agenda for social media research in IS. In PACIS 2016 Proceeding* (p. 190). Association for Information Systems.

Warren, A. M., Sulaiman, A., & Jaafar, N. I. (2014). Social media effects on fostering online civic engagement and building citizen trust and trust in institutions. *Government Information Quarterly*, *31*(2), 291–301. doi:10.1016/j.giq.2013.11.007

Weller, K. (2015). Accepting the challenges of social media research. *Online Information Review*, *39*(3), 281–289. doi:10.1108/OIR-03-2015-0069

Wirtz, B. W., Daiser, P., & Binkowska, B. (2016). E-Participation: A strategic framework. *International Journal of Public Administration*, *39*, 1–12.

Wolfswinkel, J. F., Furtmueller, E., & Wilderon, C. P. M. (2013). Using grounded theory as a method for rigorously reviewing literature. *European Journal of Information Systems*, *22*(1), 45–55. doi:10.1057/ejis.2011.51

Wukich, C., & Mergel, I. (2016). Reusing social media information in government. *Government Information Quarterly*, *33*(2), 305–312. doi:10.1016/j.giq.2016.01.011

Zhao, F., Scavarda, A. J., & Waxin, M. F. (2012). Key issues and challenges in e-government development. An integrative case study of the number one eCity in the Arab World. *Information Technology for Development*, *25*(4), 395–422.

Zheng, L., & Medaglia, R. (2017). Mapping government social media research and moving it forward: A framework and a research agenda. *Government Information Quarterly*. doi:10.1016/j.giq.2017.06.001

Chapter 2
The Role and Impact of Social Media in E-Government

Rasim M. Alguliyev
Institute of Information Technology of Azerbaijan National Academy of Sciences, Azerbaijan

Farhad F. Yusifov
Institute of Information Technology of Azerbaijan National Academy of Sciences, Azerbaijan

ABSTRACT

The rapid development of ICT has a significant impact on the lifestyle of and communication among people. Such impact tendencies alter the human activity as well as government functions and the ways these are implemented. The studies related to Web 2.0, social media, social networks, and their use in the government sector show that the issues such as the formation of social media and important role of the latter in public administration have become a broad research topic. Despite the presence of various approaches of states to social media and social media analytics in international practice, the large impact of social media on public administration is of no doubt. The chapter reviews such issues in the presence of the goal of building mutual communication between government bodies and citizens, the role of social media in building feedback between e-government and citizens, the use of social media in e-government, and the transformation of administrative mechanisms.

DOI: 10.4018/978-1-5225-5326-7.ch002

INTRODUCTION

The flow of new technologies and broad use of social media in recent years have altered the way people communicate with each other. However, the contribution of new technologies and social media to the transformation of public administration into new and open format can change the communication between governments and citizens as well.

At present, social networks and social media in general develop rapidly owing to their capacity to support broad social demand. In this sense, social media is deemed as a powerful tool based on network communications. It is a mutual communication tool between government and society which improves government transparency and facilitates the development of democratic society. It is to be noted that, the achievement of transparency in public administration can be obtained by referring to advanced information.

Social networks enable people to use networks easily; it is interactive and powerful as it facilitates the use of not only content, but also audio and video materials and is based on measures and goals for boosting this communication. Networks are largely used among private, public and non-government organizations. People wish to gather information easily and develop relationships. Interactive communication used in multimedia becomes an integral part of networks in exchange to the adoption of various approaches to the administration of government functions. It is the government's decision whether to improve networks, to become an integral part of these networks or remain as a periphery. The conduction of everyday tasks and development of long-term goals jointly with citizens are considered as government's roles. Multimedia is a powerful tools for applying information in text, as well as in visual and audio format. From this point of view, the investigation of the role of social media in public administration is considered as one of the topical research directions.

As of today, citizens utilize information and communication technologies (ICT) not only for professional purposes, but also in social lives, and analogically, they wish to communicate with governments in the same manner. Hence, the expectations of citizens regarding modern, open and effective government sector broaden. On the other hand, government bodies encountering austere economic measures and intensive budget control are forced to search for innovative tools. The growing tendency of the desire of citizens to establish more comfortable, impeccable and smooth communication with government alongside with this economic situation, as well as the demand for the access to more unbiased information give an impetus to government institutions to employ new digital technology and Web 2.0 tools. The latter would reduce financial difficulties and improve the quality of government services. In this sense, the exploration of the role of social media in shaping and effectively managing e-government is extremely topical.

The research shows that, the application of Web 2.0 technologies in e-government environment in recent years has shaped numerous topical research directions. The studies related to Web 2.0, social media, social networks and their use in government sector demonstrate that, the formation of social media and its role in public administration has become an elaborate research subject.

The literature review describes demonstrate that social media is an effective means for government to improve citizens' trust in government by enhancing their perceptions of government transparency. In case of study has explored how citizens' use of social media in government may lead them to have trust in government and by providing empirical evidence of the mediating role of perceived government transparency in linking the use of e-government to trust in government (Song, & Lee, 2016).

In research Linders, (2012) investigates the evolution of citizen coproduction in the age of social media, web 2.0 interactivity, and ubiquitous connectivity. In this work proposes a unified typology to support systematic analysis based on the overarching categories of "Citizen Sourcing," "Government as a Platform," and "Do-It-Yourself Government." In work examines a discussion of the potential implications for public administration, the remaining limitations and rising social concerns, and the public to play a far more active role in the functioning of their government (Linders, 2012). In research Park, Kang, et al. (2016) demonstrates policy role of social media in developing public trust. In study observed that tweets coming from a leading government officer (e.g., a minister) played mediation role in increasing citizens' perception of credibility in governmental Twitter feed. In research Bonsón et al. (2017) provides an initial assessment of Facebook use by Western European municipalities considering two aspects: citizens' engagement and municipalities' activity. In this case observed that the use of Facebook by Western European local governments has become commonplace. Furthermore, in research proposes a methodology that can be used in future research to measure citizen engagement on social media (Bonsón et al. 2017). In work Rodríguez-Bolivar (2017) examines governance models for the delivery of public services through the Web 2.0 technologies in local initiatives. In research discussed the current debate on Web 2.0 technologies and their implications for local governance through the identification of governance models to be adopted by local governments if Web 2.0 technologies are implemented for providing public services. The results indicate that majority government is prone to implement collaborative models of governance, whereas minority governments are in favor to implement another non-collaborative solution (Rodríguez-Bolivar, 2017).

Issues such as the role of social media in establishing feedback between e-government and citizens, the presence of a long-term agreed goal for building mutual links between government institutions and citizens, the role of social media in building feedback between e-government and citizen, the use of social media in e-government, social culture and the transformation with administrative forms are shown as main research directions. In this sense, the exploration of the role of social media in e-government environment and the development of feedback mechanisms for the efficient administration of e-government preserve high topicality.

It is evident that, the development of effective administrative mechanisms in the implementation of e-government projects is an important issue. The application of social media tools and social networks facilitates the improvement of administrative effectiveness of e-government and the establishment of feedback mechanisms. The analysis of social networks, its application in the process of transformation and development of public administration mechanisms, as well as the development of effective solution tools are considered as effective tools. The development of social media analysis tools facilitates the expansion of mutual communication between citizens and government, effective administration of e-government and development of feedback mechanisms.

This study explores the issues of use of social media tools in e-government environment and main development tendencies. It also reviews conceptual approaches to improving the efficiency of e-government services based on social media analytics and elaborating feedback mechanisms for improving the effectiveness of e-government services.

BACKGROUND

The emergence of electronic commerce in 1995 has given an impetus to new trends. Soon, governments have started to develop established and reliable electronic business practice providing customer self-service. Information access within 24 hours and citizen-government agreement processes such as updating automobile registration and paying taxes have been facilitated. While considering e-government practices, it is evident that implemented projects mainly encompass investments to the improvement of service delivery and efficiency. Today, e-government transforms the state to the electronic environment by improving the access to information and services via online channels, distributing information among organizations and rising the efficiency of business process.

Social media includes social networks such as Facebook and Google+, microblogs such as Twitter, blogs, wikis and numerous sharing web-sites such as Youtube and Flickr. Social media is deemed as an integral part of Web 2.0 technologies characterized by user content, the creation of online profile and relative network. Social media has a particularly attractive potential for electronic participation (Magro, 2012).

Many were interested in opportunities to be created in government by Web 2.0 in 2007-2009 years. Digital diversity is deemed to be eliminated in several developed countries (Couldry, 2007). However, a share of population is still concerned that, new access opportunities are not created, hence, this share remains as "second-class citizens" due to the lack of access (Couldry, 2007; Bertot, Jaeger, & Grimes, 2010; Magro, 2012). A group of people has conceived that, the use of technology for the sake of technology does not lead to civil participation (Breind, & Francq, 2008). Due to the unsuccessful implementation of some early Web 2.0 experiments and the halt of transformative initiatives, governments aspiring to apply technologies have understood that, their innovative behaviors would mostly lead to harm than to benefits (Magro, 2012).

The research conducted from the point of view of citizens has shown that, people had positive attitude and were ready for establishing mutual link with government bodies via e-government initiatives; they trust government more than private sector in terms of private information (Chang, & Kannon, 2008).

Starting from 2009, some issues under threat have been identified. Experts reckon that, participation and liability, accessible information, cooperation among government institutions, multi-channel delivery and identification must achieve success as the sectors of government.

Participation and liability were primary objectives of e-government social media projects, however, their content would lead to unexpected outcomes. Some propose that, social media provides a platform for mutual cooperation of citizens and government via information sharing and has a potential to shape a positive opinion about governments (Park, & Cho, 2009).

Experts were still deprived of the use of social media in government in 2009. It has been revealed that, social media use by government may facilitate broader opportunities for participation, or may increase the degree of satisfaction of individual and unaware citizens characterized by liability and absence of concern.

2010 was marked with the rapid growth in the number of research works on social media and e-government. More attention has been devoted to some new problems and detailed guidelines have been developed.

Social media and Web 2.0 have been used in Europe, however, their full potential has not been utilized. Government lagged behind the publicity in terms of using social media. Many have started recognize that, not only new technologies, but also a new approach is needed. Government has been forced to use everyday technologies utilized by people. Changes in leadership and policies was necessary for comprehensive use of social media (Magro, 2012).

As before, some institutions were expecting the use of social media technologies in order to increase their participation, however, as indicated by experts, digital technologies have never protected us from ourselves; those can actually amplify existing tendencies. If government does not adapt to current agenda, Web 2.0 can never be seen as a solution (Ostling, 2010). In other words, the performance of traditional government is tracked with the model of collection and limitation of information. This approach suppresses e-participation and government innovation and when success is achieved, the paradigm of information exchange must be adopted (Parvcek, & Sachs, 2010).

Web 2.0 has facilitated the transformation of passive web users into active content creators willing to share in last 5 years. Enterprises have been flexible in investing to social media in order to attract customers, gain their satisfaction, provide their participation in discussions, become familiarized with them and use their knowledge for industrial manufacturing.

Governments have been witnessing the success of these technologies in election campaigns by analyzing business sectors which apply Web 2.0 technologies; at present, they have focused their attention on investments to social media as a part of their IT strategies. However, the application of social media in government and its tracking of similar experiences and limitations employed by business sectors remains open to research.

Various approaches are necessary for government's successful investments in social media. In this case, it would be desirable that, the government does not follow the trajectory of corporate sector using social media only for the sake of using it. The use of social media by governments must be planned, just and based on promoting mutual aid and transparency (Magro, 2012).

Another approach states that, e-government approach allows to produce advanced ICT tools, existing environment and organizational changes (Magro, 2012). Experts have proposed 8 elements to be addressed for successful social media policy: employee availability, account management, satisfactory use, situation, content, security, legal issues and citizen.

Starting from 2011, the concentration of social media power in the hands of users have come evident. The analysis of early forms of e-government initiatives in the world has revealed the limited use of early e-government proposals. The expansion of social media use have been proposed as a low-level participation solution which would lead to the electronic participation of more extensive, deeper and more advanced generation (Charalabis, & Loukis, 2012).

Some agencies have detected main problems pertaining to social media proposals. For instance, if announcements on Facebook page of government contradict to the aim and challenges of the page, reliability becomes a primary issue. In addition, Facebook privacy has been an important issue for years. While using it, citizens may not be able to differentiate between social media sources and government institutions. The access to an undesirable web-site which is not a priority of social media users is another issue of concern or format and design limitations may hinder the government from reaching particular citizen groups.

Expert analysis has shown that, information about revolts known as Arab Spring in Near East has been spread via Facebook and Twitter. A report submitted by analytics has stated that, social media tools comprised online and offline identities, which have played important role in dramatic changes taking place in Arab region (Magro, 2012).

Instructions regarding the use of social media in government and non-commercial social tools such as Facebook and Twitter in particular have continued. Similar issues directs governments towards developing a particular strategy and acting according to it and presents alternative platforms providing better access (Hellman, 2011).

Studies have shown that, 65% of all enterprises (including state enterprises) does not have appropriate policy regarding the employees using social media and 50% of those does not monitor social media regularly (Mcnamara, 2011; Magro, 2012).

The number of studies oriented to the application of e-government Web 2.0 technologies in recent years has been growing. Studies are conducted as a literature review on Web 2.0, social media, social networks and their use in state sector. Primary analysis includes the evolution of social media and social media policy in long-term and issues such as important role of social media in public administration has been reviewed. Other matters covered by studies are the lack of goal for e-government, the implementation of significant changes in resource management, as well as factors for successful use of social media.

Various technologies comprised under the umbrella of Web 2.0 technologies has been located at different degrees by local, regional and national governments in USA and other advanced countries. The representative Web 2.0 technologies in government are Social cooperation and Blogs, Wikis for collaborative authoring and editing, podcasting, photo and video sharing, Social Bookmarking, News Sharing, and Tagging, Social network, Mashups, Widgets and so on. These technologies have been briefly reviewed in this section and represented placements have been identified (Accenture, 2001; Armano, 2010; Campbell, & Flagg, 2010).

Social Media Technologies in E-Government

The expansion of electronic awareness, the acceleration of e-government and development of e-administration can be considered as a noteworthy tendency oriented to the formation of information society. Regular monitoring of these tendencies is at the spotlight of many international and national organizations.

The rapid development of ICT has gained larger importance for public administration. The expenditure on e-government building in advanced countries is rapidly growing in recent years. Hence, the efficiency of the implementation of corresponding projects is among main discussion topics.

The primary objectives of building e-government programs are to increase the efficiency of economic management, as well as government and municipal administration and to establish a material-technical base and new environment for the development of civil society by providing the right of free access to information.

The implementation of e-government projects in international practice is constituted of three main conceptual models: G2G, G2B, and G2C. It provides an easy access to services for citizens and simplified use of those by enabling rapid access to government services. In addition, e-government facilitates the addressing of numerous functional issues, for instance, provision of various e-services to registries established in different spheres, e-document flow of government institutions and etc.

Social media has wide audience due to its use of visual and audio information alongside with multimedia. At present, the monitoring of public administration has become an integral part of this network in exchange for decision-making. It is a tool of mutual communication between the government and society facilitating the development of government transparency and democratic society. It is self-evident that, government transparency can be achieved by referring to advanced information. The information access of citizens must be accessible and transparent (Landsbergen, 2010; Song, & Lee, 2013; Banday, & Mattoo, 2013).

Social media rapidly develops while it meets important social demand. If government can utilize it, it must learn how social media meets these social demands in this case. People wish to acquire information easily and develop relationships. Interactive communication used in multimedia is becoming a part of networks in exchange for adopting various methods of the administration of government's affairs. It is the government's decision to improve or support networks, become an integral part of these networks or remain at a periphery. The conduction of daily transactions and development of long-term goals with its citizens is deemed as the role of government. Multimedia is powerful in applying text, as well as visual and audio information (Landsbergen, 2010; Banday, & Mattoo, 2013).

The trust in public administration is considered as a balance between decision makers and citizens or the trust of citizens to each government decision. Administrative bodies must trust in the sovereignty of civil democracy. Unlike web-pages, social media tools may send appeals and proposals to citizens. It creates social networks with stricter position supporting the reliability of government. Social media strongly supports network communication and facilitates the communication in unofficial networks existing within government. More effective utilization of sources and trust raising are among the methods to make social media useful for government.

Alongside being a tool of information technologies, social media has advantages for government and people. This sort of communication can be prompt, mutual or individual. It remains as a desirable issue for citizens, however, the government is in need of new avenues on how to build communication with citizens and monitor their activities. Social media develops networks and uses them appropriately. At last, social media is a communication tool and a strategy for managing communication channels. Commercial organizations, scientific institutions and individuals use social media for online participation, promotion of goods and services, gathering customer feedback, expertise exchange, consumption and mutual customer relations, creation of joint content, electronic education, communication, social links, etc. (Banday, & Mattoo, 2013).

The primary power of social media pages is cooperation, participation, competence and time. It serves as a tool of comprising government institutions, citizens, activities of institutions and information by promoting government information, services and cooperation. Social media expands the avenues of Internet use in order to implement all benefits of electronic administration. It not only proposes benefits for electronic administration regarding the intensification and monitoring of services, but also reduces costs by raising efficiency. Governments can post job announcements, promote services, announce market measures, seek for public feedback and cooperate with geographically different institutions by using these web-pages. Broader use can increase transparency which, in turn, leads to growing reliability of government (O'Reilly, 2005).

The electronic transparency in social media implies the activities of people, groups and institutions outside organization and the ability to monitor decisions adopted within organization. It includes tendencies about which organizations tend to share information regarding their performance and outcomes, as well as the openness of organizations to its evaluations and criticism by outside groups and individuals. Government transparency can be obtained by active information sharing. The provision of government transparency leads to the reduction of corruption case in government (O'Reilly, 2005).

Internet has a potential role in expanding the government's transparency. It is because large-volume information can be demonstrated with lower costs and people can acquire information as long as they are connected to Internet. Governments make effort to raise the openness and transparency of their activities via electronic administration. Despite the potential strategy employed by governments in order to raise the transparency, both practitioners and scientists have drawn attention to the potential of social media to be an alternative channel for electronic transparency. Social media enables to reach the groups lagging behind in using online government services. Social media has affected mutual links between governments and citizens, as well as the methods of increasing the transparency of governments significantly.

Although in slow tempo, government institutions adopt social technologies better in order to reach assigned goals. These technologies offer more opportunities, and hence, may alter the old model of state sector gradually. Newly proposed opportunities can raise the transparency and reliability of government, establish new forms of civil participation and engagement in public issues, as well as inter- and intra-organizational cooperation. The cooperation between a provider and a receiver, government and citizens in our case, alters (Karakiza, 2014).

Nowadays, citizens use ICT not only for professional, but also for social lives and want to establish similar links with governments analogically. Hence, the expectations of citizens rise regarding a modern, open and effective government. On the other hand, government institutions encounter harsh economic measures and intensive budget control, which leads to the search for new and innovative forms. Alongside with this economic situation, the growing tendency of citizens willing to establish more comfortable, impeccable and smooth communication with government alongside with this economic situation, the demand for the access to more unbiased information gives an impetus to government bodies to apply new digital technology and Web 2.0 tools which will reduce financial difficulties and improve the quality of government services (Karakiza, 2014).

O'Reilly (2005) has described Web 2.0 as a platform comprising interlinked devices. It is characterized by Transparency, Honesty, Trust and Authority and based on simple, usable and centralized model. The use of static pages of Web 1.0 by Web 2.0 can be deemed as an important shift to more usable web tools. Web 2.0 has "participation architecture", which makes information and services suggestions from different sources and this information and services can be updated, used and remixed by others (O'Reilly, 2005). Main aspects of Web 2.0 are to create and exchange. Web 2.0 possesses a potential to mutually expand the intelligence of participants collectively. In general, it can be considered as an Internet software used for the purpose of online sharing archived for media demonstration by social media users, as well as for easy access of other impressive users. Social media ca be characterized in two ways: social participation / media abundance and self-introduction / self-explanation. According to another classification, those can be grouped in two broad classifications regardless their goal: a) impressing social media; here, users express themselves by sharing texts, images and videos, b) Cooperative social media; users work together by sharing their knowledge and work for a common purpose in general here. Social media proposes a unique opportunity for reconstructing the relations between government and population, such that, it is a transition from one-direction or two-direction information exchange to a communication process taking place among many. Government institutions try to become citizen-centred and social media proposes powerful tools for increasing the engagement of publicity. In fact, "digital citizens – are social media users" and it is the place of communication of government with them, surely, in case if the government desires to communicate. Thus, government must develop own Web-software in order to broaden its capacity (Karakiza, 2014).

Alongside new technologies oriented to the expansion of openness, participation, transparency and cooperation, Gov 2.0 integrates the changes in organizational culture. Gov 2.0 provides mutual cooperation between the government and citizens at greater extent which are main generators of government information (Karakiza, 2014). Moreover, Government 2.0 is defined as "IT application for the purpose of publicization and commodification of state services, processes and information". In addition to broad application of ICT, this notion also emphasizes the terms of socialization and commodification. As a result, the boundaries between government and citizens become blurred. In some cases, Gov 2.0 and Open Government terms are used interchangeably, although Open Government underlines the information openness and civil participation. Open Government is defined as "a transparent, accessible and responsible administration system where information freely flows from various channels to and / or from the government". If Open Government is focused on information, it is necessary to define Open Government Information term in this case: a) Government Information is "any information generated by society", b) Open information is "the information easily used and shared information multiple times". While we are oriented to We-Government, citizens actively participate and become partners: citizens and government generate information and resources once again (Ubaldi, 2013).

Impact of Social Network Websites in E-Government

Information and communication tools have not only started to play an important role in people's life, but also the use of the technologies has increased, and Internet significantly influences the mutual communication and cooperation among people in particular. The development of blogs, web-sites and social networks such as Facebook, Twitter and Google Plus creates a favourable environment for the government to benefit from these new methods by registering in these web-sites. On the other hand, social media becomes a platform facilitating easy access to Internet for everyone which enables governments to communication with its citizens by joining these pages and raises the level of participation and employment level of citizens (Abu-Shanab, 2012).

The use of social media web-pages and information tools by people, private enterprises and government institutions forces the government to ponder carefully regarding the possibilities of how to benefit from use of social media by raising the level of employment and participation of those people. E-government web-sites are created for the use of citizens, whereas social networks are a place of communication among people; the registration in these pages enables governments to become closer with its citizens (Khasawneh, & Abu-Shanab, 2013).

Social media has become easily accessible for everyone with Internet access and a favorite communication tool of broad audience. It has forced governments to meditate about benefitting from social media by employing these methods via strategic ways in order to manage their trade, communicate with their citizens more effectively and efficiently.

Social media is being largely used by people and offers to create online mutual communication between them in an easier and more affordable way (Khasawneh, & Abu-Shanab, 2013). Harris and Rea (2009) have described social media as a project facilitating second-generation web development and Internet communication, contacts and cooperation and enabling information sharing. According to the definition, it is evident that, primary functions of social media is communication and mutual links where electronic government has historically evolved as information exchange and communication in two main stages.

One of the benefits of social media is that it offers new modes of communication in order to enable information exchange from private profiles of people and describe content (Khasawneh, & Abu-Shanab, 2013). Social media transforms people from content readers into content creators and publishers which have become an important feedback mechanism of people possessing two-sided information flow. Various contents such as news, advertisements, documents, videos and music can be shared in and obtained from social media (Nica, & Grayson, 2011). Users obtain an opportunity to share and disseminate their information with others via their networks.

The rapidly growing use of social media web-sites, as well as various social media websites with customized and attractive features is capable to draw people's attention and joining these websites. Based on aforementioned, social media web-sites can be group in 4 main categories according to various functions (Khasawneh, & Abu-Shanab, 2013):

- Checklists serving to the function of writing a resume which contains skills indicated by customers and their colleagues. LinkedIn is the best example of this sort of networks;
- A communication channel with the feature of disseminating current or updated valid information or content; the best example for this sort of networks are twitter and all blogs (like bloggers)
- Public and rating websites usable for event promotion and serving to less formal mutual communication with similar websites; Facebook and fan pages are best examples for websites with aforementioned features.

- Archive and sharing websites with active feedback channels used for the sharing and storage of documents and slides, as well as videos; the best websites with these features are Youtube and slideshare websites.

Social media is not only a website, but also a communication tool facilitating the mutual interaction and communication among people and to share audio, video files and content. Moreover, social media provides people with tools to obtain the required information in an easy way and establish relationships. According to information obtained from multiple sources, a brief overview of some social networks are given below.

- **Facebook:** Is one of the rapidly developing media web-pages; this easily usable page with an interface and a broad range of features was established in 2004 (Khasawneh, & Abu-Shanab, 2013). Facebook has numerous applications where people can create own accounts and communicate with friends, family members and work colleagues in a more effective manner. Facebook also has professional applications where corporations and organizations can create fan pages in order to establish communication with customers via feedback and active communication channel. Facebook brings into life the intent of corporations to attract millions of customers with minimum time and costs. Research has shown that, Facebook occupies the first place in the list of top popular 10 social networks (Khasawneh, & Abu-Shanab, 2013).
- **Twitter:** Twitter is another rapidly growing social network website; established in 2006; the website offers an opportunity to people to open a free account and communicate by using short messages and 140-symbol "Tweets". Twitter can be described as large information storage available to use for socio-political and marketing purposes and electronic "word of mouth" (e-WOM) in another form (Khasawneh, & Abu-Shanab, 2013). Research has demonstrated that, Twitter is in the second position among 10 top popular social networks.
- **MySpace:** Is one of the general social network web-pages; it was established by the executive director of eUniverse Internet company in August, 2003. Research has shown that, MySpace occupies the third place among 10 top popular social networks (Khasawneh, & Abu-Shanab, 2013).
- **LinkedIn:** Is among business-oriented social network websites used for professional matters. It was established in 2002 and started to be used in an executive form of social networks in 2003. Members of the LinkedIn website must fill their profiles in the form of Resume, for instance, some private information, employment record, current work experience and professional

skills, etc. Research has revealed that, LinkedIn occupies the fourth place among 10 top popular social networks (Khasawneh, & Abu-Shanab, 2013).

- **Other Websites:** Other social network websites include ning, Tgged, Friendster, Hi5, Meetup, MyYearbook and other existing in virtual space. Each of these web-sites has special and unique features distinguishing them among others.

E-government implies the use of information and communication technologies by government in order to establish mutual communication with citizens and pursue state affairs by using various electronic media such as telephones, tablets, fax, smart cards, self-service shops, email, Internet and EDI (Electronic Data Exchange) (Almarabeh, & AbuAli, 2010). The conceptual model of e-government is categorized according to proposed services and the provision of the efficiency of those. These range of categories covers government institutions, social and political organizations, business, employees and non-governmental organizations.

Social media has a significant impact on the implementation of government affairs. Moreover, social media offers strategic opportunities for attracting citizens, business sector and organizations. When the government decides to join social media web-pages, it must take into consideration some important points; governments must be cautious while pursuing these activities by creating Facebook and twitter accounts and fan pages. It is necessary for the government to become an active user of these web-pages by providing timely, sustainable and updated information and establishing mutual communication with citizens.

Experts reckon that, social media will help governments to become more transparent by providing citizens with better services and information access, opening active communication channel with them and assigning competences to citizens (Khasawneh, & Abu-Shanab, 2013). Moreover, if governments use these webpages effectively, it will encourage citizens to become more influential and active participants in their society. In terms of e-participation, social media provides new communication tools for governments to deliver any message or news rapidly and effectively. Citizens can participate in online discussions on public matters with local or national governments. This will facilitate more open, transparent and mutual relations between citizens and governments.

In order to provide such relations to citizens, governments must carefully ponder on how to manage social media websites and use such channels effectively. Social media management can be implemented by using various approaches; the best example is used by corporations in order to manage social media present. "Four R" approach is based on following 4 actions: React, pay attention to monitoring of what people say online: Respond, be sure that, its active communication channel is existent; and Redirect to another address, allow other people with similar issues and problems to benefit from similar situation. Hence, governments must speculate about how to benefit from these approaches in social media websites in effective and easy way (Khasawneh, & Abu-Shanab, 2013).

It is absolutely necessary for government to be present in social media websites, especially if governments wish to maintain people's trust at high level and use social media in order provide them with active information channel. In addition, social media websites allow governments to communicate citizens and use valuable resources present in these websites effectively by employing more creative and innovative methods.

Feedback Tools for Improving the Efficiency of E-Government Services

Governments pursue noteworthy efforts for the purpose of expanding citizen participation in decision making and political processes. In order to understand the needs of citizens, government institutions devote much attention to their capability to use e-services. Recently, social media offers opportunities for higher transparency of governments by providing better services to citizens and expanding their information access.

E-government employs information and communication tools in order to achieve higher citizen satisfaction by using useful services in a better way. The experience shows that, governments can be more efficient by being more interactive with their citizens.

Social media services have become a main tool in expressing thoughts and sharing the content and are deemed as a valuable source helping to collect all necessary information about society in recent years. Experts state that, governments possess capability to benefit from social media popularity and its use by wide audience in order to improve their strategies and efficiency indicators. Large interest and engagement in social media use shows that, there exists a great potential for the expansion of online participation. According to statistical figures, the number of users of online government services has increased from 39% in 2005 to 57% in 2011 (Kacem, Belkaroui, & Jemal, 2016).

Social media still plays an important role in the emergence of political protests in some countries. For instance, Tunisia, Iran, Egypt and other countries marked with Arab string revolt can be shown as examples of the impact of social media on government and on shaping opinions. Moreover, social media offers strategic opportunities for attracting individuals, as well as corporations and public organizations. This enables governments to offer better opportunities and Internet access to citizens and be more transparent by providing active communication channels.

Customization of information is applied for meeting the citizens' needs in a better way by assisting the acquisition of corresponding information among big data via the individualization of government services in e-government sector. The previous research on the issue of user profile in e-government does not include user activities extracted from social media. Those mainly employ demographic information or feedback. Notwithstanding this, the profile content of a user may be determined from his/her online activity in social media websites. In fact, the systems of knowledge detection in recent times benefit from blogs, micro blogs and social networks created by users (Hussain, 2014). This type of contents is not used in e-government sphere widely.

Latest research utilizes user contents created on the platform of government services. For example, researchers propose a customized platform corresponding to the services suggested to each user profile (Kacem, Belkaroui, & Jemal, 2016). After a user profile is created, those utilize two profiles: a long-term profile storing static information about user and a short-term profile storing the data detected from current session.

The majority of lately conducted studies uses social media as the customization of government services (Bista, Nepal, & Paris, 2013). The studies on the analysis of social media presents new elements such as the exploration of online societies, social networks and contents created by user to e-government (Reddick, 2010). They reckon that, Web 2.0 is essential for the cooperation aspect as it comprises communication, mutual links, content sharing and social networks.

When combined with the power of social media, open and big data offers significant capabilities to accelerate the civil activeness and social innovations. Open data is also called the information of open government sector and adopts important decisions to increase the transparency, participation and government effectiveness. Researchers present open data as the latest phenomenon at the initial stage of open data development (Kacem, Belkaroui, & Jemal, 2016). They analyze the benefits and obstacles of open data system by synthesizing their experience with open data.

Currently, there exist big data projects successfully applied in large corporations, including Adobe, Amazon, Yahoo, Facebook, etc. The issues considered by these corporations can be applied in e-government environment as well. Big data and Hadoop are employed in various spheres including data storage, healthcare, education, trade, energy, logistics, travel, financial services, politics, etc. Some of Big data issues applied in practice bear a large importance for e-government in particular.

Given the popularity of social networks, the analysis of those is an important issue. Analytical tools possessing broad capabilities enable to analyze unstructured data in social media and determine the user interest and profile regarding a particular matter. For instance, those can be used for improving the accuracy of big data analysis for identifying the effectiveness of various marketing campaigns.

The use of big data compiled in social networks can be proposed as below for finding effective e-government solutions (Yusifov, 2016):

- **Aim:** Analysis of user profiles by using big data compiled in e-government system.
- **Importance:** Establishment of feedback with e-government portal users; expansion of government services provided for users.
- **Data Sources:** Social media, electronic applications of citizens and other sources.
- **Analysis Outcomes:** Various information on e-services (for example, ratings, efficiency, required services, etc.); suggestion of recommendations for improving the effectiveness of government services based on data acquired; establishment of feedback mechanism.

The rapid development of proposed services and technologies, especially mobile communication, internet of things, social media and e-service sectors has led to the generation of large-volume unstructured data. The analysis of such data bears importance not only for business sector, but also for science, public administration, education and the society in general. Nowadays, it is practically unattainable to process large-volume data generated in e-government systems and social networks with traditional methods. The purposeful use of big data will allow to improve the effectiveness of e-government system, to find effective e-government solutions, to expand relations between citizens and government institutions, to develop effective feedback mechanisms and to achieve high level of civil society development overall.

The capabilities and potential of big data play an important role in improving the effectiveness of digital government services and service delivery via mutual relations of governments with citizens and private sector. The adoption and benefits of solution avenues of big data facilitate the process of government decision-making in various government projects (Kim, Trimi, & Chung, 2015).

One of the important and topical issues is the exploration of citizen profiles for the development of e-government services. Such that, a conceptual structure is proposed for exploring citizen profiles in order to develop state services, the decision making, information sharing, transparency and communication with citizens Kacem, Belkaroui, & Jemal, 2016. By studying this experience, a conceptual model consisting of six main components can be proposed which suggests most appropriate recommendations in order to meet citizens' demands. It can be applied in various government institutions such as education, tourism and healthcare (Yusifov, 2016). The proposed model presents three forms of appropriate information for citizens, business sector and politicians, respectively (Figure 1).

Figure 1. Proposed conceptual model of e-government

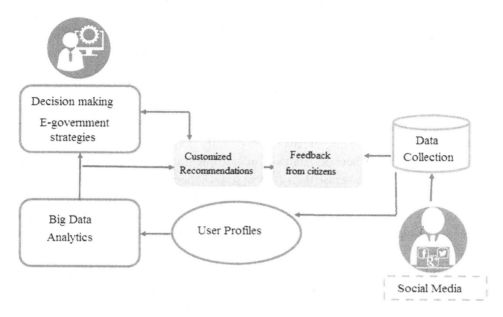

- **For Citizens:** Customized recommendations corresponding to profiles are proposed to citizens for improving the government services provided to citizens.
- **For Business Sector:** Formation of a transparent environment in business sector, establishment of new and interactive links between citizens and business sector, investigation of user profiles by considering the citizen satisfaction and requirements for shaping business solutions.
- **For Politicians:** It proposes the investigation of profiles based on meeting the demand of citizens for improving the decision making, e-government strategies, transparency and cooperation.

The creation of customized interface provides mutual communication between citizens and the system. The inclusion of each citizen in government structure takes place by providing the username and password during registration. The private information of a user is gathered with demographic information (name, age, personal interests and information regarding the preference of e-government services) entered during the registration. User has an option to update information on his/her personal page regularly. Context-related information (personal and public) is obtained from public profiles of users and their activity in social media.

Profiles are formed which detect use profiles, use the activity of citizens in social media websites and based on the integration of mutual communication of citizens.

Users freely express their opinions and preferences and share the contents they are interested in. As the existing approach is the most common social network among Facebook and Twitter users, their activity can be analyzed here.

If use a representation based on key words for the structure of user profile in which key words are provided from online activities of each user in social media.

After the terms used in profile creation are compiled, it is possible to identify the term frequency providing the overview of daily frequency of terms distribution. "Hashtags" are used in Facebook status in order to integrate the mutual communication of citizens effectively and grasp their current state. Especially, the gist of each hashtag can be reviewed separately. Thereafter, we obtain general discussion collection by using various methods, for instance, a decision tree. At second phase, we analyze all discussions in all Facebook shares of users and determine the category collection identifying the subject of interest of user profile. We grade each category for creating profile subject by using frequency grading function. Thereafter, profile subject is defined as main categories which is based on ranking function. The outcome of this phase is used for enriching user and public profiles by accelerating interests and preferences matching main categories and user and public profiles.

It can be generalized that, one of the most important issues in the establishment of e-government is the development of effective administrative mechanisms. The application of social networks helps to improve the administrative effectiveness of e-government and enhance public administration mechanisms such as feedback mechanism. The application of social networks can facilitate the centralized administration of resources pertaining to e-government, content monitoring, number of applications and the investigation of user and expert forums. In general, the application of social networks enables the improvement of e-government administrative mechanisms.

Social networks bring together people with similar interests in Internet environment and constitute an integral part of our lives. Today, virtual networks supported by blogs and Wiki technologies constitute the majority among websites.

Let's consider a particular example related to the application of social networks in e-government administration process: assume that, any legislative institution contemplates the adoption of a specific law. Applied social network can boost mutual information exchange among legislative institutions and the consideration of user opinion at discussion phase in advance.

Moreover, the position of users is specified in the process of network analysis which is very important for determining their role in network. Several principal phases can be indicated during the process of network analysis. Each phase addresses its specific methodological problem. Firstly, indicators characterizing the features of network links are developed. On this basis, requests are generated for network users. Compiled data is analyzed and network is constructed. The measurement of indicators reflecting the structural characteristics of network is developed at next phase. The results are analyzed in the end.

SOLUTIONS AND RECOMMENDATIONS

It is to be noted that, alongside the high sensitivity of governments regarding legal and ethical aspects of the application of technology, privacy attacks to state institutions on social media amplify the inclinations to compile and use the contents created by online users. Despite the existence of such threats, social media is an ideal solution for supporting the awareness and future-oriented policy making; hence, the benefits of social media tools for governments must not be overlooked.

Different advantages of social media such as collaboration, empowerment, and participation have attracted various governments to utilize social media in governance for uniting citizens, agencies, and local municipalities information and organisations. It is utilized to the expansion of government services, improve governmental trust, democracy mechanisms and increase transparency. When implemented in e-governance, or using in e-government social media might also pose various risks of exclusion, addiction, reputation, isolation, privacy violation, fraud and scams, security threats and potentially results in lost productivity.

Governments have to develop comprehensive frameworks, best practices, guidelines, feedback mechanisms and policies to work as a key enabler for local government agencies for the implementation of social media in e-government. Various policies focus on different components and the majority of them indicate the adapting of existing rules and regulations for securing information and data.

The application of social network is considered as a new direction in conducted research and empirical applications targeting the effective administration of e-government which is based on the outcomes of the analysis of electronic documents massive and the monitoring of information space. Proposals are developed regarding administrative decision making based on the information acquired at the stage of data analysis and outcomes are obtained. After a report is prepared based on feedback according to the evaluation conducted, the last phase – is the adoption of a decision based on acquired information.

It can be noted that, e-government building and development of effective administrative mechanisms constitute a priority of the development of states. In accordance with the stages of transformation and development of public administration, e-government building is among vital issues. The achievements acquired in e-government building foster economic growth, connect remote provinces with urban centers and improve the standard of living.

FUTURE RESEARCH DIRECTIONS

The development and application of new methods and mechanisms in e-government administration is not only confined to increasing the number of electronic services and building internal networks and database in public administration institutions. It also denotes the provision of transparency in the activity of government institutions and freedom of information, the increase in the efficiency of the activity of government institutions, development of democracy and close participation of citizens in public administration regardless their physical abilities, the formation of direct democracy, provision of state services in online environment and the maintenance of security. In this regard, social media bears a great importance in e-government environment. The analytics of social media and social networks and the consideration of those among the mechanisms of e-government administration mechanisms is one of topical problems and the expansion of studies in this direction is deemed as purposeful.

Considering the popularity of social media, the implementing and analysis of social media tools is an important issue. Analytical tools possessing broad capabilities enable to analyze unstructured data in social media and determine the user interest and profile regarding a particular matter. Those can be used for improving the accuracy of big data analysis for identifying the effectiveness of various marketing and political campaigns. In future research focus on development of feedback tools for improving the efficiency of e-government services based on social media analytics. More in detail analysis can be formed based on citizen information gathered in social media for representing user groups sharing similar interests, characters and e-government domains. This content can be used for forecasting and recommending most corresponding services among existing ones. Corresponding services will be created as a customized outcome based on citizen interests and requests obtained from their profiles for improving their level of satisfaction.

CONCLUSION

As a result, it is to be noted that, the rapid development of ICT influences the lifestyle of people, their interaction and communication significantly. Such noteworthy changes alter the modes of people's activity, as well as the implementation of government functions. On the other hand, existing media tools and websites such as blogs and social media widely used by many people and organizations force e-government administrators to ponder on the possible benefits of joining these sort of websites.

The growing importance and role of social media in many societies, as well as in political communication and civil activity enables the social media analysis, the analysis of social networks, knowledge detection, creation of user profiles and the use of mechanisms such as feedback and facilitates the expansion of services provided by government and the improvement of administrative efficiency. Hence, social media analytics tools are mostly used in political process and by private companies for commercial purposes, the tools enabling the analysis of social media in general have been reviewed in this study. Despite the presence of various approaches to social media and social analytics tools in international practice, it is no doubt that, it has a large influence on improving public administration. Several governments express interest for promoting the positions of social media, however, they also use social media for obtaining feedbacks on their activities.

ACKNOWLEDGMENT

This work was supported by the Science Development Foundation under the President of the Republic of Azerbaijan - Grant № EİF-KETPL-2-2015-1(25)-56/05/1.

REFERENCES

Abu-Shanab, E. (2012). Digital Government Adoption in Jordan: An Environmental Model. *The International Arab Journal of e-Technology*, 2(3), 129-135.

Accenture. (2001). *Accenture Public Service Value Governance Framework*. Retrieved June 13, from www.accenture.com

Almarabeh, T., & AbuAli, A. A. (2010). General Framework for E-Government: Definition Maturity Challenges, Opportunities, and Success. *European Journal of Scientific Research*, 39(1), 29–42.

Armano, D. (2010). Six Social Media Trends for 2010, 2009. *Harvard Business Review*. Retrieved June 18, from http://blogs.hbr.org/cs/2009/11/six_social_media_trends.html

Banday, M.T., & Mattoo, M.M. (2013). Social Media in e-Governance. *Scientific Research Journal*, 47-56.

Bertot, J. C., Jaeger, P. T., & Grimes, J. M. (2010). Using ICTs to create a culture of transparency: E-government and social media as openness and anti-corruption tools for societies. *Government Information Quarterly*, 27(3), 264–271. doi:10.1016/j.giq.2010.03.001

Bista, S. K., Nepal, S., & Paris, C. (2013). The human touch of government services. In *Proceedings of the Late-Breaking Results, Project Papers and Workshop Proceedings of the 21st Conference on User Modeling, Adaptation, and Personalization (UMAP'13)*. Rome, Italy: Springer International Publishing.

Bonsón, E., Royo, S., & Ratkai, M. (2017). Facebook Practices in Western European Municipalities. An Empirical Analysis of Activity and Citizens' Engagement. *Administration & Society*, 49(3), 320–347. doi:10.1177/0095399714544945

Breind, Y., & Francq, P. (2008). Can Web 2.0 applications save e-democracy? A study of how new internet applications may enhance citizen participation in the political process online. *Int. J. Electron. Democr, 1*(1), 14–31. doi:10.1504/IJED.2008.021276

Campbell, S., & Flagg, R. (2010). *Examples of Agencies Using Online Content and Technology to Achieve Mission and Goals*. Retrieved June 10, from www.usa.gov

Chang, A., & Kannon, P. K. (2008). *Leveraging Web 2.0 in government. E-Government Technology Series*. IBM Center for the Business of E-Government. Retrieved June 10, from www.businessofgovernment.org

Charalabis, Y., & Loukis, E. (2012). Transforming government agencies' approach to e-participation through efficient exploitation of social media. *Proceedings of the 2011 European Conference on Information Systems*, 1–12.

Couldry, N. (2007). New media for global citizens? The future of the digital divide debate. *The Brown Journal of World Affairs, 14*, 249–261.

Harris, A., & Rea, A. (2009). Web 2.0 and Virtual World technologies: A Growing impact on IS Education. *Journal of Information Systems Education*, 20(2).

Hellman, R. (2011). The Cloverleaves of Social Media Challenges for e-Governments. *Proceedings of eChallenges e-2011 Conference*, 1–8.

Hussain, Y. (2014). *Social Media as a Tool for Transparency and Good Governance in the Government of Gilgit-Baltistan*. Crossroads Asia Working Paper Series, 22.

Kacem, A, Belkaroui R., & Jemal D. (2016). Towards Improving e-Government Services Using Social Media-Based Citizen's Profile Investigation. *ICEGOV '15-16*.

Karakiza, M. (2014). The impact of Social Media in the Public Sector. *Proceedings of the International Conference on Strategic Innovative Marketing*, 384-392.

Khasawneh, R. T., & Abu-Shanab, E. A. (2013). E-Government and Social Media Sites: The Role and Impact. *World Journal of Computer Application and Technology*, *1*(1), 10–17.

Kim, G.-H., Trimi, S., & Chung, J.-H. (2015). Big-Data Applications in the Government Sector. *Communications of the ACM*, *57*(3), 78–85. doi:10.1145/2500873

Landsbergen, D. (2010). Government as part of the revolution: using social media to achieve public goals. *Electron J e-Govern*, *8*(2), 135–147.

Linders, D. (2012). From e-government to we-government: Defining a typology for citizen e-participation in the age of social media. *Government Information Quarterly*, *29*(4), 446–454. doi:10.1016/j.giq.2012.06.003

Magro, M. J. (2012). A Review of Social Media Use in E-Government. *Adm. Sci.*, *2*, 148-161. Retrieved June 5, from www.mdpi.com/journal/admsci

Mcnamara, J. (2011). *Social Media Strategy and Governance: Gaps, Risks and Opportunities*. Sydney, Australia: University of Technology Sydney.

Nica, M., & Grayson. (2011). M. Effects of Teaching Business Web 2.0 Style. *International Journal of Business and Social Science*, *2*(18).

O'Reilly, T. (2005). *What Is Web 2.0 Design patterns and business models for the next generation of software*. Retrieved June 30, from http://oreilly.com

Ostling, A. (2010). ICT in politics: From peaks of inflated expectations to voids of disillusionment. *Eur. J. ePractice, 9*, 49–56.

Park, J., & Cho, K. (2009). Declining relational trust between government and publics, and potential prospects of social media in the government public relations. In *Proceedings of EGPA Conference 2009*. The Public Service: Service Delivery in the Information Age.

Park, M. J., Kang, D., Rho, J. J., & Lee, D. H. (2016). Policy Role of Social Media in Developing Public Trust: Twitter communication with government leaders. *Public Management Review*, *18*(9), 1265–1288. doi:10.1080/14719037.2015.1066418

Parvcek, P., & Sachs, M. (2010). Open Government—Information Flow in Web 2.0. *Eur. J. ePractice, 9*, 57–68.

Prajapati, M., & Sharma A. (2014). *Role of Web 2.0 in E-Governance*. Academic Press.

Reddick, C. G. (2010). *Citizens and E-government: Evaluating Policy and Management*. IGI Global. doi:10.4018/978-1-61520-931-6

Rodríguez-Bolivar, M. P. (2017). Governance Models for the Delivery of Public services Through the Web 2.0 technologies: A political view in large Spanish Municipalities. *Social Science Computer Review*, *35*(2), 203–225. doi:10.1177/0894439315609919

Song, Ch., & Lee, J. (2013). *Can Social Media Restore Citizen Trust in Government*. Omaha, NE: School of Public Administration.

Song, C., & Lee, J. (2016). Citizens' Use of Social Media in Government, Perceived Transparency, and Trust in Government. *Public Performance & Management Review*, *39*(2), 430–453. doi:10.1080/15309576.2015.1108798

Ubaldi, B. (2013). Open Government Data: Towards Empirical Analysis of Open Government Data Initiatives. *OECD Working Papers on Public Governance*, *22*, 15-35.

Yusifov, F. (2016). Big Data in E-Government: Issues, Opportunities and Prospects. *16th European Conference on e-Government*, 352-355.

KEY TERMS AND DEFINITIONS

Big Data: Big data is high volume, high velocity, and/or high variety information assets that require new forms of processing to enable enhanced decision making, insight discovery, and process optimization.

E-Government: E-government is the use of information and communication technologies (ICTs) to improve the activities of public sector organisations. Some definitions restrict e-government to internet-enabled applications only, or only to interactions between government and outside groups.

Gov 2.0: Refers to government policies that aim to harness collaborative technologies and interactive internet tools to create an open-source computing platform in which government, citizens, and innovative companies can improve transparency and efficiency.

Open Government: Open government is the opening up of government processes, proceedings, documents, and data for public scrutiny and involvement and is now considered as a fundamental element of a democratic society.

Social Media: Social media are websites and applications that enable users to create and share content or to participate in social networking.

Social Networks: The websites or other application that enable users to communicate with each other by posting information, comments, messages, images, etc.

Web 2.0: The second stage of development of the WWW, characterized especially by the change from static web pages to dynamic or user-generated content and the growth of social media.

Web-Users Profile: Analyzing web user profiles and making decisions and predictions are possible with data mining techniques. For example, user profiles can be used to analyze user's behaviour and predict what kind of actions should be served to the website user.

Chapter 3
Saving Democracy:
Populism, Deception, and E-Participation

Robert Niewiadomski
Hunter College – The City University of New York, USA

Dennis Anderson
St. Francis College, USA

ABSTRACT

The recent rise of populism around the world, often accompanied by nationalism and isolationism, is a trend that presents a serious threat not only to liberal democracies but also to global peace and security. Populist forces have already shown their influence through the British referendum on membership withdrawal from the European Union and the election of Donald J. Trump as the U.S. President in 2016. These two events alone had ripple effects and were felt by the international community. The causes of populism are being currently revisited. It appears that socioeconomic and cultural aspects are key contributors. Even though the persistent existence of populist elements within societies comes from the very core of the democratic experiment, the current trend in social media technologies allowed demagogues to utilize viral deception on a considerable scale. The authors argue that social media technologies could be employed through e-participation to inhibit populism by bolstering civic empowerment, transparency, progressive inclusiveness, fact-based analysis, and informed decision making.

DOI: 10.4018/978-1-5225-5326-7.ch003

"THE CROOKED TIMBER OF HUMANITY"

To abandon facts is to abandon freedom. -Timothy Snyder, On Tyranny: Twenty Lessons from the Twentieth Century

Large sections of Western societies fell prey to a particularly malignant version of populism that is often nationalistic and isolationistic in nature. This worldwide trend presents a serious threat not only to liberal democracies but also to global peace and security. Forces that fuel these tendencies are multifaceted. The sections of the population susceptible to populism often experience economic scarcity, largely due to globalization and inevitable automation. Additionally, they also frequently experience cultural exclusion and sense of disconnect from prominent progressive lifestyles. This might be accompanied by limited access to factual information, lack of cultural capital, and training to process information critically. Thus, they may display anti-intellectual and traditionalist attitudes, sometimes with racist undertones. On the other hand, even populations with a rising solid middle-class turn to demagogues driven by, both real and perceived, external fears and cultural insecurity.

The frequent resurgence of populism is not particularly rare in Western democracies. What is worth noting, however, is that the proliferation of social media technologies allowed political demagogues to mobilize the "silent majority" to advance their agenda through viral deceptive campaigns. These actions are not only employed to spread confusion, deceit, and mistrust of government but also to activate deep emotional need for symbolic identification with the demagogue. Among the wide repertoire of tactics at the populists' disposal, one strategy is supremely pernicious and poses a grave threat to liberal democracies by ushering in tyranny. This strategy could be described as a deliberate effort to dismantle the notion of objective reality and verifiable knowledge.

We argue that a strategy involving social media technologies could be employed by the e-participation to inhibit populism by bolstering civic empowerment, transparency, progressive inclusiveness, fact-based analysis, and rational decision-making. In order to promote such a process, creating a nonpartisan e-participation platforms is essential. These platforms would support a collective voice by engaging communities into a deliberative, fact-based, rational, and transparent decision-making process. An effective e-participation on the local community level could be gradually expanded all the way to the regional and, eventually, to federal levels. Nonpartisan e-participation has the potential to prevent the further disintegration of trust in the political process and the further erosion of high ideals of objective truth and reason. Especially the latter process is sending us back into the pre-Enlightenment epistemic murk. We make a case that civic empowerment through e-participation has the potential to mitigate the effect of populism, and consequently, prevent tyranny.

Democracy was born with a peculiar form of "congenital defect" which makes it intrinsically fragile and ephemeral. Democracies worthy of that name that sustained for a historically significant period of time are extremely rare. Virtually every single one eventually experienced deterioration and most collapsed, and now we find ourselves in the midst of yet another crisis. At the very core of every democratic system lies the perpetual susceptibility to nefarious forms of populism. The Founding Fathers, informed by the spectacular examples of collapses of ancient republics, understood that threat and, a system of checks and balances "to avoid the evil that they, like the ancient philosophers, called tyranny" (Snyder, 2017, p. 10). Snyder continues, "The European history of the twentieth century shows us that societies can break, democracies can fall, ethics can collapse, and ordinary men can find themselves standing over death pits with guns in their hands. It would serve us well today to understand why" (Snyder, 2017, p. 11-12). The constant possibility of tyranny is not necessarily an external threat; it comes chiefly from within the democratic system itself. One cannot help but wonder what is it about the nature of human societies that fall so easily for populist sentiments?

The Paradoxes of Representative Democracy

The democratic process had Janus face features from its inception - a need for rational knowledge -driven and informed deliberation and a tribal crave for the emotional identification with the community. These two elements are not necessarily mutually exclusive but a conflict between them arises if the need of symbolic identification contradicts rational judgment based on factual information. The enduring presence of the latter irrational component provided a constant source of nutrients for various critics of democracy who found this intrinsic "messiness" unsettling. They argue that the system breeds dysfunction, corruption, instability, oppression by the majority, and anarchy, among others. Plato (2008) worried that that out of excesses of democratic freedom, tyranny naturally arises. Some came to the conclusion that the irrationality and demagoguery eventually always takes over, and thus democracy is untenable.

On the other hand, optimists strongly relied on the notion that ultimately people are inherently rational, and in spite occasional impediments of reason, under right circumstances, they make decisions that benefit the well-being of the community as a whole. The extreme version of such optimism is exemplified by teleological narratives developed on the onset of two waves of globalization -at the end of 19th century and at the end of 20th century. It was believed that free global exchange of good and ideas will to promote capitalistic economy and liberal democracy virtually across the globe culminating in a utopian bliss -"the end of history," as Francis Fukuyama (1992) put it.

This idea of the democratic utopia received can be traced to the age of Enlightenment belief that individuals possess the innate capacity for reason and critical deliberation. The idea laid the ideological foundations for American and French Revolutions and became a widely accepted grand narrative of the West. The premise that participants of the democratic process are always rational, act in self-interest, and are well-informed is difficult to defend. The immense traumas of the twentieth century, particularly the rise of Nazism, culminating in the Holocaust, greatly eroded the solid foundations of this great narrative. However, it did not result in a complete disillusion with democracy but rather served as a motivating factor. It maximized efforts to ensure its future success by creating a network of mutual support through an incremental unification of Europe. As Churchill put it in the House of Commons on 11 November 1947,

Many forms of Government have been tried, and will be tried in this world of sin and woe. No one pretends that democracy is perfect or all-wise. Indeed it has been said that democracy is the worst form of Government except for all those other forms that have been tried from time to time...

Nevertheless, the traumas of the degeneration and subsequent collapse of Western democracies in the first part of the 20th century warranted serious relitigation of the rationalist ideas of the Enlightenment. It became clear that even if the grant that humans are innately rational, that does not takes into account the moral aspect of their character. One can be perfectly rational and still commit morally repugnant acts. And yet it is not entirely clear if the moral failures are not connected to the shortcomings of our rationality. Hannah Arendt in *Eichmann in Jerusalem: A Report on the Banality of Evil* (1963) entertains the possibility that the phenomenon of evil stems from the tendency of ordinary people to obey orders and conform to mass opinion without a critical evaluation. The Milgram experiment on obedience to authority seems to point in this direction, as well. Zygmunt Bauman in his acclaimed *Modernity and the Holocaust* (1989) derives the barbarism of the Holocaust directly from the rationalistic projects. Earlier, Bauman developed an argument that Europeans agreed to sacrifice a level of freedom in order to receive the benefits of increased individual security. Bauman argued that modernity was fixated on removing unknowns and uncertainties. This involved control over nature, hierarchical bureaucracy, rules and regulations, control and categorization in the effort to make human life appear well-ordered and familiar. Holocaust should be seen, he argues, as a direct result of this order-making efforts. Procedural rationality, the division of labor into small tasks, the obsessive taxonomy of various species, and obedience to rules as morally good, contributed to the Holocaust since the image of a Jew as the ultimate "other", whose very existence was perceived as subversive to the modern order.

In the post-WWII world, outbursts of populism were usually associated with fragile non-Western quasi-democracies. The West became complacent and took it as a fact that it gained an immunity from the painful lessons of pre-war totalitarian regimes and their genocidal consequences. This might explain the disbelief, denial, and anger present in vast strata of the Western societies when confronted with the recent outbursts of populism. Trump, Brexit, autocratic governments in Venezuela, Philippines, Turkey, Hungary or Poland might be spectacular successes of populism but, as previously mentioned, populism is some way, was always present, like an "evil twin" of democracy. To shed a light on this problem, it's important to try to understand what is this phenomenon we call populism.

However, populism is notoriously difficult to define. Christa Deiwiks (2009) in her comprehensive of review of scholarly literature on populism notes that "Strikingly, even some of the works on populism regarded as groundbreaking and substantial like Ionescu and Gellner ... fail to state explicitly what they mean by the term" (p.1). After an exhausting review Christa Deiwiks compresses the multitude of scholarly views on the topic to the core characteristics of the phenomenon, "First, the 'people' is of paramount importance. Here, a feeling of community is stressed, and horizontal cleavages (such as left-right) are played down while vertical ones are played up for the purpose of excluding particular groups, e.g. elites and immigrants. Second, populists claim that the 'people' have been betrayed by the elites through their abuse of power, corruption, etc. Third, populists demand that the 'primacy of the people'... has to be restored. In short: the current elites would have to be replaced and in their place, the new leaders (the populists) would act for the good of the 'people' " (p. 2). Thus, the concept of "people" is the central imagined entity. Deiwiks claims further that,

Mudde...provides ... the most to-the point definition by limiting himself to the 'people' and its antagonistic 'other.' He conceives of populism as an ideology that considers society to be ultimately separated into two homogeneous and antagonistic groups, 'the pure people' versus 'the corrupt elite', and which argues that politics should be an expression of the volonté générale (general will) of the people ... To sum up, these definitions show us that the core aspects of populism are, first, the focus on the 'people' - whatever this term may refer to – and its sovereignty, and second, the antagonism between this 'people' and its 'other' – whatever this 'other' may be, the elite in a representative democracy, foreigners, or others. (p. 2)

Additionally, Deiwiks (2009) stresses other accompanying elements of populism. They include a sharp distinction between elites and masses, distrust towards institutions, and a charismatic leader who tries to close the apparent gap between the people and the establishment by directly appealing to the voters and presenting himself as one of the 'people": "I am one of you", "I alone can do it", "I am your voice" etc. The phrases were actually used by Donald J. Trump during his presidential campaign.

It is also crucial to stress that the nature of the democratic paradox lied in the fact that populism is, in a way, a product of the tensions that lie at the very core of representative democracy,

The inclusion of an increasing amount of people in the decision-making process leads to an increase in the level of opaqueness as to who rules whom, and how. The growing gap between the voters and their representatives results in populist leaders claiming to close that gap by 'putting the power back' into the 'people's' hand. (Deiwiks, 2009, p. 4)

The more power is dispersed between many actors in a democratic, the less visible it actually becomes who is in charge. This leads to the appearance as if the power was taken away from the people. Thus, the goal of a demagogue is to "bring back" the power to the people and provide it with certain visibility by putting a face on it, typically his/her own. Ultimately, populists use their own charisma, propaganda, and manipulation to lure followers and advance their own agenda that is hardly ever aligned with the interest of the community. The opposing view sees populism not as a pathological phenomenon but rather as a justifiable signal sent to the establishment that the system has defects. It is a sort of a "mirror of democracy in the sense that it reflects the nature of democracy and so renders problems visible" (Deiwiks, 2009, p. 4).

Economic Inequality and Cultural Anxiety

In order for this apparent intrinsic ability of democracy to produce populism, there has to be a fertile ground in a form of a real or manufactured gap between the establishment and the "people." The nature of this "gap" is complex. It is, most likely an aggregate of a deep sense of social inequity and the thirst for "meaning," -a sort of symbolic community "glue." The latter is often described as "cultural" aspect. There is a tendency in the media to stress the former, but it becomes clear that the latter plays an equally important role. Especially, when we consider societies with a robust and educated middle class, former strong supporters of globalization, that are now strongly infatuated with forms of populism -often openly hostile to liberal democracy.

In the broadest sense, both are a reaction to globalization. Even though on the surface, this allergic reaction to globalization might appear like a new phenomenon, the is quite illuminating historical analogon. As Snyder (2017) explains,

History can familiarize, and it can warn. In the late nineteenth century, just as in the late twentieth century, the expansion of global trade generated expectations of progress. In the early twentieth century, as in the early twenty first, these hopes were challenged by new visions of mass politics in which a leader or a party claimed directly represent the will of the people ...both Fascism and communism were responses to globalization: to the real and perceived inequalities it created, and the apparent helplessness of the democracies of addressing them ... They put a face on globalization, arguing that its complex challenges were the result of a conspiracy against the nation. (p. 11-12)

Since the two waves of globalization were both economic and cultural phenomena inextricably intertwined, the backlash consequently was corresponding to both spheres.

In their paper *Trump, Brexit, and the rise of Populism*, Inglehart and Norris (2016) concentrated on the two most widely held views on mass support of populism -the economic insecurity perspective and the cultural backlash thesis in order to establish which of them played the primary role in recent European and American politics.

The "economic inequality" perspective focuses on the consequences for electoral behavior arising from profound changes transforming the workforce and society in post-industrial economies. There is overwhelming evidence of powerful trends toward greater income and wealth inequality in the West, based on the rise of the knowledge economy, automation, and the collapse of manufacturing industry, global flows of labor, goods, peoples, and capital, outsourcing, compounded especially by the inflow of migrants and refugees, the erosion of labor unions, shrinking welfare safety-nets, and the corporate bottom-line. Some of these phenomena could be seen as a contingent, some as a result of deliberate policies and political actions (Inglehart & Norris, 2016). In *Requiem for the American Dream*, Chomsky (2017) unapologetically claims the neoliberal ideology and describes the principles of those who benefit from this status quo: reduce democracy, shape ideology, redesign the economy, shift the burden onto the poor and middle classes, attack the solidarity of the people, let special interests run the regulators, engineer election results, use fear and the power of the state to keep the rabble in line, manufacture consent, marginalize the population. Chomsky's view is worth nothing even if is nothing short of a claim that there is a colonization of a middle class.

In short, the "economic inequality" thesis stresses the popular resentment of the establishment fueled by economic insecurity and social deprivation. This makes the economically disadvantaged strata of society "susceptible to the anti-establishment, nativist, and xenophobic scare-mongering... parties, and leaders, blaming 'Them' for stripping prosperity, job opportunities, and public services from 'Us'" (Inglehart & Norris, 2016, p.2).

On the other hand, the "cultural backlash" thesis suggests that the surge in votes for populist parties can be explained not as a purely economic phenomenon but in large part as a reaction against progressive cultural change,

Extensive research indicates that since about 1970, affluent Western societies have seen growing emphasis on post-materialist and self-expression values among the younger birth cohorts and the better-educated strata of society. This has brought rising emphasis on such issues as environmental protection, increased acceptance of gender and racial equality, and equal rights for the LGBT community. This cultural shift has fostered greater approval of social tolerance of diverse lifestyles, religions, and cultures, multiculturalism, international cooperation, democratic governance, and protection of fundamental freedoms and human rights. Social movements reflecting these values have brought policies such as environmental protection, same sex marriage, and gender equality in public life to the center of the political agenda, drawing attention away from the classic economic redistribution issues. But the spread of progressive values has also stimulated a cultural backlash among people who feel threatened by this development. Less educated and older citizens, especially white men, who were once the privileged majority culture in Western societies, resent being told that traditional values are 'politically incorrect' if they have come to feel that they are being marginalized within their own countries. As cultures have shifted, a tipping point appears to have occurred. (Inglehart & Norris, 2016, p. 29)

After examining the cross-national evidence at the individual level for the impact of the economic insecurity and cultural values as predictors of voting for populist parties and combing through the robust body of data and research, Inglehart and Norris found the most consistent evidence supporting the cultural backlash thesis. This is further supported by data from other reports. According to Pew Research (Kochhar, 2017), even though, "From 1991 to 2010, the middle class expands in France, the Netherlands and the United Kingdom," in all of these countries populism is on the rise to varying degrees. It is presumed that this could be attributed to cultural anxiety associated with an influx of migrants, both economic and refugees.

Thus, the sense of social disenfranchisement and disappointment with the "system" that stems from the unfulfilled promise of globalization amplified by real or manufactured sense of social external threat, whether it is terrorism or global conspiracy, makes even the most impregnable democratic system vulnerable to demagoguery, malignant populism, and ultimately a form of a tyrannical rule.

The issue of value-based voting, against one's self-interest, has been litigated extensively by George Lakoff. In his work with Mark Johnson, *Metaphors We Live By* (2003), Lakoff developed an argument that individuals' decision- making are mostly guided by the central metaphors they use to explain complex phenomena. When applied to political reality, this theory has startling consequences. People are not interested in facts, says Lakoff, but rather in values they can emotionally relate to. That is not to say that facts are not important, they matter but they always follow and support values (Lakoff, 2016). The superior role of values in political decision-making leads voters to make decisions that are economically not in their own interest. They would rather vote and support a leader who they symbolically identify with and offers a clear path to strengthen their communal identity.

Lakoff's approach explains, for example, why some Trump supporters, often without health insurance or underinsured had a positive response to Trump's rhetoric against the Affordable Care Act. The answer is simple, says Lakoff, "All politics is moral. Supporting Trump – and gutting public health care resources in order to provide tax cuts for the wealthy – fits perfectly within the strict conservative moral worldview, which is hierarchical in nature. Voters don't vote their self-interest. They vote their values" (Lakoff, 2017).

As Lakoff argues, human thinking, including our moral reflection, manifest itself through metaphors,

We may not always know it, but we think in metaphor. A large proportion of our most commonplace thoughts make use of an extensive, but unconscious, system of metaphorical concepts, that is, concepts from a typically concrete realm of thought that are used to comprehend another, completely different domain. (Lakoff, 1995)

The conservative metaphor for morality is the "Strict Father Model" (Lakoff, 2016) This makes the notion of an authoritarian leader such as a "strong man" or a "father of the nation" more palatable for voters inclined to identify with conservative values.

If voters make up their minds mostly informed by their values and their deep subconscious archetypes, then the management of their emotions is naturally the primary concern of any potential demagogue. If we are hardwired in such way, decisions of immense gravity are made not primarily based on the scrutiny of facts and logical calculation but rather on the basis whether we can relate to the politicians emotionally, whether they fill our symbolic void. Any rational justification comes after.

The Age of Epistemic Murk

If it is the case, as Lakoff claims, that values matter more that fact, the truth is the first victim of demagogues in the process of dismantling democracy. We know this phenomenon under the name of "fake news", "alternative facts" or "dishonest media." It is a very familiar tool employed populists and has been known simply as propaganda, disinformation, hogwash, newspeak, indoctrination, among others.

In the era of social media and mobile applications, it takes a form of what has need recently called a "viral deception." This deception appears to be so pervasive that some are willing to concede that we are living in a pos-truth reality. We are drowning in a cyber- ocean of quasi-informational "stuff" that makes is for many people virtually impossible to discern between reality and fiction. It effectively makes us as uninformed as we were before the spread of literacy. As Daniel Dennett (Cadwalladr, 2017) puts it, "People have discovered that it's much easier to destroy reputations for credibility than it is to maintain them. It doesn't matter how good your facts are, somebody else can spread the rumor that you're fake news. We're entering a period of epistemological murk and uncertainty that we've not experienced since the middle ages."

Before we look closely what the strategy of viral deception exactly look like, it is appropriate to ask a question: Why the assault on truth is so crucial in in the process leading to tyranny? The analysis of the problem is voluminous but Snyder (2017) summarizes it with an aphoristic simplicity and precision,

If nothing is true, then no one can criticize power because there is no basis upon which to do so. If nothing is true, then all is spectacle. The biggest wallet pays for the most blinding lights. You submit to tyranny when you renounce the difference between what you want to hear and what is actually the case. The renunciation of reality can feel natural and pleasant, but the result is your demise as an individual -and thus the collapse of any political system that depends on individualism ... It is your ability to discern facts that makes you an individual, and our collective trust in common knowledge that makes us a society. The individual who investigates is also the citizen who builds. The leader who dislikes the investigators is a potential tyrant. (p.65-73)

The abandonment or unwillingness of pursuit of truth brings back an individual to a state of immaturity, both intellectual and civic. Thus, an individual who cannot navigate the epistemic murk finds herself in a sort of Enlightenment à rebours - unable to use her own "understanding without the guidance of another" and "lack of resolution and courage to use it without the guidance of another" (Kant, 1784). This makes her an ideal candidate to become a follower of an autocratic leader.

Certainly, the concept of truth is not unproblematic from the philosophical perspective. In the political reality, however, there are certain basic epistemic commitments that are absolutely vital in order to prevent a total collapse of the democratic system. First, one must accept that there is such thing as an objective reality, that there are facts of the matter. Second, that we are capable of, with a certain degree of accuracy, to discern what these facts are. Third, that there is a way to communicate these facts in ways that are unbiased and objective (or intersubjective) to the best of our abilities. Fourth, that we all agree that the ultimate judge of the veracity of our utterances is their level of correspondence to reality.

In a world devoid of a sense that there are actual facts one can refer to and based one's judgment on, the power of persuasion cannot be based on reason and knowledge. Therefore what is left are competing narratives, alternative stories, often contradictory and incompatible that are placed on display to lure potential buyers. And without any confidence in the existence in factual reality that would verify them, we are left alone roaming like children in a toy store searching for objects that are the most appealing, the most flashy, the most stimulating our senses. What is true does not matter anymore; what matters is which narrative satisfies our biases, which story makes us feel good, and which of them aligns with our emotions and values that we are already committed to.

Thus, the Enlightenment's principles, no matter how fragile, that we are all capable of critical thinking and rational deliberation matters a great deal for the preservation of the democratic experiment. This conviction echoed in Hillary Clinton's commencement speech delivered at Wesleyan College in 2017,

If our leaders lie about the problems we face, we'll never solve them. It matters because it undermines confidence in government as a whole, which in turn breeds more cynicism and anger … the belief that people, you and I, possess the capacity for reason and critical thinking … is the lifeblood of a democracy.

Viral Deception

Viral deception plays a particularly pernicious role in creating the environment of epistemic murk. It was a term proposed on CNN's "Reliable Sources" by Kathleen Hall Jamieson, director of the Annenberg Public Policy Center at the University of Pennsylvania, to more precisely capture the phenomenon of "fake news." While asked about them, Jamieson told host Brian Stelter,

I'd like to call them 'viral deception,' and I'd like to use the VD acronym because I'd like to associate it with venereal disease. We don't want to get venereal disease. If you find someone who's got it, you want to quarantine them and cure them. You don't want to transmit it. By virtue of saying 'fake news,' we ask the question, well, what is real news – and you invite people to label everything they disapprove of 'fake news.' As a result, it's not a useful concept. What are we really concerned about? Deception. And deception of a certain sort that goes viral. Much of that deception isn't actually imitating news. It's imitating news like structures, its narrative, and form. But nonetheless, if we say we are only concerned with "fake news", we may be missing a lot of things that are going viral that are deceptive. And many things that are found in quasi-fake news sites, that is the appropriating the credibility of news; trying to look like the CNN website, for example, aren't only found there. Sometimes, aren't found there at all. There are found in other kinds of channels. (Jamieson, 2017)

Viral deception, therefore, is a wider concept than "fake news." It captures both the mendacity of the phenomenon and the nature of its proliferation. The latter matters because viral deception differs from its predecessors in a way that it spreads faster, often globally, and similarly to viruses, has the ability to mutate, effectively being sometimes resistant to potential "vaccines" that arrive too late to prevent the damage.

Viral deception could be seen, in a way, as a special falsehood-carrying type a "meme" - a unit of cultural transmission coined by Richard Dawkins in his book *The Selfish Gene* (1990). Memes are cultural equivalent to genes and possess similar properties: self-replication and mutation in response to evolutionary selective pressures. While discussing the "Trump phenomenon", Daniel Dennett (Cadwalladr, 2017) notes the potentially detrimental role of memes, especially in a political discourse,

one of the most powerful and unsettling parts of Dawkins's vision is that memes have their own fitness. In the same way that germs and viruses have their own fitness. That means that there can be a very, very successful meme, which is really dangerous.

Robert Proctor, a Stanford historian, while studying the practice of calculated deception practiced by the tobacco industry, created a term for the study of the deliberate propagation of confusion, doubt, and deceit, typically for mercantile purposes at that time. The term is "agnotology" -a hybrid of two Greek words: agnosis (ignorance) and ontology. "I was exploring how powerful industries could promote ignorance to sell their wares. Ignorance is power... and agnotology is about the deliberate creation of ignorance" Proctor explains (Kenyon, 2016).

Agnotology seems more important now than ever since the techniques that it describes are ubiquitous tools of choice of political demagoguery. As one example we could refer to Donald Trump's questioning Obama's birth certificate. Despite the evidence provided to put an end to the campaign, "birtherism" still persists. Another example includes Trump's claim of a massive voting fraud or a vast number of gruesome crimes committed by "illegal aliens." It would be tempting to just brush off these deceptive practices as a political nuisance if it was not for their real and serious consequences. The two latter examples of deceit served as a reason to warrant the creation of Voter-Fraud Commission and another body within the U.S. Immigration and Customs Enforcement called VOICE (Victims of Immigration Crime Engagement). And obviously, we cannot ignore the elephant in the room -

climate change "skepticism" that lead Trump to withdraw U.S. from Paris Climate Agreement.

Viral deception exacerbated by the proliferation of social media leads to the predicament of the public drowning in the murky ocean of "radical ignorance" -and as Proctor's said, "the marvel is that any kind of truth cuts through the noise" (Kenyon, 2016). The Cartesian "evil demon" of doubt is no longer a theoretical construct to test the foundations of knowledge, it is the reality of our daily experience.

Populism vs. Pluralistic Empowerment

As we stressed previously, the nature of the paradox of representative democracy is that populism is the product of that very democratic process. Namely, the dispersion of power within the technocracy and different centers of political establishment creates a high level of murkiness regarding the decision-making process. This leads to the growing gap between the voters and their representatives, atrophy of the sense of citizen's political agency and a deterioration of a sense of symbolic community. The society separates into homogeneous and antagonistic camps -"the people" and 'the corrupt elite" (Mudde, 2004). The result is the rise in populist leaders, who under the banner of putting the power back into people's' hand and a skillful use of deceptive techniques, bond with voters by appealing to their emotional needs of belonging to a community of shared values, and ultimately clinch the political power with devastating effect for democracy itself. Populism is not attached to any side of the political spectrum - it can arise from the right of left, indiscriminately.

Typically, elitism has been considered to be the direct opposite of populism but Cas Mudde and Cristóbal Rovira Kaltwasser (2013), argue that populism has, in fact, two direct opposites: elitism and pluralism. When we try to entertain the possible solution to mitigate the possibility of populistic insurgencies, elitism is not the candidate of choice. As Kaltwasser (2013) points out,

Those who adhere to elitism share the Manichean distinction between 'the people' and 'the elite', but think that the former is a dangerous and unwise mob, while the latter is seen as an intellectually and morally superior group of actors, who should be in charge of the government – technocrats are a key example of this.

Even though the technocratic rule has a certain appeal and a veneer of preserving a level of competence and rationality that are desirable in a democracy, reliance on technocratic governance would further deepen the gap mentioned earlier that is a breeding ground of populism in the first place. The second direct opposition - pluralism acknowledges the fact that society comprises of diverse groups and individuals. As opposed to populism that seeks uniformity and excludes those who resist by placing them in the category of "enemies", pluralism, in its ideal form, is inclusive and celebratory, respects the interests of minorities, and seeks mediation and agreement.

The desired model is to empower more direct, deliberative, inclusive and informed participation in order to fill the gap between the citizens and the political establishment and circumvent the remove the need for a "strong man" or a populist party that present themselves as the embodiment of "will of the people." Properly implemented e-participation provides a platform for such pluralistic empowerment by encouraging inclusive participation, fact-based rational deliberation, transparency, and civic education. An effective e-participation has the highest chance of success on the local community level but it could be gradually expanded all the way to the regional and even the federal levels.

Towards a New Model of Civic Empowerment

John Mathiason in his concept paper *Information and Communication Technologies and eParticipation for the Empowerment of People and eGovernance* (2013) provides an overview of various initiatives in social development undertaken mostly from the 1960s in order to strengthen democratic cultures and achieve social mobilization in the post-WWII Europe. Mathiason also includes a useful definition of empowerment established by the 2012 Expert Group meeting as

... effective participation by members of society, as individuals and groups, in decisions about their lives, that is conditioned by a supportive enabling environment, and leads to the solution of economic and social problems confronting them. (Department for Economic and Social Affairs, Division for Social Policy and Development [UNDESA], 2012, p. 5)

Historically speaking, the progress of civic empowerment is closely interwoven with the history of major technological inventions. They provided the necessary means for such engagements to expand. Initially, participation relied primarily on a physical presence at meetings, protests, and other types of gatherings, and thus, was extremely localized. Subsequent expansion had to do with the growing popularity of written petitions, letters, etc. The true acceleration on a large scale dates to the invention allowing mass communication, particularly -the printing press. Successive expansions correlate to the advent and proliferation of newspapers (which was furthered by public education and growing literacy), voice recording, telephone, radio, television, and, finally, the Internet. Naturally, the nature of the Internet allows for an unprecedented level of human interaction and as such is used as an avenue to spread viral deception and contributes to the dissemination of detrimental populistic ideas. Lucky, it also became a tool for an unparalleled possibility for civic empowerment. And the same strategies involving social media technologies could be employed through e-participation to make democratic process more transparent, inclusive, informed, and educational.

The term "empowerment" seems to capture the spirit of civic engagement more adequately than "participation" since emphasizes more strongly the element of agency in a democratic process. Perhaps then, in current debates, it would be more appropriate to use the term "eEmpowerment" but conceivably because of its linguistic oddness, the term "e-participation" is widely used.

The UN's E-Participation Index describes e-Participation as "...fostering civic engagement and open, participatory governance through Information and Communications Technologies (ICTs). Growing evidence points to the rapid expansion of e-Participation as a tool for engagement and strengthened collaboration between governments and citizens. Its objective is to improve access to information and public services as well as to promote participation in policy-making, both for the empowerment of individual citizens and the benefit of society as a whole" (UNDESA, 2017).

The same source also establishes a framework with three crucial components, that are, in fact, levels of e-participation, with e-decision-making being the highest:

- **E-Information:** Enabling participation by providing citizens with public information and access to information without or upon demand.
- **E-Consultation:** Engaging citizens in contributions to and deliberation on public policies and services.
- **E-Decision-Making:** Empowering citizens through co-design of policy option and co-production of service components and delivery modalities (UNDESA, 2017).

Even though E-participation is an evolving concept and practice, the "United Nations E-government Survey" (UNDESA, 2016) stresses that, "there is vast evidence that e-participation technologies expand opportunities for civic engagement, including increased possibilities for people to participate in decision-making processes and service delivery to make societies more participatory, inclusive, and deliberative."

Particularly, its role in promoting citizen's empowerment cannot be overestimated. Greater engagement and participation in policy-making has an intrinsic value, among other more practical reasons, in terms of deepening democracy and making governance more responsive and transparent, providing the citizens with a sense of agency, shared governance, and increase trust in their governments (Kim & Lee, 2011). The sense of agency is vital to in the process of creating a sense of community, both on a political and on a symbolic level by fulfilling the emotional need to belong.

E-participation, in its high level, "goes beyond merely requesting people to provide their views about decisions and services proposed by the government. It mobilizes and shapes action" (Kim & Lee, 2011). It can harness the citizens' capacities and ideas. Thus, its is exactly the opposite of past ideas where the citizens were merely passive recipients of government's policies and solutions,

E-participation is more than simply informing or consulting citizens, it is about engaging the citizens in the decision-making process and empowering them to participate in democratic governance so that a common goal is achieved. In that aspect, it is not a simple top down the way for the government to inform citizens about things that matter to them. It is a give-and-take process that has to be integrated into all levels of decision making from local to regional to the federal government. It is also about building consensus, which is necessary to make proper decision to act on. Otherwise, it can result in an ineffective and chaotic stalemate situation where no big decisions can be made. (Anderson, 2013)

While e-information and e-consultations are equally valuable participation forms in their own right, e-decision-making is the logical pinnacle of e-participation. E-decision-making denotes "a process in which people provide their own inputs into decision-making" in a variety of means that include, but are not limited to e-voting and eliciting policy proposals, and identifying popular preferences that may lead to policies (UNDESA, 2016).

Examples of e-decision-making initiatives are quite numerous and most have been thoroughly studied to assess both their benefits as well as challenges. The portal eparticipation.eu documents various e-participation initiatives both on the local and national level. Some well-studied cases that are worth mentioning included the Scottish Government e-government program (2011) and the e-participants initiative in the city of Seoul. The results of the assessments of the Korean program showed that there is "a positive association between e-participants' assessment of government transparency and their trust in the local government that provides the e-participation program" (Kim & Lee, 2011, p. 2).

In 2010, Finland, a pioneer in providing its citizens with access to digital tools and services, became the first country to pass legislation making the broadband connection one of the citizens' legal rights. Finnish initiatives could serve as a model of using crowdsourcing in e-decision-making. One of the most important e-participation initiatives in Finland was the adoption of *The New Citizens' Initiative Act* in March 2012 (Aitamurto, Landemore, Lee, & Goel, 2014). The act

Introduced an element of direct democracy ... by allowing Finnish citizens to submit an initiative to the Parliament. The rules are simple: any citizen of voting age can

start a petition to propose to the government either a change to an existing legislation or a completely new bill, formulated through crowdsourcing methods. This petition must receive 50,000 signatures in six months, in paper form or online (by using an online bank user identification), in order for the Parliament to discuss it. Although it is mandatory for the Parliament to take into consideration the successful initiatives, it can still decide to amend or reject the proposals... (p. 18)

Between the adoption of the act in 2016 and 2016 nine

Successful initiatives reached the parliament (e.g. stricter penalties for drunk driving, changes to the energy certification law, copyright reform), among which the only one has been turned into law so far (equal marriage rights for gay couples). (p. 18)

Research conducted on the Finnish Citizens' program revealed both a positive role of e-participation in invigorating participatory democracy and some challenges that will need to be addressed in future initiatives. It was concluded that the program

Enhanced participation by involving citizens in policy-making... For example, the initiative on equal marriage rights gathered more than 120,000 supporters within 24 hours of being launched (to put this into perspective, Helsinki has less than 600,000 inhabitants). (Aitamurto et al., 2014, p. 19)

However, the initiative appealed only to a specific segment of the population since the supporters were mostly urban, young, educated males, and as such cannot be considered representative of the whole Finnish society. This segment of the population tends to be more familiar with digital tools and generally more engaged than older citizens, hence the results can be hardly surprising.

Nevertheless, the initiative of blending traditional democratic process with direct e-democracy invited innovative ideas into a political decision-making process and served as a learning experience for both the citizens and lawmakers. Moreover, crowdsourcing overall contributed to enhancing

legitimacy by creating more trust in the decision-making process. Even if the participants did not receive the desired outcome of their initiative, they kept their faith in the system if they perceived the whole process was fair. (Aitamurto et al., 2014, p. 19)

In addition to the mentioned lack of Internet access in some section of the population, major challenges observed during the course of the initiative had to do with the risk of possible misrepresentation of populations' preferences and difficulties with the authentication process. As far as recommendations for future improvements are concerned, ensuring that all sections of the populations are included in crowdsourcing is crucial. The authentication process challenge is a purely technical issue. Furthermore, some measure to guarantee that citizens' opinion will matter at the final step of the process would prevent any potential frustration and dissolution" (p. 23).

The challenges discovered during the Finnish initiative, are somewhat reflective of challenges encountered while implementing e-participation in general. A study on potential and challenges of e-participation in the European Union (Lironi, 2016) echoed by UN's E-government Survey (2016) provides a non-exhaustive list of needs that would have to be met in order to implement e-participation successfully: necessary infrastructure and legal framework for implementation, inclusion of all sections of the society (especially vulnerable groups), improvement of digital literacy, addressing the disinterest of some sections of citizens in political, and igniting the political will to implement elements of e-government.

If e-participation is to succeed in combating the threat of populism, several conditions should be met. First, the decisions makers in representative democracies have to realize that limiting citizens' participation only to traditional elections is untenable. The proliferation of cybersphere change people's expectations and raised their demand for more instantaneous results. Second, they need to ensure that both a necessary structure and legal framework to make sure that e-participation reaches all strata of the populations and that the process is fruitful -in other words: people's voice must matter. Third, the citizens should show a willingness to embrace this new opportunity and overcome the inertia of non-engagement. An example is set by the way people, as clients, interact with businesses, and this new digital and instantaneous modes of interaction put pressure on the democratic states to embrace it as well. This process is expected to accelerate which means governments have to pay attention and meet the citizens' needs and expectation.

"Nothing Beautiful Without Struggle"

Populism is the child of the paradoxical nature of representative democracy. The inevitable complexity and dispersion of power in different centers of the political establishment, sharp economic inequalities, create a gap between the voters and decision makers. This leads to growing frustration, sense of disenfranchisement and loss of political agency by the citizens. The symbolic identification with the government, state, and the community deteriorate. The society tends to separates into antagonistic camps - often describes as "the people" and "the corrupt elite." This provides an opportunity for leaders with populist inclinations to gain political control by using a variety of deceptive techniques and emotional manipulations to convince the voters that they alone restore the sovereign power of the "people." Assault on the notion of truth is a major technique of such manipulation. Populists strategy is twofold: first, using viral deception in order to create an image of the world that is far from reality but suits their goal and replacing the notion of objective truth with a multitude of "narratives"; second, appeal to the irrational, the emotional, and the symbolic human needs. Ultimately, as they concentrate power, they take a stance against political pluralism and democratic institutions that are put in place to protect the people against tyrannical rule. This has a devastating effect on liberal democracy that, in the end, implodes.

The strategy outlined in this essay is a reversal of the populist's maneuvers, and it is twofold. First, populists use viral deceptive by utilizing social media campaigns. We argue that the same strategy involving social media technologies could be employed to bolster civic empowerment, transparency, progressive inclusiveness, and rational decision-making. In order to promote such a process, creating a nonpartisan e-participation is essential.

Nonpartisan e-participation has the potential to prevent the further erosion of trust in the political process, and most importantly stop the spread of populism and isolationism by filling the gap between the citizens and the political establishment. It can also remove the need for a "strong man" or a populist party that present themselves as the embodiment of "will of the people." An effective e-participation has the highest chance of success on the local community level but it could be gradually expanded all the way to the regional and even the federal levels.

Moreover, it is imperative that e-participation needs to address the emotional need of the people by providing a sense of community, shared purpose, and values. Perhaps when we succeed in tapping into deep emotional and symbolic needs of the citizens, we might have a chance to compete with demagogues on the democratic value market. In short, e-participation could strengthen democracy and energize citizens by injecting both solid factual information to drive fact-based decision-making and creating an environment conducive to a building a sense of identity around common goals.

The rise of populism we currently experience is a global trend and no single group of people or even a country is going to solve it alone. We must learn from the experiences of our peers from other countries. E-participation must be a global effort, and perhaps then this strategy, as we hope, will give democracy a chance of survival. Continuous occurrence of populism will continue but strengthening immunity to it through engaged and informed society is the most promising strategy to avoid a tyrannical form of government. The success is never guaranteed but, in the words of Plato (2008), χαλεπὰ τὰ καλά -nothing beautiful could be achieved without struggle.

REFERENCES

Aitamurto, T., Landemore, H., Lee, D., & Goel, A. (2014). *Crowdsourced Off-Road Traffic Law in Finland*. Retrieved from https://www.eduskunta.fi/FI/tietoaeduskunnasta/julkaisut/Documents/tuvj_1+2014.pdf

Anderson, D. (2013). *E-participation: Innovative Strategies, Emerging Trends and Services for the Empowerment of People*. Retrieved from http://www.un.org/esa/socdev/egms/docs//2013/ict/DennisAnderson.pdf

Arendt, H. (1963). *Eichmann in Jerusalem: A Report on the Banality of Evil*. Penguin Classics.

Bauman, Z. (1989). *Modernity and the Holocaust*. Cornell University Press.

Cadwalladr, C. (2017). Daniel Dennett: 'I begrudge every hour I have to spend worrying about politics'. *The Guardian*. Retrieved from https://www.theguardian.com/science/2017/feb/12/daniel-dennett-politics-bacteria-bach-back-dawkins-trump-interview

Chomsky, N. (2017). *Requiem for the American Dream: The 10 Principles of Concentration of Wealth & Power*. Seven Stories Press.

Dawkins, R. (1990). *The Selfish Gene*. Oxford University Press.

DeiwiksC. (2009). *Populism*. Retrieved from https://www.ethz.ch/content/dam/ethz/special-interest/gess/cis/cis-dam/CIS_DAM_2015/WorkingPapers/Living_Reviews_Democracy/Deiwiks.PDF

Fukuyama, F. (1992). *The End of History and the Last Man*. New York: Free Press.

Inglehart, R., & Norris, P. (2016). *Trump, Brexit, and the Rise of Populism: Economic Have-Nots and Cultural Backlash*. HKS Working Paper No. RWP16-026. Retrieved from https://ssrn.com/abstract=2818659

Ionescu, G., & Gellner, E. (1969). Introduction. In G. Ionescu & E. Gellner (Eds.), *In Populism - Its Meanings and National Characteristics*. London: Weidenfeld & Nicolson.

Jamieson, K. H. (2017). New name for fake news: 'viral deception'/Interviewer: B. Stelter. *Reliable Sources, CNN, CNN.com*. Retrieved from http://www.cnn.com/videos/tv/2017/03/05/new-name-for-fake-news-viral-deception.cnn

Kaltwasser, C. R. (2013). *Populism, its opposites, and its contentious relationship with democracy*. Retrieved from https://www.opendemocracy.net/can-europe-make-it/crist%C3%B3bal-rovira-kaltwasser/populism-its-opposites-and-its-contentious-relationsh

Kant, I. (1784). *Answering the Question: What is Enlightenment?* Retrieved from http://library.standrews-de.org/lists/CourseGuides/religion/rs-vi/oppressed/kant_what_is_enlightenment.pdf

Kenyon, G. (2016). *The Man Who Studies the Spread of Ignorance*. Retrieved from http://www.bbc.com/future/story/20160105-the-man-who-studies-the-spread-of-ignorance

Kim, S., & Lee, J. (2011). *E-Participation, Transparency, and Trust in Local Government*. Retrieved from https://spaa.newark.rutgers.edu/sites/default/files/files/Transparency_Research_Conference/Papers/Kim_Soonhee.pdf

Kochhar, R. (2017). *Middle Class Fortunes in Western Europe*. Retrieved from http://www.pewglobal.org/2017/04/24/middle-class-fortunes-in-western-europe/

Lakoff, G. (1995). Metaphor, Morality, and Politics, Or, Why Conservatives Have Left Liberals in the Dust. *Social Research*, *62*(2).

Lakoff, G. (2016). *Moral Politics: How Liberals and Conservatives Think*. University Of Chicago Press. doi:10.7208/chicago/9780226411323.001.0001

Lakoff, G. (2017). *Two Questions About Trump and Republicans that Stump Progressives*. Retrieved from https://georgelakoff.com/2017/07/01/two-questions-about-trump-and-republicans-that-stump-progressives/

Lakoff, G., & Johnson, M. (2003). *Metaphors We Live By*. University Of Chicago Press. doi:10.7208/chicago/9780226470993.001.0001

Lironi, E. (2016). *Potential and Challenges of E-Participation in the European Union*. Retrieved from http://www.europarl.europa.eu/RegData/etudes/STUD/2016/556949/IPOL_STU(2016)556949_EN.pdf

Mathiason, J. (2013). *Information and Communication Technologies and eParticipation for the Empowerment of People and eGovernance*. Retrieved from http://www.un.org/esa/socdev/egms/docs//2013/ict/BackgroundPaper.pdf

Mudde, C. (2004). The Populist Zeitgeist. *Government and Opposition*, *39*(4), 541–563. doi:10.1111/j.1477-7053.2004.00135.x

Mudde, C., & Kaltwasser, C. R. (2013). Populism. In M. Freeden, L. T. Sargent, & M. Stears (Eds.), *The Oxford Handbook of Political Ideologies* (pp. 493–512). Oxford, UK: Oxford University Press.

Plato, . (2008). *The Republic* (B. Jowett, Trans.). United States: Simon & Brown.

Snyder, T. D. (2017). *On Tyranny: Twenty Lessons from the Twentieth Century*. Tim Duggan Books.

The Scottish Government. (2011). *Scotland's Digital Future: A Strategy for Scotland*. Retrieved from http://www.gov.scot/Resource/Doc/343733/0114331.pdf

United Nations Department of Economic and Social Affairs. (2012). *Report of the Expert Group Meeting on "Promoting People's Empowerment in Achieving Poverty Eradication, Social Integration and Decent Work for All"*. Retrieved from http://www.un.org/esa/socdev/csocd/2013/egm-empowerment-final.pdf

United Nations Department of Economic and Social Affairs. (2016). *United Nations E-government Survey 2016*. Retrieved from http://workspace.unpan.org/sites/Internet/Documents/UNPAN96407.pdf

United Nations Department of Economic and Social Affairs. (2017). *E-Participation Index*. Retrieved from https://publicadministration.un.org/egovkb/en-us/About/Overview/E-Participation

Section 2
Case Studies of Social Media in Developing Countries

Chapter 4

Participation With Social Media:
The Case of Turkish Metropolitan Municipalities in Facebook

Cenay Babaoglu
Nigde Omer Halisdemir University, Turkey

Elvettin Akman
Suleyman Demirel University, Turkey

ABSTRACT

By improving ICT within the scope of administration, new terms like e-government, m-government, e-governance, e-participation appeared in the field of public administration. The concept of e-government affects municipalities—closest service units to the citizens—and with this effect developed the term e-municipality. Municipalities in Turkey began to use the new technologies for the delivery of services, and terms like e-participation and e-governance are widening rapidly. This chapter investigates whether Facebook pages are an effective tool for local participation. The social media-citizen relationship that is claimed to be more effective, especially at the local level, has been evaluated through the Facebook pages of the municipalities. This chapter focuses on the role of social media in participatory administration.

DOI: 10.4018/978-1-5225-5326-7.ch004

INTRODUCTION

The steady growth at air transportation and communication sector after 1950s and the revolution by computer and internet technologies in 1990s have led people around the world get closer. Especially, services which emerged with internet technologies, such as e-mail and video-conference, are increasingly connecting overseas countries. In this way, every corner of the world becomes more accessible that this situation accelerates inter-country interactions and makes it easier for people to connect other countries. Therefore, changes and developments in a country show themselves in other countries in a very short time.

The information and communication technologies (ICT) creates difference in connecting local to global, increasing opportunities for communication, participation to politics and opens doors for direct political participation. Social media communication, on the other hand, has transformed these interactions into interactions, resulting in reciprocity and continuity.

Developments in the field of ICT effect the classic bureaucratic structures in the positive way and a new structure are forming, which make faster, easier and lower cost act and transactions possible. New developments especially effect mutual obligations between state and citizen. Administrations aim to form transparent, accountable, deliberative, effective, efficient institutions and citizens expectations support these goals. Transferring duties and services to e-channels is being a useful instrument in this process.

By improving ICT within the scope of administration, new terms like e-government, m-government, e-governance, e-participation appeared in the field of public administration. Concept of e-government effect municipalities –closest service units to the citizens- and with this affect develop the term of e-municipality. Municipalities in Turkey began also use the new technologies for the delivery of services, and the terms like e-participation and e-governance are widening rapidly. In these developments could be accepted as an organizational development, and technology as an instrument for participatory administration. In this study, it is investigated whether Facebook pages are an effective tool for local participation. The social media-citizen relationship that is claimed to be more effective, especially at the local level, has been evaluated through the Facebook pages of the municipalities. In this study, it is also aimed to show what kind of a communication channel preferred by municipalities by considering the interaction between municipalities and citizens on Facebook. Especially, it is aimed to show whether this interaction is one-sided or two-sided as of the Social Media's nature. After inspecting lots of materials, especially Rutgers E-Governance Performance Index Report prepared by Rutgers University School of Public Affairs and Administration National Center for Public Performance in 2010 and investigating the structure of Facebook pages, some questions are graded from 0 to 5, while others are graded 0 and 1 as indicating "no" and "yes" in order. It is very important to present the level of interaction between the metropolitan municipalities and citizens by this study.

LITERATURE REVIEW

Recently 'electronic state' approach has been developed with the use of information technology as a means of presentation of state services and citizen-state relations. The use of e-government has become widespread throughout the world in the last two decades, and in many countries technological changes have been marked by state-citizen relations. It is also recorded that about 45% of the population in Turkey is communicating with public institutions via computer and internet (TURKSTAT, 2015). The fact that new technologies are being used for communication by nearly half of the population shows that the use of e-government in Turkey has reached a certain level. This situation also points to a change in state-citizen relations in Turkey.

The facilitating role of technology in state-citizen relations is particularly effective in reducing the negative belief that democratic representation is a problem of pluralism and loss of representation (Gokce and Orselli, 2012: 41-42). E-elections, voting in the referendum, requests and tendency surveys increase the state-citizen interaction. The flow of information towards citizens, the possibility of independent campaigning of political actor candidates, the opportunities for direct citizen accessibility are qualities that can improve democracy (Korac-Kakabadse and Korac-Kakabadse, 1999: 214-216). The Internet is often referred to in the literature of potency to promote political and civic engagement and to improve the political participation which is a need for a democratic society (Weber, Loumakis and Bergman, 2003: 28). Today, it is possible to evolve from a parliamentary body to a more real, less hierarchical and democratic legitimacy to a higher level of participation, where civil society is directly involved. Thanks to this new structure, it will be possible for the decision-making phases to draw a wider frame than the central points (Armstrong and Gilson, 2011: 6).

As it is seen, there are various possibilities for ICT and citizens or organized pressure groups to be involved in the solution processes of the discussions on social issues, especially the process of policy making (Karkin, 2011: 13-16). Especially in recent years, the use of information technology has become a means of implementing reforms in the public sector (Bonsón, Royo and Ratkai, 2015: 52). In addition, new possibilities are emerging in the creation of new ways to increase public administrations' interaction with citizens and in increasing the effectiveness of service provision through pro-active citizens (OECD, 2007: 13).

This is because there are three main components to ensure transparency in the policy making process: access to information and dissemination of information (where the state is a competent actor and the public is only provided information), public consultation (at this stage there is bilateral interaction but the decisions are still taken by state organs, citizens only give feedback about policies) and active participation (citizens are actively involved in decision-making processes and they are in all the processes from creating policy to its implementation) (OECD, 2001). With ICT, participation in the policy making process gains a new dimension and the processes by which the citizen can intervene are increasing rapidly. Social networks can be used effectively both in policy advocacy and political candidacy processes (Bonsón et al., 2012: 126). Not only citizen-state but also citizen-citizen cooperation and co-production opportunities occur.

Along with the emergence of social media, the one-way roads have become bi-directional, and new networks have begun to develop. The closed information transfer process for citizens starting with Web 1.0 has become more interactive with Web 2.0. (Chun and Cho, 2012: 130-133). With Web 2.0 technologies, interfaces for both political processes and policy processes are formed. A social media that integrates with the e-government system will provide opportunities in improving public services, developing new solutions to problems, improving decision-making processes with more information and more interaction. It can undertake a role as a tool towards democratic state with information provision, participation opportunities, opportunities for public debate (Zheng and Zheng, 2014:107).

In addition, the problems of access with social media decreased and the solution of the problem of equality before participation started to develop (Gokce and Orselli, 2012: 54-56). Social media (Facebook, Twitter, various web forums, etc.) function as an area where public debate can be held as an easily accessible and fast-talking environment (Mentzas et al., 2011: 25). Social media links of public institutions have become an instant information shares and feedback platform for citizens and government.

Social media has changed the citizens' information sources; and carried local, national, or global information shares to another dimension. It can be argued that the Internet carries disabled people to the public sphere and increases their visibility and accessibility (Ellis and Kent, 2011: 50). For example, young people with physical disabilities can participate in social life especially via Facebook (Koten and Erdogan, 2014: 336). In some countries, electronic processes are beneficial in increasing disadvantaged women's education and participation opportunities (Kumar and Sharma, 2012: 194). Social networks are also instrumental in bringing young people together and moving towards active roles in the virtual arena (Koten and Erdogan, 2014: 353-354).

In Lysenko and Desouza's research on social media use and influence on citizen participation in Moldova it has been found that the use of information and communication technologies does not provide direct participation, but it can be achieved by bringing appropriate conditions to the political sphere (Bershadskaya, Chugunov and Trutnev, 2014: 77). Sobaci and Karkın's (2013) survey of mayor candidates in Turkey examining the use of Twitter also revealed similar results, it is seen that Twitter is not being used for transparency, participation, or citizen-focused service delivery, but rather for candidates 'election campaigns and candidates'.

Musso, Weare, and Hale (2000: 2) argue that the opportunities that technology brings are particularly responsive in local governments. However, when the local governments in Germany use social media to communicate via Facebook is investigated, it is seen that the citizen interaction is not used appropriately in the social media potency; rather the unilateral information flow is presented (Hofmann, et al., 2013: 390-395). In a survey conducted by Ikiz and his colleagues on Twitter usage of the candidates of the metropolitan municipalities in Turkey 2014 Local Governments' Elections; it is seen that the rate of messages that candidates sent to citizens to communicate was only 16.6% through the election, the rate of activities that candidates were generally involved was 32.8% and (18.74%) messages related to election campaigns were sent (Ikiz et al. 2014: 44-45). Even though the works of Sobaci and Altinok (2010); Karkin (2011); Karkin and Calhan (2011) and (2012); Karkin (2012); Sobaci & Karkin, (2013); Sobaci & Eryigit, (2015); Yildiz, et al. (2016) there is not enough example about Turkish case, which focused on social media and participation relationship at local level. Sobaci and Altinok (2010) analyzed municipalities' web sites with a participative aspect. Karkin and Calhan (2011) also completed a similar analysis about local governments' and special provincial administrations' web sites. And Karkin again, published an important conceptual framework about e-participation and its effects on public policies. Sobaci and Karkin (2013) again, focused on Turkish Mayors' Twitter usage and effects on better public service. Yildiz et al. (2016) also exerted usability tests on three biggest metropolitan municipalities' Facebook pages. So that, web 2.0 technologies –especially social media- will be a very important indicator to analyze effects of this relationship. This analyzes focus on the role of social media on the way of participatory administration.

Thus, it can be said that there are differences in application of the use of ICT and the assessment of the opportunities for participation between countries. In the survey conducted by Bonsón et al., status of municipal Facebook pages that let shareholders post on the wall selected from different countries were taken as independent variables and an investigation was conducted for 15 countries (Bonsón, Royo and Ratkai, 2015: 56). As a result, Anglo-Saxon, Germanic and Scandinavian local governments were found to be more effective in using Facebook. Citizens selected from the country of origin are allowed to share on the Facebook page of the stakeholders and interactive use is made possible. However, the most successful citizen intervention rates are seen in Scandinavian countries and municipalities in Southern Europe (Bonsón, Royo and Ratkai, 2015: 59).

METHODOLOGY

According to the results of Household Information Technologies Usage Survey made by Turkish Statistical Institute (TSI) in 2016, when the aim to use Internet is taken into consideration, in the first three months of the year, 82,4 per cent of the individuals that use Internet to create profile, sent message or share photos, 74,5 per cent to watch video from video channels, 69,5 to read online news or magazines, 65,9 to search information on health, 65,5 to search information on gods and services and 63,7 to listen to music via Internet (TSI, 2016). Internet usage in rural areas is less then cities. It is necessary for metropolitan municipalities to use their Facebook pages actively in an era when internet and especially social media are intensely used.

According to 'Digital in 2017 Global Overview'[1] published by *We Are Social and Hootsuite,* 48 million people which constitute 60% penetration of the population connect internet in Turkey. In the report, the number of active social media user is 48 million, but it is necessary to state that this number is not individual use. While the number of mobile user in Turkey is 71 million, the number of people who connect to social media via mobile devices is 42 million. Also, users spend 7 hours in front of a computer, 3 hours connecting internet via mobile phone and 3 hours on social media platforms.

The most used social media channel in Turkey is YouTube (every registered Gmail user is already registered as a YouTube user too.) with a rate of 57 per cent and Facebook is the second with 56%. It is a significant lack that a local government does not have a Facebook page that's a commonly used social media channel in Turkey. This study also aims to share the results with the directors of the metropolitan municipalities and informing them in which areas to on Facebook page and how to use it.

Likewise, many institutions in Turkey have official accounts on Facebook. So, Facebook will be a good sample for social media analysis. Within this scope, Facebook pages of 30 metropolitan municipalities in Turkey were researched, and the criteria such as liking figures, shares situations, mutual interaction, and content of the shares were evaluated.

The study started with the question of how metropolitan municipalities' activities effect citizens' electronic participation. This study aims to make an evaluation about Facebook pages of 30 metropolitan municipalities in Turkey which are one of their social media accounts. Firstly, metropolitan municipalities' web pages were entered and it was controlled whether Facebook connection was available or not. Facebook pages were entered in undetected situations and necessary controls were made. In the research, it is determined whether they shared any kind of video application, weather report or night pharmacy on their Facebook pages by grading with 0 and 1. Then it is graded from 1 to 5 according to the criteria determined by analyzing some cases as whether they have link of their Facebook pages on their website, or as whether they give place for communication information by evaluating each one on its category. For example, it is taken into consideration whether they have phone number, address, mail address and web address in communication section. Then, a lot of studies were made about a lot of subjects such as interacting, informing, request, complaint and expectation. This study aims to reveal in what level metropolitan municipalities that provide the closest service to the public use Facebook that a social media in a citizen-centered and effective way is considering that 75 per cent of Turkish citizens live within the borders of metropolitan municipalities[2]. In order to examine the participative role of Facebook pages, a content analysis scale and sub-indicators evolved with the help of the scales from Holzer; You & Manoharan (2010) Holzer & Manoharan 2016); Bensghir, (2002). With the help of these scales contents and participation possibilities will be searched.

FINDINGS

The study shows that 14 metropolitan municipalities (Aydın, Denizli, Muğla, Tekirdağ, Trabzon, Şanlıurfa, Kahramanmaraş, Balıkesir, Van, Manisa, Hatay, Malatya, Mardin and Ordu) that have become metropolitan municipalities according to the Law no. 6360[3] and Mardin that gained the metropolitan municipality status by a legislative regulation have not got an official Facebook page. This situation shows that the necessity of the digital age has not been understood enough and it must also be investigated in what reasons metropolitan municipalities have not opened an official Facebook account. Because it is estimated that literacy rate in this region is low[4] (9.9%) and digital literacy rate could be revealed by the studies to be done. Even if there is such a situation, it could be expected that the metropolitan municipality should develop alternative solutions such as shares videos or photos in different languages by taking into consideration the recent condition of the citizens.

Evaluation of General Issues About Facebook Pages

The populations of the metropolitan municipalities according to the TUIK statistics 2016 are given in Figure 1[5]. It is seen that the population of 9 metropolitan municipalities (Erzurum, Eskişehir, Malatya, Mardin, Muğla, Ordu, Sakarya,

Figure 1. Population of Metropolitan Municipalities

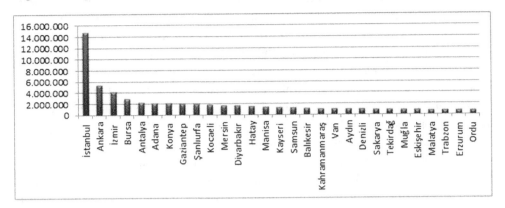

Tekirdağ ve Trabzon) are below 1 million. 38 per cent of 62 million people living in 30 metropolitan municipalities live within the borders of three metropolitan municipalities (İstanbul, İzmir, Ankara). When compared, Ordu Metroplitan Municiality that has the lowest population among metropolitan municipalities, that's 5 per cent of the population of Istanbul Metropolitan Municipality that has the highest population. This rate shows that the difference among the population of metropolitan municipalities in Turkey is high.

Metropolitan Municipalities in Figures; 1- İstanbul, 2- Ankara, 3- İzmir, 4- Bursa, 5-Antalya, 6-Adan, 7-Konya, 8-Gaziantep, 9- Şanlıurfa, 10-Kocaeli, 11- Mersin, 12- Diyarbakır, 13- Hatay, 14- Manisa, 15- Kayseri, 16- Samsun, 17- Balıkesir, 18- Kahramanmaraş, 19- Van, 20- Aydın, 21- Denizli, 22- Sakarya, 23- Tekirdağ, 24- Muğla, 25- Eskişehir, 26- Malatya, 27- Trabzon, 28- Erzurum, 29- Ordu

While taken into consideration that 60 per cent of Turkey's population use Internet and most of these users are also social media users, population density is a disadvantage in the number of average Facebook page likes. In Figure 2, average number of like was detected by dividing the population of metropolitan municipalities into the number of Facebook like. According to this, the like performances of the metropolitan municipalities whose like rates are high are low. When the Figure is examined, it is seen that Kayseri Metropolitan Municipality with 350 averages like rate shows the lowest performance. Kayseri is followed by Istanbul Metropolitan Municipality with 227 averages like rate, Ankara with 128 and Trabzon with 123. It is necessary to point out that although Antalya Metropolitan Municipality has about 75400 like number, it has disadvantage of high population. It is also seen that Kayseri Metropolitan Municipality is used by the name of the mayor and it is a negative state for institutionalization. When the number of people who like is examined, the number of people who like Facebook pages of Metropolitan Municipality in Erzurum

Figure 2. Like rates of Metropolitan Municipalities

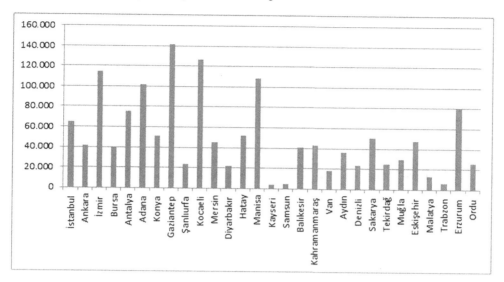

that has the population of 762021 is 80317 and it is the city that shows the highest performance by the average rate 9. Erzurum is followed by Manisa (average like rate 12) and Gaziantep (average like rate 13). When taken free from population, the metropolitan municipality with the highest number of like is Gaziantep Metropolitan Municipality with 141569 likes. It shows that the rate of like is high and the shares appeal to the citizens. Also data show that the followers in these cities are more interactive and open to interaction than other cities.

Evaluation About the Functioning of Facebook Page

The evaluations about the functioning of Facebook pages of metropolitan municipalities are given in this part. Within this context, the number of monthly shares of metropolitan municipalities between June, 19, 2017 and July, 19, 2017 are given. Then an evaluation is made within the context of giving information about Facebook pages on official web pages of metropolitan municipalities (easily access to logo, direct connection to Facebook page etc.). Also it is searched whether there are evaluation sections on Facebook pages. 29 metropolitan municipalities are evaluated according to their shares numbers in a month (June, 19, 2017- July, 19, 2017). According to this evaluation, it is seen that Trabzon Metropolitan Municipality did not make any shares between these dates, Ankara Metropolitan Municipality made four shares and Samsun Metropolitan Municipality made only

Figure 3. The number 9 monthly shares (June, 19, 2017- July, 19, 2017)

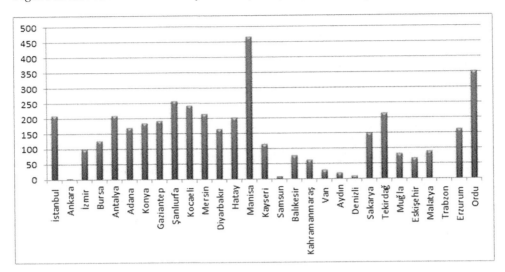

8 shares. Facebook account of Manisa Metropolitan Municipality is the most active account with 467 shares.

In Figure 4, it is studied whether there are the logos of social media accounts in their official web pages of metropolitan municipalities and if it is possible to enter official Facebook account via these logos. Within the scope of these studies, metropolitan municipalities are graded from 1 to 5 based on their performances. 23 metropolitan municipalities are graded with 5 because their social media logos are

Figure 4. Access to Facebook page through Official Municipality Web Page

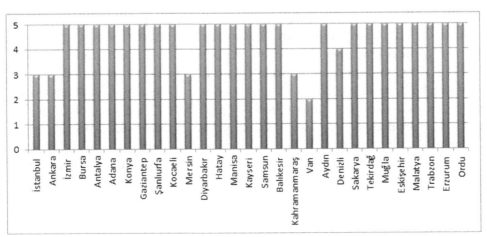

easily available and it is possible to enter the social media accounts directly. Van Metropolitan Municipality has the lowest performance with 2 points.

In Figure 5, it is dealt that whether there is assessment section in official Facebook pages of metropolitan municipalities. According to this, only 12 metropolitan municipalities (Adana, Antalya, Denizli, Diyarbakır, Erzurum, İstanbul, Kocaeli, Mersin, Trabzon, Sakarya, Samsun, Şanlıurfa) out of 29 metropolitan municipalities[6] have "assess the Facebook page" section.

Figure 5. Facebook Assessment Section

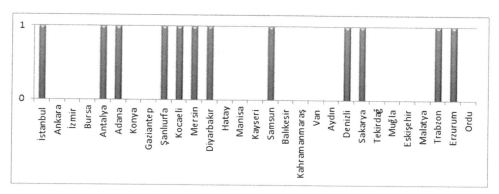

Table 1. Metropolitan Municipalities According To Facebook Evaluation

Metropolitan municipalities that have Facebook evaluation	Metropolitan municipalities that do not have Facebook evaluation
Adana	Ankara
Antalya	Aydın
Denizli	Balıkesir
Diyarbakır	Bursa
Erzurum	Eskişehir
İstanbul	Gaziantep
Kocaeli	Hatay
Mersin	İzmir
Sakarya	Kahramanmaraş
Samsun	Kayseri
Şanlıurfa	Konya
Trabzon	Malatya
	Manisa
	Muğla
	Ordu
	Tekirdağ
	Van

Among the metropolitan municipalities that have Facebook page assessment, Mersin Metropolitan Municipality has the highest rate with 4.9 assessment score on a 5 point scale. Samsun Metropolitan Municipality with 2.6 assessment scale has the lowest rate. As seen in the Figure 5, it is remarkable that Istanbul, Antalya, Adana, Diyarbakır, Erzurum, Kocaeli, Mersin, Sakarya and Samsun metropolitan municipalities that became metropolitan municipalities before the legal regulation no. 6330 do not have Facebook evaluation.

Figure 5 shows us that among the metropolitan municipalities in Turkey that have Facebook pages, 59 per cent of them have evaluation sections.

Evaluation About Facebook Page Setup

The Facebook page setup of metropolitan municipalities is examined in this part of the study. It is searched whether there is message button, contact information of municipality, connection links to the service units of the municipality, the links of other social media accounts, activity calendar, blue tick, information about the city and the mayor. If there is, 1 point is given; if not, 0 is given.

Public relations works are common nowadays. Within this scope metropolitan municipalities form some units under different names and another mechanism by which people convey their demands, complaints and ideas is social media. It is significant that there must be message button in Facebook pages of metropolitan municipalities when considered the personal privacy. Within this scope, it is seen in the Figure 6 whether there is message button in official Facebook accounts. 9 metropolitan municipalities have not got message button in their Facebook pages.

Figure 6. Existence of Message Button

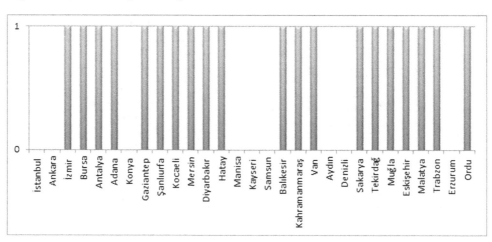

31 per cent of Facebook pages of metropolitan municipalities do not have message buttons. Istanbul and Ankara Metropolitan Municipalities are among the metropolitan municipalities that have not got message button.

The data that is about contact information and comprises of four criteria are below. These criteria are telephone numbers in Facebook accounts, address, e-mail address and how many of the official web site information it provides. These criteria are formed by grading from 0 to 4. Eight metropolitan municipalities (Samsun, Şanlıurfa, Sakarya, Adana, Antalya, Diyarbakır, Kocaeli, and Mersin) provide the criteria and are graded with 4. Ankara and Kahramanmaraş Metropolitan Municipalities provides only one criterion that's the official web site information (Figure 7).

Only four metropolitan municipalities provide connection to their service units' Facebook pages (water and sewerage administration etc.), these are Tekirdağ, Sakarya, Gaziantep and Bursa Metropolitan Municipalities (Figure 8).

Figure 7. Existence of General Contact Information

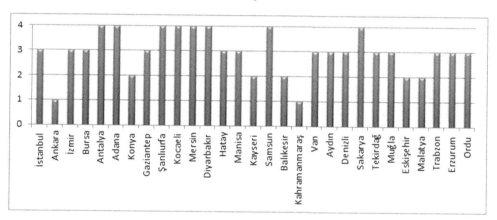
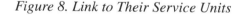

Figure 8. Link to Their Service Units

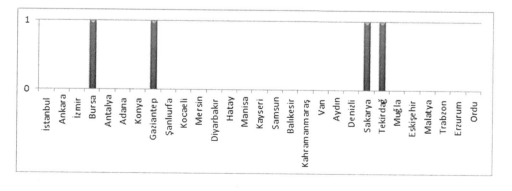

89

15 metropolitan municipalities have connection from their Facebook pages to other social media accounts of theirs such as Twitter and Instagram (Figure 9). This issue is significant in terms of metropolitan Municipalities' following the social media. The possibility of followers to follow other social media via a social media is high.

When taken the prevalence of social and cultural activities into consideration, it is seen that reaching the citizens via different channels is significant. One of these is making an activity calendar in social media accounts. When it is thought that social media via cell phones is a part of daily life, it grows in importance. In the Figure 10 it is evaluated whether there is activity calendar in Facebook accounts grading from 0 to 1. According to this, 19 metropolitan municipalities form activity calendar and reach the citizens. These metropolitan municipalities are Adana, Antalya, Bursa, Denizli, Diyarbakır, Eskişehir, Gaziantep, İzmir, Kahramanmaraş, Kocaeli, Malatya, Manisa, Mersin, Muğla, Ordu, Sakarya, Samsun, Şanlıurfa and Tekirdağ.

Figure 9. Existence of Other Social Media Links

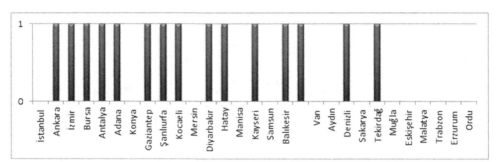

Figure 10. Application of Activity Calender

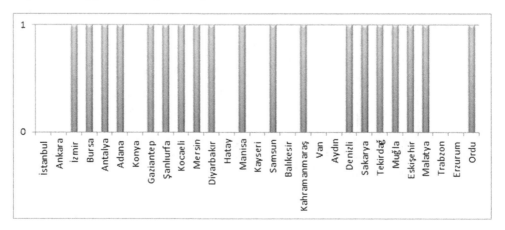

Metropolitan municipalities try to introduce their cities via different channels such as YouTube, web pages and city information system. Within this scope, it is dealt whether metropolitan municipalities give information about their cities in their Facebook accounts. According to this, only Adana, Gaziantep, Kocaeli and Tekirdağ Metropolitan Municipalities give information about their cities in their Facebook accounts (Figure 11).

In the Figure 12 it is evaluated whether there is a separate section about the mayor for informing the citizens. It is seen that only Ankara and Kayseri Metropolitan Municipalities inform the citizens about their mayors. As mentioned above, the

Figure 11. Access Info about The City

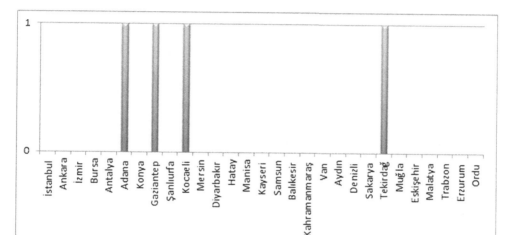

Figure 12. Using Blue Teak

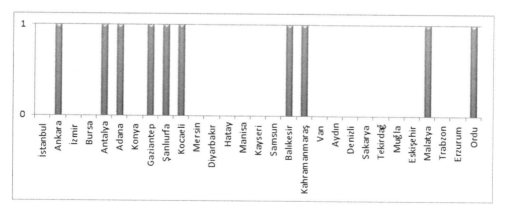

official Facebook page of Kayseri Metropolitan Municipality was opened by the name of the Mayor.

The performances of metropolitan municipalities about shares video that is a kind of public informing are rather high except Trabzon and Van Metropolitan Municipalities. Trabzon and Van Metropolitan Municipalities have never shared a video since they opened Facebook accounts.

It a significant issue in terms of institutionalism for metropolitan municipalities to have Facebook authorities certify their Facebook pages. Within this scope, only 33 per cent of metropolitan municipalities have got Facebook blue tick. These cities are Adana, Antalya, Ankara, Balıkesir, Kahramanmaraş, Kocaeli, Manisa, Ordu and Şanlıurfa.

Evaluation About Facebook Shares

The control and shares of Facebook pages are significant from the point of view of the metropolitan municipalities' interaction with the citizens. An evaluation about informing the citizens about the local services, information shares via videos about the projects made by the municipality based on the comments or demands via Facebook, information of night-pharmacy and weather forecast to avert for a natural disaster is made. An evaluation "has" or "has not" is made for the shares of metropolitan municipalities' Facebook pages (Figure 13).

Another criterion of this study that is carried out on Facebook pages of metropolitan municipalities is whether they share in a foreign language or not. It is also significant that metropolitan municipalities that take important actions in internationalization

Figure 13. Video Application

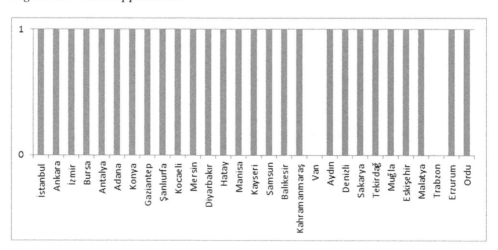

by some applications such as town twinning etc. should share in a foreign language. Within this scope, it is seen that 29 metropolitan municipalities have not shared anything in any foreign language. When it is taken into consideration that people who speak different languages live in our country, we are in internet era and metropolitan municipalities aim at internationalization, it is a great lack not to share in a foreign language for people to be informed.

Metropolitan municipalities' considering citizens' demands, complaints and offers are as significant as their informing citizens via Facebook pages. It is significant for metropolitan municipalities to answer citizens' comments fast in terms of mobile municipals. Only 6 metropolitan municipalities (Eskişehir, İzmir, Kahramanmaraş, Manisa, Mersin ve Şanlıurfa) out of 29 metropolitan municipalities inform for citizens' demands, complaints and complaints. For instance, a citizen comment on Eskisehir Metropolitan Municipality's Facebook page at 19[07], July 2017 that he must be informed about wrong parking on the pavement and garbage collecting in his new neighborhood. Eskisehir Metropolitan Municipality officials answered this comment in 3 minutes and informed the citizen. A comment was written on Izmir Metropolitan Municipality's Facebook page at 14. in 01 August, 2017 about the place of travelling children's theatre. The necessary information was given about 25 minutes later. But when metropolitan municipalities' Facebook pages are examined, it is seen that they do not answer citizens' comments (Figure 14).

It was examined in the Figure 15 whether metropolitan municipalities share weather forecast reports or not. It is significant for metropolitan municipalities to inform citizens about the weather conditions of the city by using technology.

Figure 14. Answering Comments

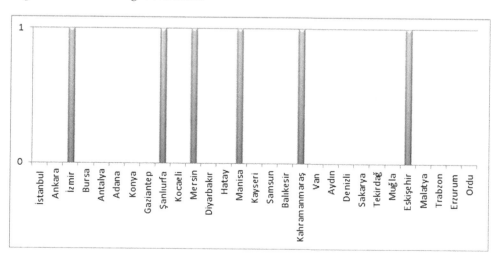

Figure 15. Shares Weather Forecast Reports

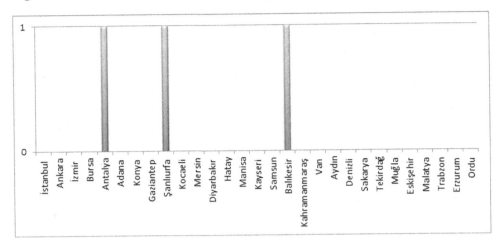

Especially, it is more significant in case of rain, snow and freeze. Antalya, Şanlıurfa, Balıkesir metropolitan municipalities share weather forecast reports and inform citizens about weather conditions.

It is not suitable for understanding of social municipals that only 25 per cent of metropolitan municipalities share night pharmacy information. This is another example of some municipalities that misunderstand to inform people. Metropolitan municipalities that share the list of night pharmacies are Adana, Ankara, Aydın, Balıkesir, Denizli, Kahramanmaras, Sanlıurfa and Tekirdag (Figure 16).

Figure 16. Shares the list of Night Pharmacies

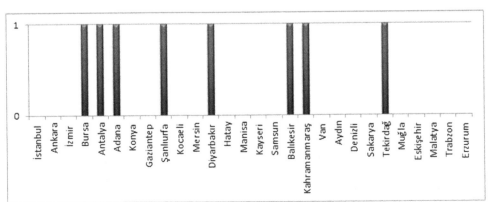

Among the criteria, sharing photos are the only criteria with which all metropolitan municipalities comply. All of 29 metropolitan municipalities share photos on their Facebook pages. Photos that are shared by metropolitan municipalities are generally about their works and activities.

DISCUSSION

In fact, it is not possible to say that the possibilities of participation in the global sense are fully assessed. In the study by Bonsón, Royo and Ratkai (2015), it is found that 79% of city municipalities which are the five biggest cities of European Union's top 15 member countries have Facebook pages. However, it is noted that very few of them are applications for citizen participation (Bonsón, Royo and Ratkai, 2015: 59). In terms of Turkey, it can be argued that there are still significant disruptions in civilian intervention due to costs, bureaucratic resistance and severe legal regulations to create access (Karkin, 2011: 17). Norris and Reddick (2013: 173-174) state that a social media account doesn't contribute to democratization immediately. Likewise, it is understood that the difference can only be understood by investigating the extent to which participation in action at local level has contributed. From this point, the situation in Turkey has been examined through Facebook pages.

The metropolitan municipality with the highest number of Facebook favorites is Gaziantep Metropolitan Municipality with the liking of 141569. The contribution of the mayor, Fatma Sahin, in terms of effective use of social media for years, including her previous ministry, is also great. Fatma Sahin is messaging with her followers on Twitter and Instagram, even arranging meetings from time to time. In this respect, it is significant that Gaziantep Metropolitan Municipality's headquarters Facebook page is the metropolitan city with the highest rating. It also shows that mutual interaction promotes diffusion. On the other hand, it has been noticed that the likes of many municipalities on Facebook pages show some sort of overlap with the activities of the mayors in other social media areas. This creates a kind of problem in terms of corporate social accounts. It is unclear what the circumstances of these Facebook accounts will be after the presidencies that may change with the elections in 2019. The fact that institutions in Turkey do not yet have social media vision documents also shows the institutionalization dimension of the problem. It is possible to encounter similar problems in many public institutions, since there is no provision of some sort of institutional social media accounts at the national level. It is possible to talk about a more isomorphic structure of Facebook pages. A municipality or mayor who takes place on the agenda that succeeds with his social media account is also pursuing other institutional structures. On the other hand, these changes seem to remain only in the formal dimensions.

The fact that shares on Facebook pages is usually one way also supports this argument. Comments on the shares are generally not answered. It is not possible to talk about mutual interaction except for shares and liking. It is even possible to say that half of the official Facebook pages are already in a passive position. There is not any information about owner or controller of Facebook pages and also municipalities did not answer our questions about that. It is significant whether the people who share are digital natives[7] or digital immigrants. When the shares are taken into consideration, it can be said that the users of Facebook ages of metropolitan municipalities in Turkey are still digital immigrants. It is also significant that these digital immigrants should get education about social media literacy in terms of quality and effectiveness of shares.

When the municipalities' web pages are examined, it is seen that the unit that deal with the social media is not known and pages of departments of municipalities give only short information. Even unilateral data such as daily weather shares, pharmacy information on duty, and information about the city where the municipality is located, information about the mayor were not found on the pages except for exceptions. This shows that these pages are not used even for one-way information transfer.

In such a case, the likes on the pages can be explained with the information and interaction requests of the citizens. With approximately 48 million accounts, Turkey-based account holders located on the Facebook network demand to be in touch with the public institutions in this area rightly. Institutions have assessed this claim solely for the sake of existence and non-existence, and many institutions have limited their possibilities to use these accounts when opening official accounts. It is seen that contact information such as phone, fax, and e-mail appear on Facebook pages of corporations. Likewise, they seem to direct directly to the municipal web pages. In this case, Turkey shows that metropolitan municipalities have not yet seen Facebook pages as a service area. On the contrary, it is possible to say that they are used as a kind of directional plate conveying the classical communication methods.

Today, information and communication technologies provide opportunities for more successful democracy experiences and participation experiences. It is possible to increase the level and quality of public participation with information technology. What is important is the extent to which ICT is used to influence public decisions. As stated by Hood, ICT is not a utopian solution. ICT offers opportunities, but results vary depending on implementation (Hood, 2008: 476). In terms of Turkey, it is possible to say that a popular approach only evaluates metropolitan municipalities' Facebook usage. As is stands, these pages show similarities with the German study presented by Hofmann, et al. (2013) and can be considered as a one-way information transmission tool that is far from interactive, as is the case in Germany. It is depicted in the study how social media effects e-participation (electronic participation) in developing countries by the research carried out on Facebook. The answer is, as mentioned, that it has the same results with the research held in Germany.

As Yildiz, et al (2016) cited that there are still no online services available on the Facebook pages ever since 2015. The reality stated by Norris and Reddick (2013), and the fact that the existence of the social media accounts is not a stand-alone success has been revealed once again with this work. Babaoglu, Akilli and Demircioglu (2012: 71) mentioned about the importance of human capital for the success of e-government projects and Garson (2006) points that governments doesn't pay any attention to the education and training activities about e-government services and Turkish case confirms these arguments again. There is not any social media expert or institutional structures in local governments in Turkey to control and manage social media accounts. The lack of institutional policies and technical knowledge lead the experience of metropolitan municipalities' participative Facebook to the downfall. In this context, technological tools are not enough alone. Technological tools can be considered as means of technical participation under various participation methods. On the other hand, it is thought that a study that will evaluate the other social media accounts will reveal whether this situation is specific for Facebook accounts or it is a general tendency of institutions in Turkey.

REFERENCES

Armstrong, D., & Gilson, J. (2011). Introduction: Civil Society and International Governance. In D. Armstrong, V. Bello, J. Gilson, & D. Spini (Eds.), *Civil Society and International Governance* (pp. 1–13). New York: Routhledge.

Babaoglu, C., Akıllı, S., & Demircioglu, M. A. (2012). E-Government Education at the Public Administration Departments in Turkey. In R. Gil-Garcia, N. Helbig, & A. Ojo (Eds.), *ICEGOV-Open Innovation of Global Change* (pp. 71–85). New York: ACM. doi:10.1145/2463728.2463745

Bensghir, K. T. (2002). Web'deki Belediyelerimiz: Eskişehir Büyükşehir Belediyesi [Our municipalities on the Web: Eskisehir Metropolitan Municipality]. *Çağdaş Yerel Yönetimler Dergisi, 11*(1), 107–124.

Bershadskaya, L., Chugunov, A., & Trutnev, D. (2014). Evaluation of E-Participation in Social Networks: Russian E-Petitions Portal. In M. W. A. Janssen, F. Bannister, O. Glassey, H. J. Scholl, E. Tambouris, M. A. Wimmer, & A. Macintosh (Eds.), *Electronic Government and Electronic Participation* (pp. 76–83). Amsterdam: IOS Press.

Bonsón, E., Royo, S., & Ratkai, M. (2015). Citizens' Engagement on Local Governments' Facebook Sites. An empirical analysis: The impact of different media and content types in Western Europe. *Government Information Quarterly*, *32*(1), 52–62. doi:10.1016/j.giq.2014.11.001

Bonsón, E., Torres, L., Royo, S., & Flores, F. (2012). Local e-Government 2.0: Social Media and Corporate Transparency in Municipalities. *Government Information Quarterly*, *29*(2), 123–132. doi:10.1016/j.giq.2011.10.001

Chun, S. A., & Cho, J.-S. (2012). E-participation and Transparent Policy Decision Making. *Information Polity*, *17*, 129–145.

Turhan, D. G. (2016). *Digital Natives and Digital Activism in the Framework of Information Society Context* (Unpublished PhD thesis). Suleyman Demirel University, Social Sciences Institute, Department of International Relations.

Ellis, K., & Kent, M. (2011). *Disability and New Media*. New York: Routledge.

Garson, D. G. (2006). *Public Information Technology and E-Governance: Managing the Virtual State*. London: Jones and Bartlett Pub.

Gokce, O., & Orselli, E. (2012). E-Demokrasi Vatandaşların Siyasete İlgilerinin ve Katılımlarının Arttırılmasının Bir Aracı Mı? [Is e-Democracy a Tool to Arise the Interest of Citizen to Politics and for Participation]. in. E-Devlet. Ankara: Nobel.

Hofmann, S., Beverungen, D., Michael, R., & Becker, J. (2013). What Makes Local Governments' Online Communications Successful? Insights From A Multi-Method Analysis Of Facebook. *Government Information Quarterly*, *30*(4), 387–396. doi:10.1016/j.giq.2013.05.013

Holzer, M., & Manoharan, A. (2016). Digital Governance in Municipalities Worldwide ~ A Longitudinal Assessment of Municipal Websites Throughout the World. E-Governance Institute National Center for Public Performance, Rutgers University.

Holzer, M., You, M.-B., & Manoharan, A. (2010). Digital Governance in Municipalities Worldwide ~ A Longitudinal Assessment of Municipal Websites Throughout the World. E-Governance Institute National Center for Public Performance, Rutgers University.

Hood, C. (2008). The Tools Of The Government. In *The Information Age. In The Oxford Handbook of Public Policy*. Oxford, UK: Oxford University Press.

Ozdesim, Sobaci, Yavuz, & Karkin. (2014). Political Use of Twitter: The Case of Metropolitan Mayor Candidates in 2014 Local Elections in Turkey. *ICEGOV '14 Proceedings of the 8th International Conference on Theory and Practice of Electronic Governance*, 41-50.

Karkin, N. (2012). e-Katılım Kavramı ve Süreci: Kamu Siyasa Oluşum Sürecine Vatandaş Katkısının Olabilirliği [e-Participation Concept and Practice: The Feasibility of Citizen Engagement in Public Policy Formulation]. *Sosyo-Ekonomi Dergisi, 2012*(1), 41-62.

Karkin, N., & Çalhan, H. S. (2012). An Interactive e-Participation Model for the Public Administration System in Turkey: SIBIYO. *Ege Akademik Bakış, 12*(1), 107-125.

Karkin, N., & Çalhan, H. S. (2011). Vilayet ve İl Özel İdare Web Sitelerinde E-Katılım Olgusu [The E-Participation Concept in the Web Sites of Turkish Governorships and Special Provincial Administrations]. *Süleyman Demirel Üniversitesi Sosyal Bilimler Enstitüsü Dergisi, 13*(1), 55-80.

Karkin, N. (2011). The Critical Analysis of Civic Engagement in Public Policy Formation in the Light of the Stakeholder Theory. *Bulletinul, 2011*(1), 9-18.

Kavanaugh, A. L., Fox, E. A., Sheetz, S. D., Yang, S., Li, L. T., Shoemaker, D. J., ... Xie, L. (2012). Social Media Use by Government: From The Routine To The Critical. *Government Information Quarterly, 29*(4), 480–491. doi:10.1016/j.giq.2012.06.002

Koten, E., & Erdoğan, B. (2014). Sanaldan Gerçeğe Ağlara Tutunmak: Engelli Gençlerin Facebook'ta Sosyalleşme Deneyimleri [Transition from Sticking to Virtual to Real Networks: The Socilisation Experiences of Disabled Young People]. *Alternatif Politika, 6*(3), 333-358.

Korac-Kakabadse, A., & Korac-Kakabadse, N. (1999). Information Technology's Impact on the Quality of Democracy: Reinventing the 'Democratic Vassel.' In Reinventing Government In The Digital Age. London: Routledge.

Kumar, R., & Sharma, M. K. (2012). Impact of ICT For Women Literacy In Indian Rural Areas Of e-Governance. *Journal of Information and Operations Management, 3*(1), 194–195.

Metzas, G., Apostolou, D., Bothos, E., & Magoutas, B. (2011). Information Markets For Social Participation in Public Policy Design and Implementation. *Proceedings of Fifth International AAAI Conference on Weblogs and Social Media*. Retrieved from https://www.aaai.org/ocs/index.php/ICWSM/ICWSM11/paper/view/3862

Musso, J., Weare, C., & Hale, M. (2000). Designing Web Technologies for Local Governance Reform: Good Management or Good Democracy? *Political Communication, 17*(1), 1–19. doi:10.1080/105846000198486

Norris, D., & Reddick, C. G. (2013). Local E-Government In The United States: Transformation or Incremental Change? *Public Administration Review, 73*(1), 165–175. doi:10.1111/j.1540-6210.2012.02647.x

Organisation of Economic Cooperation and Development (OECD). (2007). *Participative Web and User-Created Content: Web 2.0, Wikis and Social Networking.* Paris: OECD. Retrieved from http://www.oecd.org/sti/ieconomy/participativewebandusercreatedcontentweb20wikisandsocialnetworking.htm

Organisation of Economic Cooperation and Development (OECD). (2001). Engaging Citizens in Policy Making: Information, Consultation and Participation. *OECD Public Management Brief.* Retrieved from http://www.oecd.org/dataoecd/24/34/2384040.pdf

Sobacı, M. Z., & Karkın, N. (2013). The Use of Twitter by Mayors in Turkey: Tweets for Better Public Services? *Government Information Quarterly, 30*(4), 417–425. doi:10.1016/j.giq.2013.05.014

Sobaci, M. Z., & Altınok, R. (2011). Türkiye'de Büyükşehir Belediyelerinin E-Katılım Uygulamaları: Website İçerik Analizi [E-Participation Applications of Metropalitan Municipality in Turkey: A Webside Content Analysis]. Kamu Yönetimi Forumu, Ankara, Turkey.

Sobaci, M. Z., & Eryigit, K. Y. (2015). Determinants of E-Democracy Adoption in Turkish Municipalities: An Analysis for Spatial Diffusion Effect. *Local Government Studies, 41*(3), 1–25. doi:10.1080/03003930.2014.995296

Turkish Statistical Institute (TURKSTAT). (2016) *Household Informatics Technology Usage Research.* Retrieved from http://www.tuik.gov.tr/PreHaberBultenleri.do?id=21779

Weber, L., Loumakis, A., & Bergman, J. (2003). Who Participates and Why? An Analysis of Citizens on the Internet and the Mass Public. *Social Science Computer Review, 21*(1), 26–42. doi:10.1177/0894439302238969

We Are Social. (2017). *The Digital in 2017 Global Overview.* Retrieved from https://wearesocial.com/special-reports/digital-in-2017-global-overview

Yildiz, M., Ocak, N., Yildirim, C., Cagiltay, K., & Babaoglu, C. (2016). Usability in Local E-Government: Analysis of Turkish Metropolitan Municipality Facebook Pages. *International Journal of Public Administration in the Digital Age*, *3*(1), 53–69. doi:10.4018/IJPADA.2016010104

Zheng, L., & Zheng, T. (2014). Innovation Through Social Media in the Public Sector: Information and Interactions. *Government Information Quarterly*, *31*(1), S106–S117. doi:10.1016/j.giq.2014.01.011

ENDNOTES

[1]   The Digital in 2017 Global Overview report could be accessed at https://wearesocial.com/special-reports/digital-in-2017-global-overview

[2]   Turkish Statistical Institute, 2016 Address Based Population Registration System.

[3]   Turkish Metropolitan Municipality Law

[4]   http://www.dontwasteyourfuture.eu/turkiyede-illere-gore-okur-yazarlik/?lang=tr Access date: 10/08/2017.

[5]   TUİK, 2016 Address Based Population Registration System.

[6]   Mardin Metropolitan Municipality was excluded because of lack of official Facebook page.

[7]   For more information about digital natives: Durmuş Gökhan Turhan, "Digital Natives and Digital Activism in the Framework of Information Society Context", Suleyman Demirel University, Social Sciences Institute, Department of International Relations, Unpublished PhD Thesis.

APPENDIX

Table 2. Facebook Accounts of Metropolitan Municipalities

METROPOLITAN MUNICIPALITIES	Population/The rate of Like °Oram	Evaluation of Facebook?	Message Button°	Monthly Share Number	Contact Information	Other Institution Contact	S.MedHes. Bağ.	Activity Calender	Information about the city	Info about the mayor	Vide share	Picture share	Answer to comments	Blue Tich	Weather Forecast	Share in a foreign language	Night pharmacy
İstanbul	227	1 (3.5)	0	210	3	0	0	0	0	0	1	1	1	0	0	0	0
Ankara	128	0	0	4	1	0	1	0	0	0	1	1	0	0	0	0	1
İzmir	36	0	1	99	3	0	1	1	0	0	1	1	0	1	1	0	1
Bursa	73	0	1	126	3	1	1	1	0	0	1	1	0	1	0	0	1
Antalya	30	1 (3.6)	1	211	4	0	1	1	0	0	1	1	0	0	0	0	0
Adana	21	1 (3.9)	1	170	4	0	1	1	1	0	1	1	0	1	0	0	0
Konya	42	0	0	185	2	0	0	0	0	0	1	1	1	1	1	0	1
Gaziantep	13	0	1	193	3	1	1	1	1	0	1	1	0	1	0	0	0
Şanlıurfa	82	1 (3.6)	1	258	4	0	1	1	0	0	1	1	1	0	0	0	0
Kocaeli	14	1 (4)	1	242	4	0	1	1	1	0	1	1	0	0	0	0	1
Mersin	39	1 (4.7)	1	215	4	0	0	1	0	0	1	1	0	0	0	0	0
Diyarbakır	76	1 (4.5)	1	164	4	0	1	1	0	0	1	1	1	0	0	0	0
Hatay	29	0	1	202	3	0	1	0	0	1	1	1	0	0	0	0	0
Manisa	12	0	0	467	3	0	0	1	0	0	1	1	0	0	0	0	0
Kayseri	350	0	0	115	2	0	1	0	0	0	1	1	0	1	1	0	1
Samsun	95	1 (2.6)	0	8	4	0	0	1	0	0	1	1	1	1	0	0	1
Balıkesir	29	0	1	76	2	0	1	0	0	0	0	1	0	0	0	0	0
Kahramanmaraş	25	0	1	63	1	0	1	1	0	0	1	1	0	0	0	0	0
Van	59	0	1	29	3	0	0	0	0	0	1	1	0	0	0	0	0
Aydın	29	0	0	20	3	0	0	0	0	0	1	1	0	0	0	0	0
Denizli	43	1 (3.2)	0	10	3	0	1	1	0	0	1	1	0	0	0	0	1
Sakarya	19	1 (3.2)	1	149	4	1	0	1	0	0	1	1	0	0	0	0	0
Tekirdağ	38	0	1	216	3	1	1	1	1	0	1	1	1	0	0	0	0
Muğla	31	0	1	82	3	0	0	1	0	0	1	1	0	1	0	0	0
Eskişehir	17	0	1	68	2	0	0	1	0	0	0	1	0	0	0	0	0
Malatya	60	0	1	90	2	0	0	1	0	0	1	1	0	0	0	0	0
Trabzon	123	1 (3.3)	1	0	3	0	0	0	0	0	1	1	0	1	0	0	0
Erzurum	9	1 (3.7)	0	163	3	0	0	0	0	0	1	1	1	0	0	0	0
Ordu	29	0	1	354	3	0	0	1	0	0	1	1	0	0	0	0	1

Chapter 5
Boosting E–Participation:
The Use of Social Media in Municipalities in the State of Mexico

David Valle-Cruz
Universidad Autónoma del Estado de México, Mexico

Rodrigo Sandoval-Almazan
Universidad Autónoma del Estado de México, Mexico

ABSTRACT

In this chapter, the authors show two case studies of the use of social media in municipal governments: Lerma, a small municipality with a significant growth, and Metepec, an important municipality of the State of México. The purpose of this chapter is to provide empirical evidence of how social media improves government to citizen relationship and promotes e-participation in municipal governments. The results are based on semi-structured interviews applied to public servants and a survey to evaluate e-government services by citizens. So, the citizen perception is contrasted with public servants' interviews. Citizens consider that electronic procedures and services implemented by their municipalities do not generate value. The efforts of governments should focus on avoiding corruption, making governments transparent, opening data, and properly managing the privacy of information.

INTRODUCTION

Social media is an important tool that foster citizen to government interaction (G2C) (Bertot, Jaeger, & Hansen, 2012; Khan, 2017), so that the government is closer the people. Social media has been used as a mechanism to increase openness and transparency (Sandoval-Almazán & Gil-García, 2014). In this sense, governments

DOI: 10.4018/978-1-5225-5326-7.ch005

around the world have used Facebook, Twitter, Instagram and YouTube as an alternative communication channel with citizens.

Traditional governments have been transformed into E-Governments 2.0 (Khan, 2017), and E-Government is transforming into E-Governance (Dadashzadeh, 2010). For many municipalities in México, social media has represented an emergent technology that has changed G2C improving efficiency in communication (Valle-Cruz, Sandoval-Almazán, & Gil-García, 2016) since citizens have used this kind of technologies to make information request and complaints.

In the State of Mexico, a central state, near Mexico City, each municipality has at least a Facebook account useful for disseminating information about social programs, supports, cultural and political events, and to improve interaction with citizens. Some years ago, citizens had to go to the municipal office to request information or to know about the different events promoted by municipal governments.

Nowadays, with the advantages that social media provides, citizens can interact with governments virtually from their homes, and through their smartphones. One of the functions of governments is to respond to the citizens' needs so that some governments have tried to improve citizen participation. Furthermore, engaging citizens in government decision making is an important value and priority in a democratic society (Huang & Feeney, 2016). For this reason, social media is a useful mechanism to improve E-Participation towards an Electronic Empowerment Participation (E2P) (Chesnevar, Maguitman, González, & Estevez, 2016).

Different scholars have studied the use of social media to foster E-Participation in municipalities (Al-Aama, 2015; Bershadskaya, Chugunov, & Trutnev, 2014; Bonsón, Royo, & Ratkai, 2015), but it is important to compare the citizens' use of municipal social media, against the objectives and strategies that public officials pretend. In this manner, we will be able to answer the question: How do social media affects citizen's participation?

In this chapter, the authors show two study cases regarding the use of social media in municipal governments. Lerma a small municipality with a significant growth, and Metepec an important municipality of the State of México, which are part of the metropolitan zone of Toluca's Valley. The purpose of this chapter is to provide empirical evidence of how social media improves G2C, and boosts E-Participation in municipal governments.

E-Participation occurs, when citizens read information in the municipalities' Facebook and make an opinion about municipal information. In this manner, ICTs disseminate information and helps the government to citizen interaction. Citizens' opinions represent a feedback for governments.

The chapter structure is divided into five stages including the foregoing section. The second stage shows the literature review. The third section will describe the two study cases and data collection based on interviews applied to government officials, and a survey applied to citizens, in order to compare perspectives. The fourth section shows the results. Finally, the fifth section presents the discussion and conclusions.

LITERATURE REVIEW

Citizen participation empowers people and represents power redistribution to consider citizens' opinion to economic and political decisions. In this manner citizens can produce social reforms in order to share the benefits to society.

According to Arstein (1969) there are different levels of participation classified into a ladder. At the lowest level, there is the nonparticipation forms (1. Manipulation and 2. Therapy), here citizens are used by powerful actor to impose their agenda. Tokenism occurs when participants hear about interventions and may say something about them (3. Informing, 4. Consultation, and 5. Placation), and finally the higher level of the ladder is represented when citizens have more power to negotiate and change the status quo (6. Partnership, 7. Delegated Power, and 8. Citizen Control).

White (1996) argues that there are four forms of participation: 1) nominal, often used by more powerful actor to give legitimacy to develop plans; 2) instrumental, sees community participation being used as a means towards a stated end – often the efficient use of the skills and knowledge of community members in project implementation; 3) representative, involves giving community members a voice in the decision-making and implementation process of projects or policies that affect them; and 4) transformative, results in the empowerment of those involved, and as a result alters the structures and institutions that lead to marginalization and exclusion.

Macintosh (2004) conceptualizes E-Democracy as the use of ICTs to support the democratic decision-making processes, furthermore argues that E-Participation enables citizens to access to policy information and request comment on it, providing people with the capacity to participate and influence decision-making.

However participation in developing countries, is confined to administrative processes, payment of fiscal obligations, but not in participation, nor in the elaboration and design of policies (decisions), since only the government is evaluated by assigning scores to the service provided (Bannister y Connolly, 2014).

Although there are significant advances in government to citizen interaction, for example: using and implementing social media (Twitter, Facebook, YouTube and Instagram), since governments at different levels (federal, state and municipal) use social media for citizens' services.

Social media is an emergent mechanism for citizens' services and a fast communication channel. As a result, government agencies such as municipalities have begun adopting Facebook and Twitter to "be in the citizens' place of residence." Since Facebook and Twitter offers new opportunities for the fast dissemination of information and dialogue with the public, foster transparency and boost E-democracy (Magnusson, Bellström, y Thoren, 2012).

In general, organizations have adopted social media mechanisms into their campaigns, product designs aimed at improving the user experience (Tuten, Wetsch, y Munoz, 2015), hence there is an approach between organizations (city councils) and clients (citizens), as well as access to information in "real time".

However, consumption and decision-making are induced, as some organizations in their campaigns promote the purchase of attractive but unnecessary products. In addition, some governments are bombarding citizens with information in order to legitimize government actions and policies.

Moreover, the use of social networks allow the ubiquity of today's society, in addition they have become mechanisms to boost the organization or call for major citizen movements such as the occupation of Wall Street, the Arab Spring and the movement #YoSoy132 (Welp and Breuer, 2014). They have even served as a mechanism to counter the information that is institutionalized in the mass media (radio and television).

So, social media influences human behavior in different domains such as politics, health, environmental sustainability, collective activism, and other areas of education, consumer behavior and government (Kamal et al., 2013).

Understanding the factors that influence the dynamics of social media allows generating more efficient services, as well as providing valuable information to the content generators (Figueiredo, Almeida, Gonçalves, and Benevenuto, 2014).

The propagation of opinion through social media has become a widespread phenomenon. There are several applications of this phenomenon such as: viral marketing, electoral campaigns and government to citizen interaction (Cercel and Trausan-Matu, 2014). Although these applications have also been used as mechanisms of persuasion, or to disseminate "the citizens' needs" to understand and accept government decisions, for example in the case of Mexico: political campaigns, problems with gasoline's price, budget cuts in health, education and research (Picazo et. al, 2017).

Consequently, mobile technology has been linked to the use of social media, users spend time on their phones to find information, entertainment and communication (Au, Lam, and Chan, 2015). Thus, E-Government is transformed into mobile government (M-Government), and the use of social media is important to transparency, anti-corruption initiatives (Bertot, Jaeger, y Grimes, 2010) and citizen participation.

In addition, social media initiatives are increasingly being used by governments to encourage user interaction. Particularly in cities with high ICT infrastructures and high Internet penetration rates, social media platforms are valuable tools to reach a large number of citizens (Mainka, Hartmann, Stock, and Peters, 2014).

Mobile technology has served as an enabler mechanism for the use of social media in citizenship, so that mobility is no longer a technological revolution. In this sense, the current trend is about how companies and governments can provide a better social infrastructure through mobile applications and services.

E-Government is an important milestone given by different governments, nowadays the provision of services through mobile technologies is unavoidable. Public demand for mobility, as well as gains in efficiency and productivity of the public sector through mobility, lead to a natural move from E-Governments to mobile governments: mobile technology applied to E-Government (Emmanouilidou y Kreps, 2010; Kushchu, 2007), which translates into the ubiquity of government.

Also, some scholars have studied the benefits and capabilities that citizens obtain through the flexibility offered by mobile technology (Rossel, Finger, and Misuraca, 2006), although the problem of accessibility remains a challenge for governments —equal services for all citizens everywhere (Emmanouilidou y Kreps, 2010),— as factors such as the digital divide and lack of connectivity affect, in particular, most entities in developing countries.

Other scholars have developed site customization and recognition techniques to efficiently select smart mobile government services (Al-Khamayseh, Hujran, Aloudat, and Lawrence, 2006). Likewise, there are works such as the one made by Sandy and McMillan (2005) report on the usefulness of mobile technology in the government health services of Australia, where they identify factors of success. In turn, Antovski and Gusev (2005) propose a framework for mobile governance based on five principles: interoperability, security, openness, flexibility and scalability.

Similarly, Sundar and Garg (2005) argue that the key feature of these mobile government (M-Government) solutions is "the catch levels required to provide faster, more cost-effective and scalable services for citizens through mobile technologies, rather than mere computerization in local offices. "As a result, mobile government is one of the most important developments in E-Government (Kesavarapu and Choi, 2012) and the development of government mobile applications will be in the following years in Mexico.

The term M-Government, therefore, appears as a powerful component of electronic administration, to facilitate the provision of more and better services for citizens, in a personalized way and through different devices: mobile phones, tablets and laptops (Nava & Dávila, 2005). Hence, both E-Government and M-Government should be exploited for the automation of services, as well as to avoid duplication of information (Maumbe and Owei, 2006), create public value and improve services.

As a result, mobile government increases operational efficiency, as well as quality and transparency in government services, where the city of Seattle pioneered the use of wirelessly connected users (Fidel, Scholl, Liu, and Unsworth, 2007).

In Mexico, there have been studies on social media and mobile technology applied to E-Government since 2011. Sandoval-Almazán, Gil-García, Luna-Reyes y Diaz-Murillo (2011) analyzed the use of Web 2.0 in the websites in Mexico. In 2012, Sandoval-Almazán y Gil-García conducted a study on the use of Twitter in state governments. In addition, Sandoval-Almazán, Gil-García, Luna-Reyes and Rojas-Romero (2012) describe how web and mobile applications are useful for citizens, through open data.

Again, Sandoval-Almazán and Gil-García (2013) conducted a study of cyber-activism, through Twitter and YouTube related to the "Yo Soy 132" movement (I am 132), showing how social media serve to organize the civil society. Criado, Sandoval-Almazán y Gil-García (2013) argue that the use of social media works as a mechanism of governmental innovation.

Specifically in the State of Mexico, Sandoval-Almazán, Cruz, and Armas (2015) carried out a qualitative study on the use of social networks in municipalities in the State of Mexico. Likewise, Sandoval-Almazán (2015) describes how Twitter is useful in political campaigns. Sandoval-Almazán y Valle-Cruz (2016) analyzed the case of the report of the governor of the State of Mexico, where they classified the different participants in social media, how information is disseminated and how the use of Twitter represents a promotional mechanism for the governor. These types of technologies are gradually implemented in governments in the State of Mexico. For some, this is an innovative (emerging) process, but for others, they are already established or enacted technologies.

Finally, Sandoval-Almazán, Gil-García y Valle-Cruz (2017) carry out a study on the implementation of mobile applications by using "gamification" techniques to involve citizens in the mapping of transport routes in Mexico City. Mapatón (SETRAVI-INEGI, 2007) is a clear example of citizen participation and collaboration and the use of emerging technologies in government. The methodology is shown in the following section.

METHODOLOGY

The research carried out in this paper follows the case study methodology (Remenyi, 2013; Stake, 1998; Yin, 2009), which is based on current events, in general to answer questions such as: How? and Why? The research question is: How do social media affect citizen's participation?

The results are based on semi - structured interviews applied to nine participants (key informants), to collect qualitative data. These results are useful to triangulate the information between the interviewees and the secondary data found in statistics, social media and webpages.

Interviewees include key stakeholders linked to the use of social media, considering officials of the transparency departments; systems, web page and social networks; and E-Government. Each interview had a duration between 50 and 70 minutes and were conducted between January 2017 and March 2017. But the researchers had some difficulties in applying the interviews, however the key informants in the government were contacted. According to Schellong (2007) key informants in government are policymakers, managers, administrators, operators and workers un government.

Municipalities were selected in order to compare and two different contexts. With differences in the educational level, connectivity, poverty and use of technologies. Metepec represents an example of E-Government 2.5 and Lerma represents an example of E-Government 1.0.

The use of qualitative methods offers the flexibility to draw a variety of complementary and convergent data from multiple sources of consultation such as: semi - structured interviews, focus group sessions, documental analysis and the exploration of technological artifacts (Yin, 2009). Table 1 shows the profile of the interviewed public officials.

Table 1. Public officials profile (key informants)

Interview	Position	Profession	Administrative	Technician	User
1	Head of Transparency Unit in Lerma	Master in Business Management.	☑		☑
2	Head of Transparency Unit in Metepec	Bachelor of Political and Social Sciences.	☑		☑
3	Head of the Systems Development and Support Department in Lerma	Bachelor of Computer Science.	☑	☑	☑
4	Technical Support in Lerma	Systems engineer		☑	☑
5	Head of the Planning Unit in Lerma	Bachelor in graphic design	☑		☑
6	Head of the Social Media Department in Lerma	Systems engineer	☑	☑	☑
7	Software developer in Metepec	Systems engineer		☑	☑
8	Deputy Director of Digital Government in Metepec	Master in Public Administration and Bachelor in Territorial Planning	☑		☑
9	Director of Government Innovation in Metepec	Master of Public Administration	☑		☑

Furthermore, this survey was also applied to citizens in order to evaluate E-Government services. This way, the citizen perception was contrasted with public servants' interviews. To carry out the citizen perception survey, a 43-item instrument was designed and applied to evaluate the perception of procedures and services of the municipal government (n = 61). The items were grouped by six factors, according to Valle-Cruz et al (2016) research: a) anti-corruption, b) social media, c) web portals, d) access to information, e) public value, and f) virtual agency. The instrument evaluated each item on a Likert scale from 0 to 5 (0 = I do not know, 1 = very bad, 2 = bad, 3 = acceptable, 4 = good, and 5 = excellent). For this research, the authors evaluated three kind of factors: 1) technological aspects conformed by social media, web portals, and virtual agency items; 2) transparency and access to information: conformed by anti-corruption and access to information items, and 3) public value items.

Since the instrument was designed for citizens who use information technologies, it was applied to Twitter users who follow their municipal government. The average age of the respondents in the municipality of Lerma was 32.11 years, the youngest 19 and the oldest 53 years. Regarding the educational level, 50.0% has a bachelor degree, 32.1% high school studies, 10.7% a master's degree, 3.6% a doctorate degree, and another 3.6% only secondary school. The predominant occupations were employed (35.7%) and student (35.7%), then teachers (17.9%), and traders (7.1%) and finally social educator (3.6%). 64.3% of the respondents were women and 35.7% men.

For the municipality of Metepec, the average age of the respondents was 28.39 years, the oldest 18 years old and the youngest 46. Regarding the educational level, 75.8% has a bachelor's degree, 15.2% high school studies, 6.1% a master degree and 3.0% secondary school. The predominant occupation was employee (45.5%), student (39.4%), then trader (9.1%) and finally teacher (6.1%). 60.9% of the respondents were men and 39.4% were women (Table 2).

Comparing Metepec with Lerma, the municipality that uses more social media is Metepec; it is a municipality with a greater technological development, besides having a better educational level and lower poverty compared to Lerma (Table 3). Thus, for case studies with a higher educational level and a lower level of poverty, there is a greater use of emerging technologies in the implementation of public services. Therefore, new communication channels, collaboration and citizen participation are generated, as well as new forms for tax collection.

Lerma lags in implementing technology-related policies, compared to Metepec, but Lerma is a municipality with many areas of opportunity. They are trying to use their resources efficiently, generating new policies and giving continuity to municipal projects. Social media is used to inform citizens about different activities of the town hall. Lerma's poverty level is higher compared to Metepec.

Table 2. Demographic data of citizens' survey

	Lerma	Metepec
Surveyed	28	33
Average age (years)	32.11	28.39
Educational Level		
Secondary school	3.6%	3.0%
High School	32.1%	15.2%
Bachelor's degree	50.0%	75.8%
Master's degree	10.7%	6.1%
Doctor's degree	3.6%	0.0%
Profession		
Employee	35.7%	45.5%
Merchandiser	7.1%	9.1%
Professor	17.9%	6.1%
Student	35.7%	39.4%
Other	0.0%	0.0%
Genre		
Male	64.3%	60.9%
Female	35.7%	39.4%

Regarding Facebook users, Metepec has almost 4.5 times more Facebook users than Lerma. So, the difference between the two municipalities is notable (in the same region), one with few implemented technologies and the other, with a small extension area, has a higher level of technological development.

Metepec has advantages to be a small municipality in territorial extension and with many citizens with access to Internet (high connectivity), so that it facilitates the implementation of technologies to support their processes and services oriented to citizenship. Although the municipality of Lerma has had continuity in the last two administrations, the context of the municipality does not allow it to have a development which can be compared to the Metepec.

Thus, Metepec, a municipality with foreign investment and tourism, with a lower level of illiteracy and lower poverty, represents the municipality that has developed more social media policies over time.

The territorial extension and the number of localities of Metepec allow the city council to have greater coverage when implementing technologies for procedures and services throughout the municipality. So, in Lerma it is more complicated, since

Table 3. Municipalities' demographic data

Factor	Lerma	Metepec
Classification according to localities' size	Mixed	Middle urban
Land area	228.64 km	70.43 km
Main economic activities	Industry, agriculture and farming	Foreign capital, tourism, handicrafts
Municipal GDP 2014 (millions of pesos)	29023.6	34899.1
Inhabitants	134,799	214,162
Households	39,618	53,540
Average number of inhabitants per dwelling	4.4	3.9
Localities	70	25
Population in poverty	52.30%	26.30%
Population in extreme poverty	11.20%	3.20%
Average grade of education of 15 years or more	9	11.4
Population of three years or more speaking an indigenous language	2,334	822
Illiterate population 15 years and overs	4,660	2,884
Likes (Facebook) (11/03/2016) (07/04/2017)	4,370 4,532	22,470 22,834
Followers (Twitter) (11/03/2016) (07/04/2017)	960 1,720	12,400 12,700
YouTube (Subscribers) (11/03/2016) (07/04/2017)	36 37	70 105

Source: GEM (2015); INEGI, (2015); SEDESOL (2015a, 2015b, 2015c).

it is a municipality six times greater in territorial extension, in addition that it needs more urban and technological development.

Despite this situation Metepec has a comparable number of users connected to the social media with Toluca (the capital of the State of Mexico). Thus, social media initiatives or policies are more useful in Metepec than in Lerma.

RESULTS

The number of citizens that use municipalities' social media are increasing (Figure 1, 2, 3 and 4), but Metepec has more likes and followers, because it is a municipality

Figure 1. Lerma's Facebook likes

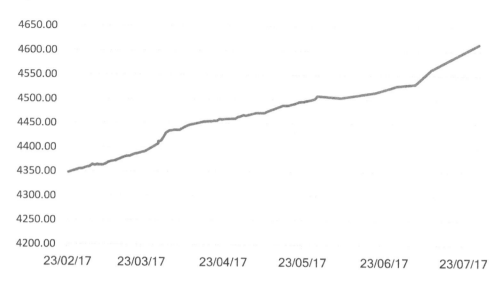

Figure 2. Metepec's Facebook likes

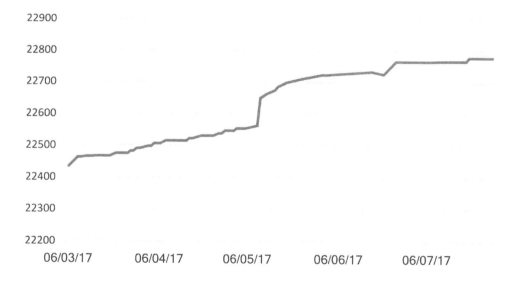

with more connectivity, less illiteracy and poverty. So, the Metepec's city council has used more social media initiatives to foster G2C interaction.

Despite of this situation, Lerma is boosting the use of technologies like social media in the government. For the Lerma's major, it is important to improve G2C

Figure 3. Lerma's followers

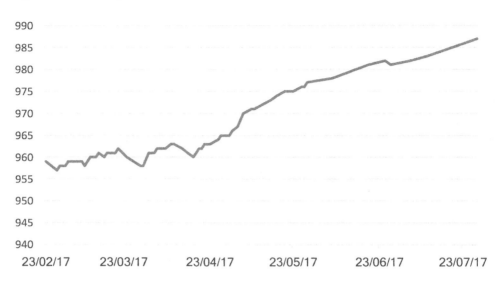

Figure 4. Metepec's followers

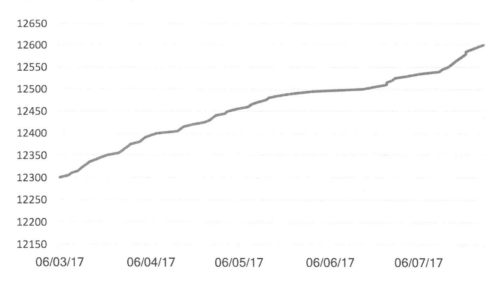

interaction. So, the use of social media is important. For this reason, the major continually reviews his account. This way he follows up on the requests, complaints and suggestions of citizens. Interviews supports this concept.

[...] Since the campaign, the city council has been concerned that the municipality maintains institutional social media and it does not get lost with the change of administration. The municipal government has transferred the institutional social media and the new government did not miss the approach that already had or the work that had been done previously [...](interview 6).

There is also a protocol of care and eventuality for social media in general with 20 participants in the administration

The use of social media is an important mechanism to G2C interaction, although Lerma does not have an important advance in technological initiatives, they think that the use of technology improves G2C interaction. According to Interview 5:

[...] previously, without the use of social media, the citizens had to come and issue a document with their requirements. It took quite a long time till their requests could be answered. This does not happen with social media, it is almost immediate [...].

Social media improves interaction between public servants and represents an effective and informal communication channel, according to interview 1:

Now with the new boss [...] municipal government has started using the new technology from the very beginning and now municipal government have a better communication between all the members. if something important happen to someone, the event is communicated through this type of technology.

The use of social media has created faster communication channels between government and citizens, and represents an emerging mechanism for G2C interaction interviewers supports this argument. For example: according to interview 3:

Practically at the beginning of the triennium the municipal government implemented a procedure to generate social media accounts (the most important) Lerma city council and some dependencies (the logo, type of behavior, politics). In no more than 5 minutes the citizen must be attended.

Interview 2 supports this fact: "The benefits of technology are that it helps you reduce times, processes and have greater communication". Also interview 5 mentions something related:

[...] previously, without the use of this technology, the citizens had to come and hand in their requirements in writing. In order to be able to answer, a long process had to be fulfilled. With social media this does not happen, it is almost immediate [...].

Another path to support interaction through social media is to provide a channel for transparency. According to interview 6: "The use of social media has made the use of resources transparent, as well as having more efficient times, as citizens can make their requests more directly". Also, social media help for disaster management; according to interview 4:

It serves to predict risks: for example, the flood of Lerma river, or to know of some movement or public discontent ... In addition to deny news, for example, the march against the gasoline price: as for the looting of businesses.

In this year (2017), they have the plan to increase participation by including citizens who do not use technologies. According to interview 7:

In this year, public officials want to know about the opinion of citizens, not only through technology, but to go to the neighborhoods and communities to take an urn and vote for projects that are of interest to them.

Metepec's city council uses different technologies to improve interaction between officials and for citizens' care. Being a municipality with a high level of connectivity (almost 90% of the population), the use of social media is fundamental to improve services and procedures. According to interview 7:

In this municipality that has high connectivity and the conditions to access technology, it is important to generate applications to serve citizens. In other municipalities where there are deficiencies in technology or rural municipalities, there would be no case to develop applications and systems, since the needs of the citizens would not be addressed.

Metepec is considered to have a complicated administration regarding social media, since there are more users (compared to Lerma).

The social media topic is a very strong and dynamic one and you have to be very close to them because this issue is a topic of ongoing dissemination and information to the community [...]. There is a committee of social media where each direction has a link. So, this committee reports everything relevant to its coordinator in the committee sessions [...] the coordinator is responsible for spreading the relevant issues of the 27 dependencies. (interview 7).

Another finding confirms the use of technology to supports and improve public management. According to interview 8:

Technology improves processes, simplifies work and brings benefits to the community [...] today electronic tools reduce time and reduce distances. Currently, with expenditure containment policies, municipalities are working on results-based budgeting (PBR in Spanish). It is necessary to make processes efficient, reduce costs and times, as well as generate more and better services for citizens. Metepec is a clear example of how government organizations and citizens have evolved.

Finally, the use of social media is a generation trend in government. According to interview 9:

The application that citizens suggest being done with part of the budget. So, it shows a more democratic government [...] It is not the same as 20 years ago, where the politicians were the only ones to know everything. Now millennials citizens can collaborate to carry out projects [...].

New generations and the age of citizens in municipalities will improve G2C interaction through social media, and E-Participation.

According to citizens' perception survey the authors found that the average evaluation of anti-corruption strategies is 1.8, public value is 2.3, social media use is 1.8, web portal is 2.2, virtual agency is 2.3, and public value is 2.3. These values are low, since the maximum evaluated in the survey is 5. Table 4, shows correlation between factors and public value, based on the citizens' perception survey.

In conclusion, according to findings the use of social media in Lerma is only informative, and they do not use it to improve citizen participation. However, Metepec's social media accounts boost citizen participation with a better interaction responding posts and collecting citizen's opinions (Figure 5).

Table 4. Correlation between factors and public value

Factors	Public Value
Anti-Corruption	.778**
Social Media	.444**
Web Portal	.646**
Access to information	.761**
Virtual agency	.537**

** Significant at 0.01

Figure 5. Facebook's government to citizen interaction

DISCUSSION AND CONCLUSION

According to key Informants and demographic data from Lerma and Metepec, the researchers found that Metepec is more advanced in terms of ICTs' policies, first, because Metepec has more connectivity than Lerma, and is an Urban municipality. Lerma has less citizens connected to Internet and less Social Media's users. Metepec is a smaller region with more educated citizens and high income population, these elements could explain because Metepec's government boost E-Participation.

On the ladder of citizen participation, Metepec is one step forward of Lerma, although Social Media in the case studies are in the tokenism level. Metepec municipality has more Government to Citizen interaction and this situation foster citizen participation, because government consider citizens' opinion, and engage to citizens through technology and traditional communication channels.

As in private organizations, the products generated focus on their clients, in government organizations the procedures and services are focused on citizens.

Gradually, governments have included citizens in terms of citizen participation and collaboration (through technologies). In addition, they have increased government - citizen interaction.

In terms of Governance e-participation has evolve in three different ways. The participatory budget usually is through technology – a website or an App – to collect citizens needs and decision for the budget. The Lerma and Metepec municipalities have not introduce this technology yet for such purpose, however, they consider some online surveys as an informal referendum to capture citizens' opinions in specific areas. Finally, the use of Facebook platforms and posts to provide information about new public policies or services and improve the interaction is a path to transform the digital governance step by step.

On the other hand, very few has been done in updating laws and regulations that imply the use of technology in government. Only tax payments online, by federal government has important transformations in the recent years, like send PDF and XML files of all expenses citizens perform, every companies of any size should send this files on a single government platform to make it valid and able government to cross reference between sellers and buyers. In sum, governance on the use of social media interaction is only on favor of government payments nor to provide more services to citizens or enhance the service quality.

With the support of social media, citizens consider governments more important. Information is disseminated in a quicker way and the communication mechanisms that can be on both sides are facilitated: government to citizen (G2C) and citizen to government (C2G) interaction. At the same time, channels for citizen participation and collaboration are provided.

Despite of this, and public servant's interviews results (according to the perception survey on E-Government services) citizens consider that electronic procedures and services implemented by their municipalities, do not generate value. The efforts of governments should focus on avoiding corruption, making governments transparent, opening data, and properly managing the privacy of information.

The implementation of information technologies creates changes in government to citizen interaction and different mechanisms of communication, since the traditional and the new ones are supported by technologies. This situation accelerates the information delivery for citizens, and generates more requests for the government. It also creates the need to better manage and organize the information that must be provided among the different government areas and that must be handed out to citizens. As stated on the different interviews from Lerma and Metepec these municipalities must adapt their organizations to use social media efficiently.

The evolution of information technologies into mobile government allow citizens to interact with government all the time; using smartphones and Apps, the communication become more efficient and fast for the government and citizens; the Metepec experience compared with Lerma is important to boost e-participation in their municipalities.

Thus, by improving citizens' perception over their governments, a greater citizen commitment will be generated to use the new mechanisms implemented by government's social media. In addition, citizen participation and collaboration should be encouraged, as well as improving citizens' confidence in their governments. The cases of Lerma and Metepec describe two different situations, one with an initial stage of boosting e-participation through social media; the second with large experience on engaging citizens to participate using technology. However, both cases are working to adapt and create new solutions to improve their relationship with citizens.

Public value is an important issue that concerns to governments (regardless of whether it is generated with electronic mechanisms or not). It was pointed out that the use of technologies in municipalities has generated new communication channels and interaction between government and citizens. And municipal governments have been concerned to make their processes efficient to generate more and better services oriented to citizenship and to foster E-Participation.

It was found that the city councils of both case studies made their first attempts to improve citizen participation and public value through social media. However, this study shows that municipalities are just aware the use of technology to communicate with citizens.

Regarding citizen perception, it is emphasized that, citizens do not have confidence in municipal E-Governments, the value generated by governments is not enough, despite the efforts that are made for the delivery of digital services. Particularly, the citizens' lack of confidence is explained by the contextual factors in Mexico, and the problems of corruption, lack of transparency, lack of citizens' engagement, and lack of citizens' participation. Furthermore, some citizens do not know about the existence of E-Government services and others do not perceive the use of municipal social media as useful in terms of citizen participation and collaboration.

The distrust of municipal social media stems from the same distrust of governments, cyber fraud and lack of culture in using electronic services in Mexico. However, the most important issue for citizens' perception is transparency and access to information. Therefore, for the citizens of the municipalities of Lerma and Metepec, policies of transparency and anti - corruption are significant for improving public value and to boost citizen participation. Thus, governments must promote such policies, both by traditional and electronic means.

However, municipalities should encourage the use of social media and generate strategies for citizens' participation and collaboration, so that citizens find value in their use, not only using social media to denounce politicians about their bad practices or frauds, or make claims about the disagreements of the citizens against the government. Since the information provided by citizens, in social networks, is useful for the design and generation of useful public policies for society.

REFERENCES

Al-Aama, A. Y. (2015). The use of Twitter to promote e-participation: Connecting government and people. *International Journal of Web Based Communities*, *11*(1), 73–96. doi:10.1504/IJWBC.2015.067082

Al-Khamayseh, S., Hujran, O., Aloudat, A., & Lawrence, E. (2006). *Intelligent M-Government: Application of Personalisation and Location Awareness Techniques*. Mobile Government Consortium International LLC.

Antovski, L., & Gusev, M. (2005). *M-Government Framework*. Mobile Government Consortium International LLC.

Arstein, R. (1969). A ladder of citizen participation. *Journal of the American Institute of Planners*, *35*(4), 216–224. doi:10.1080/01944366908977225

Au, M., Lam, J., & Chan, R. (2015). Social Media Education: Barriers and Critical Issues. Springer Berlin Heidelberg. doi:10.1007/978-3-662-46158-7_20

Bannister, F., & Connolly, R. (2014). ICT, public values and transformative government: A framework and programme for research. *Government Information Quarterly*, *31*(1), 119–128. doi:10.1016/j.giq.2013.06.002

Bershadskaya, L., Chugunov, A., & Trutnev, D. (2014). *Evaluation of E-Participation in Social Networks: Russian E-Petitions Portal* (Vol. 21). Retrieved from http://www.medra.org/servlet/aliasResolver?alias=iospressISSNISBN&issn=1871-1073&volume=21&spage=76

Bertot, J. C., Jaeger, P. T., & Grimes, J. M. (2010). *Crowd-sourcing transparency: ICTs, social media, and government transparency initiatives*. Digital Government Society of North America. Retrieved from http://dl.acm.org/citation.cfm?id=1809874.1809887

Bertot, J. C., Jaeger, P. T., & Hansen, D. (2012). The impact of polices on government social media usage: Issues, challenges, and recommendations. *Government Information Quarterly*, *29*(1), 30–40. doi:10.1016/j.giq.2011.04.004

Bonsón, E., Royo, S., & Ratkai, M. (2015). Citizens' engagement on local governments' Facebook sites. An empirical analysis: The impact of different media and content types in Western Europe. *Government Information Quarterly, 32*(1), 52–62. doi:10.1016/j.giq.2014.11.001

Cercel, D.-C., & Trausan-Matu, S. (2014). Opinion Propagation in Online Social Networks: A Survey. New York: ACM. doi:10.1145/2611040.2611088

Chesnevar, C. I., Maguitman, A. G., González, M. P., & Estevez, E. (2016). *Opinion Aggregation and Conflict Resolution in E-Government Platforms: Contrasting Social Media Information through Argumentation* (P. Novais & D. Carneiro, Eds.). IGI Global. doi:10.4018/978-1-5225-0245-6.ch011

Criado, J. I., Sandoval-Almazan, R., & Gil-Garcia, J. R. (2013). Government innovation through social media. *Government Information Quarterly, 30*(4), 319–326. doi:10.1016/j.giq.2013.10.003

Dadashzadeh, M. (2010). Social media in government: From eGovernment to eGovernance. *Journal of Business & Economics Research, 8*(11), 81. doi:10.19030/jber.v8i11.51

Emmanouilidou, M., & Kreps, D. (2010). A framework for accessible m-government implementation. *Electronic Government, an International Journal, 7*(3), 252–269.

Fidel, R., Scholl, H. J., Liu, S., & Unsworth, K. (2007). Mobile government fieldwork: A preliminary study of technological, organizational, and social challenges (Vol. 228). Digital Government Research Center.

Figueiredo, F., Almeida, J. M., Gonçalves, M. A., & Benevenuto, F. (2014). On the Dynamics of Social Media Popularity: A YouTube Case Study. *ACM Trans. Internet Technol., 14*(4), 24:1–24:23. 10.1145/2665065

GEM. (2015). *Producto Interno Bruto Municipal*. Toluca, México. Retrieved from http://igecem.edomex.gob.mx/sites/igecem.edomex.gob.mx/files/files/Archivos PDF/Productos Estadisticos/Índole Económica/PIB/PIB_municipal2015.pdf

Huang, W.-L., & Feeney, M. K. (2016). Citizen Participation in Local Government Decision Making: The Role of Manager Motivation. *Review of Public Personnel Administration, 36*(2), 188–209. doi:10.1177/0734371X15576410

INEGI. (2015). *Encuesta Intercensal 2015*. INEGI. Retrieved from http://www.beta.inegi.org.mx/proyectos/enchogares/especiales/intercensal/

Kamal, N., Fels, S., Fergusson, M., Preece, J., Cosley, D., & Munson, S. (2013). *Designing Social Media for Change*. New York: ACM. doi:10.1145/2468356.2479642

Kesavarapu, S., & Choi, M. (2012). M-government - A framework to investigate killer applications for developing countries: An Indian case study. *Electronic Government: An International Journal*, 9(2), 200–219. doi:10.1504/EG.2012.046269

Khan, G. F. (2017). Social-Media-Based Government. In Social Media for Government (pp. 7–20). Springer. doi:10.1007/978-981-10-2942-4_2

Kushchu, I. (2007). *Mobile Government: An Emerging Direction in E-government* (1st ed.). Hershey, PA: IGI Publishing. doi:10.4018/978-1-59140-884-0

Macintosh, A. (2004). Characterizing E-Participation in Policy-Making. In *Proceedings of the 37th Annual Hawaii International Conference on System Science.* Computer Society Press. Retrieved from http://csdl2.computer.org/persagen/DLAbsToc.jsp?resourcePath=/dl/proceedings/hicss/&toc=comp/proceedings/hicss/2004/2056/05/2056toc.xml&DOI=10.1109/HICSS.2004.1265300

Magnusson, M., Bellström, P., & Thoren, C. (2012). *Facebook usage in government – a case study of information content.* Retrieved from http://aisel.aisnet.org/amcis2012/proceedings/EGovernment/11

Mainka, A., Hartmann, S., Stock, W. G., & Peters, I. (2014). *Government and Social Media: A Case Study of 31 Informational World Cities.* Academic Press.

Maumbe, B. M., & Owei, V. (2006). *Bringing M-government to South African Citizens: Policy Framework, Delivery Challenges and Opportunities.* Mobile Government Consortium International LLC.

Remenyi, D. (2013). *Case Study Research (2nd ed.).* Academic Conferences and Publishing International Limited.

Rossel, P., Finger, M., & Misuraca, G. (2006). "Mobile" e-Government Options: Between Technology-driven and User-centric. *Electronic Journal of E-Government,* 4(2), 79–86. Retrieved from http://www.ejeg.com/volume-4/vol4-iss2/v4-i2-art5.htm

Sandoval-Almazan, R. (2015). Using Twitter in political campaigns: The case of the PRI candidate in Mexico. *International Journal of E-Politics*, 6(1), 1–15. doi:10.4018/IJEP.2015010101

Sandoval-Almazan, R., Cruz, D. V., & Armas, J. C. N. (2015). Social Media in Smart Cities: An Exploratory Research in Mexican Municipalities. *Proceedings of the 48th Hawaii International Conference on System Sciences (HICSS-48).* doi:10.1109/HICSS.2015.284

Sandoval-Almazan, R., & Gil-Garcia, J. R. (2013). *Cyberactivism through Social Media: Twitter, YouTube, and the Mexican Political Movement*. IEEE Computer Society.

Sandoval-Almazan, R., Gil-Garcia, J. R., Luna-Reyes, L. F., & Diaz-Murillo, D. E. L. G. (2011). The use of Web 2.0 on Mexican State Websites: A Three-Year Assessment. *Electronic Journal of E-Government*, *9*(2), 107–121.

Sandoval-Almazan, R., Gil-Garcia, J. R., Luna-Reyes, L. F., Luna, D. E., & Rojas-Romero, Y. (2012). *Open Government 2.0: Citizen Empowerment Through Open Data, Web and Mobile Apps*. New York: ACM; doi:10.1145/2463728.2463735

Sandoval-Almazan, R., & Gil-Garcia, J. R. R. (2012). Social Media In State Governments: Preliminary Results About The Use Of Twitter In Mexico. Trauner Verlag.

Sandoval-Almazan, R., & Ramon Gil-Garcia, J. (2014). Towards cyberactivism 2.0? Understanding the use of social media and other information technologies for political activism and social movements. *Government Information Quarterly*, *31*(3), 365–378. doi:10.1016/j.giq.2013.10.016

Sandoval-Almazan, R., Ramon Gil-Garcia, J., & Valle-Cruz, D. (2017). Going Beyond Bureaucracy Through Gamification: Innovation Labs and Citizen Engagement in the Case of "Mapaton" in Mexico City. In A. A. Paulin, L. G. Anthopoulos, & C. G. Reddick (Eds.), *Beyond Bureaucracy. Public Administration and Information Technology* (pp. 133–149). Cham: Springer International Publishing; doi:10.1007/978-3-319-54142-6_9

Sandoval-Almazán, R., & Valle-Cruz, D. (2016). Understanding Network Links in Twitter: A Mexican Case Study. *Proceedings of the 17th International Digital Government Research Conference on Digital Government Research - Dg.o '16*, 122–128. doi:10.1145/2912160.2912204

Sandy, G. A., & McMillan, S. (2005). *A Success Factors Model For M-Government*. Mobile Government Consortium International LLC.

Schellong, A. (2007). *Extending the Technology Enactment Framework*. PNG Working Paper No PNG07-003, Program on Networked Governance, 3.

SEDESOL. (2015a). *Informe anual sobre la situación de pobreza y rezago social 2015: Lerma, México*. Retrieved from http://www.gob.mx/cms/uploads/attachment/file/42816/Mexico_051.pdf

SEDESOL. (2015b). *Informe anual sobre la situación de pobreza y rezago social 2015: Metepec, México*. Retrieved from http://www.gob.mx/cms/uploads/attachment/file/42819/Mexico_054.pdf

SEDESOL. (2015c). *Informe anual sobre la situación de pobreza y rezago social 2015: Toluca, México*. Retrieved from http://www.gob.mx/cms/uploads/attachment/file/42871/Mexico_106.pdf

Stake, R. E. (1998). *Investigación con estudio de casos*. Ediciones Morata.

Sundar, D. K., & Garg, S. (2005). *M-Governance: A Framework for Indian Urban Local Bodies*. Mobile Government Consortium International LLC.

Tuten, T., Wetsch, L., & Munoz, C. (2015). Conversation Beyond the Classroom: Social Media and Marketing Education. Springer International Publishing. doi:10.1007/978-3-319-11797-3_182

Valle-Cruz, D., Sandoval-Almazan, R., & Gil-Garcia, J. R. (2016). Citizens' perceptions of the impact of information technology use on transparency, efficiency and corruption in local governments. *Information Polity, 21*(3), 1–14.

Welp, Y., & Breuer, A. (2014). *ICTs and democratic governance: The Latin American experience*. Academic Press. 10.1109/ICEDEG.2014.6819946

White, S. (1996). Depoliticising development: The uses and abuses of participation. *Development in Practice, 6*(1), 6–15. doi:10.1080/0961452961000157564

Yin, R. K. (2009). *Case study research: Design and methods (Rev.)*. Newbury Park, CA: Sage Publications.

Chapter 6
E-Participation in Developing Countries:
The Case of the National Social Insurance Fund in Cameroon

Ransome E. Bawack
Catholic University of Central Africa, Cameroon

Jean Robert Kala Kamdjoug
Catholic University of Central Africa, Cameroon

Samuel Fosso Wamba
Toulouse Business School, France

Aime Fobang Noutsa
Catholic University of Central Africa, Cameroon

ABSTRACT

This chapter on e-participation in developing countries uses Cameroon as a case study to demonstrate the realities of practicing Web 2.0 and social media tools to drive collaborative initiatives between government agencies and citizens in developing countries. The case study was guided by the incentives for e-participation using social media technologies, the tools used by a government to drive such initiatives, the level of participation from citizens, and the challenges and risks faced in implementing these technologies. A study of Cameroon's National Social Insurance Fund (NSIF) confirmed the main incentives of e-participation initiatives in developing countries and the major challenges they face in implementing them.

DOI: 10.4018/978-1-5225-5326-7.ch006

BACKGROUND ON E-PARTICIPATION
IN DEVELOPING COUNTRIES

In this age of social media, the relationship between governments, citizens, employees, and businesses have evolved to a more participatory level in decision-making and nation-building (Komito, 2005). These stakeholders now perform the role of a partner rather than a customer in the delivery of public services (Linders, 2012). However, this scenario of developed countries should not be generalized in the context of developing countries, where other realities like the digital divide are very much evident (Islam, 2008). Nevertheless, e-participation has become an integral part of e-government initiatives worldwide with the ultimate goal of supporting and stimulating good governance (Basu, 2004).

According to the United Nations e-government survey (United Nations, 2016), there has been a sharp rise in the number of countries using e-government to facilitate access to public services. Many governments are trying to ensure public institutions are more accountable and transparent by making their data more available to the public. Thanks to easy access to social media by everyone, more countries are moving towards participatory decision-making, with many developing countries making good progress in the same direction though still struggling with substantial regional disparities and a persistent digital divide. Thus, most developing countries have e-government development index (EGDI) levels below 0.5. This proves that, though e-participation is a global phenomenon, simply importing e-participation systems and related organizational concepts from developed to developing countries cannot deliver the expected results (Schuppan, 2009). Given the mismatch between the realities of developing countries and those of developed countries in which the systems were designed, transferred e-participation initiatives in developing countries are often bound to fail. The risk of failure increases as the economic, cultural and other contextual differences between these countries widen (Heeks, 2001, 2002). However, social media surpass those barriers because they naturally adapt to their context of use.

There is limited public information and research on e-participation through social media in developing countries as compared to that available on developed countries. That which is available is very dispersed making these contexts difficult to understand and making existing research harder to exploit. In an attempt to summarize what has been done so far on the state of social media research for e-participation in developing countries, previous research were categorized into 7 main groups which are: actors, social media technologies, contextual issues, objectives, research methods, theoretical approaches, and legal issues (Dini & Sæbø, 2016). The key actors of e-participation research in developing countries include citizens, governments, and politicians. Social media technologies are identified to be an attractive alternative to traditional media though both need to subtly coexist to achieve maximum impact. However, contextual issues such as cultural characteristics, ICT infrastructure, and type of governance may influence the use of social media for e-participation in these countries.

This chapter presents e-participation in developing countries using the case of the National Social Insurance Fund (NSIF) of Cameroon to exemplify the major characteristics, opportunities, and challenges faced by e-participation initiatives implemented in such countries. Cameroon is a country that has always perplexed the international community in terms of its level of development vis a vis its economic potential. Despite its telecommunication and information and communication technology (ICT) infrastructure, the country still performs very poorly in e-participation and e-government surveys. Its government agencies show typical characteristics of e-participation initiatives in developing countries identified in literature. Thus, this chapter places these characteristics in a real-life context to show clear boundaries between the e-participation phenomenon and the context in developing countries. Therefore, this chapter will present Web 2.0 tools and technologies used for e-participation; the role of Web 2.0 tools and Social Media in e-participation; opportunities and challenges faced; and e-participation strategic frameworks and models for developing countries.

SETTING THE STAGE

The International Labor Organization (ILO) defines Social Security as *the protection that a society provides to individuals and households to ensure access to health care and to guarantee income security, particularly in cases of old age, unemployment, sickness, invalidity, work injury, maternity or loss of a breadwinner* (International Labor Organization, 2001). Thus, adequate social security policies are important factors in the process of socio-political development and economic growth of developing economies. However, many developing countries are unable to implement effective social security programs due to the level of complexity required during and after implementation. This fundamental issue is often mismanaged by governments in developing countries, leading to increased deprivation and loss in human and physical capital (Justino, 2007), often causing civil unrest and lack of trust in government agencies, such as with the case of the NSIF.

Social security in Cameroon was born on December 15, 1952, before the country gained its independence, and with the promulgation of the French Labor Code in French overseas territories (CNPS, 2008). This code which granted social benefits to the French citizens working in Cameroon was later extended to Cameroonian citizens. In 1956, the Compensation Fund of Family Allowance was created, with the first code of family benefits enacted on April 11, 1959. This was followed by the issuing of decree number 59/100 of December 31, 1959, on the compensation and prevention of industrial accidents and occupational hazards, which entrusted the management of occupational risks to private insurance companies. After its independence in 1960, Cameroon as a member state of the ILO was called upon to adapt its legislation to meet international standards. Thus, the legal framework of social security was adjusted through a series of laws, among which was Law No. 67-LF-08 of June 12, 1967, creating the National Social Insurance Fund (NSIF) as an independent body in charge of managing social security in Cameroon. It was entrusted with managing the advantages provided by the legislation on social protection, the compensation and prevention of industrial accidents and occupational hazards, and the coverage and management of occupational risks.

Today, NSIF is a parastatal organization under the Ministry of Labor and Social Security in Cameroon. It has over 3015 permanent employees with 37 branches across the national territory. Its head office is in Yaoundé, the political capital of Cameroon. The mission of NSIF is to implement the government's social security and social protection policies. It is managed by a tripartite Board of Directors, composed of employee representatives, employers' representatives, and government representatives. It covers 04 categories of social security namely: family benefits; old-age, disability and death pensions; occupational risks and hazards; health and social affairs. NSIF is financially autonomous with 80% of its financial resources obtained from social contributions collected from affiliated companies. The main source of these collections is social contributions that employers pay-in monthly on behalf of their employees. Other sources include penalties paid by employers for delayed payments, income from financial investments and assets, contributions from voluntary insurance, revenues from other investments such as buildings, hospitals and schools, and an operating budget allocated by the State (CNPS, 2017).

NSIF experienced enormous financial difficulties due to the economic and financial crisis that stormed Cameroon in 1983, leading to the bankruptcy and massive downsizing of several companies (Mbu Daniel, 2015). This resulted in a huge decline in the financial resources of NSIF, making it unable to meet-up with its social obligations and to cover its operating costs. This had a tremendous impact on the confidence stakeholders had in the agency. Clients of the NSIF did not fail to manifest their disgruntlement by protesting and requesting immediate refunds and more transparency. Recovery measures were proposed with the support of foreign organizations and donors, some of which included forceful collections of social contributions from employers and employees.

The arrival of a new management team at the head of NSIF in 1999 began a new era, marking the beginning of a vision that revolved around 03 main objectives: revitalizing and refocusing NSIF on its sovereign missions; bringing the services of

NSIF closer to its clients; progressively paying clients' benefits unpaid since 1996. The strategy put in place was to reinstate a climate of trust with social partners such as employers by allowing them to negotiate the procedures for clearing their debts, and with pensioners by improving their payment and pay-collection conditions. These efforts had significant positive effects because many recalcitrant clients started trusting the NSIF again, and started paying in their social contributions. This relationship of trust kick-started the effective reconciliation between NSIF and its clients.

Since then, the NSIF has presented itself as an agency that believes very much in collaborating with its employees and beneficiaries because of the positive effects thereof, especially when it comes to gaining the trust of its beneficiaries and social partners. Its core values include social coverage, growth, cohesion, change, transparency, neat environment, perfection, participation, performance, selection, solidarity, and quality service. To improve the collection of social security contributions, NSIF partnered with the country's tax administration which is now involved in the collection process. As a result, claims on social security contributions treated as tax claims are collected under the same conditions and time limits (CNPS, 2015). The reforms undertaken in this partnership remarkably increased social security contributions collected. This led to the increase in the organization's revenues, allowing its management team in 2003 to initiate the progressive resorption of pension recalls frozen since 1996.

In 2008, the NSIF's management decided to leverage Information and Communication Technologies (ICTs) to maintain an ever-increasing clients' trust in the organization, by improving the quality of its services, increasing transparency and disclosure of public information, and increasing participation from its clients in decision-making. In fact, they sought to digitize and automate as many organizational processes as possible to meet up with demand. It manages its internal operations essentially using an Enterprise Resource Planning (ERP) software, with the main objective of speeding up file processing and ensuring secure and reliable settlements. The organization makes use of a website (www.cnps.cm) to interact with clients. It has a very active and dynamic website with an average of over 37000 visitors a week. The organization, therefore, decided to make use of this website and other web technologies to increase interaction between the organization and its clients.

The section that follows presents a vivid description of e-participation in developing countries and uses the case of the NSIF's e-participation experience to exemplify findings brought out by previous research. Web 2.0 and social media tools used for e-participation in developing countries and the role these tools play in e-participation initiatives are presented.

The experience of the NSIF was obtained from existing documentation on the NSIF's e-participation initiative, and from 03 interview sessions with an Internal auditor of the organization. Given that it is a qualitative study, the interviews were coded, transcribed and analyzed using the content analysis method (Sobaci, 2010), alongside the content of the project's documentation, the organization's Website, Facebook, Twitter and YouTube profiles. An online questionnaire built on Google Forms was also used to capture and assess the opinion of some NSIF's clients on the relevance of the services rendered for information purposes and to better formulate recommendations.

CASE DESCRIPTION

To improve the quality of services rendered by the organization, the NSIF's senior management decided since 2010 to make use of Web 2.0 tools and social media. It upgraded its website to an interactive Web 2.0 platform and created social media accounts on multiple tools. The subsection that follows presents the Web 2.0 tools and technologies used by the NSIF in its e-participation initiative.

Web 2.0 Tools and Technologies

Web 2.0 social sites such as Facebook, Twitter, and YouTube have brought significant changes and opportunities to both citizens and governments in developing countries. Through various platforms enabled by Web 2.0 technologies, citizens can collectively create public information, provide services, and take part in policy making (Kuzma, 2010; Nam, 2012). This makes social media very attractive to developing countries and contrary to many imported e-participation tools, they are not costly, they can easily be tailored to the needs of citizens and governments, and they can easily penetrate the age groups of active citizens (Papaloi, Staiou, & Gouscos, 2012). Thus, citizens become active agents in creating, organizing, combining and sharing Web content through social media (Chun, Shulman, Sandoval, & Hovy, 2010). Table 1 presents Web 2.0 tools and technologies used at each stage of e-participation initiatives in developing countries.

Many governments are using social media more for information dissemination (e-informing) than for interaction (e-involving, e-collaborating, e-empowering) (Thompson, 2008). As a result, they are missing opportunities to better serve their citizens and reach the growing number of internet users. Instead of avoiding the fundamental challenges these technologies are most likely to pose, governments could rather develop strategic plans so that all their agencies can participate in social networks and come up with a coordinated effort to develop and implement their policies. By so doing, Web 2.0 technologies can be leveraged to accelerate service innovation, augment bureaucracy with crowd wisdom through government

Table 1. Levels of participation and Web 2.0 tools and technologies of e-participation (Adapted from (Al-Dalou & Abu-Shanab, 2013))

Level of Participation	Description	Web 2.0 Technologies and Social Media Tools
E-informing	A one-way communication that provides citizens with online information concerning policies and citizenship.	E-mail (mailing list), e-meetings, virtual communities/online community networks (social networks), e-participation chat rooms, mobile phones/devices (text messages), Webcasts, GIS-tools, RSS Feeds, Online newsletters, FAQs, web portals, weblogs (blogs), video conferencing, Alerts, Wikis, Podcasting.
E-consulting	A limited two-way channel that has the objective of collecting public feedback and alternatives.	E-survey, feedback forms, e-mail, e-polls, newsgroups, weblogs (blogs), mobile phones/devices, virtual communities/online community networks, consultation platforms, text-to-speech technology (natural language processing), e-panels, Podcasting, Wikis, e-participation chat rooms, video conferencing, e-referenda, instant messaging
E-involving	The stage before the e-collaboration to ensure that the concerns of the public are understood and taken into consideration	E-mail, virtual e-meetings, chat-rooms, discussion forums/boards, online virtual communities (social networks), video conferencing, mobile phones/ devices (text messages), consultation platforms, online citizen juries
E-collaborating	enhanced two-way communication between citizens and government, and a full partnership that enables citizens to actively participate in the development of alternatives and the identification of preferred solutions	E-debates, Web virtual meetings (chat-rooms, discussion forums/boards), decision-making games, virtual communities/online community networks (social networks, data analysis tools)
E-empowering	A delegation of final decision-making rights to the public, and implementing what citizens decide	E-petition, e-voting tools, e-bulletin boards, e-polls, virtual e-meetings, chat-rooms, discussion forums/boards, e-Panel, Virtual communities/online community networks (social networks), Argument Visualization Tools. Natural Language Interfaces.

crowdsourcing, manage private sector participation in service delivery, and incite citizens to be co-producers of public services (Tapscott, Williams, & Herman, 2008). Table 2 presents some applications of Web 2.0 and social media tools for e-participation in developing countries.

The NSIF essentially implements the Government to Citizen (G2C) type of e-participation. In addition to recommendations made by clients, the NSIF found Web 2.0 and other social media tools very attractive because most of the country's active population has access to internet services and are familiar with social media technologies. Thus, it is more cost-effective and appealing to both the NSIF and

Table 2. Applications of Web 2.0 and social media tools in developing countries (Authors, 2017)

Country/Government/ Institution	Type of E-participation	Web 2.0/Social media Tool	Initiative/ Purpose	Citation
Egypt, Morocco, Bahrain, Tunisia, Iran, and Libya	Citizen to Citizen	Blogs, YouTube	e-democracy	(Cropf, Benmamoun, & Kalliny, 2012; Sandoval-Almazan & Gil-Garcia, 2013)
Mexico	Citizen to Citizen	Twitter, YouTube	Political and Social Activism	(Sandoval-Almazan & Gil-Garcia, 2013)
Indonesia	Citizen to Citizen	Facebook	Public Advocacy	(Murti, 2013)
Egypt	Government to Citizen	Forums, Survey, RSS, Blogs External Channels, YouTube, Twitter, Wiki page, LinkedIn, Skype	Information dissemination and civic engagement	(Abdelsalam, Reddick, Gamal, & Al-Shaar, 2013)
Peru	Government to Citizen	Google Docs, blog, Facebook	Decision-support (broadband project)	(Bossio, 2012)
Ethiopia	Government to Citizen	WoredaNet, SchoolNet, EthERNet, justice information system, transport management information system	Government transparency, education, open justice system, open transport system	(Belachew, 2010)
Indonesia	Government to citizen	YouTube	Government transparency	(Chatfield & Brajawidagda, 2013)

its clients. The agency uses these technologies to overcome infrastructural barriers and to improve the quality of its services. Table 3 presents the Web 2.0 and social media tools used by the NSIF and the target levels of e-participation. It also makes use of Facebook, Twitter, and YouTube, which are the most popular social media used for e-participation initiatives in developing countries.

Figure 1 illustrates how the Web 2.0 and social media tools relate with the NSIF website. The website provides access to the organization's Web2.0 tools and provides links to its Facebook and Twitter pages.

According to NSIF, their Web 2.0 services are frequently used and very appreciated by its users. NSIF's Facebook page (www.facebook.com/cnps.cm/) was launched in

Table 3. Technology components of NSIF's e-participation systems (Authors, 2017)

Web 2.0/ Social Media Platform	Tool	Role	Management practices and philosophies	Level of E-Participation
Web 2.0	Follow up of files	Facilitate client's ability to monitor their files submitted for processing	transparency, performance, quality services	E-consulting
	Consultation of individual accounts	Create a forum through which users can verify previous individual salary declarations	Transparency, participation, performance, and quality services	E-consulting
	Denouncer	Platform through which employees can denounce cases of fraud, bribery, corruption or any illegal practices concerning their social insurance activities especially from their employers	Cohesion, change, transparency, participation, solidarity, and quality services	E-involving
	Registration verifier	Verification of worker registration	Transparency, and quality services	E-consulting
Social Media	Facebook (www.facebook.com/cnps.cm)	Public access to information and interaction between the organization and its clients	Visibility, relevant information, cohesion, change, transparency, participation, solidarity	E-collaborating
	Twitter (www.twitter.com/cnpscameroun)	Inform and interact with users promptly	Visibility, relevant information, cohesion, change, transparency, participation, solidarity	E-collaborating
	YouTube (CNPS Cameroun)	Share videos on the agency's activities	Visibility	E-informing

2014. It is very active from the organization's end with an average of 01 posts per day, though most of the posts are feeds from the organization's Twitter page. As of July 1, 2017, the page had 3119 likes, 3144 followers, 87 reviews and was rated 3.6 of 5 stars (5 stars – 35 votes, 4 stars - 16 votes, 3 stars – 17 votes, 2 stars – 8 votes, and 1 star – 11 votes). While NSIF uses the page mostly to inform its clients, its clients use the page mostly to lay complaints concerning the services rendered by the organization. After analyzing posts on the Facebook page, it was observed that NSIF was quite prompt at responding to comments made on its posts. However, it took an average of 30 days to respond to posts from clients seeking information or complaining about services. Nevertheless, NSIF responded to all such posts from its clients. NSIF's Twitter page was created in January 2015, and it has been very active

Figure 1. Web2.0 tool connections with the main organizational website (Authors, 2017)

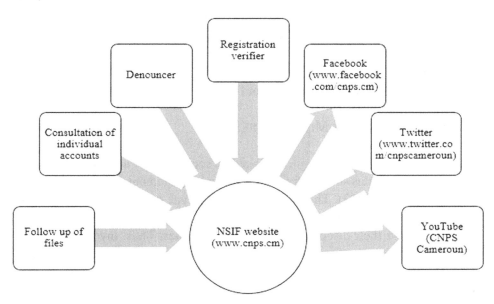

since then. As of July 1, 2017, it had made 1420 tweets, followed 2499 accounts, had 2464 followers and obtained 1208 likes. The organization's YouTube channel is practically inactive. It was created in 2016 and since then, only 5 videos have been uploaded, with only 05 subscribers as of July 1, 2017.

Though summarized in table 3, the subsection that follows presents the role played by each of the Web 2.0 and social media tools used by the NSIF in its e-participation initiative. The perspectives of this initiative by NSIF's clients will also be presented, particularly from the perspective of employers and employees registered with the agency.

Role of Web 2.0 and Social Media

Citizen participation is generally agreed to be an essential part of a healthy democracy. Though widespread participation is not easy to achieve in practice, there is no doubt today that citizens play a primary role in politics. They can either participate directly (without recourse to representation) or indirectly (through an elected representative) (Bullock, 2014). Direct participation is that which is gaining grounds in developing countries. It is motivated by distrust of government and the belief that citizens have a duty to keep a watch on government. This enthusiasm for direct democracy reflects what people find lacking in a representative democracy (Bowler, Donovan, & Karp, 2007). However, for direct participation to be effective, there needs to be extensive technological support for citizen participation (Chun et al., 2010).

E-participation initiatives are mostly driven by youths who make up most of the population in developing countries (Lam, 2006). The main objectives of e-participation initiatives in these countries include more civic engagement and mobilization, better government services, and transparency and accountability (Dini & Sæbø, 2016).

Civic Engagement and Mobilization

The use of social media has led to changes in social norms and behavior at the societal level in domains such as civic and political engagement, privacy and public safety (Aksoy et al., 2013). This has created a new type of citizen participation in socio-political issues through social media, which has opened opportunities for citizens to express their discontent on democratic issues. Thus, involving citizens with politics is important for the emergence of democracy in developing countries (Sandoval-Almazan & Gil-Garcia, 2013). Social media have the potential to influence youth civic engagement (Aksoy et al., 2013). However, the political environment in developing countries, often characterized by restrictions on freedom of expression, can influence how social media are used by citizens (Aksoy et al., 2013; Shirazi, 2012).

Nevertheless, social media and virtual communities are without parallel in their ability to mobilize vast numbers of the public. They are the foundations for implementing e-democracy in developing countries (Maciel, Roque, & Garcia, 2010), especially Facebook (Robertson, Vatrapu, & Medina, 2009). These tools have also demonstrated their potential in the Arab Spring, where social media have become the main mobilization platform where young and educated people who are disappointed with the socioeconomic and political conditions in their countries discuss and exchange information (Kamel, 2013). As a result, the NSIF is striving to make the most of these technologies to improve and better coordinate civic engagement and mobilization with its clients.

As years go by, the NSIF gets more and more recognition for its efforts towards making a difference in the civic life of communities in Cameroon through its efforts towards developing knowledge, skills, and values that can improve the quality of life of workers and their households. NSIF has 04 health facilities and 02 schools. Through these schools and hospitals, it is very active in its commitment to participate and work for social changes that can improve the living conditions and opportunities for children, families, and communities. To prevent the mishaps the organization faced with its clients in 1983, it has developed strategies through which clients can express themselves and come together as a virtual community to channel complaints and requests to the organization in a non-violent manner. This strategy largely involves the use of social media, particularly Facebook through which it obtains and responds to complains, remarks and recommendation from its clients.

Better Government Services

Government services can be difficult to access in an offline environment, which is especially problematic for people in remote locations in developing countries. In Cameroon, many remote locations exist and workers there find it difficult to benefit from the services of NSIF. E-participation offers a potential to dramatically increase access to information and services and makes it easier for citizens to participate in, and contribute to governmental issues (Chen, Chen, Huang, & Ching, 2006). In addition, the availability of social media allows the population greater access to government services (Meso, Musa, Straub, & Mbarika, 2009), especially in those remote areas.

Web 2.0 technologies are faster, cheaper, and effortless compared to obtaining the services directly from the government office (Basu, 2004; Kumar & Best, 2006). As a result, they have considerable social and economic value for the citizens. In addition, these media can also help reduce corruption during the delivery of these services (Kumar & Best, 2006). Thus, NSIF's decision to use Web 2.0 technologies and social media to provide the proper governance of public services is positively associated with the rate at which citizens obtain and appreciate some of its services. However, information quality, system management, and service delivery strongly influence citizens' satisfaction in e-participation services (Marković, Labus, Vulić, & Radenković, 2013).

NSIF is the official social security agency in Cameroon and all legal employers in Cameroon must register their employees so that their monthly savings can be deducted from their salaries. Self-employed citizens can also voluntarily get insured with NSIF. This agency, therefore essentially provides social security services to all workers in the country. For NSIF to properly accomplish this goal, it should make sure that its services are reliable, timely, responsive, and consistent. To achieve these results, the NSIF makes use of its website to provide online access to its services, which is very beneficial to its citizens, especially in terms of accessibility for those in remote areas of the country.

Transparency and Accountability

Transparency is an essential element of the e-participation initiatives that governments in developing countries have employed to promote openness and reduce corruption. It limits many opportunities for corrupt practices, which is a serious issue in developing countries. Lack of transparency can make corruption less risky and more attractive, prevent the use of public incentives to make public officials act responsibly and in the public interest, create informational advantages to privileged groups, instill and perpetuate control over resources, spur opportunism and undermine cooperation, and hinder social trust and therefore development (Andersen, 2009; Cuillier & Piotrowski, 2009; Dawes, 2010; Kolstad & Wiig, 2009; Kolstad, Wiig, & Williams, 2009; Stiglitz, 2002, 2003).

For many years, transparency and accountability have not been one of the strengths of the Cameroon government and its agencies. With a perceived level of public sector corruption score of 26 on a scale of 100 (0 -highly corrupt; 100 very clean), Cameroon has been ranked 145th most corrupt country relative to 176 countries in the index by Transparency International (Transparency International, 2016). Most citizens do not have a good understanding of the laws governing most government structures, nor do these structures feel accountable to the citizens. Such governance fuels a lot of corrupt practices in the government and ignites considerable anger from the citizens. Thus, the government in its attempt to fight corruption is promoting transparency and accountability initiatives. The NSIF as a government agency has implemented, through its e-participation initiatives, the *Denouncer* system that can help increase its transparency and the level of accountability of the services it provides to its clients. This system and Facebook have played a major role in fighting corruption in the NSIF, making the clients and the agency more aware of corrupt practices (CNPS, 2016).

Using social media effectively can help governments and citizens with the issue of transparency and accountability (Polat, Bakıroğlu, & Sayın, 2013) by fostering collaboration between them (Relly & Sabharwal, 2009). According to Chun (Ae Chun et al., 2012), there are several key roles that social media can play in collaborative e-government to help improve government transparency and increase anti-corruption. However, the laws and policies that government agencies enforce on the use of social media shape the role social media play on government transparency (Bertot, Jaeger, & Hansen, 2012).

Client Perspectives NSIF's e-Participation Initiatives

Most of NSIF's clients are legal employers and organizations that pay in social contributions on behalf of their employees. These employers are most satisfied with the "Consultation of insured individual account" platform. They found the rest of the services very ineffective. However, they believe that these services can be very relevant if used as presented in Table 4.

Over 70% of the employers who participated in the study were very satisfied with the compatibility of the system with their social practices, and with the possibility

Table 4. Employer perception of the relevance of the technological components of NSIF's Web 2.0 and Social Media tools (Authors, 2017)

Relevance	Technology Component
Access to Information	Follow-up files system
Transparency	Facebook page, Twitter page
Trust	Consultation of individual accounts
Irrelevant	Denouncer

of giving feedback on their appreciation of the systems. They were also satisfied with the availability of the systems, and with their added value. However, they were unsure of their level of satisfaction when it came to accessibility and relative advantage over manual procedures and technological complexity. To encourage them to better use these Web services and social media, they recommended that NSIF should communicate more on the availability of these services using traditional media such as radio, TV, and newspapers. As concerns transparency and trust, employers recommended that NSIF should communicate more through Facebook and Twitter on the actions they are taking towards achieving these goals.

Facebook is the social media tool used by over 66% of the employees who responded to the questionnaire used in this study. They also appreciated the follow-up file system, consultation of insured individual account, and the denouncer system. Table 5 presents their perception of the relevance of each technological component considered during this study.

80% of employees are most satisfied by the relative advantage these Web 2.0 and social media tools offer over manual procedures. They are also satisfied with the accessibility and availability of the services, their compatibility with social practices, their technological complexity, and their ability to receive feedback

Table 5. Employee perception of the relevance of the technological components of NSIF's Web 2.0 and Social Media tools (Author, 2017)

Relevance	Technology Component
Access to Information	Facebook, Twitter, Consultation of individual accounts
Transparency	Denouncer, Consultation of individual accounts
Trust	Follow-up of files, Denouncer
Decision/Policymaking	Tele-declaration, Pre-registration of employers, Pre-registration of the insured, Account Activation

on the quality of services offered. To promote the use of these online services, employees recommended that NSIF should communicate more on the existence of these services online. They also requested a system for the declaration of family insurance, and a system through which one can verify how much they have saved and how much they will receive as pension each month when they retire. Finally, they recommended that the organization should make available online complete access to information concerning individual accounts, especially their savings, and should communicate back on complaints made concerning reported cases of fraud, bribery, and corruption.

Management and Organizational Concerns

Overall, NSIF's clients who know about the systems and who use the systems find them effective. However, many employees are not aware of the availability of these systems online. In 2010, NSIF organized several seminars and training on the use of its online services. Today, it claims that all employers are very comfortable using these services and that practically most cannot do without them. As a result, though the organization is confident of the effective use of its systems by employers through its website, it cannot assume the same for employees. Also, there is no formal mechanism put in place to determine the effectiveness of these systems. However, each system provides the organization with statistics on the rate at which they are used, making the information available for decision makers whenever it is needed. Meanwhile, the fact that users can provide feedback on the quality of services offered enables the organization to improve its services continuously. According to the internal auditor, sensitization campaigns are being carried out regularly to make clients aware of the necessity of using the organization's e-participation initiatives, especially the advantages and legal obligations attached to them.

Given how active the organization's website and Twitter accounts are, the organization has successfully increased access to public information. Together with its Denouncer system, the organization has dramatically increased its efforts towards transparency to gain the trust of its clients. The organization has a very agile communication department that updates clients at least once a day using social media. It also responds promptly to user complaints received through social media and redirects issues or concerns to the departments directly concerned and informs the hierarchy accordingly. However, users do not know if their participation through these media have been considered in decision-making. This is mainly because the organization has no formal or systematic procedure of integrating user participation into decision making. This sometimes makes users feel like their opinions do not matter.

Given the main Web 2.0 and social media tools and the role in e-participation initiatives in developing countries, the section that follows presents the opportunities and challenges they present to the countries.

OPPORTUNITIES AND CHALLENGES

The range of choices and opportunities ICTs offer to developing countries is expanding. Nevertheless, they represent a high risk of widening the digital divide, which may lead to information poverty and increase the gap in economic status and competitiveness (Ndou, 2004). E-participation initiatives have flourished in many developing countries such as Brazil, Argentina and the Philippines (Ndou, 2004). However, more than a third of such initiatives have failed in Sub-Saharan Africa, and half of them in Eastern Europe can be considered partial failures (Heeks, 2003). Though e-participation offers great potential and opportunity for developing countries to improve their governance and citizen satisfaction levels, governments need to put in place the conditions necessary to manage the challenges that tag along to make the most of these initiatives (Ndou, 2004).

The e-participation initiatives implemented by NSIF has provided the organization with numerous opportunities to regain citizen's trust and interaction with the organization. This is mainly because the political and organizational leadership had the will to promote the initiatives. As a result, they ensured that strategies and policies were formulated to guarantee the adaptability of these initiatives to the Cameroonian context. Thus, they could prioritize the initiatives, allocate the necessary financial resources, and define the right public-private partnerships to ensure the successful implementation of these initiatives. These carefully-thought initiatives were implemented and well-integrated into the organization's back-end processes, making it easy for the NSIF to quickly respond to user requests. These are challenges that most developing countries face when designing their e-participation initiatives which the NSIF overcame (Almarabeh & AbuAli, 2010; Belachew, 2010; Ebrahim & Irani, 2005; Furuholt & Wahid, 2008; Ndou, 2004; Nkwe, 2012; Ornager & Verma, 2005; Rashid & Rahman, 2010; Sæbø, 2012; Schuppan, 2009). Despite the opportunities these initiatives have presented to the NSIF, the organization still faces several challenges. The subsections that follow present the opportunities, challenges, and risks encountered by e-participation initiatives in developing countries and exemplified using the case of the NSIF.

Opportunities

1. Cost Reduction and Efficiency Gains (Ndou, 2004; Nkwe, 2012; Schuppan, 2009)

Since the implementation of the organization's e-participation initiatives, NSIF claims to have made significant gains in efficiency and in dramatic cutting down on cost. Since most of its client-end processes have been automated, the organization has been able to economize a lot on paper, ink and other indirect costs, getting the job done better and faster.

2. Quality of Service Delivery (Ndou, 2004; Nkwe, 2012; Schuppan, 2009)

Thanks to NSIF's e-participation initiatives, services are delivered to clients wherever they are if they have access to the internet. Because the services are reported to be always available, accessible online and faster than the manual procedures, they provide NSIF with the opportunity of providing quality services to its clients.

3. Transparency, Anti-corruption, Accountability (Ndou, 2004; Nkwe, 2012)

Transparency, anti-corruption, and accountability are key elements of the e-participation initiatives implemented by NSIF. Since the implementation of these initiatives, clients have instant access to their personal information without having to pay a dime. They also have the opportunity through the system to see who is handling their file at any given time. Furthermore, clients have the possibility to use the system to either denounce cases of fraud, bribery or corruption; or to write an e-mail directly to the General Manager if they are not satisfied with any service provided.

4. Network and Community Creation (Ndou, 2004; Nkwe, 2012)

Thanks to its social media accounts especially Twitter, which is active, NSIF could create a huge network and virtual community that can drive its vision and mobilize many citizens to support its goals, thereby proposing ways in which it can improve its services to the community.

5. On-Time Information Delivery (Ndou, 2004; Nkwe, 2012)

The e-participation initiatives implemented by NSIF provide the opportunity for timely information delivery thanks to the wide coverage provided by its services.

Thanks to its website and Twitter account, clients and citizens could obtain reliable information on time from the organization.

CHALLENGES

1. Infrastructural Development (Almarabeh & AbuAli, 2010)

NSIF has struggled to develop basic infrastructure to take advantage of Web 2.0 technologies and Social Media as communication tools that can improve the quality of their services. Despite the will of its leadership, Cameroon does not have the infrastructure necessary to immediately make NSIF's online services available throughout the national territory. Though Cameroon has made significant progress in many areas of infrastructure, the country still faces several important infrastructural challenges, including poor road quality; expensive and unreliable electricity, which occasionally is absent in some parts of the country, and a stagnating and uncompetitive ICT sector. The country loses over 60% of its infrastructural budget due to mismanagement, thereby significantly slowing down development (Dominguez-Torres, 2011). Similarly, only about 20.7% of the population uses the internet (CIA, 2017). As a result, the country's infrastructure is not very conducive for these initiatives to be fully enjoyed by the wider public.

2. Law and Public Policy (Almarabeh & AbuAli, 2010)

Though the legislation in Cameroon allows electronic documents to be recognized by NSIF, this can be quite challenging for clients when they make errors during online declarations. In such situations, the client often has to present the original hard copy of the documents to the nearest NSIF branch for verification before the error can be rectified. It gets even more complicated with the unavailability of online payment services. This is because, despite the multiple electronic payment transactions going on in the country, especially via mobile phones, many clients are not aware of the position of the law vis-à-vis such transactions. Yet, clients, especially those who desire to register voluntarily, are demanding for e-payment services to be provided across these platforms.

3. Digital Divide (Almarabeh & AbuAli, 2010)

The digital divide in Cameroon is very significant. Given the comparatively slow internet penetration rate in the country, many people do not have internet access, so that they cannot access information and services that NSIF provides online. With services such as Tele-declaration, which are only available online, NSIF has to spend a lot of resources to get clients in such areas registered.

4.   E-Literacy (Almarabeh & AbuAli, 2010; Nkwe, 2012; Zukang, 2012)

Though Cameroon has a literacy rate of about 75% (CIA, 2017), its e-literacy rate is as low as about 29% (Bediang et al., 2013). This implies that about 70% of the population is unable to make use of ICTs due to computer illiteracy. With its digital evolution, NSIF faces the challenge of dealing with this category of clients, especially the adults, who are not computer literate. Not only do they not share in the benefits of the e-participation initiatives, they also miss out on a lot of information communicated on these media.

5.   Accessibility (Almarabeh & AbuAli, 2010)

Even though NSIF's services are generally always available to regular users, their interfaces do not make provision for people with physical disabilities such as the blind and deaf. As a result, such people need to be assisted by someone, who may not always be available to them.

6.   Marketing and Benchmarking (Almarabeh & AbuAli, 2010)

E-participation initiatives are effective only if people know about them and use them according to design and purpose. Since the launching seminars and workshops organized to train clients on the organization's e-participation initiatives in 2010-2011, NSIF's support services to its clients remain very active through targeted sensitizations and an available service desk.

The major challenge NSIF faces on this point is the incapability to pinpoint the degree of effectiveness of its e-participation initiatives. As a result, besides determining the rate of access to the system, evaluating the performance, the effective use, and the impact of each system objectively and with precision is practically impossible.

7.   Social and Political Instability

Like in most developing counties, terrorist attacks and civil unrest are major challenges faced by the NSIF. The political stability index of Cameroon was as weak as -0.99 in 2015, according to data collected by The Global Economy (The Global Economy, 2016) from the World Bank. This socio-political instability has greatly increased with the attacks from the Islamic insurgency Boko Haram, and the tension between the English-speaking regions of the country and the government. This hinders effective participation from citizens in the affected regions of the country.

DISCUSSION

While e-participation continues to increase citizen participation in the promotion of good governance, the challenges faced are serious barriers to e-participation development in developing countries. This chapter supports the fact that the potential of e-participation in developing countries remains largely unexploited (Ndou, 2004). The adoption of e-participation initiatives in developing countries promises a sharp paradigm shift where public institutions will be more responsive and transparent, promote efficient Public Private Partnerships (PPP), and empower citizens by making knowledge and other resources more directly accessible (Bwalya, 2009). Though the initiatives have failed in many of these countries, they have flourished in many others as well. Given that the penetration rate of mobile phones is higher than that of internet access in these countries, mobile technology could be used to narrow the digital divide, and by so doing improve the success rate of e-participation initiatives in developing countries (Ahmed, 2006).

Like in most developing countries, ICT infrastructure is a huge barrier to e-participation initiatives. Given that there isn't much an agency like NSIF can do about the infrastructural limitations of the country, they can consider adapting their initiatives to the realities of the country. For example, they could periodically go to enclaved areas or areas with no electricity with kiosks and mobile centers so that clients there could benefit from their services without having to cover long distances themselves. Doing this will improve both the quality of service and the image of NSIF. Therefore, it could consider providing its online services via mobile applications. According to Cameroon's Telecommunications Regulatory Agency (ART in its French Acronym), about 80% of Cameroonians owned smartphones. This could help make the services agiler and more accessible to many people who cannot access them from computers.

As concerns challenges posed by law and public policies, consulting with stakeholders to assess how existing laws may impede desired results will be a giant step towards solving the issue. Given the infrastructural limitations in Cameroon, many clients prefer using e-documents and e-payment services, especially with mobile phones during transactions. Thus, NSIF should consider improving and making available these services so that clients in remote areas would not have to cover long distances to present a document or make payments. Also, the NSIF should clarify and make available laws and procedures regulating e-documents and e-payments between the agency and its clients.

To bridge the digital divide and combat e-literacy, NSIF could combine communal access through village computer centers with instant training. That way, when a client comes to register or use the system for the first time, NSIF ensures that the person is trained well enough to be able to replicate the action alone subsequently. This can be done through outsourcing to the private sector, who could donate equipment and provide training. Furthermore, NSIF could make the interfaces to feature in both the English and French languages, the official languages of the country, and even in some local languages like Fufulde, which is widely spoken in the Northern regions of the country. Tutorials on how to use the system could be created on the website, and programs could be created on traditional media such as radio, TV and newspaper columns, where citizens will learn about these initiatives and how to make the most of them.

Concerning accessibility, the NSIF needs to consider ergonomics for users with disabilities. To make NSIF's platforms to accommodate people with disabilities, it could incorporate features such as audio options for the blind and speech recognition for the dismembered. In fact, it would look more responsible to establish a legal document ensuring that all its systems adopt technologies that can accommodate the physically disabled.

NSIF's clients have identified Facebook and Twitter as very relevant social media tools as concerns facilitating access to information and promoting transparency. However, NSIF is not benefiting from its Facebook page as much as it should. The organization will benefit more from regularly posting engaging information that will prompt users to generate content through participation, that the organization can use to better understand its clients' needs and to support decision making. Also, responding promptly to requests or complaints posted on Facebook by clients will be very beneficial for NSIF. Many people who complain using Facebook are those who are highly impacted by the digital divide. When they are opportune to find themselves where they have access to the internet, they take advantage to post complaints. When NSIF does not respond promptly, the client may not see the response provided by NSIF until the next time the client has access to the internet, which may be many months later when the response may be obsolete. As a result, such clients would not have a positive image of the organization's e-participation services, which might be transmitted to other clients. Given that many clients also mentioned the unawareness of some tools, the NSIF could develop more publicity and training campaigns that will increase awareness and engage the public about the initiatives. These campaigns could target the older generation that is not very familiar with ICT. For example, sensitization can be done each time an elderly person arrives an office requesting for a service available online.

It is worth noting that developing countries still lack a comprehensive framework that will enable them design e-participation systems that add value to the public

(Murti, 2013). Due to the considerable differences between developed and developing countries, the latter cannot directly adopt e-participation strategies used in developed countries (Chen et al., 2006). As a result, several conceptual frameworks that include critical success factors influencing e-participation strategies and implementations in developing countries have been developed. The model-based paradigm is the dominant theoretical framework used in e-participation research in developing countries because it is an effective means of evaluating the development of e-participation in a given context (Dini & Sæbø, 2016; Heeks & Bailur, 2007). These models suggest that there are a number of distinct phases in the development of e-government which include: limited Internet presence in the first phase of development, dynamic and enhanced online information is made available to the citizen during the second phase, more interactive interfaces between all stakeholders is provided during the third phase, and finally, customized and secure services such as passwords and other security features are added to the characteristics of the third phase to make up the fourth phase (Ngulube, 2007). Thus, social media begin to feature as tools in e-participation initiatives from the third phase of the e-government development model. Mkude and Wimmer (Mkude & Wimmer, 2013) summarize e-participation and e-government frameworks found in literature designed for developing countries.

CONCLUSION

The aim of this chapter was to use the case of Cameroon's National Social Insurance Fund (NSIF) to exemplify the realities of e-participation in developing countries. The case study has made it clear that e-participation initiatives using Web 2.0 and social media tools provides new opportunities for meaningful participation in good governance in developing countries. However, the success of such initiatives depends on modern and reliable communication networks and the political will of the government. Facebook, YouTube, and Twitter are the most popular social media used in e-participation initiatives, alongside other Web 2.0 platforms designed for specific purposes such as for transparency and anti-corruption. These platforms are mostly used for information, consultation and to some extent involvement. Nevertheless, platforms that allow meaningful collaboration, delegation of final decision-making rights to the public, and the implementation of what citizens decide (e-empowering) are almost absent. Indeed, e-participation initiatives foster civic engagement and mobilization, better government services, and transparency and accountability. Consequently, instead of being afraid of it, governments in developing countries should embrace it and work towards using it to their advantage. This implies developing countries should take advantage of the opportunities presented by Web 2.0 and social media tools, and face the challenges that come with these tools accordingly.

As concerns the NSIF, the government still needs to commit more resources to the development of ICT infrastructure and human capital, and address the nation's digital divide, while the NSIF should focus on making its e-participation initiatives better known to the population, more accessible and more compliant with organizational and national objectives.

REFERENCES

Abdelsalam, H. M., Reddick, C. G., Gamal, S., & Al-Shaar, A. (2013). Social media in Egyptian government websites: Presence, usage, and effectiveness. *Government Information Quarterly*, *30*(4), 406–416. doi:10.1016/j.giq.2013.05.020

Ae Chun, S., Luna-Reyes, L. F., Sandoval-Almazán, R., Carlo Bertot, J., Jaeger, P. T., & Grimes, J. M. (2012). Promoting transparency and accountability through ICTs, social media, and collaborative e-government. *Transforming Government: People, Process and Policy*, *6*(1), 78–91.

Ahmed, N. (2006). *An Anthology of E-Participation Models*. Paper presented at the E-Participation and E-Government: Understanding the Present and Creating the Future. Report of the Ad Hoc Expert Group Meeting, Budapest, Hungary.

Aksoy, L., van Riel, A., Kandampully, J., Bolton, R. N., Parasuraman, A., Hoefnagels, A., ... Komarova Loureiro, Y. (2013). Understanding Generation Y and their use of social media: A review and research agenda. *Journal of Service Management*, *24*(3), 245–267. doi:10.1108/09564231311326987

Al-Dalou, R., & Abu-Shanab, E. (2013). *E-participation levels and technologies*. Paper presented at the 6th International Conference on Information Technology (ICIT 2013).

Almarabeh, T., & AbuAli, A. (2010). A general framework for e-government: Definition maturity challenges, opportunities, and success. *European Journal of Scientific Research*, *39*(1), 29–42.

Andersen, T. B. (2009). E-Government as an anti-corruption strategy. *Information Economics and Policy*, *21*(3), 201–210. doi:10.1016/j.infoecopol.2008.11.003

Basu, S. (2004). E-government and developing countries: An overview. *International Review of Law Computers & Technology*, *18*(1), 109–132. doi:10.1080/13600860 410001674779

Bediang, G., Stoll, B., Geissbuhler, A., Klohn, A. M., Stuckelberger, A., Nko'o, S., & Chastonay, P. (2013). Computer literacy and E-learning perception in Cameroon: The case of Yaounde Faculty of Medicine and Biomedical Sciences. *BMC Medical Education, 13*(1), 57. doi:10.1186/1472-6920-13-57 PMID:23601853

Belachew, M. (2010). E-government initiatives in Ethiopia. *Proceedings of the 4th International Conference on Theory and Practice of Electronic Governance.*

Bertot, J. C., Jaeger, P. T., & Hansen, D. (2012). The impact of polices on government social media usage: Issues, challenges, and recommendations. *Government Information Quarterly, 29*(1), 30–40. doi:10.1016/j.giq.2011.04.004

Bossio, J. (2012). Using Web 2.0 to Influence PERU's ICT Sector. *IMPACT 2.0,* 63.

Bowler, S., Donovan, T., & Karp, J. A. (2007). Enraged or engaged? Preferences for direct citizen participation in affluent democracies. *Political Research Quarterly, 60*(3), 351–362. doi:10.1177/1065912907304108

Bullock, K. (2014). *Citizen Participation and Democracy. In Citizens, Community and Crime Control* (pp. 25–49). Springer.

Bwalya, K. J. (2009). Factors affecting adoption of e-government in Zambia. *The Electronic Journal on Information Systems in Developing Countries,* 38.

Chatfield, A. T., & Brajawidagda, U. (2013). *Political will and strategic use of YouTube to advancing government transparency: An analysis of Jakarta government-generated YouTube videos.* Paper presented at the International Conference on Electronic Government. doi:10.1007/978-3-642-40358-3_3

Chen, Y., Chen, H., Huang, W., & Ching, R. K. (2006). E-government strategies in developed and developing countries: An implementation framework and case study. *Journal of Global Information Management, 14*(1), 23–46. doi:10.4018/jgim.2006010102

Chun, S. A., Shulman, S., Sandoval, R., & Hovy, E. (2010). Government 2.0: Making connections between citizens, data and government. *Information Polity, 15*(1), 1.

CIA. (2017). *The World Factbook - Africa: Cameroon.* Retrieved 01-07-2017, 2017, from https://www.cia.gov/library/publications/resources/the-world-factbook/geos/cm.html

CNPS. (2008). *General information on social security in Cameroon.* Retrieved from http://www.cnps.cm/index.php?view=article&id=78:immobilier&format=pdf

CNPS. (2015). *Reserved for Employers*. Retrieved from http://www.cnps.cm/index. php?option=com_content&view=article&id=83&Itemid=105

CNPS. (2016). *Disclosure of false news about CNPS: The General Manager reassures and invites vigilance 2017*. Retrieved from http://www.cnps.cm/index. php?option=com_content&view=article&id=585%3Adivulgation-de-fausses-nouvelles-sur-la-cnps--le-dg-rassure-et-invite-a-la-vigilance&catid=4%3Aarticles-actualites&lang=en

CNPS. (2017). *History of CNPS*. Retrieved from http://www.cnps.cm/index. php?option=com_content&view=article&id=78&Itemid=97&lang=en

Cropf, R. A., Benmamoun, M., & Kalliny, M. (2012). The Role of Web 2.0 in the Arab Spring. *Cases on Web 2.0 in Developing Countries: Studies on Implementation, Application, and Use: Studies on Implementation, Application, and Use*, 76.

Cuillier, D., & Piotrowski, S. J. (2009). Internet information-seeking and its relation to support for access to government records. *Government Information Quarterly, 26*(3), 441–449. doi:10.1016/j.giq.2009.03.001

Dawes, S. S. (2010). Stewardship and usefulness: Policy principles for information-based transparency. *Government Information Quarterly, 27*(4), 377–383. doi:10.1016/j.giq.2010.07.001

Dini, A. A., & Sæbø, Ø. (2016). *The current state of social media research for eParticipation in developing countries: a literature review*. Paper presented at the System Sciences (HICSS), 2016 49th Hawaii International Conference on. doi:10.1109/HICSS.2016.339

Dominguez-Torres, C. F. (2011). *Cameroon's Infrastructure: A Continental Perspective*. Academic Press.

Ebrahim, Z., & Irani, Z. (2005). E-government adoption: Architecture and barriers. *Business Process Management Journal, 11*(5), 589–611. doi:10.1108/14637150510619902

Furuholt, B., & Wahid, F. (2008). *E-government Challenges and the Role of Political Leadership in Indonesia: The Case of Sragen*. Paper presented at the Hawaii International Conference on System Sciences. doi:10.1109/HICSS.2008.134

Heeks, R. (2001). *Understanding e-governance for development*. Institute for Development Policy and Management Manchester.

Heeks, R. (2002). e-Government in Africa: Promise and practice. *Information Polity, 7*(2-3), 97-114.

Heeks, R. (2003). *Success and failure rates of eGovernment in developing/transitional countries: Overview.* IDPM, University of Manchester. Retrieved from http://www.egov4dev.org/sfoverview.htm

Heeks, R., & Bailur, S. (2007). Analyzing e-government research: Perspectives, philosophies, theories, methods, and practice. *Government Information Quarterly,* *24*(2), 243–265. doi:10.1016/j.giq.2006.06.005

International Labor Organization. (2001). *Facts on Social Security.* Retrieved from http://www.ilo.org/wcmsp5/groups/public/---dgreports/---dcomm/documents/publication/wcms_067588.pdf

Islam, M. S. (2008). Towards a sustainable e-Participation implementation model. *European Journal of ePractice, 5*(10).

Justino, P. (2007). Social security in developing countries: Myth or necessity? Evidence from India. *Journal of International Development, 19*(3), 367–382. doi:10.1002/jid.1298

Kamel, S. H. (2013). The Value of Social Media in Egypt's Uprising and Beyond. *The Electronic Journal on Information Systems in Developing Countries,* 60.

Kolstad, I., & Wiig, A. (2009). Is transparency the key to reducing corruption in resource-rich countries? *World Development, 37*(3), 521–532. doi:10.1016/j.worlddev.2008.07.002

Kolstad, I., Wiig, A., & Williams, A. (2009). Mission improbable: Does petroleum-related aid address the resource curse? *Energy Policy, 37*(3), 954–965. doi:10.1016/j.enpol.2008.09.092

Komito, L. (2005). e-Participation and Governance: Widening the net. *The Electronic. Journal of E-Government, 3*(1), 39–48.

Kumar, R., & Best, M. L. (2006). Impact and sustainability of e-government services in developing countries: Lessons learned from Tamil Nadu, India. *The Information Society, 22*(1), 1–12. doi:10.1080/01972240500388149

Kuzma, J. (2010). Asian government usage of Web 2.0 social media. *European Journal of ePractice,* (9), 1-13.

Lam, D. (2006). The demography of youth in developing countries and its economic implications. Ann Arbor, 1001, 48106.

Linders, D. (2012). From e-government to we-government: Defining a typology for citizen coproduction in the age of social media. *Government Information Quarterly*, *29*(4), 446–454. doi:10.1016/j.giq.2012.06.003

Maciel, C., Roque, L., & Garcia, A. C. B. (2010). Interaction and communication resources in collaborative e-democratic environments: The democratic citizenship community. *Information Polity, 15*(1-2), 73-88.

Marković, A. M., Labus, A., Vulić, M., & Radenković, B. (2013). *Using social networks for improving egovernment services.* Academic Press.

Mbu Daniel, T. (2015). Economic Growth, Crisis, and Recovery in Cameroon: A Literature Review. *Journal of Industrial Distribution & Business*, *6*(1), 5–15. doi:10.13106/ijidb.2015.vol6.no1.5.

Meso, P., Musa, P., Straub, D., & Mbarika, V. (2009). Information infrastructure, governance, and socio-economic development in developing countries. *European Journal of Information Systems*, *18*(1), 52–65. doi:10.1057/ejis.2008.56

Mkude, C. G., & Wimmer, M. A. (2013). Strategic Framework for Designing E-Government in Developing Countries. In M. A. Wimmer, M. Janssen, & H. J. Scholl (Eds.), *Electronic Government: 12th IFIP WG 8.5 International Conference, EGOV 2013, Koblenz, Germany, September 16-19, 2013. Proceedings* (pp. 148-162). Berlin: Springer Berlin Heidelberg.

Murti, D. C. W. (2013). Keyboard Action End up Political Party: Understanding the Intertwining Relations of Social Media Activism, Citizenship, and the Dynamics of Democracy in Indonesia. *Online Journal of Communication and Media Technologies*, *3*(2), 32.

Nam, T. (2012). Suggesting frameworks of citizen-sourcing via Government 2.0. *Government Information Quarterly*, *29*(1), 12–20. doi:10.1016/j.giq.2011.07.005

Ndou, V. (2004). E-government for developing countries: Opportunities and challenges. *The Electronic Journal on Information Systems in Developing Countries*, 18.

Ngulube, P. (2007). The nature and accessibility of e-government in Sub Saharan Africa. *International Review of Information Ethics*, *7*(9), 1–13.

Nkwe, N. (2012). E-government: Challenges and opportunities in Botswana. *International Journal of Humanities and Social Science*, *2*(17), 39–48.

Ornager, S., & Verma, N. (2005). *E-Government Tool-Kit for Developing Countries.* UNESCO.

Papaloi, A., Staiou, E. R., & Gouscos, D. (2012). *Blending Social Media with Parliamentary Websites: Just a Trend, or a Promising Approach to e-Participation? In Web 2.0 Technologies and Democratic Governance* (pp. 259–275). Springer.

Polat, B., Bakıroğlu, C. T., & Sayın, M. E. D. (2013). E-Transformation of Municipalities and Social Media's Role on e-Participation in European e-Municipalities. *Academic Journal of Interdisciplinary Studies, 2*(9), 386.

Rashid, N., & Rahman, S. (2010). *An investigation into critical determinants of e-government implementation in the context of a developing nation.* Paper presented at the International Conference on Electronic Government and the Information Systems Perspective. doi:10.1007/978-3-642-15172-9_2

Relly, J. E., & Sabharwal, M. (2009). Perceptions of transparency of government policymaking: A cross-national study. *Government Information Quarterly, 26*(1), 148–157. doi:10.1016/j.giq.2008.04.002

Robertson, S. P., Vatrapu, R. K., & Medina, R. (2009). The social life of social networks: Facebook linkage patterns in the 2008 US presidential election. *Proceedings of the 10th Annual International Conference on Digital Government Research: Social Networks: Making Connections between Citizens, Data and Government.*

Sæbø, Ø. (2012). *E-government in Tanzania: current status and future challenges.* Paper presented at the International Conference on Electronic Government. doi:10.1007/978-3-642-33489-4_17

Sandoval-Almazan, R., & Gil-Garcia, J. R. (2013). *Cyberactivism through Social Media: Twitter, YouTube, and the Mexican Political Movement" I'm Number 132".* Paper presented at the System Sciences (HICSS), 2013 46th Hawaii International Conference on.

Schuppan, T. (2009). E-Government in developing countries: Experiences from sub-Saharan Africa. *Government Information Quarterly, 26*(1), 118–127. doi:10.1016/j.giq.2008.01.006

Shirazi, F. (2012). Measuring the Efficiency of Digital Communities: A Case Study. *Measuring the Efficiency of Digital Communities: A Case Study*, 95-101.

Sobaci, Z. (2010). What the Turkish parliamentary web site offers to citizens in terms of e-participation: A content analysis. *Information Polity, 15*(3), 227-241.

Stiglitz, J. E. (2002). Information and the Change in the Paradigm in Economics. *The American Economic Review, 92*(3), 460–501. doi:10.1257/00028280260136363

Stiglitz, J. E. (2003). On Liberty, the Right to Know, and Public Discourse: The Role. *Globalizing Rights: The Oxford Amnesty Lectures*, *1999*, 115.

Tapscott, D., Williams, A. D., & Herman, D. (2008). Government 2.0: Transforming government and governance for the twenty-first century. *New Paradigm, 1*.

The Global Economy. (2016). *Cameroon: Political stability*. Retrieved 02-07-2017, 2017, from http://www.theglobaleconomy.com/Cameroon/wb_political_stability/

Thompson, M. (2008). ICT and development studies: Towards development 2.0. *Journal of International Development*, *20*(6), 821–835. doi:10.1002/jid.1498

Transparency International. (2016). *Corruption Perceptions Index 2016*. Retrieved from https://www.transparency.org/country/CMR#

United Nations. (2016). *United nations e-government survey 2016: E-government in support of sustainable development*. Retrieved from https://publicadministration. un.org/egovkb/en-us/reports/un-e-government-survey-2016

Zukang, S. (2012). *E-Government Survey 2012: E-Government for the People*. United Nations Report.

Chapter 7
Networks for Cyberactivism and Their Implications for Policymaking in Brazil

Christiana Soares de Freitas
University of Brasilia, Brazil

Isabela Nascimento Ewerton
University of Brasilia, Brazil

ABSTRACT

Networks for cyberactivism have been developed in Brazil since the end of the 20th century. This chapter presents results of a three-year research about networks for digital political participation developed by civil society. The research analyzed 41 networks according to specific analytical categories to deepen the understanding about their potential to foster citizens' engagement in political initiatives and strengthen democracy. Several mechanisms that considerably stimulate a culture of political participation were clearly observed. Possibilities for political acting through those networks tend to narrow the gap between citizens' claims and government actions but that is not always the case. There is a lack of synergy between citizens' demands and strategic planning of public policies and other political outcomes. Some hypotheses are discussed to understand this context and reflect on the trends and challenges to digital democracy in the twenty-first century.

DOI: 10.4018/978-1-5225-5326-7.ch007

INTRODUCTION

Brazil has experienced three decades of uninterrupted democracy. That context fostered the birth of specific political conceptions and practices. The notorious crisis of representativeness in the country also contributed to the emergence of specific and alternative ways of political activism using information and communication technologies as powerful allies to generate more outreach and penetrability of the organized actions. Non-government citizen networks, mainly from civil society, mobilize internet resources to achieve political goals. Those resources enable projects and practices that tend to offer more possibilities for citizens to engage in political mobilization, potentially contributing to strengthen and deepen participatory democratic practices (Bonsón, Royo & Ratkai, 2015).

In the mentioned historical period government strategies were adopted to stimulate citizens´ participation in political processes through cyberspace (Freitas, 2016). Such strategies were adopted in digital governance practices implemented with the goal of deepening the relationship between public administration representatives and citizens by improving political mechanisms for participation. However, research results have shown that government initiatives tend to have a limited range fostering effective citizens´ participation through cyber interactive channels of communication. The initiatives tend to guarantee institutional stability to the organizations rather than effectively promote citizens´ engagement and legitimize democratic processes (Freitas, Fiuza & Queiroz, 2015).

Civil society also plays a strategic role in that political scenario. This chapter will present the results of a research that aimed at investigating the conditions created by non-government actors to legitimize participatory democratic practices through different strategies in cyberspace. The research mapped and analyzed non-government networks that developed digital platforms alongside other initiatives to stimulate political activism and cyberactivism.

Digital democratic initiatives are usually implemented by non-government and in some cases non-institutional actors organized in social movements and political actions. They reveal a political environment in which strategies to improve digital participatory democracy play a fundamental role. Digital democracy, in this sense, can be defined as

the process of using devices, apps, digital communication artifacts and technologies in general to supplement, reinforce or improve aspects of social and political practices – coming from the State or the citizens – in the benefit of the democratic substance of political communities. (Gomes, 2011, p. 27).

Some indicators were developed to comprehend the possibilities offered by digital platforms for citizens´ engagement. It was crucial to understand how those resources offer effective mechanisms for participation in political processes. The best example was the set of digital environments that promote collaborative production of actions, projects, programs, politics and laws. Seven analytical categories were outlined with their respective indicators to analyze the scenario: legal and normative institutionalization; coordination and resources; types of digital environment and strategies for the systematization of citizens´ demands; effects and implications of demands in formal political processes[1]; social capital; transparency and sustainability of the initiative.

This article presents the results of two analytical categories that are directly related to mechanisms developed to enable and stimulate digital democratic practices: the specific strategies for systematizing citizens´ demands in digital platforms as future outputs and possible implications of those demands in formal political processes. The research analyzed forty-one initiatives created and coordinated by non-government actors in Brazil for the period of three years. It also involved mapping thirty-seven initiatives of the federal and state governments in the country, which are discussed in other articles (Freitas et al., 2015).

THEORETICAL FRAMEWORK

Networks of contemporary societies transcend traditional boundaries and static conceptual divisions such as the notion of civil society. In the network society, practices, norms and identities are fluid and sometimes fragmented. Networks are understood as a web of relationships established among actors that work – collaboratively or not – to transform or maintain contexts, processes and practices. Networks are not restricted to an institutional space, but conform a dynamic set of interactions that can encompass diverse institutions and disperse individuals and groups not necessarily associated to an institutional context. Those networks – depending on their power, range, and legitimacy – tend to become transnational and to transcend jurisdictional frontiers and national conventions (Castells, 1996; Eisenstadt & Vincent, 1998; Wellman & Berkowitz, 1988; Wellman, Salaff & Gulia, 1996).

The network actors that structure and sustain digital environments for cyberactivism are diverse and can be considered part of the civil society but not exclusively. This research confirmed the same idea pointed out in previous studies. As said, there is an increasing difficulty to fix rigid frontiers between the State, market and civil society (Maia, 2011, p. 51). Instead, Maia considers the existence of a "hybrid terrain of power sharing and acting" where various interests, intentions and identities are intertwined. To make this scenario even more complex there is the increasing presence of transnational advocacy networks identified as fundamental actors defining political norms and practices in the beginning of the twenty-first century. Those networks can be defined as "transborder networks of activists distinguishable largely by the centrality of principled ideas or values in motivating their formation" (Mueller, 2013, p. 39).

Such principles are not necessarily present in government agendas. Some of the networks have as one of their principles not to establish any type of bond, connection or alliance with government representatives or agencies. According to Mueller,

transnational advocacy networks are linked to the concept of 'global civil society', which views international politics as driven not entirely by the security needs and self-interest of sovereign states, but also by internationally accepted norms and conceptions of the public good promoted by 'sovereignty-free' actors (Mueller, 2013, p. 39).

The basic goal of transnational advocacy networks is granting to powerless social groups the capacity to vocalize their demands in formal political processes within national and international contexts.By playing a fundamental role in countless actions, transnational advocacy networks tend to contribute to effective results that increase citizens´ engagement and improve political mechanisms of participation.

Theoretical references associated to the analysis of political processes enabling digital participatory democracy were fundamental to analyze the research results. Cyberactivism and their implications to the public sphere were analyzed according to principles of Science and Technology Studies (Freitas, 2016; Coleman, 2017; Coleman & Sampaio, 2016; Gomes, 2011; Silva, 2011). That theoretical framework centers its analysis in subjective mechanisms observed in collective and connective actions, often not institutionalized, related to representations that guide established practices which reveal social characteristics that would not be possible to grasp just through the analysis of formalized and institutionalized norms and practices (Hoffman, Katzenbach & Gollatz, 2014; Epstein, Katzenbach & Musiani, 2016). The concepts of *habitus* and *symbolic capital* were also essential to understand those specific mechanisms not perceived in institutional environments or formal political outcomes but in strategies and sometimes informal actions with significant political potential to promote changes (Bourdieu, 2011).

By allowing the convergence of different media formats, facilitating interactive and dialogic communication and offering spaces for freedom of expression and political opinions, the internet contributes to increase possibilities for political and collective action. As a result, individuals, networks, and organizations are progressively adopting specific methods of cooperation and collaborative production of content resulting in the production of commons (Freitas & Aranha, 2017; Silveira, 2017).

Political movements mobilizing these specific resources are usually developed as networks with a polycentric structure. When digital platforms are used independently from a hierarchical coordination distinct economic and political logics are observed (Coleman, 2017, p. 19). Actors responsible for this environment tend to focus on organizing without organizations, not relying on traditional leaderships (Bennett & Segerberg, 2013). Such process suggests new meanings of being politically engaged and characteristics that can indicate specific tendencies guiding citizens´engagement, political movements and democratic practices in Brazil.

Coleman highlights a fundamental tension related to the limits of connective action that is central for understanding the purpose of this article. On one hand, connective networks have significant penetration in social movements´ actions and attract the younger population because of their versatility, agility and independence from traditional organizations. They are able to coordinate decentralized, fluid, dispersed and polycentric networks of individuals and groups. On the other hand, their maintenance, sustainability and penetrability pose a challenge.

That challenge encompasses two different possibilities: it can provide the conditions to enable short term mobilizations or to generate a specific political scope for policy development in the long run. That aspect differentiates one cyber activist network from another. While most cyber activist networks provide spaces for complaints, few of them offer a long term project for citizens to engage in discussions that will lead to proposals for policies or law enforcement. That difference has been crucial for the analysis of the results here presented.

In democratic processes, inputs and outputs are usually results of political engagement. While inputs – as Coleman pointed out – are "the expression of political demands" in a broader sense, outputs "refer to the decisions and actions of political authorities: the policies that are implemented and the social effects that are realized" (Coleman, 2017, p. 21). Most importantly,

the democratic quality of outputs is best evaluated in terms of the extent to which they reflect public inputs. A political system that encourages public input into the policy process but ignores such input when it comes to producing outputs lacks democratic legitimacy (Coleman, 2017, p. 21).

To what extent do cyber activist networks in fact contribute to legitimate democracy in Brazil? This is the main inquiry of the research that has been carried out. As pointed out, one of the fundamental goals was to analyze the possibilities of different levels of interaction in the digital platforms. It was verified how those levels can restrict or enable the penetrability and range of citizens´ demands (inputs) in government instances responsible for decision-making processes and the formulation of government actions, projects or public policies (outputs).

METHODOLOGY

A website created by a research group at *Fundação Getúlio Vargas* (FGV/SP) was the first reference to map the networks responsible for the digital platforms (Cunha, Guise & Teixeira, 2015). Other networks – more or less directly related to the previous ones – were also identified. A third step of this mapping process was the verification of the existence and continuity of each platform. The result was forty-one active initiatives that constituted the research sample[2].

Virtual ethnography was essential for collecting secondary data (Hine, 2000; Segata, 2015). The gathered data included institutional documents related to their networks´ creation and constitution. Information about formal and informal rules, coordination, structuring, and functioning of the digital platforms were also collected. Each platform was observed through a period of ninety days to identify their dynamics and actions. Daily reports of activities were produced to understand the process of organizing citizens´ demands and the strategies used afterwards to maximize their political implications.

Primary data were obtained by semi-structured interviews conducted with coordinators of the initiatives that stood out as spaces for effective participation checked by their penetrability, range and innovative features. The explicit intention of the initiative to present a process of systematizing demands and its capacity of generating effective repercussions in formal political processes were the basic criteria applied to select coordinators of seven specific digital platforms.

The results of the research are presented in a perspective that points out the importance of communicational practices and technologies as determinant means of structuring and exercising power nowadays. The various modes of communication and manifestation of political willingness – promoted by digital environments – entail different possibilities of citizens´ engagement through spaces in which the creation and systematization of demands (inputs) are possible. Those spaces, however, vary significantly. Some are closer to offering possibilities of effectively transforming those demands into political actions and proposals that will be considered by government instances and may become outputs. It means that the design of a digital environment may favor – in various degrees – the transformation of inputs into outputs and may significantly interfere in future political scenarios.

Two main analytical categories were adopted to analyze the process of gathering and organizing citizens´ demands (inputs) in digital platforms and also to understand their influence in the elaboration of government actions, public policies and other possible outputs.

STRATEGIES TO PRODUCE INPUTS AND POSSIBLE OUTPUTS IN DIGITAL PLATFORMS FOR CYBERACTIVISM

Indicators were developed to evaluate the strategies used by each network fostering its digital platform. The research conducted by Silva was particularly important for the methodological framework here suggested even though its focus was on government initiatives. The author explores three possibilities of government digital platforms´ configuration.

The first one would be publicity, when there is the explicit intention of government instances to make public or transparent their conceptions, actions and practices. The main characteristic of this requirement is that it is a space for publicization with information generated from government organizations to citizens (G2C). The second possibility of configuration – responsivity – emphasizes a more deepened relationship between government representatives and citizens, conforming a dialogic communication. The State becomes more responsive to citizens´ demands. The last one – porosity – implies the possibility of intense citizens´ participation in decision-making processes (Silva, 2011, p. 137). In this analytical category, the set of demands generated by citizens (*inputs*) tends to be heard and incorporated into formal political processes thus becoming outputs.

Based on that theoretical framework, digital platforms developed by citizens to citizens (C2C) were analyzed to identify different levels of interaction that vary according to the mobilization strategies adopted. Depending on the strategies adopted they can collaborate – in a more or less intense way – to an effective citizen` participation in formal political processes (Coleman, 2017).

In the scope of publicity – or publicization – we identified initiatives in which citizens can publish or publicize complaints, opinions and reports. Those platforms can offer information to citizens, sometimes encouraging their engagement in several topics. They are also a means of collecting data, impressions and general information about a certain theme without promoting interaction. There is usually no feedback nor interaction related to what is posted by individuals and groups. Communication is unidirectional and not related to an action plan or any other strategy to change the unwanted scenario. However, outputs can be an unpredictable result of the initiative´s existence.

In the responsivity level there are digital environments where citizens can communicate with public authorities and the published content can become concrete action plans. In those spaces citizens are usually encouraged to express their opinions and demands. Dialogic communication is observed but the possibilities for interaction are limited. There is no explicit intention of coproducing a possible output such as proposals for a draft bill or a public policy. Coordinators of the initiatives implement campaigns to solve specific problems. Projects and actions linked to mobilizations are developed from citizens´ demands (inputs) without necessarily having confirmed effects in political formal processes.

A few initiatives that promote political actions were identified in the responsivity level. Usually focused on a specific topic or fact, they do not show the explicit intention of being a space for collaborative production of proposals to transform the political scenario in the long term. There is no deliberate action or strategy to stimulate citizens to being part of a broader policymaking process even though that could eventually happen. Nevertheless, there is an effort from coordinators to provide the ones that join the networks with information about the consequences of their cyber activist practices.

One example is the platform *Votenaweb* – a digital platform developed to monitor draft bills in progress in the Brazilian Parliament. Citizens can vote for or against a bill. That creates a map of acceptance and rejection of each proposal that can be very relevant for a member of the Parliament. Draft bills are publicized and open for public scrutiny and control. Besides, citizens can also read all the proposals and send messages to the members of Parliament. In this digital environment it is possible to see clearly a feedback of citizens´ actions and demands.

The third possibility – designated as porosity – is related to the digital platforms´ configuration that enables the penetrability of citizens´ demands in policymaking processes. In those spaces citizens effectively join processes destined to elaborate collaboratively a draft bill, a specific political action, a political program or a public policy. The explicit intention of the initiative is to gather inputs and transform them into outputs in formal political processes. The networks that create those spaces offer a wide range of possibilities for engagement and empowerment. Citizens feel as part of a web that truly offers a means of consolidating participatory democratic practices. Citizens´ empowerment happens because there is the

transfer of influence, control, proposition and policy formulation that happens based on the desire of citizens; there are mobilizing actions that use technological tools, means of mass communication and also the development of offline actions such as awareness campaigns (Araújo, Penteado & Santos, 2015, p.1607).

Those platforms offer expanded possibilities for citizens to interfere in political decision-making processes. Their main characteristic is to foster a clearly defined space for collaborative production of proposals that can become outputs in formal political processes. It is also possible to find spaces to express complaints and start a specific protest or claim. So in the digital platforms that promote effective penetrability of citizens´ demands there are also spaces for other political activities.

Cidade Democrática is an initiative that represents this type of digital platform. It offers the possibility of exposing a problem, proposing solutions for it and debating them with others that join the network. The initiative organizes contests to give more visibility to the proposals considered to be more interesting and more related to the majority's will. There are several different spaces to interact and propose actions and policies.

Results of the conducted research show that the majority aims at creating environments to allow citizens to post complaints, claims and reports. Thus the publicity type of configuration represents 61% of the initiatives studied. The ones that develop spaces where there is a clear interaction with citizens' demands – stimulating responsivity and dialogic communication – represent 22% of the total[3]. Digital platforms aiming at developing porosity environments – where inputs are deliberately gathered to become part of policymaking processes – are 17% of the studied sample[4].

REPERCUSSIONS OF DEMANDS IN FORMAL POLITICAL PROCESSES

The other central analytical category aimed at identifying the implications of citizens' demands after they were systematized in the digital platforms. A research carried out by Araújo, Penteado and Santos (2015) has also been important for the elaboration of this methodological framework. The authors analyzed digital platforms coordinated by several organizations in São Paulo. The main goal of the research was to understand how web activism influences the cycle of public policy development. In other words, the goal was to understand "how civil society is making use of internet resources to promote citizens' participation and to transform the process of public policy development" (Araújo, Penteado & Santos, 2015, p. 1606).

In order to analyze the relation between policy development and cyber activism the authors developed a methodological tool called Index for Political Participation and Influence (IPPI). The index was built in five levels. The focal point of this work will be on the ones related to mobilization strategies and the implications of citizens' actions for public policies (Araújo et al., 2015, p. 1607).

A different perspective concerning the concept of public policy development led this research to a distinct approach. According to our perspective, the traditional notion that establishes a cycle of public policy development is not an efficient analytical tool. Policymaking processes are not developed in a sequential and ordered way as it is often introduced by that traditional theoretical conception. Authors such as Surel and Muller (2012) state that the traditional approach can mask issues and phenomena that are not necessarily associated to each stage of the mentioned cycle

(Surel & Muller, 2002). In this sense non-linear dynamics responsible for public policies´ constitution could be left out of the traditional analysis and that could restrict studies´ reach and depth (Lindblom, 1980).

That non-linear perspective suggests what was later developed by further science and technology studies: the premise that non-institutionalized, subjective and informal mechanisms also shape practices and norms of political and social reality. Those elements are deeply responsible for social dynamics, their characteristics and configurations (Epstein et al., 2016). Also the notion of outputs here adopted offers a broader analytical tool that allows the analysis of the whole set of implications of cyber political mobilizations. In this sense the notion of outputs can encompass several other political results such as draft bills and localized government actions.

The proposals analyzed were classified into two categories to understand the implications of citizens' demands after being posted and systematized as specific proposals in digital platforms. The first category identified the proposals that were not considered as outputs. The second one identified the proposals incorporated into political processes as outputs or that offered data for future outputs. Figure 1 summarizes the methodological tools applied to analyze the studied networks and their digital platforms.

The results reveal the capacity of each initiative to promote effective and legitimate participatory democratic practices. The implications of citizens´ demands were analyzed based on the monitoring of the proposals presented by the networks in order to verify the legitimacy of those democratic practices. Were inputs really being considered as outputs by government agencies or as part of formal political processes?

From the forty-one digital platforms analyzed nine of them presented some sort of output. Among those nine there were six initiatives configured according to the porosity type. It means that the platforms were already built with the explicit intention of producing outputs for formal political processes. It was observed that most of those environments – destined to formulate an action, a public policy or a draft bill – tend to generate outputs based on citizens´ demands[5].

The digital platforms that were not created with that explicit intention can also produce outputs as an unpredictable effect. Two initiatives at the responsivity level[6] and one at the publicity dimension[7] produced outputs by establishing partnerships and offering their data to public administration. One example is the digital platform *Chega de Fiu Fiu*. Even though its initial goals were not directly related to the elaboration of outputs, *Chega de Fiu Fiu* ended up doing that. The initiative was created by the NGO *Olga* to collect testimonials and statements from women victims of sexual harassment. Interesting to note that the platform works with crowdsourcing strategies. All data are inserted by the users´ platform.

Figure 1. Analytical categories and indicators

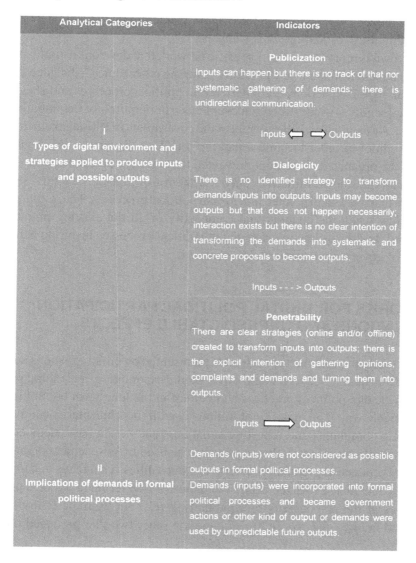

The Public Ministry of São Paulo established a partnership with the NGO *Olga* responsible for its creation. The idea was to systematize data collected through the digital platform and produce awareness campaigns for the population involved with sexual harassment against women. So the initiative now generates clear repercussions in formal political processes without that being established in its beginning.

One network responsible for the production of several outputs was *Nossas*. It is a non-profit association characterized as a laboratory for activism and mobilization projects. The association coordinates a network of networks composed by different groups of citizens in each town of the country that has already joined the movement called "our cities" or *Rede Nossas Cidades*.

Each town is represented by its specific network that develops a digital platform. In the digital environment they publicize – among other topics – the goals achieved by several organized actions that interfered in political processes and changed that particular locality. Twenty-three achievements – or outputs – of the initiatives were identified. An example was the attempt of the government of Rio de Janeiro to destroy a public school in order to build a parking lot. With the support of thousands of citizens, the organized movement prevented the action to be carried out.

From all the studied initiatives only 9 of them – or 22% of the total – submitted proposals that were incorporated into formal political processes. The results obtained are still few when the quantity and complexity of all the existing initiatives are considered. Even so some interference in political processes inspiring actions and projects of government agencies was observed.

NETWORKS FOR DIGITAL POLITICAL PARTICIPATION: IMPLICATIONS AND UNPREDICTABLE EFFECTS

It is interesting to point out that demands represented by broad questions and topics – such as transparency, social control over public expenditure or electoral processes – tend to change political practices and culture in the long term but not in a clear and verifiable way. The majority of initiatives with this characteristic aims only at publicizing complaints and reporting situations that violate basic democratic and human rights. Nevertheless, their results can be used by government organizations since they produce unpredictable effects or externalities. That tends to happen with initiatives not created with the explicit intention of interfering in political processes – the ones at the responsivity and publicity levels. An example is the initiative mentioned before – *Chega de Fiu Fiu* and the other two that produced outputs – *Mapa do Acolhimento* e *A Voz do Cidadão*.

Therefore, the initiatives that were not created with the intention of producing outputs may contribute to the elaboration of new government actions or public policies in the long term. They can also generate unpredictable effects and collaborate to the emergence of alternative political practices and specific symbolic capital. In some cases, the digital platforms themselves can be considered as a political outcome or a political intervention.

Conceptions and practices of citizens involved with the creation and continuity of the analyzed networks point out the tendency of expanding possible ways of political actions and mobilizations. The diversity of possibilities are developed in a context characterized by the fragmentation of decision-making processes; the loss of centrality of traditional political institutions; and the reconfiguration and restructuring of democratic control practices.

Other common features conform the networks built from citizens to citizens. One of them is the strategy observed of creating specific digital tools to organize their political acts. The use of those tools provides means of mobilizing citizens in more direct ways. *Nossas*, for instance, uses two digital tools that effectively collaborate to enable the penetrability of citizens´ demands. The first one is called *Panela de Pressão*. It provides citizens with the possibility of "creating their own campaigns and mobilizing supporters of their causes to directly apply political pressure to decision makers (through emails and messages in social networks)[8]". Another platform developed by the network is called *Legislando*. The tool allows citizens to post proposals of draft bills and to suggest changes in other proposals posted by citizens. In the platform it is also possible for a member of Parliament to adopt a proposed bill and try to transform it into law. After some negotiations, *Nossas* decided to adopt another platform and abandon *Legislando*. They started using the app *Mudamos* which has the same goals of the former initiative.

Mudamos was launched in 2014 by researchers of the Institute of Technology and Society (ITS) in Rio de Janeiro. The initiative also received the Google Impact Challenge Award in 2016 and is financially supported exclusively by those resources. An interesting trend observed is the clustering of successful networks. That tends to strengthen even more their initiatives and the political movement usually related to a specific cause. The gathering helps to create favorable conditions for the sustainability and continuity of these networks – a major challenge for all of them.

The networks studied tend to be totally independent from government organizations. They sustain their actions only by *crowdfunding* supported by citizens and non-government organizations. Joining political parties or traditional organizations is not a goal for the networks´ cyber activists. This characteristic suggests a particular conception of doing politics implemented through specific ways of acting on movements and campaigns in Brazil nowadays.

Also observed as a characteristic of the studied networks was the activists´ perception related to their capacity to change. According to that perspective, political change is not seen as something to be planned and implemented in the future by abstract entities such as government agencies but it must happen through citizens´ activism and political engagement.

The constant negotiation with all citizens involved in political proposals is an example of that perspective. Citizens are always invited to join the whole process of political mobilization – from the initial proposal to the final decision with representatives. There is a clear process of constant negotiation established to define strategies and plans of action. One of the coordinators who were interviewed explained a recent negotiation that took place in the state of Rio Grande do Sul. The founder of *Minha Porto Alegre* explained how that dynamics usually works:

citizens are the main political player; we act in partnership with other groups and associations. We are constantly consulting them. For example, we are trying to build an office in order that all the NGOs / Aids can work in a common place. So we define strategies with the involved actors; we join the commission of health that takes care of this issue and also the mortality committee; we had a hearing with the Secretary of Health. We made a proposal, he made a counter proposal and now we will take that to the community (groups and associations) to decide whether they accept it or not. Because it´s their protagonism. The decisions have to be their decisions. The idea is to make people feel that they are the major players that conduct the city´s paths (C. Soares, personal communication, July 24, 2017).

Some activists do volunteer work. When asked about why one of the coordinators was working voluntarily for the network, she told us that she herself couldn´t understand or explain. In her statement there is a clear sense of civic duty conducing her practices:

you know... for me it is a natural thing... so natural that I cannot do differently any more... I cannot not do what I do... after realizing that I could do something to change my city... I can – we can – promote micro-revolutions, you know... I can do small things that cause impacts on a place... (A. Helena, personal communication, July 26, 2017).

Besides the sense of civic duty there is also the acquisition of power and recognition by the individual involved in those political arrangements. Even though the sense of civic duty can be observed, the symbolic capital acquired with the conducted activities also guides and motivates the activists´ practices.

Another characteristic pointed out by the research results was the activists´ perception of misrepresentation associated to the players of the formal political system. That tends to produce a certain detachment of political activists´ practices from the formal political processes. On the one hand, this scenario can reveal innovative practices that enable the production of democratic actions and conceptions that appear as completely different and revolutionary. On the other hand, it can limit the reach of inputs from citizens thus hindering the possibilities of promoting effective change by turning those inputs into projects, programs and actions (outputs) in the formal political scenario. Reinforcing the idea presented earlier, the willingness of political activists to negotiate with this formal system is fundamental for the effectiveness and repercussions of their actions and proposals (Castells, 2013).

Networks for cyberactivism tend to be non-partisan – maybe as a result of the crisis of representativeness experienced not only in Brazil but in all Latin America. Therefore, the networks cannot receive financial or political support from government organizations, public companies or political parties. Their main support comes from crowdfunding strategies – citizens´ and other non-governmental organizations´ donations. This principle is seen as fundamental to guarantee the legitimacy of their way of exercising social and political control.

As an implication of this crisis most networks stablish a clear differentiation between the concept of "power" – associated to political and government representatives – and the concept of "strength" – that results from social and political movements organized by citizens. Power, according to what the network disseminates, is centralizing, concentrated and privatizing. That is why, according to their conception, it only exists if badly distributed. Power is represented by institutions, political parties, labor unions, members of Parliament, presidents and the militaries. Power is seen as built by "structures that exist to dominate individuals, limiting their potential to create, recreate and transform (M. Isabel, personal communication, July 25, 2017).

The term "strength", on the other hand, suggests fluidity, distribution and decentralization. Strength is represented by mobilized and engaged citizens that *create and share commons, that make institutions internalize continuous changes faced by society; strength only survives in this shared place, acting for collective solutions to social and political problems (M. Isabel, personal communication, July 25, 2017).*

Cyberactivism plays a major role in forming that singular conception of political action nowadays. It is important to highlight that the protests and mobilizations that tend to really influence and change political processes – by contributing to the enforcement of democratic practices and enabling outputs – are organized offline as well. Such conclusion was also reached in the research conducted by Araújo, Penteado and Santos – in 2013 – based on the analysis of the initiatives for cyberactivism developed by civil society in the city of São Paulo (Araújo et al., 2015).

Digital environments for political activism tend to be under-explored by networks. This is notorious in spaces created by some very active networks. They may have great influence in political processes but they do not encourage that such influence be materialized in actions, programs, projects, laws or public policies for the coproduction of outputs in their digital environments.

Some challenges tend to threaten the continuity and sustainability of the networks and their initiatives. Some of them are related to unequal distribution of gender-based power; prejudice against the activists' age (usually between 20 and 25); lack of a regular financial support, which hinders planning in the long term and threatens the stability of goals´ and the implementations of actions. The occasional absence of financial remuneration for activists and coordinators of the networks also tends to create instability and high turnover of coordinators and other similar participants who play important roles in the networks.

The last characteristic observed is the tendency to use crowdsourcing strategies to develop and maintain the digital platforms. The dynamic interaction between actors brings citizens´ participation as one of the main characteristics of the social and political arrangements observed nowadays. Collaborative production of political actions is increasingly perceived as a means of generating public value and guaranteeing legitimacy to democratic processes. The possibility of directly engaging in the coproduction of a specific product or proposal can alter political processes and consolidate a tendency of implementing crowdsourcing practices in government and non-government networks. Practices are not limited to cooperative production to raise material resources – observed in crowdfunding practices – but also to acquire immaterial resources such as knowledge and information to develop proposals, content or artifacts (Freitas & Aranha, 2017).

Crowdsourcing – or the process of coproduction of ideas, content and artifacts – is significantly used nowadays as a means of organizing movements, political actions, and proposals. Internet is the main channel to enable that practice. It implies strategies of gathering information or other material or immaterial resources that come from an undefined number of individuals who aim at achieving specific goals or implementing a certain project. There is usually an open call for everyone interested in joining the network – online or not. Crowdsourcing is a mechanism to gather resources that allows coordinated actions among individuals, organizations and networks. By being able to generate public value in the most diverse ways, crowdsourcing is becoming a very common practice in the public sphere.

Public administration has been using such strategy frequently to formulate public policies, laws and other political outputs. It has been regarded as an efficient means of improving public management. The Finnish parliament, for instance, issued a document in 2012 to determine the best practices of crowdsourcing in the world and to carry out a strategic plan for action. Some examples of public administration´s use of that strategy are the implementation of the participatory budget in Canada and the constitutional reform in Iceland (Aitamurto, 2012; Cepik & Canabarro, 2014; Pinho, 2008).

Eighteen (44%) of the forty-one digital platforms adopt crowdsourcing as a strategy to build their database. As seen, there are several goals that guide those initiatives. They can be designed to report violence against women or bad conditions of public transport; to monitor parliamentary activities, electoral processes or public expenditures.

Although government agencies may eventually use the collected information to formulate and implement policies or actions, public administration lacks long term well-structured strategies to use them. The digital platforms provide politicians and public administrators with accurate and updated information directly related to citizens' demands. If well applied by public administration those database may contribute to increase efficiency of administration management and policymaking processes. Besides they may bring government actions closer to citizens' demands thus enhancing and amplifying legitimate democratic processes in Brazil.

CONCLUSION

The implications of cyberactivism can be understood as expressions of a historical period in which participatory democratic practices were highly stimulated in Brazil. Possibilities of improving the design of those practices were also observed. Even though only a few initiatives aim at enabling an effective citizens´ engagement, the existence of a significant number of sustainable networks reveals the trend to consolidate and expand the arena for political action and democratic deliberation.

It was observed that even the initiatives that are not explicitly designed to produce outputs are fundamental to strengthen citizenship by allowing political participation and awareness. In this sense, transformation means not only influencing formal political processes but also changing – in a broader sense – social and political mechanisms. Those digital platforms – not created to interfere directly in formal political processes – can eventually produce unpredictable effects especially because of the data produced which can be used to elaborate several outputs. Increasing the use of those outputs can also increase the legitimacy of democratic processes in Brazil.

Future research is necessary to deepen the analyses related to the outputs produced by each network studied. A typology will be developed to identify and explore possible outputs. That could support government agencies on the development of strategies for data gathering which could in turn collaborate for the elaboration of public policies and other more efficient outputs better coordinated with citizens´ demands.

The possibilities for participatory democratic practices studied can promote an increase in the diversity of actors engaged in public discussions. They can foster the development of a wide range of possibilities for minorities´ expectations to be considered and represented in the formal political system. Networks for cyberactivism – created from citizens to citizens – tend to consolidate and reinforce a democratic society. However, that goal is not always accomplished. As it was discussed here, those initiatives are instruments that can either legitimate democratic practices or not.

The expansion of those cyber activist networks – as well as the consolidation of other mechanisms of political participation – were the result of decades of democracy in the country. The continuity of the process encouraging those mechanisms will depend on the future political scenario which will guide the strategies to be adopted.

The networks for cyberactivism tend to consolidate and strengthen democratic inclusive practices and encourage citizens towards a more effective participation in policymaking processes. The larger the penetration of social demands in the formal political spectrum the greater are the chances of securing that those initiatives effectively become legitimate instruments fostering democratic practices in Brazil.

ACKNOWLEDGMENT

This research was supported by the Conselho Nacional de Desenvolvimento Científico e Tecnológico – CNPq, Brazil (grant number 456.347-2014-3).

REFERENCES

Aitamurto, T. (2012). Crowdsourcing for Democracy: A New Era in Policy-Making. *Publications of the Committee for the Future, Parliament of Finland*. Available at: https://papers.ssrn.com/sol3/papers.cfm?abstract_id=2716771

Araújo, R., Penteado, C., & Santos, M. (2015, December). Democracia Digital e Experiências de e-Participação: Webativismo e políticas públicas. *Historia, Ciencias, Saude--Manguinhos, 22*(supl.), 1597–1619. doi:10.1590/S0104-59702015000500004 PMID:26785869

Bennett, W., & Segerberg, A. (2013). *The logic of Connective Action: Digital Media and the Personalization of Contentious Politics*. Cambridge, UK: Cambridge University Press. doi:10.1017/CBO9781139198752

Bonsón, E., Royo, S., & Ratkai, M. (2015). Citizens' engagement on local governments' Facebook sites. An empirical analysis: The impact of different media and content types. *Western Europe Government Information Quarterly, 32*(1), 52-62.

Bourdieu, P. (2011). O campo político. *Revista Brasileira de Ciência Política, Brasília, 2011*(5). 10.1590/S0103-33522011000100008

E. Brousseau, M. Marzouki, & C. Méadel (Eds.). (2012). *Governance, regulations, and powers on the Internet*. Cambridge, UK: Cambridge University Press. doi:10.1017/CBO9781139004145

Castells, M. (1996). *The Rise of the Network Society, The Information Age: Economy, Society and Culture* (Vol. I). Malden, MA: Blackwell.

Castells, M. (2013). *Redes de Indignação e Esperança: Movimentos sociais na era da Internet*. Rio de Janeiro: Zahar.

Cepik, M., & Canabarro, D. (Eds.). (2010). *Governança de TI: transformando a Administração Pública no Brasil Rio Grande do Sul: CEGOV/UFRGS*. Retrieved from http://www.lume.ufrgs.br/bitstream/handle/10183/78940/000764826. pdf?sequence=1

Coleman, S. (2017). *Can the Internet Strengthen Democracy?* Cambridge, UK: Polity Press.

Coleman, S., & Sampaio, R. (2016). Sustaining a democratic innovation: A study of three e-participatory budgets in Belo Horizonte. *Information Communication and Society*, *20*, 1–16.

Eisenstadt, M., & Vincent, T. (1998). *The Knowledge Web*. Stylus Publishing Inc.

Epstein, D.; Katzenbach, C. & Musiani, F. (2016). Editorial – Doing internet governance: how science and technology studies inform the study of internet governance. *Internet Policy Review*.

Freitas, C. (2016). Sociotechnical and Political Processes shaping Digital Democracy in Brazil: the case of the project e-Democracia In Inovação, Governança Digital e Políticas Públicas: conquistas e desafios para a democracia. Belo Horizonte: Arraes Editores.

Freitas, C., & Aranha, M. (2017). Commons como Motor de Inovação nas Sociedades Contemporâneas. In *Proceedings of Communication and Policy Research Latin America Conference*. CPRLatam.

Freitas, C., Fiuza, F., & Queiroz, F. (2015). Os Desafios ao Desenvolvimento de um Ambiente para Participação Política Digital: O Caso de uma Comunidade Virtual Legislativa do Projeto e-Democracia no Brasil. *Organizações & Sociedade*, *22*(75), 639–657. doi:10.1590/1984-9230759

Gomes, W. (2011). *90 anos de Comunicação e Política* (Vol. 9). Salvador: Contemporânea.

Hine, C. (2000). *Virtual Ethnography*. London: Sage Publications. doi:10.4135/9780857020277

Hofmann, J., Katzenbach, C., & Gollatz, K. (2014) *Between Coordination and Regulation: Conceptualizing Governance in Internet Governance*. HIIG Discussion Paper Series, Berlim, n. 2014-04.

Keck, M., & Sikkink, K. (1998). *Activists beyond Borders: Advocacy Networks in International Politics*. New York: Cornell University Press.

Lindblom, C. (1980). *The policy making process*. Prentice-Hall Foundations of Modem Political Science Series.

Maia, R. (2011). Internet e esfera civil: limites e alcances da participação política. In R. Maia (Ed.), *Internet e Participação Política no Brasil*. Porto Alegre: Editora Sulina.

Mueller, M. (2013). *Networks and States: the global politics of internet governance*. MIT Press.

Musiani, F. (2015). *Nais sans géants: architecture décentralisée et services Internet* (2nd ed.). Paris: Presses des Mines. doi:10.4000/books.pressesmines.1853

Pinho, J. A. G. (2008). Investigando portais de governo eletrônico de estados no Brasil: Muita tecnologia, pouca democracia. *RAP – Revista de Administração Pública, 42*(03), 471–493. doi:10.1590/S0034-76122008000300003

Segata, J. O. (2015). Ciberespaço, a etnografia e algumas caixas pretas. *Revista Z Cultural, 1*, 5–12.

Silva, S. (2011). Exigências Democráticas e dimensões analíticas para a interface digital do Estado. In *Internet e Participação Política no Brasil*. Porto Alegre: Editora Sulina.

Silveira, S. A. (2017). Tudo sobre tod@s. Redes digitais, privacidade e venda de dados pessoais.

Surel, P., & Muller, Y. (2002). *A Análise das Políticas Públicas*. Pelotas: Editora da Universidade Católica de Pelotas.

Viana, A. (1996). Abordagens metodológicas em Políticas Públicas. *Revista de Administração Pública*.

B. Wellman, & S. Berkowitz (Eds.). (1998). *Social structures: A network approach*. Cambridge, UK: Cambridge University Press.

Wellman, B., Salaff, J., & Gulia, M. (1996). Computer Networks as Social Networks. *Annual Review of Sociology*, (22), 211–238.

ENDNOTES

[1]   By formal political processes we understand the set of mechanisms responsible for the processes of formulating, implementing and evaluating politics in a broader sense. In this set there would be representatives of the Executive, Legislative and Judiciary Branches: legislators, executors, administrative staff and judges (Viana, 1996, p. 15).

[2]   The forty-one initiatives studied are: Adote um Distrital; Adote um vereador (SP); Atlas Político; A voz do Cidadão; Cansei de Ser Sardinha; Chega de Aperto; Chega de Fiu Fiu; Cidade Democrática; Colab.re; CTRL+X; Cuidando do meu Bairro; De Olho nas Emendas; De onde vem a água?; Escola de Dados; Escola que Queremos; Eu Voto Distrital; Ficha Limpa; Gastos Abertos; Lixo Político; Mapa do Acolhimento; Meu Município; Mobilize Brasil; Mudamos; Nossas Cidades; Onde fui Roubado; Orçamento ao seu Alcance; Para onde foi o meu dinheiro?; Política.me; Politize; Radar Parlamentar; Ranking Políticos; Rede Nossa São Paulo; Retrato da Violência Contra a Mulher no Rio Grande do Sul; Serenata de Amor; Sitransp-DF; Truco; Vamos Mudar; Você Fiscal; Vote na Web; Voto Legal; Voto x Veto.

[3]   Digital platforms considered at the responsivity level were A Voz do Cidadão; Adote um Vereador SP; Cuidando do meu Bairro; #EuVotoDistrital; Escola de Dados; Mapa do Acolhimento; Mobilize Brasil; Politica.me; Vote na Web.

[4]   Digital platforms considered at the porosity level were Colab.re; Cidade Democrática; Gastos Abertos; Rede Nossas; Mudamos; Rede Nossa São Paulo; Vamos Mudar.

[5]   The six platforms were Colab.re; Cidade Democrática; Gastos Abertos; Mudamos; Nossas; Rede Nossa SP.

[6]   The digital platforms were A voz do Cidadão e o Mapa do Acolhimento.

[7]   The one mentioned here is Chega de Fiu Fiu.

[8]   Information available at: https://www.facebook.com/meurio/photos/a.459201 504112427.108939.241897672509479/632769456755630/?type=3. Accessed on September 25, 2017.

Chapter 8
Building Performance Competencies in Open Government:
Perspectives From the Philippines

Sherwin E. Ona
De La Salle University, Philippines

Ma. Beth S. Concepcion
De La Salle University, Philippines

ABSTRACT

Open government initiatives around the world have encouraged governments to be more transparent and accessible while its partners have found new venues to further participate and collaborate. However, realities on the ground have begun to show the complexities of openness, raising questions on how these initiatives could be sustained. In the Philippines, most of the open government-open government data (OG-OGD) programs are considered top-down. This means that almost all of the activities are initiated by the national government and are often funded by multilateral agencies such as the World Bank. However, due to the changes in political priorities, the future of these programs remains uncertain. Current experiences further highlight the importance of institutionalization as one of the ingredients to sustain these initiatives; thus, the authors believe that building capacities play an important part in such an endeavor. As such, this chapter presents an initial set of OG-OGD performance competencies for local government executives and their civil society partners.

DOI: 10.4018/978-1-5225-5326-7.ch008

INTRODUCTION

Opening government to greater participation and scrutiny has resulted to various opportunities and challenges. As a practice, open government has cleared the way for greater transparency and access to public transactions, thus resulting to more participation among governance stakeholders. While as an advocacy, open government has increased the clamor for governments to do more. Civil society organizations (CSOs) and citizens alike have demanded for a more proactive approach. Veering away from the usual "reactive practices" of openness, this approach highlights the importance of improving the ability of non-government actors to source, use, re-use and share data sets. Furthermore, as part of open government efforts, social media often regarded as a popular venue in pushing-pulling information and feedback from constituents. However, due to its volume and the anonymity of users, this bridging capacity of social media has often caused a dilemma among government decision makers as well as their partners and constituents regarding the reliability and accuracy of feedback. Indeed, these events can be seen as part of an ongoing shift from a regime of transparency, access to that of data intelligence, collaboration, and innovation.

In developing countries, open government-open government data (OG-OGD) initially enjoyed a certain novelty, but political and organizational realities are now showing the inadequacies of reactive approaches. Questions on its tangible benefits and long-term outcomes continue to be a controversial topic. While concerns regarding implementation and sustainability beyond political administrations remain a significant issue. Furthermore, another facet of OG-OGD enigma is the need to improve capacities. Developing human capacities on OG-OGD for data providers and users is recognized as one of the important facets of OG-OGD adoption. Moreover, building capacities at all organizational levels guarantee the ability to properly use and ensure the quality of data sets. Enhanced appreciation of OG-OGD principles also ensure the integration to the current freedom of information/right to information regimes and even to national development initiatives.

In this chapter, the authors put forward the idea of developing an OG-OGD competency matrix that can be used in developing capacity building programs. Competency-based training programs are anchored on the identification of the knowledge, skills, attitudes and values (KSAVs) that are necessary to accomplish a task. By integrating the KSAVs in the training design, these programs are seen as more responsive to organizational needs, promotes professional development and are cost effective in the long run. Competency-based programs veer away from the usual training for the sake of training approach by providing a set of performance criteria and connects these general competencies that are relevant to an organization.

As for this chapter, the first part presents an overview of the prevailing literature on OG-OGD, highlighting the need for its institutionalization and the role of building capacities. The discussion further provides a glimpse of the adoption challenges in developing countries and then examining the current implementation of OG-OGD in the Philippines. This will be followed by a brief presentation of the research design of the chapter and the discussion of results. Lastly, the chapter will provide recommendations on how OG-OGD programs can be sustained.

BACKGROUND OF THE STUDY

The practice of open government (OG) has led to new challenges and opportunities. For one, its discourse present as a product of an evolution in governance and even in democracy. Often seen as a governance philosophy, proponents of OG see it as embracing collaborative relationships, promoting transparency and use of ICTs. Interactions between the governors and the governed are characterized as having meaning access to public data/information, the presence of venues in which citizens can participate in decision-making thus allowing meaningful oversight on the functions of government (Lathrop and Ruma, 2010). As an innovative strategy, OG is presented as a set of practices that allows the free movement of information from government to multiple channels, thus increasing transparency and accountability at all levels (Karamagioli et al., 2014). Tracing its roots from the early traditions of freedom of information to its current adaptation in new public management and good governance, its proponents argue that it is a bit more than the usual. By highlighting the power of open government data (OGD), OG provides an ideal platform that can promote collaboration, transparency and participation. It can result to smarter decision-making due to the increased citizen involvement in public policy development and the implementation of programs (Trivellato, Boselli, & Cavenago, 2014). Furthermore, OG-OGD is seen as a proactive approach in governance, stressing the need for data management and the use of new technologies to achieve innovation in governance and even proposing benefits to the economy in general (Halonen, 2012).

However, numerous challenges abound regarding its implementation. For instance, the public sector continues to grapple with problems concerning policies and capacities which in turn limits its ability to share government data and address the demands of its citizens. In addition, the creation of venues (or ecosystems) that can enable unhampered access and re-use of data that provides value-added results to stakeholders remains a pressing concern (Yang, Lo, Wang, & Shiang, 2013). These problems are further highlighted in developing countries, where early OG-OGD adaptors are plagued with political, resource and human capacity challenges. On top of this, numerous barriers exist that inhibit the tapping of its full potential.

Zuiderwijk, Janssen, Choenni, Meijer, and Alibaks (2012) cite what they term as social-technical impediments. While Trivellato et al. (2014) cite issues on granularity, choices of data to be published, and technical issues on format, accessibility and quality as barriers to OGD use and adoption. Referring what they termed as data skills, their work highlighted the need to address the concerns on access, use and storage of data. On a related note, Janssen, Charalabidis, and Zuiderwijk (2012) mentioned the inability to use of data, its questionable quality and the willingness of owners to release data as obstacles for realizing the objectives of OG-OGD.

Challenges in Developing Countries: Defining the Problem

A closer look at the experiences of developing countries magnifies these challenges. OG-OGD practices are often linked to two main goals, namely: (1) good governance-governance reform and (2) national development. The first goal is usually reflected in national and local initiatives related to transparency, access and anti-corruption programs. While OG-OGD initiatives are often related to national development through programs that support inclusiveness goals. These goals are commonly reflected in the following: a) equitable access to opportunities; b) promote participation of all sectors, especially the marginalized and c) ensure that the divisions caused by existing socioeconomic and political factors are avoided or eliminated (Heckmann, 2011; Davies & Bawa, 2012).

In the 2013 study conducted by the Open Data in Developing Countries (ODDC) research network showed the serious gaps on human capacities among others. Focusing on this issue, Mejabi, Azeez, Adedoyin, and Oloyede (2015) cite the lack of appreciation of OG-OGD can be traced to the lack of basic orientation on the subject matter. The study also points to the inability of top government officials in Nigeria to adopt OG-OGD and further stressed the need to build capacities. In the Philippines, Ona, Hecita, and Ulit (2014) uncovered the existence of health datasets and its use in decision-making concerning community health (e.g. Visualization, summary, etc.). Although its use is still limited due to the inability of these communities to scale up and replicate their practices. Moreover, in relation to local government, Canares, de Guia, Narca, and Arawiran (2014) point to the intent of the national government to provide access to OGD, but lacks the capacity building component to ensure that local stakeholders are able to adopt and sustain its implementation.

In summary, these challenges can be traced to capacity-related issues being experienced from both the demand and supply sides of the OGD equation. On the demand side, government's top down approach to OGD is often characterized as a convenient approach to ensure adherence to trends rather than embracing it as part of a governance philosophy or strategy. Moreover, numerous OGD programs in developing countries also lacks the needed policy base to guarantee its institutionalization. As for the supply side, there is a clear need to empower the users of open data. Empowering means that both sides must search for ways to go beyond transparency and accountability towards building a relationship that promotes participation and collaboration.

In this chapter, the authors argue that building capacities based on competencies is one of the effective ways of mainstreaming OG-OGD in public institutions. This would allow participants and advocates to adopt OG-OGD practices and enable them to link these techniques to existing good governance/bureaucratic reform initiatives.

Building Human Capacities: What Do We Mean?

Viewing human capacity on a conceptual level, OG-OGD is seen as being mired in complexity. Key issues pertaining to capacity building are multi-faceted and associated with other concerns. A common theme in the prevailing literature implies the need to underscore the importance of people and the use of open data. On establishing its value, Reilly and Smith (2013) stressed the need to focus on people and their ability to take advantage of openness as the overarching challenge to OG-OGD while at the onset mechanisms on how to ensure effective use of open datasets must be identified (Gurstein, 2011). Another persistent theme in the prevailing discourse is the need to look at the readiness of institutions particularly the need to establish a conducive policy and government environment. Cooke, Ariss, Smith, and Read (2015) cite the need for policies, the evolving roles of stakeholders and citizen engagement mechanisms as relevant issues that should be considered in capacity building. These concerns are similar to the items previously raised by Dawes and Helbig (2010) that present policies and governance mechanisms as areas where capacities should be developed. Furthermore, the same study identified technology standards and data management as additional areas for capacity building. And on the technical skills end, Verma *and* Gupta (2012) stressed the importance of sustaining OG-OGD initiatives by ensuring the quality of datasets by relating OGD to data management. Indeed, numerous works link OG-OGD capacities to IT-related capacities. For instance, the work of Mitrovic (2015) identified what he termed as "e-skills", stressing that the absence of these skills remain one of the biggest obstacles in the successful implementation of OG-OGD initiatives. These skills are as follows: a) e-Leadership; b) e-Awareness; c) data literacy and d) e-practitioners. While the work of van Deursen and van Dijk (2009) suggest a typology that categorized these skills into the following: a) operational; b) formal; c) information and d) strategic. In addition, Evans and Campos (2013) defined skill sets related to communication, efficacy of data sources together with the need for analytical skills to effectively use of open datasets in solving governance-related problems.

A review of abovementioned works provides an excellent view on the various concerns surrounding the implementation of OG-OGD programs. Aside from establishing its value and purpose, authors stressed the need to address issues on governance and have identified possible skills that can be considered in developing training programs on OG-OGD. However, in relation to building capacities, there is a need to further bridge the need for context (purpose, value and relevance) to that of technical skills. The chapter authors believe that the definition of performance competencies can provide this vital link.

The Importance of the Identifying Competencies and Determining the Local Context

Clearly, as more datasets are being released, there is a need to ensure that these datasets result to better governance. Related to this concern is the need to address gaps in organizational capacity especially with regards to the use of these datasets for better policy-making and program implementation. The authors recognize this issue as a challenge and thus see the need to adopt competency-based training design. Sanghi (2007) defined competencies as the needed knowledge, skills and attitudes to effectively perform job-related tasks. Also, identifying the competencies demands for a validated set of training requirements, thereby making the training design more responsive and relevant (Pawlak, Way, & Thompson, 1982). In addition, competency-based training programs tend to focus on individual, task-related, contingency and environmental skills, which are all needed to describe the capabilities of good job performance (Rothwell, Graber, & Graber, 2010).

For Philippines, the authors believe that in order to mainstream and sustain OG-OGD programs, it is necessary to define performance competencies. For one, it is easier to develop a capacity building program based on these competencies. Such programs can immediately reflect organizational needs and adjust to the existing human resource programs. It can also be argued that with OG-OGD performance competencies, the integration of related training initiatives on data privacy, cybersecurity, and use of Web 2.0 tools in public institutions can be done. This integration can further increase the chances of institutionalization through the development of professional programs for public officers and employees.

Overview of Current OG-OGD: Republic of the Philippines

OG-OGD initiatives are often situated in an environment that is governed by political priorities and bounded by socioeconomic realities. In developing countries, most of these programs are linked with good governance and anti-poverty efforts often as part of a national development and bureaucratic reform agenda. In the Philippines, the Good Governance Action Plan (GGAP, 2012) cites OG-OGD as ingredients for achieving its governance reform targets. The current open data portal (data.gov.ph) and other related initiatives clearly show the government's intent to fulfill its OGP commitments. However, Davies (2014) further observed that the current public sector led OGD program is greatly influenced by its interaction with external (foreign) actors. Moreover, low literacy levels and the lack of intermediaries impede open government initiatives. This is further aggravated by the prevailing political culture that hampers reform efforts that aims to provide a greater role for non-government actors (Davies, 2014).

At present, the Duterte administration promulgated executive order (EO) number 2 which instructs national government agencies and government owned and controlled corporations to implement procedures and access points for public information. Popularly known as the "freedom of information" (FOI) order, this EO is widely seen as a commitment of the current administration to continue the tradition of good governance. There are also initiatives within the executive branch to integrate FOI with the current open data, data privacy and cybersecurity initiatives which includes the use of Web 2.0 especially social media.

There are also continuing efforts to update the open government portal and increasing the number of agencies that are uploading public data sets. The current administration is also expanding its engagement with civil society organizations on how to improve the OGD program. There are also proposals to integrate OG-OGD practices as part of the transparency seal criteria of the Department of the Interior and Local Government (DILG) for local government units. The transparency seal is an award given to local governments for meeting transparency requirements and promoting good governance practices.

However, cascading these efforts to local governments remain a daunting task. In fact, a 2012 assessment report highlighted the importance of diffusing OG-OGD efforts towards the local government units (LGUs) claiming that such moves while promising good governance benefits, would require the uncovering of local requirements and needs in relation to its governance environment. Aside from infrastructure cost, significant investments must be made on improving local capacities, establish ownership of open data initiatives through a coherent mix of policies and programs. Overall, this means that OG-OGD initiatives must find relevance and purpose in the local governance while taking cognizant of organizational and resource limitations. Simply said, the political and socio-economic benefits of OG must be made, "crystal clear".

OVERVIEW OF THE RESEARCH DESIGN

This section provides a summary of different activities that were undertaken to achieve the objectives of the project. In developing the competency-based training program, an action research stance combined with the use of qualitative data gathering and validation techniques were adopted.

The study employed the following qualitative techniques: interviews with key informants and subject matter experts, observation of their actual practices, focus group discussions (FGD), validation workshops, document reviews, content analysis of websites and social networking sites, and review of existing researches and programs related to OG-OGD (see Table 1).

Data were primarily sourced out from direct interviews with stakeholders and observations on their practices. Key informant interviews were undertaken to gather information on the existing plans, programs, and governance related practices of LGUs from different stakeholders - including LCEs, administrators, planning and development coordinators, heads of offices, and support staff. The authors also conducted direct interviews with subject matter experts (SMEs) from the academe, CSOs, media, and government partners. In addition, LGUs organizational processes and practices related to the management of data-information were observed. As part of the validation process, FGD sessions with community-based organizations, government partners and CSOs were also organized.

Secondary data were obtained from document reviews of government reports, memoranda, plans, and project documentation of the LGUs. In addition, the authors

Table 1. Data sources

Data Types	Description
Primary data	• Direct interview with the Local Government Stakeholders (Local Chief Executives, Administrator, Planning and Development Coordinator, unit heads, and staff) • Direct interview with subject matters experts from the academe, CSOs, media, Union of Local Authorities in the Philippines (ULAP), Open Government Task Force • Observation of their governance-related practices • Focus group discussion with inter-govermental organizations, government partners, CSOs, and OG-OGD advocates • Validation workshops
Secondary data	• Perusal of documents (i.e. Comprehensive Development Plan, Annual Investment Plan, Accomplishment Report, Executive and Legislative Agenda) • Examination of government reports, memoranda and articles • Examination of websites and social networking sites
Tertiary data	• Related researches on OG-OGD views and trends • Related capability building initiatives in line with OG-OGD

also conducted a content analysis of their websites and social networking sites in order to determine its characteristics, structural features, key themes, and contents.

Furthermore, related researches were considered as the tertiary data to determine the existing views, practices, trends as well as the capacity building initiatives related to OG-OGD.

For data analyis, thematic analysis was used to generate themes from OG-OGD literature, existing OG-OGD practices among LGUs, and stakeholder assessment. The generated themes led to the development of the interim competency matrix and training program. These are constantly and subsequently validated with the LGUs and SMEs coming from the academe, CSOs and media.

For the study sample, this research examined the existing practices of the Philippine LGUs in the following municipalities: Pavia, Santa Barbara, New Lucena, Zarraga, and Leganes. These municipalities belong to the second congressional district in the province of Iloilo and are considered as the major contributors in boosting the economy of the province through their agro-industrial and marine resources.

The selection of study sample is based on the initial survey criterion that sample municipalities should be recepients of the Seal of Good Housekeeping (SHG) awards by the Department of Interior and Local Government. Thus, these chosen municipalities were conferred with SGH through their observance on transparency and accountability as well as by compying with the Full Disclosure Policy (FDP).

DISCUSSION OF RESULTS

In developing the OG-OGD competency matrix (see Annex 1), this study categorized the activities into the following phases: a) Uncovering themes in OG-OGD literature; b) Uncovering practices in Philippine LGUs and c) Stakeholders Assessment (see Figure 1).

Phase 1: Uncovering Themes in Literature in OG-OGD

In this phase, the authors identified the emerging themes culled from the available literature on the area of OG-OGD. To further explain these themes, Figure 2 provides an overview of the results of review which identified three emerging themes.

In addition to the earlier themes cited in the previous section of this chapter, the works of Bauer and Kaltenbock (2011), O'Hara (2012), O'Rain, Curry, and Harth (2012), and Van Veenstra, Janssen, and Boon (2011) present OG-OGD as a movement that espouses for more transparency and ensure that new venues for participation are created. As a trend, the authors see OG-OGD being offered as a new tool for transparency and participation. It aims to add to the existing good governance

Figure 1. Phases in developing the OG-OGD Competency Matrix

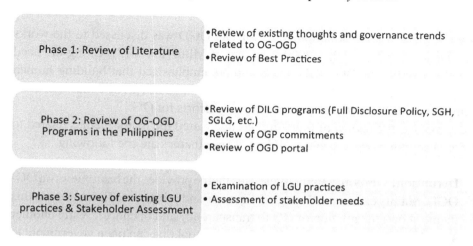

Figure 2. Emerging views on OG-OGD

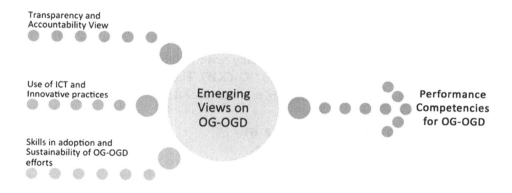

practices by highlighting the openness dimension with the intent of achieving collaboration and innovation-related goals. Related to this thought of creating new venues come the idea of using new technologies to further enlarge the opportunities for participation. The work of Chan (2013) mainly points to Web 2.0 tools. In this work, OGD is seen as an ingredient for enabling collaboration and innovation. While Reggi and Ricci (2011) stressed the need to define the value adding outcomes of OG-OGD for institutions and sectors that wish to adopt such practice. Moreover, a set of works on the area defines its basic principles and characteristics (Tauberer, 2014) (Halonen, 2012) and its dimensions (Smith & Reilly, 2014). These works provide the much needed conceptual basis and attributes necessary in defining the purpose and potentials of OGD.

Lastly, the theme on adoption skills for OG-OGD was discussed in the works of van Deursen and van Dijk (2009) and that of Mitrovic (2012). Citing the need to develop e-skills for OG-OGD, these authors emphasized that building human capacity is essential in ensuring its adoption and sustainability. The concept of civic hacking was also discussed as part of adoption efforts for OG.

In summary, the review of literature has uncovered the major themes related to OG-OGD adoption and capacity building. These themes are the following:

1. **Definition, Views and Principles:** This theme provides the basic views on OG-OGD. Mainly expressed through definitions and principles, discussions in this theme shows the relation of OG to transparency and openness, while another side of the discussion present OG-OGD as a tool that can open government to more participation and collaboration thus resulting to innovative governance practices;

2. **Governance Environment and the Role of ICT:** This literature theme emphasized the need to develop policies and governance mechanisms to ensure the adoption and the institutionalization of OG-OGD programs. This theme also stressed the importance of ICT as an enabler for OG-OGD;

3. **Technical Skills:** The works cited in the review highlighted what it termed as "digital skills" or e-skills related to OG-OGD. These skills range from digital literacy and ethics to visualization, user interface design and decision making;

Phase 2: Uncovering Practices in National and Local Government

In the second phase of development approach, this study looked at Philippine-specific practices in relation to OG-OGD both from national and local levels (see Figure 3).

On the national level, the Philippine government has embarked on numerous initiatives in relation to OG-OGD. The commitment of the Philippines to Open Government Partnership in 2011 put forward in the adoption of transparency and accountability mechanisms to strengthen governance.

For one, the creation of the Philippine OGP steering committee demonstrates the support of the national government to push open government from the national down to the local governments. Plans to mobilize civil society organizations among others show the intent to deepen and institutionalize these initiatives. For instance, the Open Data Task Force (ODTF) led by the Department of Budget and Management (DBM) with its partner agencies, oversees the open government data programs by encouraging national government agencies to open their data to the public. Another

Figure 3. OG-OGD related initiatives in the Philippines

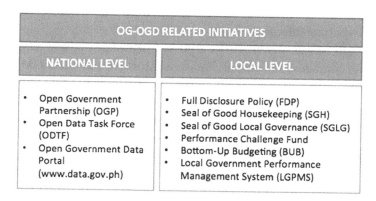

noteworthy endeavor is the Open Government Data portal (data.gov.ph), which aims to release public data sets in open format (see Figure 4).

On the local level, the Department of the Interior and Local Government (DILG) has implemented various bureaucratic reforms and initiatives to strengthen good governance and for the effective delivery of services at the municipal and city levels.

Figure 4. Open data portal of the Philippine government (Screen captured from http://data.gov.ph)

Amongst are the Full Disclosure Policy (FDP), Seal of Good Housekeeping (SGH), Seal of Good Local Governance (SGLG), and Bottom-Up Budgeting (BUB) (http://www.opengovpartnership.org).

The FDP calls for transparency in local government plans and budget. Specifically, this program encourages LGUs to provide avenues for their constituents to be informed of what their local government is doing specifically on how LGU budget is being managed, disbursed and used by posting their budgets, expenditures, contracts, loans, and procurement related documents in conspicuous places and municipal websites. In 2012, the DILG expanded these initiatives by establishing the FDP Portal where LGUs post their budget documents online.

In 2010, the DILG launched the Seal of Good Housekeeping (SGH) program that seeks to promote and incentivize good governance at the local level. The seal recognizes LGUs for their compliance with Sound Fiscal Management (no serious negative findings by COA on local financial transactions) and direct observance with FDP. In 2014, the program was updated to the Seal of Good Local Governance (SGLG) to include assessment areas on Good Financial Housekeeping, Disaster Preparedness, Social Protection, Business-Friendly LGUs, Law and Order, and Public Safety and Environmental Protection.

In 2011, the DILG also initiated an incentive-driven program thru the Performance Challenge Fund (PCF). In this project, LGUs can avail of financial support to jumpstart and sustain projects in promoting local economic development and addressing local concerns. In order to be eligible for the grant, participating LGUs must be recipients of the SGH award. Thus, this strategy encourages LGUs to put premium on performance in governance and efficient delivery of basic services before being granted with such assistance.

In addition, participation spaces were opened for civil society organizations, local special bodies and multi-sectoral groups to be part of governance. The Bottom-up Budgeting (BuB) for instance enabled inclusive participation wherein grassroots communities took part in planning, budgeting and identification of project prioritization areas. This form of citizen participation and empowerment enables local government to be more responsive to the local needs.

Furthermore, performance monitoring and feedback form part of the whole gamut of governance. Through the Local Government Performance Management Systems (LGPMS), the local governments can assess their state of local development using governance and development indicators in the following areas: administrative, economic social governance, valuing fundamentals of governance, and environmental governance (http://www.blgs.gov.ph). This tool enables LGUs to identify their capabilities and limitations, which then serves as a basis in implementing appropriate actions and in addressing local development gaps and concerns.

In summary, it can be construed that since 2010, the Philippine government has embarked on a good governance initiative intended to introduce bureaucratic reforms anchored on the principles of good governance. Popularly known as "Tuwid na Daan" (The Honest, Straight Path), this reform initiative has involved the adoption of open govern data program at the national level. The OGD program was handled by the DBM and was seen as a top-down attempt to adoption open data practices. While at the local level, open government initiatives such as the BuB, Seal of Good House-keeping and Full Disclosure Policy were meant to cascade open government practices down to the cities and municipalities. However, it can be said the both programs lack the necessary capacity building aspect that could have ensured its continuous implementation.

Phase 3: Survey of Existing LGU Practices and Stakeholder Assessment

In this phase, the authors uncovered the governance-related practices of 5 municipalities in the province of Iloilo namely, Pavia, Santa Barbara, New Lucena, Zarraga, and Leganes. In so doing, key informant interviews were conducted with LCEs, administrators, planning and development coordinators, unit heads and staff. In addition, the authors observed their actual practices and context driven initiatives in line with OG-OGD. These findings were further validated with subject matter experts (SMEs) stressing the need for OG-OGD adoption.

Existing LGU Practices

Looking into the OG-OGD practices at the local level, LGUs implemented programs and institutionalized initiatives to make governance more open, transparent and participative. Primarily, this is in pursuance with the DILG's mandates on FDP and SGH. On the other hand, other LGUs took value in advancing the initiatives through the use of various communication media and Web 2.0 technologies.

As observed, LGUs diligently comply with the FDP by posting their financial documents and transactions in order for their constituents to see how the funds were being utilized. These documents were displayed in municipal halls, markets, public terminals, and other conspicuous places (see example in Figure 5). Following additional directives on FDP, LGUs also posted these documents on their municipal websites as well in the national FDP portal (see Figures 6 and 7).

Aside from disclosing local government financial data, context driven initiatives were materialized to paved way for people to be updated of the current state and issues affecting their localities. For some, the institutionalization of the annual practice of the State of the Municipality Address (SOMA) by their local chief executives

Figure 5. Full disclosure policy report of the municipality of Zarraga, Iloilo

Figure 6. FDP Document Posted at New Lucena, Iloilo website (Screen captured from http://www.newlucena.gov.ph)

Figure 7. FDP document uploaded at the National FDP portal (Screen captured from http://fdpp.blgs.gov.ph)

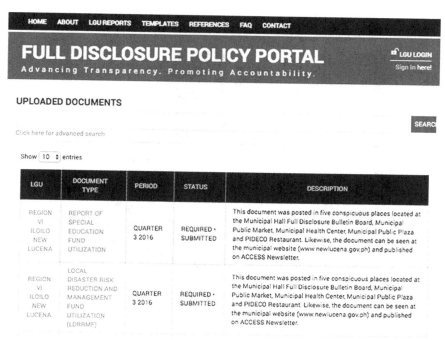

served as means to inform their constituents about the present economic, political and social conditions of their community. It is also serves as a medium for the LCEs to highlight the accomplishments, plans, and future directions of their municipality (see Figure 8).

Furthermore, LGUs also utilized various media to disseminate information and engage citizen participation. As an example, one municipality established a local radio station to broadcast news and information (see Figure 9). This is also an avenue for local government officials, municipal employees, partners, local CSOs, multi-sectoral groups, and ordinary citizens to tackle concerns on their radio programs, particularly on issues concerning the effective and efficient delivery of government and social services.

To complement the traditional approach of informing the public, some LGUs also established their own websites (see Figure 10). The prevalent contents found include the services offered, name of government officials, job postings, news and updates and FDP documents. Thus, the provision of websites is basically to promote awareness.

Figure 8. The delivery of State of Municipality Address, Santa Barbara, Iloilo (Screen captured from Santa Barbara Ugyon YouTube channel)

Figure 9. Local radio station of Santa Barbara, Iloilo (Source: https://www.facebook. com/santabarbara.ugyon)

Figure 10. Municipal website of Pavia, Iloilo (Screen captured from http://www.pavia.gov.ph)

LGUs also recognized the instant and interactive capabilities of Web 2.0 technologies to reach wide audience, increase transparency, and promote public participation. Some municipalities created their own Facebook page (Figure 11) and YouTube Channel (Figure 8). The use of social media is their way to push announcements immediately as well to make government information readily accessible. In addition, this medium advances participation wherein citizens can freely ask questions, post comments and join discussions.

In summary, the above discussions highlight the practices of LGUs to make governance more open, transparent and citizen-centric. It should be recognized that Web 2.0 technologies play a vital role in increasing reach of information and widening spaces for participation. Despite its potentials, it should be noted that the greater challenge imposes questions not only on its optimum use but also on the accuracy and reliability of data-information shared and the quality of user engagement. Thus, the authors believed that there is a need to address these concerns and furthering the OG-OGD initiatives by first identifying the competencies before conducting the capability programs. This is to ensure that feedbacks and collective intelligence

Figure 11. Facebook page of Santa Barbara, Iloilo (Screen captured from https:// www.facebook.com/santabarbara.ugyon)

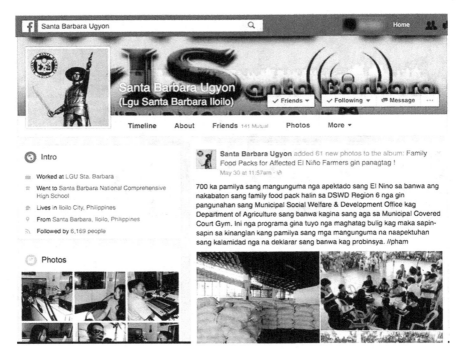

will become valuable inputs to the problem-solving and decision-making process of their local government officers, legislatures and executives.

Stakeholder Assessment

Using key informant interviews with local government stakeholders, SMEs from the academe, intergovernmental organizations, national government partners, media and CSOs, the authors identified the entities with declared or conceivable interest in OG-OGD and assessed their needs in advancing these initiatives.

The identified stakeholders were categorized into: 1) demand side and 2) supply side. The supply side constitutes the local government units (LGUs), national government, and government agencies. They are considered as the primary sources, holders and providers of data. On the other hand, the civil society organizations (CSOs), media, academia/research institutions, private/business sectors, and ordinary citizens form part of the demand side. They are considered to be the consumers of data and are expected to use data for social, political and development engagement, research purposes as well as for potential business benefit.

In conducting a stakeholder assessment, the authors identify the stakeholders' needs in realizing OG-OGD initiatives. Through key informant interviews with the local partners and SMEs, this study enumerates their concerns as detailed in Table 2.

Table 2. Stakeholder Assessment

Stakeholder	Needs Assessment and Expectations
Local Government Units • Elected Officials • Civil Servants	• Policy and regulatory framework for the nationwide adoption of OG-OGD Initiative; Enactment of Freedom of Information (FOI) Bill • Appropriation of knowledge and skills related to OG-OGD through Capacity Building Program • ICT Equipment and facilities • Access to Internet • Data standards • Data management systems that facilitates collection, storage, retrieval, analysis, publishing and reporting of data/information • Central data portal • Commitment and active involvement of other stakeholders • Champions to advocate OG-OGD • Development support or incentives from national government and international organizations for those who adopt OG-OGD
National Government and Government Agencies	• Policy and regulatory framework for the nationwide adoption of OG-OGD Initiative; Enactment of FOI Bill • Nationwide adoption of OG-OGD • Data Standards • Stable Internet Infrastructure • Champions to advocate OG-OGD • Commitment and active involvement of other stakeholders
Civil Society Organizations • Community-based organizations • Sectoral groups • Charities/Civic/Non-profit organizations • Non-governmental organizations (NGOs) • Mass Media • Print • Broadcast • New Media	• Policy and regulatory framework for the nationwide adoption of OG-OGD Initiative; Enactment of FOI Bill • Easy access to government data • Awareness on the availability and use of government data • Training for data scrapping, data analysis and data reuse • Proactive approach for civic engagement • Online platform for data sharing
Academia • Higher Education Institutions • Research Institutions • Training Centers • Students	• Policy and regulatory framework for the nationwide adoption of OG-OGD Initiative; Enactment of FOI Bill • Easy access to government data for academic and research purposes • Awareness on the availability and use of government data • Online platform for data sharing • Effective use of data (contribution to the body of knowledge)
Business/Private Sector	• Awareness and use of data • Easy access to government data for potential commercial benefit
International / Intergovernmental Organizations	• Provide interventions to support the OG-OGD Initiatives • Commitment of Stakeholders
Ordinary Citizens	• Awareness on the availability and use of government data • Easy access to government data • Make use of and benefit from data

DEVELOPING THE COMPETENCY MATRIX

After carefully examining the OG-OGD literature, uncovering the OG-OGD practices among local governments in the Philippines, stakeholder assessment as well as the constant validation activities with SMEs, the authors were able to generate themes leading to the development of interim competency matrix (see Figure 12).

Present in both literature and SME interviews were the concerns on the importance of strengthening the policy regimes that are necessary to adopt and sustain OG-OGD initiatives. With this, a suggestion was made to present the value-adding aspects of open government. This can be done to ensure that OG-OGD initiatives are grounded implying that its value adding capacities is presented as possible solutions to real problems. Furthermore, the validation points to the need to enhance the skills in data driven policy development, data management, and the use of ICT tools to harness the potentials of data-information.

Regarding digital and ICT skills, literature in open government adoption and digital skills point to this aspect as an important component for ensuring the efficacy of ICT-related programs. Particularly referring to information (or data)-digital skills, works on the area link these skills to individual productivity and organizational efficacy, especially in the public sector. Moreover, the study's field validation effort uncovered inadequacies in this area, pointing to the limitations in resources and existing policies on human resources. It is also revealed numerous challenges in ICT infrastructure, especially in the area of maximizing the use of ICT systems beyond transaction processing and information dissemination. Interviews with SMEs however, stress the importance of developing data-information standards and the need to ensure interoperability, especially among the basic services in local government.

After examining the local government practices, the authors see the use of social media networks as means to disseminate information so that constituents are updated of the current activities and concerns of the locality particularly on programs related

Figure 12. Themes leading to Competency Matrix

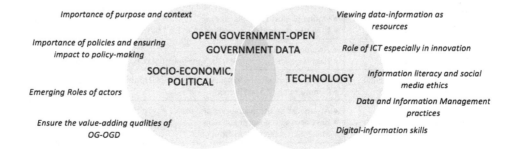

to the delivery of social services. Taking advantage of the opportunities offered by Internet technologies, there is a need to further the initiative by emphasizing the use of social media as a democratic space for participation and dialogue; not just a mere information dissemination tool. In addition, citizens should be empowered to take an active role in governance not just a receiver of information and services. Along with that, to overcome potential threats and risks, there should be a provision on information literacy and social media ethics on the proper use of social media. In this accord, LGUs ensure that citizens' comments and feedbacks will become valuable inputs to the policy development and decision-making process of their local government officers, legislators and executives.

As shown in Figure 12, the result of this study illustrates 2 intersecting domains between socio-economic and political concerns with that of technology. The product of this intersection area is OG-OGD competencies. From this, the authors identified the 3 core competencies for OG-OGD. Specifically, it is composed of the following sub-competencies: a) OG-OGD principles, b) Data Management, and c) ICT. Discussion box 1 explains each competency area.

Discussion Box 1: Description of OG-OGD Core Competencies

OG-OGD Principles Competency

This competency provides the what, why and how of OGD. It is anchored on the 14 principles of open government data (Tauberer, 2014). As such, it should address the supply side of OGD by providing appropriate justification, understanding, and application of OGD. At the end of the course, participants will appreciate the value of OGD, justify its goals and critique models/approaches of OGD. The main purpose of this competency is to increase the pool of experts and champions of OGD and to create a self-sustaining movement in the supply side of OGD.

Data Competency

This competency provides knowledge, skills, and understanding on the data lifecycle as well as the management, analysis and stewardship of data. Anchored on the 14 principles of open government data (Tauberer, 2014), this competency is needed to address the challenge of making Open Government Data available to the finest possible level of granularity as well as making an evidence-based decision-making. Moreover, it is also concerned with ensuring access and compliance to data standard, which can be used for further analysis and manipulation by interested stakeholders.

ICT Competency

This competency is needed to address the challenge of making Open Government Data accessible, non-proprietary and publishable in safe-file format with permanence, trust, and provenance. Moreover, this competency determines what information technologies will be used to support openness, participation and collaboration. It also ensures interoperability by developing shared data standard to enable data exchange and data re-use across agencies.

After identifying the 3 core competencies, the competency matrix was developed (see Table 3). It provides details on each competency and corresponding sub-competencies. The 11 sub-competencies identified define the functional components of the 3 core competencies. These sub-competencies were derived from interviews with SMEs, review of literature and benchmarking with training programs for OG-OGD. Furthermore, these sub-competencies serve as a guide in the development of

Table 3. Competency matrix for Open Government-Open Government Data (OG-OGD) for local government units

Sub-Competency	KSAVs	Performance Criteria	Existing Training Courses	Training Modules
OG-OGD COMPETENCY				
OGD principles and policies	• Define and describe the relevance of good governance • Define and discuss the relationship of eGov and OG/OGD • Demonstrate understanding OG-OGD concepts and principles • Identify and discuss relevance of OG-OGD to organizational functions	• Explain and discuss good governance concepts in relation to organizational goals and mission • Exhibit the ability to relate OG-OGD principle to organizational needs and requirements • Explain the relevance of OG-OGD principles to address organizational-related issues and concerns	• Open Data in 1 Day (OKF & ODI) • Basics of Open Data (OKF) • So What? Finding the Value in Open Data (ODI) • Open Data Project (GovLab)	OGD principles & policies (Examining open government and open government data)
OG-OGD Project management and addressing change	• Understand project management life cycle • Apply project management-related practices/techniques to OG-OGD projects • Understanding the basic concepts of change management • Employ use change management concepts to address OG-OGD implementation challenges	• Exhibit the ability to use/integrate change management concepts in planning and designing OG-OGD implementation • Demonstrate the ability to use project management-practices/techniques in managing OG-OGD projects		Change management (Implementing OG-OGD and Managing change)
Evidenced-based Policy making	• Understanding of the basic concepts relating to problem solving and the policy development process (initiation, formulation, analysis and evaluation) • Recognize the use and value of data in policy development	• Demonstrate the use of problem solving cycle/techniques in addressing organizational challenges • Ability to identify policy-related alternatives • Ability to identify and use data to support policy-related alternatives	• Open Data Management (OKF) • Open Data in Practice (ODI)	OD management (Managing OG-OGD implemen-tation)

continued on following page

Table 3. Continued

Sub-Competency	KSAVs	Performance Criteria	Existing Training Courses	Training Modules
Civic hacking	Define and discuss the various approaches and techniques related to civic hacking: participation, collaboration and the use of on-line tools	Demonstrate the ability to identify possible opportunities to use civic hacking techniques to address organizational challenges		Civic hacking & OGD
DATA COMPETENCY				
Data management	• Recognize the value of data/information • Apply the principles and concepts of data management	• Demonstrate the ability to apply and use data management principles and concepts in addressing organizational issues and challenges	• Open Data in 1 Day (OKF & ODI)	Data Management
Data analysis and presentation	• Ability to identify opportunity for data reuse • Apply the techniques in interpreting, analyzing, and presenting data • Integrate the results of data analysis in problem solving • Synthesize and use data for evidence-based policy making	• Demonstrate the ability to use data analysis techniques through the use of productivity tools • Ability to synthesize the result of data analysis for problem solving and evidence-based policy making • Ability to organize data sets for future reuse	• Data Skills Training (OKF & SOD)	• Data Analysis and Presentation • Evidence-based policy making
Data stewardship	• Understand the roles and responsibilities related to data stewardship • Identify the principles of data stewardship	• Ability to explain and discuss the roles and responsibilities of data stewards in implementing data collection programs, developing data standards and maintaining datasets • Ability to realize the individual (participant) roles in data stewardship • Ability to explain and discuss the data standards, data use and exchange, data security, data usage monitoring, and data ethics	• Open Data, Law, and Licensing (ODI) • Civic Tech for Local Legislatures and Legislators (GoVLab)	Data Stewardship
ICT COMPETENCY				
Digital literacy	• Describe and explain the computer systems (hardware, software, people, data, process) and ICT related devices that can support open government • Apply file organization and manipulation in the use of computer • Use basic functions of spreadsheet application in handling data • Convert data into open data formats for different applications	• Explain the components of computer system and its uses given the device/software • Perform file manipulation and organization given specifications • Basic functions of spreadsheet applications are properly used • Prepare data set to subscribe to open data standards		Digital literacy
Use of databases	• Use database concepts in organizing data using software application (e.g. MS Excel, MS Access) • Retrieve and organize government data sets • Use software applications to prepare, visualize and manipulate open government data • Use software application to prepare reports	• Apply database concepts in software applications • Create data capture forms to be used in organizing data sets • Download government data sets in preparation for data manipulation • Produce graphical visualization and reports	• Data Skills Training Course (OKF & SOD) • Freedom of Information Project Coaching (GovLab)	Data manipulation

continued on following page

Table 3. Continued

Sub-Competency	KSAVs	Performance Criteria	Existing Training Courses	Training Modules
Use of internet technologies	• Demonstrate the use of internet in exploring data and retrieving information • Navigate open government portals and determine the different pages • Use different web technologies to support open data government activities such as Google forms, emails and forums • Assess authenticity or (integrity) of different web pages for data sources • Use basic practices related to internet security	• Download data from open data government portals given organizational needs • Use web collaboration tools for participation and sharing of files • Web pages and sources are verified given a website • Apply basic security functions related the use of the internet	• Open Data in One Day (OKF) • Open Data Portal Technology (OKF) • Open Data Technologies (ODI)	Use of internet technologies
Interoperability	• Recognize the importance of interoperability and standards in improving service delivery and openness • Assess the advantages and disadvantages of different open data standards and architecture • Apply open data standards and architecture in information infrastructure and data within the organization	• Demonstrate the ability to identify factors and items necessary to develop its architecture and standards given the organizational needs • Recognize the use of appropriate data standards and architecture that can be applied to an organization		Interoperability
Information Literacy and Social Media Ethics	• Recognize the importance of social media in governance • Apply techniques on the effective use of social media for information dissemination, civic engagement and collaboration	• Recognize the responsible use and governance of social media • Exhibit the ability to assess the reliability of feedbacks and accuracy of information shared on social media		Information Literacy and Social Media Ethics

concrete statements describing the necessary knowledge, skills, attitudes and values (KSAVs) for a given sub-competency as well as the performance criteria that explain the specific indicators in order to achieve target performance outcomes. To ensure that the statements and indicators appear in the competency matrix reflect the elements needed in the promotion and adoption of OG-OGD, the authors constantly check with the existing literature, stakeholder practices, and series of validation activities. To complement the existing training courses on Open Data, this research further proposes the development of training modules that can comprised a competency-based capacity building program for local governments in the Philippines.

In general, the competency matrix explicitly defines the capability required for open government and open government data. Thus, the authors believed that the competency matrix designed would serve as a basis in formulating the training programs that will capacitate local government units, civil society organizations, and other stakeholders on OG-OGD.

In developing the matrix, it should be stressed that the performance measures and training modules identified the following content as vital to address the development of competencies:

1. **Information Literacy and Social Media Ethics:** This item pertains to the need to development knowledge and skills on the productive use of information. Aside from use, this measure also integrates the ethical and safe use of tools especially that of social media;
2. **Interoperability:** This topic includes the development of data-information and infrastructure standards that would enable business systems to transact with each other;
3. **Change Management:** This skill would enable OG-OGD champions and sponsors to examine how productivity can be further improved and how the organizational-human practices can adjust to these new practices as a result of OG-OGD;
4. **Civic Hacking:** This skill is essential in building the capacities of external stakeholders (e.g. civil society organizations, peoples organizations, donors, etc.) especially in the use of open data sets, maximizing social media sites of local governments, and instituting new participation practices.

Recommendations to Local Governments and Other Stakeholders

Based on the stakeholder assessment, key themes were revealed as to needs of stakeholders in advancing the initiative. The authors created a list of recommendations necessary to implement and sustain OG-OGD at the local level. The key themes are summarized as follows: 1) establishment of policy frameworks; 2) provision of stable ICT and Internet infrastructure; 3) creation of data standards; 4) capability building for LGUs, CSOs, etc.; 5) leadership and sponsorship.

Establishment of Policy Framework

The political and legislative factors can be considered as enabler in streamlining the initiatives. However, as seen at the local level, there is no policy framework and directives as to the adoption and implementation OG-OGD and the Freedom of Information Bill (FOI) has not yet enacted. It is further underscored that the principles of open governance is easy to incorporate to the system however, the lack of political capital to build enough traction for its sustainability is still a major challenge. Thus, policy frameworks and directives are needed to stimulate the initiatives as well as the oversight agency to ensure its enactment and sustainability.

Good ICT and Internet Infrastructure

Before the concept of open data will be widely appreciated, the local government should have adequate ICT resources. In addition, national government should ensure the reliable infrastructure and stable Internet connection to improve accessibility and interoperability. As observed, the existing IT systems are in silos and not interoperable, which often results to the inability of linking and reusing data sets across departments. It has been observed that there is an initial move to establish municipal websites however the contents are not regularly updated primarily because the maintenance is mostly outsourced.

The national government also embarked initiatives in the modernization of the government procedures for the effective delivery of services. The provision of electronic services by various national agencies for online registration, tax collection, membership application, and document request, among others alleviate long lines and inefficient processes. In addition, the national government also steered on the initiative to enhance government efficiency and effectiveness through iGovPhil project. The long-term plan is to develop interconnected and interoperable government applications. However, one of the major challenges in realizing this project is the country's unstable Internet connection. This problem is hope to be resolved by the creation of the Department of Information and Communications Technology, which is expected to ensure reliable, cost-effective and efficient ICT infrastructure and accessible Internet services throughout the country.

Creation of Data Standards

One of the challenges in institutionalizing OG-OGD techniques at the local level is related to the management, analysis and publication of data. The existing practices remain inadequate to deal with voluminous data. Moreover, data are not standardized and is scattered across different departments. This often results in the difficulty of culling data when someone needs it for cross-referencing and analysis. Even though there is an abundant supply of data, these do not translate into a language that speaks to the policy makers and public sector practitioners. In addition, there are existing practices that make data available online (i.e. uploading of FDP documents) but these are usually in html, pdf and picture formats. Thus, these allow citizens to only view the data, but limit its use for further manipulation and analysis.

To institutionalize the initiatives, there should have a standard mechanism on the generation and publication of data sets across national agencies and local government units. Moreover, it is also suggested the need to establish protocols in sharing data across networks.

Capability Building for LGUs, CSOs and Other Stakeholders

The adoption of OG-OGD techniques poses considerable challenge because of the inability of employees to effectively manage data-information resources and the inadequate skills in the use of ICT and Internet applications. The existing practice of using data-information is purposively for reporting (i.e. monthly, quarterly, annual reports) and oftentimes it did not reach to a level where data is used for evidence-based decision-making. This stems from the lack of understanding of the significant value of data among local government stakeholders. Also, the lack of awareness from CSOs, media and other stakeholders on the availability and use government data hindered them to take a proactive stance in making sense of data.

With this, various skills and capabilities are needed in harnessing the potentials of opening government data and creating social and economic value from it. Capability building interventions on the LGU side can be in a form of training programs that matches the needs and requirements of local chief executives (LCEs), legislators, and local government employees. In particular, there is a need to capacitate LCEs and legislators to understand the principles OG-OGD, awareness on the significant value of data-driven decision-making, and knowhow in proactively engaging civil society organizations and citizens online. Similarly, employees should possess competencies in managing data effectively and assuring its quality and integrity. They should also be equipped with appropriate ICT skills in processing, analyzing, publishing, and sharing data. It is also significant to stress the importance of information literacy and social media ethics in governance. Thus, employees should be equipped with skills on effective and responsible use social media as well as the ability to assess the accuracy of information shared on social media. Since employees have diverse ICT skills, it is necessary to include digital literacy for those who don't have the basic knowledge on ICT. On the demand side, orientations and training programs for civil society organizations, media, academicians, students, and citizens are also needed to increase data uptake. Aside from awareness, the provision of technical skills in data scrapping, data manipulation and data analysis as well as the responsible use of social media for collaboration are also needed to unlock the potentials of open data. For information technology enthusiasts this can be a good opportunity for them to develop data portal and online applications using government data.

Leadership and Sponsorship

To ensure greater gains from OG-OGD initiatives, there is a need to identify and encourage local champions that will steer bold leadership and commitment to the OGP. The existing organizational and resource capacity is not enough thus it needs sponsorship to sustain the initiatives.

FUTURE DIRECTIONS

To further validate the competency matrix, the authors intend to further look at existing OG-OGD training programs being offered by international agencies and organizations. The authors also plan to present the competency-based OG-OGD capacity program to the concerned government agencies and civil society partners for the purpose of validating the competencies. In addition, the authors call for the continuous mainstreaming of the OG-OGD programs with partner universities through its extension projects. Lastly, the authors will also explore the possible links of OGD to current local government concerns of climate change adaptation and disaster resiliency.

ACKNOWLEDGMENT

The authors would like to express its gratitude to the World Wide Web foundation and the International Development Research Corporation (IDRC) for its support to the project. And also, the authors would like to thank our mentor, Dr. Emmanuel C. Lallana for his insights and guidance. And lastly, our thanks goes to the members of the DLSU- Robredo Institute of Governance research team namely, Mr. Rabby Lavilles and Ms. Michelle Ching.

REFERENCES

Bauer, F., & Kaltenböck, M. (2011). Linked open data: The essentials. Edition mono/monochrom.

Canares, M., de Guia, J., Narca, M., & Arawiran, J. (2014). *Opening the Gates: Will Open Data Initiatives Make Local Governments in the Philippines More Transparent?* Retrieved from http://opendataresearch.org/sites/default/files/publications/Opening the Gates - Will Open Data Initatives Make Local Government in the Philippines More Transparent.pdf

Chan, C. M. L. (2013). From Open Data to Open Innovation Strategies: Creating E-Services Using Open Government Data. *Proceedings of the 46th Hawaii International Conference on System Sciences (HICSS-46)*, 1890–1899. doi:10.1109/HICSS.2013.236

Cooke, J., Ariss, S., Smith, C., & Read, J. (2015). On-going collaborative priority-setting for research activity: A method of capacity building to reduce the research-practice translational gap. *Health Research Policy and Systems, 13*(1), 25. doi:10.1186/s12961-015-0014-y PMID:25948236

Davies, T. (2014). The construction of open government data. *64th Annual Meeting of the International Communication Association.*

Davies, T. G., & Bawa, Z. A. (2012). The Promises and Perils of Open Government Data (OGD). *The Journal of Community Informatics, 8*(2), 1–6. Retrieved from http://ci-journal.net/index.php/ciej/article/view/929/926

Dawes, S. S., & Helbig, N. (2010). Information strategies for open government: Challenges and prospects for deriving public value from government transparency. *International Conference on Electronic Government*, 50–60. doi:10.1007/978-3-642-14799-9_5

Evans, A. M., & Campos, A. (2013). Open government initiatives: Challenges of citizen participation. *Journal of Policy Analysis and Management, 32*(1), 172–185. doi:10.1002/pam.21651

GGAP. (2012). *Good Governance Action Plan*. Retrieved from http://www.gov.ph/governance/wp-content/uploads/2015/04/good-governance-cluster-plan-2012-2016.pdf

Gurstein, M. B. (2011). Open data: Empowering the empowered or effective data use for everyone? *First Monday, 16*(2). doi:10.5210/fm.v16i2.3316

Halonen, A. (2012). *Being open about data. Analysis of the UK Open Data Policies and applicability of open data*. London: The Finnish Institute in London.

Heckmann, D. (2011). Open government - Retooling democracy for the 21st century. *Proceedings of the Annual Hawaii International Conference on System Sciences*, 1–11. doi:10.1109/HICSS.2011.334

Janssen, M., Charalabidis, Y., & Zuiderwijk, A. (2012). Benefits, Adoption Barriers and Myths of Open Data and Open Government. *Information Systems Management, 29*(4), 258–268. doi:10.1080/10580530.2012.716740

Karamagioli, E., Staiou, E., & Goucos, D. (2014). Can open government models contribute to more collaborative ways of governance? an assessment of the Greek opengov initiative. In Open Government: Opportunities and challenges for public governance. Springer Publications.

Lathrop, D., & Ruma, L. (2010). *Open government: Collaboration, transparency, and participation in practice*. O'Reilly Media.

Mejabi, O. V., Azeez, A. L., Adedoyin, A., & Oloyede, M. O. (2015). Challenges to Open Data Institutionalisation : Insights from stakeholder groups in Nigeria. *2015 Open Data Research Symposium*.

Mitrovic, Z. (2015, March). Strengthening the evidence-base for open government in developing countries. *Building Open Data Capacity through e-Skills Acquisition*, 1–38.

O'Hara, K. (2012). Transparency, open data and trust in government: shaping the infosphere. *Proceedings of the 4th Annual ACM Web Science Conference*, 223–232. doi:10.1145/2380718.2380747

O'Rain, S., Curry, E., & Harth, A. (2012). XBRL and open data for global financial ecosystems: A linked data approach. *International Journal of Accounting Information Systems*, *13*(2), 141–162. doi:10.1016/j.accinf.2012.02.002

Ona, S., Hecita, I. J., & Ulit, E. (2014). *Exploring the Role of Open Government Data & New Technologies the Case of the Philippines: Opportunities in Maternal Health and Child Care (MHCC) & Micro, Small, and Medium Enterprises (MSMEs)*. Open Data Research Network. Retrieved from http://www.opendataresearch.org/sites/default/files/publications/Open Data Opportunities in Maternal Health and Child Care and MSMEs-print.pdf

Pawlak, E. J., Way, I. F., & Thompson, D. H. (1982). *Assessing factors that influence skills training in organizations*. Academic Press.

Reggi, L., & Ricci, C. A. (2011). Information strategies for open government in Europe: EU regions opening up the data on structural funds. *International Conference on Electronic Government*, 173–184. doi:10.1007/978-3-642-22878-0_15

Reilly, K. M. A., & Smith, M. L. (2013). The emergence of open development in a network society. *Open development: Networked innovations in international development*.

Rothwell, W. J., Graber, J. M., & Graber, J. M. (2010). *Competency-based training basics*. American Society for Training and Development.

Sanghi, S. (2007). *The Handbook of Competency Mapping*. Vasa. doi:10.4135/9788132108481

Smith, M. L., & Reilly, K. M. A. (2014). *Open development: Networked innovations in international development*. MIT Press.

Tauberer, J. (2014). Open Government Data: The Book (2nd ed.). Academic Press.

Trivellato, B., Boselli, R., & Cavenago, D. (2014). Design and implementation of open government initiatives at the sub-national level: Lessons from Italian cases. In *Open Government: Opportunities and challenges for public governance.* Springer Publications. doi:10.1007/978-1-4614-9563-5_5

Van Deursen, A. J. A. M., & van Dijk, J. A. G. M. (2009). Improving digital skills for the use of online public information and services. *Government Information Quarterly*, *26*(2), 333–340. doi:10.1016/j.giq.2008.11.002

Van Veenstra, A. F., Janssen, M., & Boon, A. (2011). Measure to improve: A study of eParticipation in frontrunner Dutch municipalities. Lecture Notes in Computer Science, 6847, 157–168. doi:10.1007/978-3-642-23333-3_14

Verma, N., & Gupta, M. P. (2012). *Open government data: More than eighty formats.* Paper presented at the 9th International Conference on E-Governance (ICEG 2012), Cochin, Kerala, India.

Yang, T.-M., Lo, J., Wang, H.-J., & Shiang, J. (2013). Open data development and value-added government information. *Proceedings of the 7th International Conference on Theory and Practice of Electronic Governance - ICEGOV '13,* 238–241. doi:10.1145/2591888.2591932

Zuiderwijk, A., Janssen, M., Choenni, S., Meijer, R., & Alibaks, R. S. (2012). Sociotechnical Impediments of Open Data. *Electronic Journal of E-Government*, *10*(2), 156–172. Retrieved from http://www.ejeg.com/issue/download.html?idArticle=255

Section 3
Behavior of Social Media Users:
Tools, Platforms, and Apps

Chapter 9

The Use of Social Media in Facilitating Participatory Design:
A Case Study of Classroom Design

Fatimah Alsaif
Victoria University of Wellington, New Zealand

Brenda Vale
Victoria University of Wellington, New Zealand

ABSTRACT

This chapter examines the effectiveness of using social media as an aid to primary school students participating in the design of their classroom interior layout. It describes two different attempts to do this that achieved varying degrees of success. Where a blog and Facebook page were set up to provide a virtual space for classroom design to happen, and despite teachers' expressed enthusiasm for involving students in the design of their classroom layout, very few participants resulted. However, one school successfully used the virtual space to show the work of the children and this example is described in the chapter. Social media was of more use in a second example where it formed an additional channel of communication between the researcher in the role of architect and the students. However, here it built on face-to-face communication, suggesting social media can aid in participatory design but is not a substitute for the latter.

DOI: 10.4018/978-1-5225-5326-7.ch009

INTRODUCTION

Social media is fast spreading among individuals with the result that people all around the world in various environments are becoming connected. People in their home, work, on the move, and even walking along the streets are checking their social media accounts and communicating with others to get the latest news, work on unfinished jobs, get in touch with relatives and friends, or just for fun and entertainment. Officially this social media is defined as a set of applications permitted by the Internet that allow individuals to gather in virtual locations, communicate easily, and share material (Reyes & Finken, 2012; Picaza-Vela et al 2016). Social media comes in different forms, such as mobile communication through Short Message Service (SMS) and picture messaging; social networking and media sharing sites as in Facebook, Flickr, and YouTube; or open blogging tools as in Wordpress and Tumbler (Hagen & Robertson, 2010). This chapter looks at how some of these applications can be used to enable users to become part of the building design process for learning environments—normally known as participatory design (DiSalvo et al, 2017).

At present, people do not need specialized knowledge to use the Internet, although they still need to become familiar with certain basic operations. This has parallels with the idea behind participatory design, where the end users become involved early in the design process and, in the case of a building, well before any construction starts on site. Just as instructions for using the Internet are normally given in the form of a manual or on-screen instructions that are easy to use, the use of online media in participatory design needs precise and sensibly designed tools that create environments that are attractive to their potential users. Another thing to consider in using social media in enabling participatory design is the openness of discussion within social media open forums (Näkki & Antikainen, 2008). The aim behind using social media for participatory design is to increase the quality of products or services through approaches where designers and developers can communicate with and involve the users (Johnson, 2013), and some of this may need to be confidential. This means careful setting up of social media situations.

In the research described in this chapter, participatory design was not just tested and observed in the design of primary schools and classrooms in New Zealand but social media in the form of a blog set up for the purpose was also evaluated to see if it was an aid to participatory design. The aim was to see whether having a blog would encourage more communication between school users, particularly children, and architects. This need for better communication came out of an earlier survey conducted to find out how teachers in New Zealand schools and local architects regarded participatory design (Alsaif, 2015). Both parties agreed teachers and children should be involved in classroom design but felt the need for better means of communication between school users and architects. This chapter describes the process of building on this knowledge and the attempts to involve the use of social media.

BACKGROUND

Participatory Design in Learning Environments

Ideally design should be a social process that involves communication, negotiation, and agreement, and the design process itself should be as important as the finished product (Clancy et al, 2015; Zhang and Zhang, 2010). As products, including buildings, are designed in order to be used by people, designing should involve both creating the product and setting the rules for how it could be used. As a result, the designer needs to understand the language of the product (materiality, tectonics), and the users should understand how to use it or give clear descriptions of what they need (Brandt, 2006).

There is little research into teacher involvement in the design of classrooms and schools. However, some teachers and educators have participated in designing their learning environments, ranging from a kindergarten to a high school. Helen West (2007) was a primary curriculum adviser at the Inner Western Region of The Catholic Education Office in Sydney, where a team of kindergarten teachers started a programme for establishing kindergartens in inner city schools in Sydney. One of the important factors they dealt with was designing appropriate learning spaces in these, given that potential child users would be from different cultural and linguistic backgrounds. Teachers were interested in adapting play based learning and using it as the basis for the design of the learning environments. Both the educators' team and the teachers involved wanted the spaces to be flexible, accessible to all, and reflect student needs. For example, partition walls were designed to be easily moveable, so as to make larger or smaller spaces as needed. The decision was made to remove a lot of the conventional furniture to create larger, furniture free spaces inside classrooms. Bookshelves were used as partitions or dividers between different activity corners. The aim was to design settings to support interaction between peers, quiet study, and reading and listening activities.

Participatory Design and Social Media

The variety of social media applications available for public use offer methods that could be integrated in participatory design (Lukyanenko et al, 2016). Reyes (2012) indicated how a traditional method for participatory design could be interpreted and used with Facebook. His project involved the design of a mobile app that would encourage the public to become active in stabilizing and developing heritage photographs, and making these available for comments from other people as well as additional contributions to the site. The project started with several meetings that involved Reyes, the project leader, a supervisor from the research facility, and a communication advisor. The main aims were first to establish a media site using Facebook, chosen because of its popularity and ease of access. There were 18 participants including the project owners, designers and users. The Facebook workshop had a number of different phases. The critique phase allowed participants to give their opinions about the heritage photo service and to suggest improvements. There was also a fantasy phase where participants were asked to imagine and describe their ideal service, and finally an implementation phase where the best ideas from the fantasy phase as selected by the participants were improved and developed into the final service design. The study found that using Facebook enhanced the traditional methods of participatory design, especially as Facebook was well known and consequently most participants did not have to spend time becoming familiarized with different media and methods. Social media in this case also allowed more people to participate as they could access the site from home, rather than in a meeting situation, such as in typical charette type participatory design (Hanington and Martin, 2012, p.58-9). With the appropriate design of the site participants could also remain anonymous. Not having to share opinions face to face, as in traditional participatory design methods, could also encourage people to participate. Additionally, through Facebook participants could receive feedback about their work and also easily be informed about the progress of the design process. The only disadvantage seemed to be that participants were not necessarily able to meet other participants, which could cause them to miss the feeling of being in a community involved in a process of change.

Another study involving online participatory design is the open web lab Owela. This is an online media site created to enable users, customers, developers, and stakeholders to complete the design of anything they collectively desire in a participatory manner. Owela is considered to be social media, as it offers interaction between members of a society regardless of time and place. It also provides a set of tools and methods to facilitate participatory design through discovering the needs and experiences of potential users. Over 40 different types of participatory design have used this web lab and examples of completed projects include user driven software development, a consumer study of cloud software, generating ideas and concept evaluation, and public codesign of a multicultural web community called Monimos. In these projects, consumers and citizens communicated and interacted with companies and researchers to create new products or services such as a city tourism service. Most of the examples focused on the early stages of the innovation process, such as collecting information about user needs, creating ideas, and assessing new product and service concepts. Users can participate from anywhere, as they only need Internet access and basic knowledge of using social software and this saves user time and effort. With Owela, designers and developers can reach large numbers of users quickly and easily. Owela also allows different degrees of involvement as the relationships and communication through the media site can be long or short term. However, Owela does not guarantee the production of successful designs, as this will depend on the aims of each project and the effectiveness of communication between participants. Users of Owela also found this particular social media site useful, as they had the chance to obtain feedback from users and developers without having to attend direct feedback sessions (Kaasinen et al., 2013).

Participatory Design in Schools using the Internet

There are two websites that encourage more user involvement in designing learning environments and that also give tips on redesigning learning spaces. The "Classroom Architect", provides tools to help teachers with this. The first is a set of tools with which to draw the floor plan of the classroom and arrange its furniture in different layouts to achieve the best use of space. The tools provided can only draw rectangular or square floor plans, which could be a disadvantage for classrooms of different shapes, such as the not uncommon L shape. Teachers can use the furniture from the template provided on the website or draw their own furniture. However, the shapes of furniture in the template are also limited to being square, rectangular or circular. The first section in the "Classroom Architect" also gives some instruction on using the tools.

The second section provides information on how learning environments affect learning outcomes. It explains there is no ultimate design for classrooms, as each should be designed according to its students' needs and nature. A group of elements for successful classroom design are mentioned, such as having neutral colours for walls (grey, off white, beige), preventing overcrowded corners as these can result in behaviour issues, and creating different zones that serve different learning styles, such as individual and group work. The third section provides examples of classroom floor plans to instruct teachers about layout possibilities, although this link was not working at the time of writing this chapter ("Classroom architect", 2008).

The other website is linked to the "Edutopia" website, which provides more general tips about what works for education. This is written by David Bill, a designer and educator. One of the topics gives eight tips and tricks for teachers when redesigning or reorganising their classrooms. The first is to involve the students, as they are the main users of the classroom environment. Bill (2014) suggests this could take different forms, such as seeking out visual inspiration by looking for photos of classrooms from magazines or on the Internet. As another suggestion for involving students is printing the existing classroom floor plan at large scale and then allowing students to comment on how they feel about everything in their classroom. His second tip is to use research and brainstorming methods in the redesigning process. These could involve subjects such as how to create collaborative space in the classroom. The third tip is to organize volunteers to help the teacher in the participatory design process, while the fourth is to remove all unnecessary items from the classroom, and the fifth to define any new materials and settings that are required before starting the classroom redesign. The sixth tip is to recycle and reuse any available materials. For example, plastic containers from the grocery store could be used as storage units. The seventh tip is organizing the learning tools in the classroom according to their frequency of use. Colours or labels on the storage units could be used to identify each set of tools by type and how often it is used. For the last tip, Bill provided a list of links to additional resources teachers could use in their process of classroom redesign. These resources included books, photos and information about selected educational projects, together with a number of guidelines for designing learning environments.

Children, as users of schools as well as teachers, also have the right to participate in designing learning environments. Researchers claim children have good potential for participating in design processes, and that this should be a recommendation (Nesset & Large, 2004). Child and developmental psychologists (De Winter et al., 1999) claim that children can face difficulties in completing the tasks and activities set them and argue that these difficulties are related to the children's environments, as these offer them insufficient room for learning and developing. They suggest some of these problems could be prevented by enabling children to participate in designing the environments they use for learning. They also state the social participation of children affects their mental health and involving children as active components of their environments in addition to letting them manage and arrange events in their lives could contribute towards giving them confidence and mastery over their lives and health. Long term use of dependent environments may lead children to develop problems in defining their abilities to complete actions responsibly. When children are involved in decision making, they learn, gain experience and end up with confidence and self respect. Children may also have thoughts that adults might not conceive because of the practical experience of the latter of living in many different environments but this also means that some of the ideas of children could be impossible to implement. Thus, the recommendation is to limit the expectations of children before they start to generate ideas, by providing a brief description of the project and the design process (Nesset & Large, 2004). Ignoring children's participation in designing and planning their built environments makes them feel that they have no control over their learning spaces, and consequently, they may not be able to move freely in their built environment. Thus the environment may limit their actions and potential (Said, 2007). Studies show that school designs that involve student participation, through using children's imaginations in the design process, end up with good, innovative ideas not considered by either architects or teachers (Bland, 2009). Architects and designers also need recognize the importance of children's experiences and thought processes in order to be able to design effective learning spaces. Designing is, in the end, all about the attitudes of users to built environments (Nair & Fielding, 2007).

Participatory Design in New Zealand schools: A Case for using Social Media

In New Zealand, there are almost no studies of classroom layouts. Rather, the New Zealand studies on learning environments have focused on environmental issues such as acoustics, natural lighting, fresh air, and temperature. Even the Ministry of Education's learning studios pilot project only dealt with the building shell and failed to focus on furnishing these environments and creating good internal layouts. In general, it seems there is less care about the internal layout in New Zealand classroom studies. From observations made in earlier research into learning environments in primary schools (Alsaif, 2011), teachers are supposed to be responsible for the classroom layout and furniture arrangements. So on the one hand learning environments in New Zealand are not studied enough, while on the other there is also a lack of concern about the role of users in designing learning environments.

For true participatory design, users of designed environments should work alongside the designers. In the case of primary school learning environments, designers and architects might find it hard to work with young users, in addition to the difficulty of having a large number of users to include. This led to the idea of setting up a situation where the effect of social media on the participation of users in the design process of learning environments could be studied. The aim was to see the extent to which social media might be useful in enabling the participation of students and teachers in the design of their learning environments, and to reveal problems that might be encountered.

METHOD

As this research aimed at finding the effectiveness of using social media as a means of user involvement, in design an experimental methodology was selected. The creation of a blog (see section The two case studies) was based on Groat and Wang (2002) and their description of designing experiments for architectural research. Their methodology includes studying the effect of identifiable variables in the research. These variables can be manipulated or controlled by the researcher in order to create a suitable experiment. In this study the variables are the work of students uploaded to the blog and their teachers' comments and posts. The work of the students was determined by the design based exercises provided in the blog. Thus, the exercises were carefully planned given that they were dealing with young minds. For this project, a large part of the background on how to research and work with young people was taken from Thomson (2008). The research also built on the experience of working with primary school age children from earlier Master's research, through observing and interviewing them and in drawing sessions (Alsaif, 2011).

Another part of the methodology based on Groat & Wang (2002), was identifying the units of the experiment and manipulating their management. In this study, the work of the students was grouped into categories based on the main ideas behind it. For example, the work might reflect what they liked or disliked about their existing environments, or it might be complaints about the furniture in the learning environments, or ideas about future learning environments and their furniture and fixtures. Managing the ideas was accomplished by defining problems with existing learning environments and finding suitable solutions from the ideas for future ones. It was felt the blog could also help in understanding the ideas and in sorting out the problems and solutions through the online discussions it offers. Generally, lab research is more likely to take causality for granted than research that involves the reactions or behaviour of people. Thus, studies about people's reactions and behaviour tend to focus on the conditions and limitations of a causal interpretation (Groat & Wang, 2002). In order to help define the limitations and conditions of this experiment, teachers were asked to attach information to each piece of student work. The information could include the age of the student, the type of existing learning environment (single cell or open plan), how much time the students spent on the work, and the environment in which the work was completed. The blog was thus set up to encourage teachers to set the exercises in limited conditions; for example, for the suggested target group of students aged from 9 to 11 years, the work was to be completed within one school day, and the environment within which the work was done was to be the same learning environment as dealt with in their work.

The Two Case Studies

In order to explore the use of social media in participatory design involving children two case studies were conducted. These were developed consecutively. The first involved the use of a blog and a facebook page. It used a series of exercises to help children understand the issues involved in planning a classroom and developing ideas for their ideal classroom. This case study is referred to as 'the blog'. The second and later case study used a blog in addition to face to face communication between children, teacher and architect. This case study is called 'the blog plus'. The aim was to see which better aided participatory design of learning environments. The two case studies are first described and the results compared and conclusions drawn.

The Blog

An experimental blog was set up supported by exercises for the students to encourage them to produce suitable ideas for designing learning environments. It included two exercises and teachers had control of using these with their students. Teachers also had to upload the ideas and thoughts about learning environments produced by their students. The blog was designed to allow students to look at the work of other children in different schools under the supervision of the teachers. Although at this stage architects were not involved, it was envisaged that in real projects architects and designers could easily access these ideas with a view to their possible integration into designs for learning environments. Alternatively, they could discuss the ideas with the users (teachers and supervised students) through the comments in the same blog. It was hoped this experimental methodology would save time and make communication between architects and students easier than setting up face to face meetings. The blog was intended as a private place, with only invited participants having access. The two set exercises helped teachers introduce the task to students in a series of well described steps. The first aimed to encourage students to produce ideas and thoughts about their current learning environments, while the second was about future and ideal learning environments. Figure 1 shows the blog's structure. The students' work could be in individual or group format and in any medium chosen by the students, such as writing, manual or digital drawings, and video or voice recordings. The blog also provided a tutorial on how to upload and post student work.

Difficulties With the Blog

Measuring the effectiveness of the blog could not be completed as originally envisaged because of the very low response rate. In June 2013, an invitation was sent to primary school teachers throughout New Zealand to participate in the first blog. Despite the enthusiasm of teachers for involving children in participatory design from the earlier survey, it was disappointing that only 16 teachers accepted the invitation and of these only 3 posted material on the blog. The posts from the participatory design blog were supposed to be discussed in a focus group in a later phase of the research, but this was not really possible for two reasons. The first was there were too few posts that really only represented the student users of one classroom. The

Figure 1. The structure of the blog "Designing my Classroom"

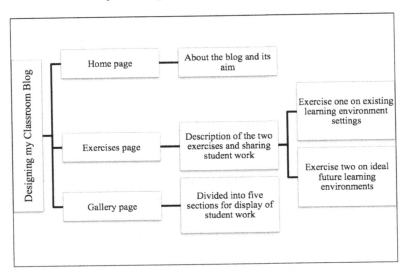

second was the difficulty in finding school architects willing to take part in a focus group, with only one enthusiastic response received. This meant there were could be no discussions about the posts and the ideas on the blog and no analysis of these in terms of the problems with and solutions for a participatory design process. The absence of measured outcomes and the lack of discussion of these meant the blog experiment was incomplete. It seemed that using social media in the form of a blog would not help participatory design of primary school learning environments.

The second step was, therefore, to set up a Facebook page the hope it would be more popular than a blog. As a result, in September 2013, a Facebook group with the same aims and exercises as the blog was initiated and invitations were again sent to primary school teachers around New Zealand. This time 27 teachers accepted the invitation. However, none posted anything related to the exercise or any previous involvement in the design process of learning environments. Some members of both the Facebook group and the blog declared they were happy to participate in these social media events and were using the exercises with their students but nothing was posted. It seems that teachers, as they said in the survey, like the idea of getting involved in collaboration and using these social media but find they are too busy for actual involvement.

As the experiment could not be completed with so few posts, a case study method was used for analysis. The posts, including the students' work, formed the case study and the material was used to answer the question: How can participants to the blog contribute in a design process through using social media? The proposition is that teachers and students do have sufficient knowledge to be able to participate in the design process of their learning environments. The units of analysis include teachers, students, and their posts on the blog. The data was collected from these posts in the form of documentation. The findings from analysis of this case study are presented below but first the second step in the attempted use of social media is described.

The Blog Plus

In the second case study the use of social media was a small part of the participatory process rather than the main method. This case study involved two classrooms in two primary schools in Wellington city, New Zealand. The exercise was to rearrange the furniture of each classroom based a revised layout devised by the users (teacher and students). Here the researcher took the role of the architect coming to the classroom with the aim of helping the students and their teacher evolve a classroom furniture layout design without any budget implications.

The design process in both classrooms started with an exploration stage in which the researcher collected information about the classroom layout and dimensions. This stage was completed from a visit supplemented with information gained from an interview with each teacher. The second stage was a brainstorming session that involved discussing general information about architecture and classroom layouts. This stage was completed via observations and discussions with the whole class, including the teacher. The third stage was the students rearranging the classroom layout on paper and discussing the new designs with each other and the teacher. All students, in addition to the teacher, were involved in this stage with the researcher as observer. The fourth stage used whole class gatherings and discussions, including the teacher to decide on the final design. The final stage was getting feedback from the students via a short questionnaire. At the start a social media blog was set up for each classroom where students could post comments and share their ideas and work. This blog was active throughout all stages of the participatory design process and its aim was to provide extra communication between students and the researcher who was taking the role of architect. All ideas and drawings could be uploaded to each of the two separate classroom blogs. Students and teachers were introduced to the blogs and how they could access and use them. Each blog gave students the opportunity to see each other's posted work and comment on this. Students thus gave design feedback through the blogs. The researcher as architect could analyse the students' comments in the blog without wasting school time.

After the brainstorming session, students had the first chance to open the blogs and participate by posting their own comments about the existing layout of their classroom. There was no given time for this task and the teachers encouraged their students to complete it during any free time in the given week. The researcher analysed these comments (see section The blog plus results) and then discussed them with the students in a face-to-face classroom session. This session was also used to introduce the students to the exercise on designing a new classroom layout. Some students were amazed that they had the chance to express their ideas through using a video camera or voice recorder. However, later, they discovered that drawings were easier than creating videos or voice recordings. As a result, most students chose to draw their ideas for the new classroom layout. Students chose to work in groups of two or three.

In the final visit by the researcher related to the design process, the ideas and comments in the form of the drawings, written work, voice recording, and videos in both classrooms were first discussed in a whole classroom session that included the teacher. Following this a discussion about the final layouts in each classroom took place. For this a floor plan of each classroom with only the fixed furniture and features was provided, together with the movable classroom furniture cut out of pieces of cardboard. The discussion was in the form of a consultation, where the architect (the researcher) consulted the students and teacher about the location of each zone and piece of furniture and then placed the cardboard cut-outs

to create a series of options. This was the point at which the issue of scale was discussed. Students became especially aware of this problem at this stage, because of the scale cardboard furniture cut-outs. As some students suggested ideas for the layout other students and the teachers voted for the ideas they liked. This part was important, as the researcher wanted to find a way of all users participating in a decision. The researcher as architect also gave opinions as an 'expert' on the design of spaces. The last part of this stage was moving the furniture cut-outs to create a final layout based on the whole class discussion.

For the last stage of this second case study, a final visit was made to each classroom after the furniture had been changed and the new layout put into place. A short presentation including photographs of students working on the classroom layout project was given and discussed with the students. Finally the students and the teachers were given a feedback sheet that asked for their opinions of the new layout. The feedback sheet for students consisted of a floor plan of the old furniture layout, a floor plan of the new one, three questions and a space for general comments.

RESULTS

The Posts in the Blog

In June 2013, the blog opened to participants. It has been previously introduced through the survey sent to all primary schools in New Zealand. In the survey 50 teachers responded positively to being part of the blog but as stated above only 16 accepted the invitation to join, and only 3 posted work.

In the first post (post 1), a teacher and her students completed exercise one. However, there were no drawings, sketches, or photographs submitted. They started the exercise with a brainstorming session about the current layout of their single cell classroom. It had one wall of windows, a front door, an art bay, and a door leading to the cloakroom bay. The teacher mentioned not having a veranda and expressed her feelings about that with a 'sad face'. The students then listed what they liked and did not like in the learning space. Likes included the interactive settings in the classroom, such as the interactive whiteboard, the computers, iPads, and a fishbowl with two fish. Students liked the fact that they changed seats every week. They also liked the natural light coming through the windows and the desks located by these. They liked some of the storage units, as they felt these provided a good place for classroom stuff such as the iPads, laptops, maths equipment, and classroom books. The teacher said that they liked the teacher's desk being in the art bay (in the cave area). Students liked the fact they could change their seats and did not have a fixed place for the whole school term. In addition, they liked having the option of sitting on cushions on the floor. In terms of their dislikes, they did not like the location of some settings, such as the bookshelf at right angles to the computer cupboard or having a shoe rack inside the classroom by the window. They also disliked the mess created by the cords by the computer tables. They would have liked to add to and change some of the existing furniture, and change the location of other pieces. However, there was no discussion of why they had these likes and dislikes, although some of this emerged in the students' drawings from the second exercise. They had, however, already changed from desks to tables, as they found the tables encouraged students not to be attached to one particular workspace (the student's desk). Instead, they had the choice of changing workspaces during activities. The teacher also claimed that the tables were easier to move than desks when they wanted to create a furniture free space for certain activities. They wanted to add more tables and storage boxes to the classroom, as unlike desks, the tables had nowhere to store books and pens. They wanted to move the jelly-bean shaped tables to the reading corner. They also mentioned changing the location of the interactive whiteboard, as when the sun entered the room it shone into their eyes when they looked at it.

In terms of participating in the classroom design the teacher said the students had the option to work in any setting inside the classroom such as at desks, at tables, on the floor, move around, or with laptops/iPads. However, the students would not normally choose the layout of the classroom furniture or the location of the settings inside the classroom.

The second post (post 2) was also about the first exercise on the existing learning space. The teacher and her students started by talking about the layout of their classroom. This was a fully carpeted room with a sink, shelving, wireless controller, "two work stations", high windows, individual desks grouped in fours, and an interactive whiteboard. The classroom had a door leading to a veranda with some seating, and the other door led to the cloakroom bay and toilets. They also listed what they liked and disliked about the classroom. Likes included the interactive board, the two workstations and the wireless service, as it enabled them to use the laptops at any time and in any place, and they liked the large area on the walls for display of things that help students to learn, such as the world map that showed where all the students' families were from. They liked that they had a fishing net hung from the ceiling and that they used it for learning purposes, such as catching the vocabulary words that were new to students. The teacher said that they liked having the books in desk trays. On the other hand, they disliked not having a proper wet area, as this made the sink area a mess, the fact there was not enough space in the mat area and that the colours of the classroom were dull (they would have liked bright colours). They also had an overheating problem, as not all windows had proper shading treatment, and this meant afternoon sun would heat up the classroom. The students claimed the desks were too low for some students and the chairs were uncomfortable.

In the third post (post 3), the teacher (the same teacher, students, and classroom of post 1) asked her students to redesign their existing classroom in a way they would like. The teacher gave them a floor plan as the basis for redesigning the existing internal layout. Not all the students of the classroom participated in this exercise. Students worked in pairs or individually and produced 11 redesigned floor plans (Figures 3 and 4). Students completed the exercise whilst inside their current classroom.

In the first drawing (Figure 2A) the student drew the existing layout of the classroom, as she liked it as it was. In this existing layout the cave area contained the teacher's desk in addition to the art bench that included a sink and tables were located in the centre of the classroom for group work. There were a number of storage units and a small furniture free area for mat time. Having this drawing was very useful, as the ideas of other children could be compared against the existing layout. This highlights the importance of having a drawing of the existing classroom layout at the start of any participatory design activity. In the second drawing (Figure 2B) the student kept the teacher's desk in the cave area. However, there was less furniture than in the existing classroom layout, which created a larger furniture free space for mat time or free movement of students. The desks and tables were arranged for students to work in groups. In the third drawing (Figure 2C) the cave was used for student activities rather than for housing the teacher's desk. In this layout, there were desks and tables for individual and group work. The fourth drawing (Figure 2D) divided the classroom into mini rooms for different activities, such as a reading room, play room, writing room, and a "treat" room. This layout had windows on all

Figure 2. (A-F) student drawings from post 3 on the blog

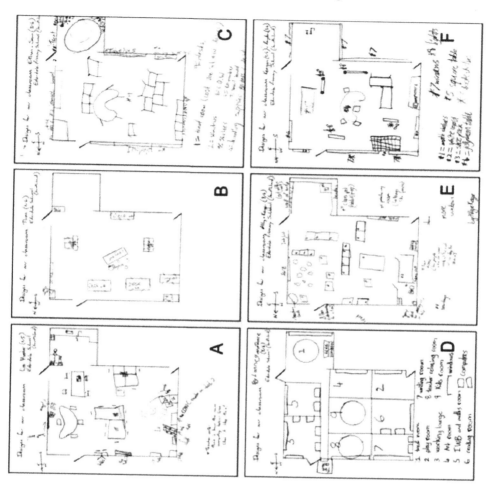

the classroom walls in order to light all these rooms. Some rooms have no furniture, which creates more space for students to move, learn, and play freely. In Figure 2E the cave was also converted to cater for student activities. The whiteboard and mat area were obvious in this layout in the top left corner. The students furnished the mat area with cushions and arranged the desks to serve both individual and group work. There were also furniture free spaces for free movement. In Figure 2F there was even less furniture to create more empty space for moving around. The students who completed this drawing included various design details, such as the lighting units and location of windows. Windows were located in all classroom walls for maximum natural light.

Figure 3. (G-K) student drawings from post 3 on the blog

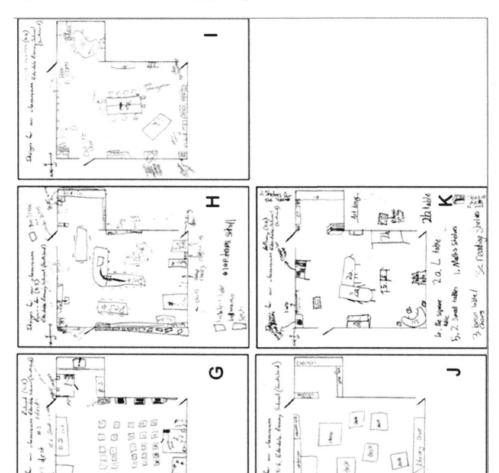

In Figure 3G the student made the cave into an area for student activities and moved the teacher's desk to another corner. Also included were various activity corners and settings around the classrooms. The main observation from this drawing was that the desks were arranged in the traditional way, with rows of individual desks facing one side of the classroom. In another design (Figure 3H) the students also suggested group tables for student group work and included activity corners around the classroom. Details covered the location of the heat pump. Figure 3I shows very similar ideas to the previous drawings, including having group-work tables and a number of activity corners. Noticeably, a couch was introduced in this

Figure 4. Student's written work from one of the rearrangement case studies

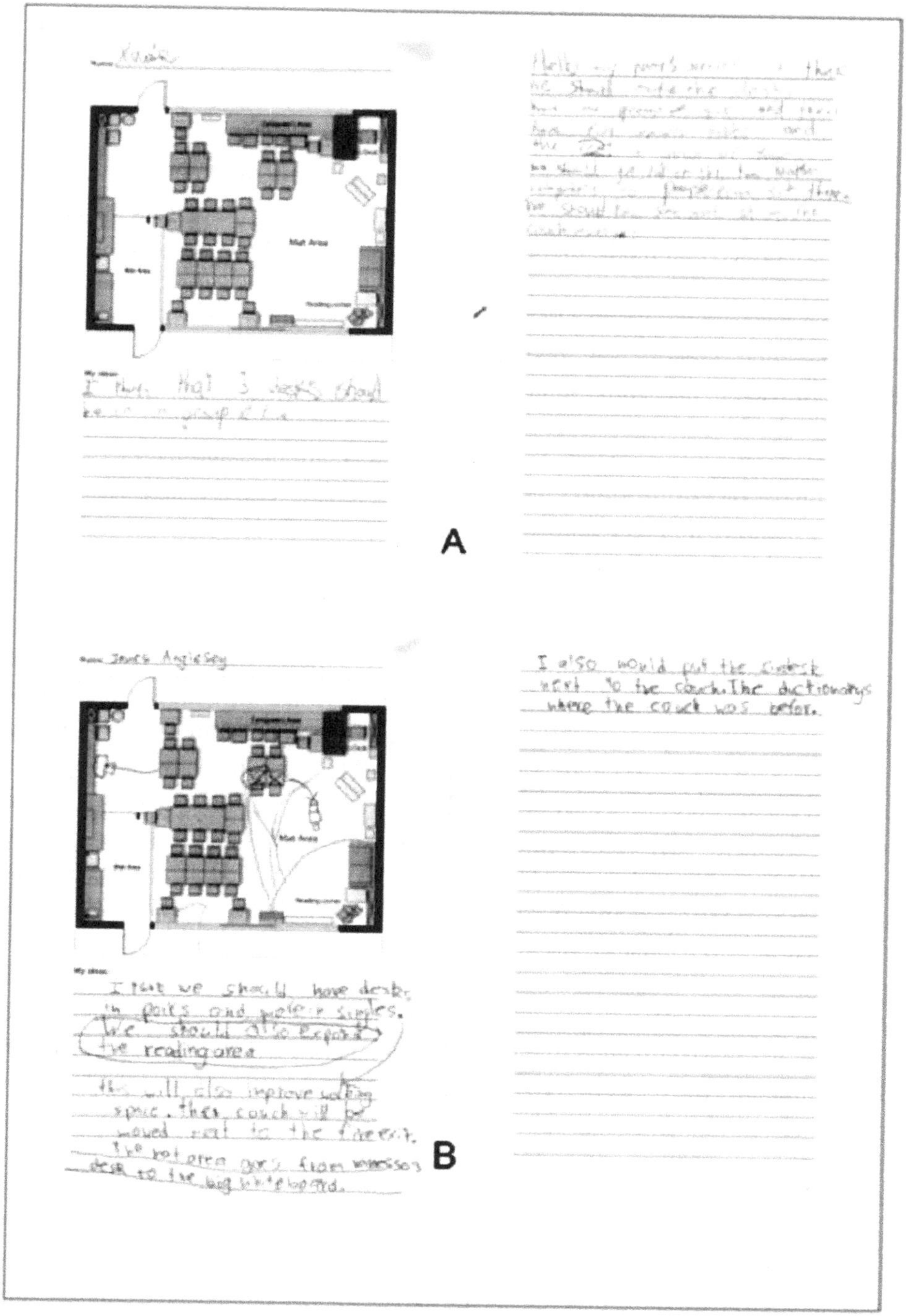

layout. The last two drawings (Figures 3J and 3K) were also similar to the others, with group-work tables and activity areas. The teacher's desk was kept in the cave area in both these drawings.

The Blog Plus Results

Students readily posted comments about their existing classrooms in the second case study. In one classroom these comments on could be put into three categories. The first contained comments on the desk arrangement and almost all comments in this category were about how crowded the desks were. Some students commented on the desk arrangement being boring. "They need [to be] dynamic," one student said. The second category was about the mat area. Although this was observed to be slightly crowded in use, some students commented it was too big. Others said they would like the location of the mat area changed. The third category was random comments. A student commented on the window treatments and the fact there are no curtains to block the sunlight when using the data projector. Other students suggested creating a bigger library/reading area. Some students suggested adding more soft settings such as beanbags.

As a result of the exercise on redesigning the classroom layout the students produced two pieces of written work, one voice recording, two videos, and nine completed drawings (Figures 4 and 5). In the written work, students suggested changing the layout of the desks, getting rid of the broken computers, having a bigger reading area and more circulation space, as well as some changes in the overall layout (Figure 4).

In the drawings, all students suggested changing the desk arrangement (Figure 5). They also wanted more space free of furniture than in the existing layout. However, students who used the paper furniture to test out their ideas had less furniture-free space in the revised work (Figure 5C & D). In Figure 5A the student drew the furniture at a similar scale to the actual furniture. So when he tested his work he achieved a similar layout to the existing (Figure 5B). Most drawings did not change much in terms of the overall locations for settings. Some drawings suggested changing the teacher's desk to another corner between two mat areas (Figure 5G). In general, the drawings focused on changing the desk arrangement. The voice recording and videos replicated the ideas in the drawings and written work of changing the desk arrangement and having more space for circulation.

Comparison of the Design Results

This discussion first considers the commonalities in the posts and drawings from both case studies and then the limitations of the exercises. The posts reveal common ideas when it comes to the likes and dislikes within the existing learning environments.

Figure 5. Student drawings from one of the rearrangement case studies

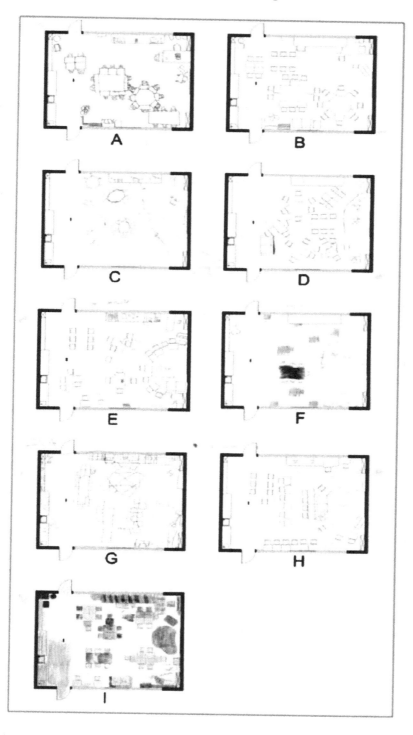

Teachers and their students liked the use of technology inside the classroom, such as the interactive whiteboard and the laptops. It is also obvious children want to use laptops wherever they like in the classroom, including on the floor. What also emerges is that there are problems using IT equipment, both from glare and in terms of dealing with wires. Students also liked having some space free of furniture for various activities, and this is reflected in the drawings, as students drew less furniture than the existing and created new furniture free spaces. This liking for the latter could be because it gives young students more freedom to play, move around and be creative in completing their set activities, rather than being stuck in a chair. However, there was a problem with scale in all the students' drawings. Students found it difficult to understand and draw the true size of familiar classroom furniture items. This led to some students suggesting more furniture free space within the same furniture and settings. However, some students had created more empty space by putting fewer pieces of furniture in the classroom, which could indicate that these students preferred working and learning on the floor more than using furniture. The designs from blog plus perhaps have more realism because the researcher as architect was able to ensure the children understood about scale, and the use of furniture cut-outs was a simple way to do this.

Students created group-work stations in nearly all drawings in both case studies, which probably underlines how much they like working in groups, although it may also reflect what they already have in their existing classroom. In the third post from the first case study, some students converted the cave area, which was used for art and to house the teacher's desk, into a space only for student activities. This perhaps indicated a student preference for having a semi private corner for quiet activities such as thinking or reading. Students also showed in their drawings that they wanted natural light as they drew windows in walls even where these would not be possible (Figures 3D and 3F). This was also mentioned in one of the posts, where the teacher said that students like to sit by the windows. Only one student suggested a traditional desk arrangement (Figure 4G), which may indicate that the majority of students prefer modern layouts that involve different activity settings that cater for different teaching and learning styles. Children also picked up on details such as giving the heat pump a location (Figure 4H). This suggests children of this age are well able to participate in the design of their classrooms. In terms of what children want in their classrooms the simple answer is a variety of spaces for working and for most children having space that is free of furniture so they can easily move around and work on the floor.

The majority of students in both case studies liked classrooms with specialized corners. Additionally, having spaces for separate activities was also liked, and this could well represent how students like to learn in different ways and that they have different needs inside the classroom, as the theory of multiple intelligences argues (Armstrong, 2009).

In terms of limitations, students may have not been in other types of classroom, so their ideas were extensions of what their current or previous classrooms offered. The exception was the two students who divided the space into many separate rooms for different functions (Figure 3D). The schemes from blog plus are also more realistic and having the researcher as architect may have limited the imaginations of the children compared to the first blog case study. This is where social media could have another role, as suggested by Bill (2014), by putting together a gallery of different types of learning environments for students to look at before they did their own designs. In the drawings from the first blog case study, the teacher gave her students the outline of the classroom for them to draw their different layouts on and she said that this might be the reason that no student tried to change the classroom shape, although the students who proposed drawing 3D did change its architecture. In the blog plus case study the students had to use the same shaped classroom as the aim was to change the classroom layout. It is also noticeable that student ideas were expressed only in plan form and no student drew either a section or three dimensional representation of the classroom. This may be the fault of the exercises in both the blog and blog plus case studies in not suggesting both plan and section of the existing classroom should be the starting point for the student work.

Comparison of the Blog and Blog Plus Methods

Using social media in different situations will probably give different results. The first blog experiment in participatory classroom design did not work as planned. However, the blog in the blog plus case study where a real project was involved worked well, or at least better than in the first experiment. The first point to emerge from the comparison is that using social media worked where there was a clear goal, which was changing the internal layout of classrooms with zero budget implication and with the researcher acting in the role of the architect. Having an aim or problem to solve seemed to generate more practical ideas and solutions in comparison to discussing general ideas or imagining ideal classrooms. Users, especially children, have little or no experience in interior design or architecture but giving them a project where they could see the results of applying their design ideas to a classroom setting gave them the chance to learn more about designing their learning spaces.

The second issue from the comparison is that in both experiments social media and online communication worked as a facilitator for saving time and effort for some activities. That said, participatory design using social media worked best where the researcher (as architect) was present in the classroom for almost all the stages in the experiment. The researcher could analyse the comments the students made on the blog but also had the chance to discuss issues with participants directly. The researcher also had the opportunity to change terms and words to simplify the tasks and discussion according to the students' abilities. Students and teachers could also chat with the researcher about many things, including some not directly related to the research. This built trust and made the communication friendlier than just giving instructions and orders. This changing of things as the design progressed was not possible when setting up the first blog and Facebook page, and it may be the communication about what was expected was not always clear. Although the researcher worked hard to simplify the tasks and exercises in the blog, there was no assurance that the teacher and students read them as intended.

The last point is that working with social media when the researcher acted as architect was only a small part of the study while in the first blog case study the whole work depended on the social media. It seems a mixture of social media and face-to-face communication worked much better. In the second blog plus study the students had a number of communication options. As well as social media they could engage in direct discussions, have hands on task sessions (such as physically rearranging the classroom layout), and use different media to express their ideas (videos, voice recording, writing, and drawing). Having these multiple communication options gave the classroom users a chance to participate in the way they liked. This again reflects the needs of students for multiple ways of learning in the classroom. Figure 6 summarises how social media was used in both methods.

CONCLUSION

The main and perhaps most important comment is that the students produced, with the help of their teacher only in the first blog case study, architectural floor plans. For their age, these drawings indicate that students were ready to participate in the design process of learning environments. They understood what the classroom layout meant and could deliver their ideas for this, both in discussion sessions and through their drawings.

The fact that most students in the two classrooms chose to draw as a way to express their ideas may indicate that drawing is the easiest method for students. It also may indicate that students can express their design ideas through drawings better than in any other way. This is, after all, the way architects work.

The case studies showed how students like to be involved in a design process. Students learned many things about their learning environment by completing the

Figure 6. The difference in using social media in the blog and blog plus case studies

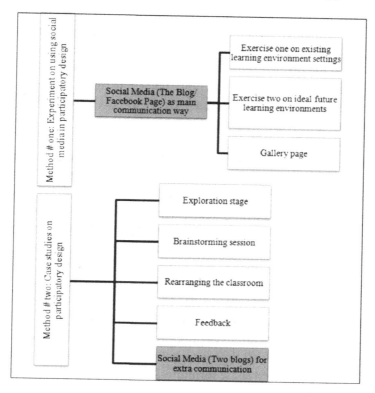

design process of rearranging the furniture of their classrooms and perhaps the most important thing they learned was that they had the right to talk about their ideas. Students could deliver ideas in the ways they found best. The design process also had a positive effect on the students' attitudes toward designing learning environments. Students learned that their ideas could be applied in the real environment if they were suitable and other users agreed with them. Students learned how to think about their needs, how to design layouts that would meet these, and how to negotiate towards a final agreed layout.

When it comes to the use of social media in the two case studies in the blog case study it seems teachers did not have the time to get involved in these online social media sites in order to explore classroom design with children as a general learning topic. Given the contrasting success in giving student users control over their classroom design with the more hands-on approach, this suggests that using online social media may not be the best way to increase user involvement in the design process of New Zealand primary schools. However, this conclusion may be influenced by the fact the very few participants in this study were currently involved in a school building or renovation project. If children did, with the help of their teacher, rearrange their classroom layout at the start of every year or after a period of use (perhaps after the first half-term), then social media is a useful way of collecting together proposals and comments on these, providing again the teacher has time to analyse these and feedback the results. This will only happened if designing a classroom is part of the regular curriculum, and what students learn from doing this is seen as useful and relevant (Bill, 2014). Additionally, the results produced by the children (mostly drawings) in these two case studies would allow architects, teachers, and the Ministry of Education to use their ideas in new designs, find solutions to common problems in existing classrooms, or form a base for guidelines for the design of learning environments in primary schools. For instance the Ministry of Education needs to know that children want to use IT but find problems with its use in existing classrooms. The search for ideal furniture for primary schools (Watson, 2017) may be an inappropriate waste of money if children would rather work on the floor.

The posts completed by students revealed that they were ready to have a role in the design process of learning environments. Students can understand the elements of designing spaces. They thought about the shell, which is the architectural borders of the space, by deciding the locations of doors and windows and by creating different rooms. They also thought about the use of interiors for learning when they changed the space layout and removed some furniture. The use of social media was perhaps a small part of their design achievements.

REFERENCES

Alsaif, F. (2011). *Intelligence-friendly environments: A study of New Zealand primary school classroom design in relation to multiple intelligences theory* (Master's thesis). Victoria University of Wellington.

Alsaif, F. (2015). *New Zealand learning environments: The role of design and the design process* (PhD thesis). Victoria University of Wellington.

Armstrong, T. (2009). *Multiple intelligences in the classroom*. Alexandria, VA: ASCD.

Bill, D. (2014, August). *8 Tips and Tricks to Redesign Your Classroom*. Retrieved October 3, 2014 from: http://www.edutopia.org/blog/8-tips-and-tricksredesign-your-classroom

Bland, D. C. (2009). Re-imagining school through young people's drawings. *Proceedings of the 1st International Visual Methods Conference University of Leeds.*

Brandt, E. (2006, August). Designing exploratory design games: A framework for participation in participatory design? In *Proceedings of the ninth conference on Participatory design: Expanding boundaries in design* (vol. 1, pp. 57-66). Trento, Italy: Academic Press. doi:10.1145/1147261.1147271

Clancy, G., Fröling, M., & Peters, G. (2015). Ecolabels as drivers of clothing design. *Journal of Cleaner Production, 99*, 345–353. doi:10.1016/j.jclepro.2015.02.086

Classroom Architect. (2008). Retrieved October 3, 2014 from: http://classroom.4teachers.org/index.html

De Winter, M., Baerveldt, C., & Kooistra, J. (1999). Enabling children: Participation as a new perspective on child health promotion. *Child: Care, Health and Development, 25*(1), 15–23. doi:10.1046/j.1365-2214.1999.00073.x PMID:9921418

DiSalvo, B., Yip, J., Bonsignore, E., & DiSalvo, C. (2017). *Participatory Design for Learning.* New York: Routledge.

Groat, L., & Wang, D. (2002). *Architectural research methods.* New York: John Wiley &Sons, Inc.

Hagen, P., & Robertson, T. (2010). Social technologies: challenges and opportunities for participation. In *Proceedings of the 11th Biennial Participatory Design Conference* (pp. 31-40). ACM. doi:10.1145/1900441.1900447

Hanington, B., & Martin, B. (2012). *Universal Methods of Design: 100 Ways to Research Complex Problems, Develop Innovative Ideas, and Design Effective Solutions.* Beverly, MA: Rockport Publishers.

Johnson, M. (2013). *How social media changes user-centred design: Cumulative and strategic user involvement with respect to developer–user social distance.* Aalto University Publication Series. Retrieved September 17, 2014 from: http://inuse.fi/2013/03/15/johnson-2013-how-social-media-changes-user-centred-design/

Kaasinen, E., Koskela-Huotari, K., Ikonen, V., & Niemeléi, M. (2013). Three approaches to co-creating services with users. In J. C. Spohrer & L. E. Freund (Eds.), Advances in the Human Side of Service Engineering (pp. 286–295). Academic Press.

Lukyanenko, R., Parsons, J., Wiersma, Y. F., Sieber, R., & Maddah, M. (2016). Participatory design for user-generated content; Understanding the challenges and moving forward. *Scandinavian Journal of Information Systems, 28*(1), 37–70.

Nair, P., & Fielding, R. (2007). *The language of school design: Design patterns for 21st century schools*. Minneapolis, MN: Design Share.

Näkki, P., & Antikainen, M. (2008). Online tools for codesign: User involvement through the innovation process. *New Approaches to Requirements Elicitation,* (96), 92–97.

Nesset, V., & Large, A. (2004). Children in the information technology design process: A review of theories and their applications. *Library & Information Science Research, 26*(2), 140–161. doi:10.1016/j.lisr.2003.12.002

Picaza-Vela, S., Fernandez-Haddad, M., & Luna-Reyes, F. L. (2016). Opening the black box: Developing strategies to use social media in government. *Government Information Quarterly, 33*(4), 693–704. doi:10.1016/j.giq.2016.08.004

Reyes, L. F. M., & Finken, S. (2012, August). Social media as a platform for participatory design. In *Proceedings of the 12th Participatory Design Conference: Exploratory Papers, Workshop Descriptions, Industry Cases* (vol. 2, pp. 89-92). ACM. doi:10.1145/2348144.2348173

Said, I. (2007). Architecture for Children: Understanding Children [sic] Perception towards Built Environment. In *Proceedings of International Conference Challenges and Experiences in Developing Architectural education in Asia*. Islamic University of Indonesia. Retrieved March 1, 2012, from http://eprints.utm.my/3575/

Thomson, P. (2008). *Doing visual research with children and young people*. London: Routledge.

Watson, D. (2017). The seat of learning (quest for the ideal school chair) (Talking Point). *Times Educational Supplement,* (5232), 44-45.

Zhang, J., & Zhang, Z. (2010). The Knowledge Management of Furniture Product Design and Development. *Proceedings 3rd International Conference on Information Management, Innovation Management and Industrial Engineering, 1*, 464-467.

KEY TERMS AND DEFINITIONS

Cave Area: A small area inside a classroom originally created for quiet reading and study.

Interactive Whiteboard: An instructional tool that allows computer images to be displayed on a board using a digital projector; teachers or students then can manipulate the elements on the board digitally.

Mat Area: A furniture free area inside a classroom usually used for class gathering and whole class activities.

Multiple-Intelligences: A theory proposed by Howard Gardner that suggests the existence of eight types of intelligences that people use variously when they learn.

Wet Area: An area inside the classroom used for messy and wet work such as painting and working with clay.

Chapter 10
Task Technology Fit in Online Transaction Through Apps

Naser Valaei
KEDGE Business School, France

S. R. Nikhashemi
Sultan Qaboos University, Oman

Hwang Ha Jin
Sunway University, Malaysia

Michael M. Dent
Sunway University, Malaysia

ABSTRACT

The purpose of this chapter is to examine what aspects of task-technology characteristics are most relevant to fit, satisfaction, and continuance intention of using apps in mobile banking transactions. Applying the SEM approach to a sample of 250 Malaysians, the findings of this chapter imply that the task characteristic of transaction-based apps is more relevant than technology characteristics. The results suggest that degree of fit is highly associated with mobile apps user satisfaction. Furthermore, the higher the degree of fit, the higher is the continuance intention to use apps for online transactions. Surprisingly, the findings show that the task characteristics are not relevant to continuous intention to use apps for online transactions.

DOI: 10.4018/978-1-5225-5326-7.ch010

INTRODUCTION

With the advent of Web 2.0 technologies (Valaei and Rezaei, 2017), the rapid development of applications has evolved and electronic devices are becoming smarter and smaller. Nowadays, companies are struggling to provide improvements to their services in order not lag behind their competitors. Mobile applications, as a new channel, have become a daily necessity for many of the human race (Rezaei *et al.*, 2017). Furthermore, consumer orientation towards online banking has changed. A study by Sangle and Awasthi (2011) indicated that mobile banking is crucial when considering the importance of the use of various channels of financial and banking companies. Customers prefer to perform transactions, transfer funds, pay their bills, and see their statements 'on the go' (Wannemacher and L'Hostis, 2015, Nikhashemi *et al.*, 2017), and they favour a 24/7 banking service through mobile apps (Rezaei and Valaei, 2017).

Mobile banking is defined as the act of making a financial transaction through a mobile device such as a tablets or smartphone. Consumer behaviour is being increasingly influenced by mobile banking (Taghavi-Fard and Torabi, 2010). Rahmani *et al.* (2012) indicate that wireless communication channel and affordable Internet data plans by telecommunication providers encourage customers to move towards mobile banking. Previous research shows that mobile banking allows banks to reduce their costs, stay competitive, and retain customers (Laukkanen *et al.*, 2008).

Anticipating the trajectories of new technologies is critical to the investment strategies of governments (Alcaide–Muñoz *et al.*, 2017) and banks. Research is limited on both the adoption and use of mobile apps for banking transactions. As banks develop their apps and provide most of their services online, previous studies have not recognized the importance of understanding under what circumstances customers would use mobile apps for their banking transactions. To address this gap, it is important to examine task-technology fit theory in the context of banking apps to comprehend the extent to which task characteristics and technology characteristics would give a better fit in banking apps and the degree to which they are associated with user satisfaction and continued intention to use banking apps.

Goodhue and Thompson (1995) claim that if the technology achieves a good fit, performance will be more effectively meet user needs. Task-technology fit will be higher when the functionality of technology fits the needs of customers. According to Lin and Wang (2006), customer satisfaction is the key element to determine the continuous intention of customers to use a technology. If apps meet consumer needs, they will be satisfied and continue using the apps (Rezaei and Valaei, 2017). The aim of this research is to examine what facets of task-technology fit impacts on satisfaction and continuance intention to use apps in mobile banking. This research tries to bridge this gap by answering the following question:

- What aspects of task-technology fit are more relevant to fit, satisfaction, and continuance intention of using apps in mobile banking transactions?

LITERATURE REVIEW AND HYPOTHESES

Task-technology fit is a model used to determine the concepts of fit and utilisation. Task-technology fit theory focuses on the representation of problem and tasks which must have a suitable fit to solve the problem. Task-technology fit is used to determine the intersection between the correct technological tool and the required task (Goodhue and Thompson, 1995). According to Goodhue and Thompson (1995), there are three key elements in Task-technology fit model, where "task characteristics" and "technology characteristics" will fit together to form the "task-technology fit".

Task characteristics are defined as behaviour performed by individuals to satisfy their information needs by changing inputs to outputs (Goodhue and Thompson, 1995). Relying on Schrier *et al.* (2010), a completion of a task is linked to the individual performance and the increasing of the task can enhance the effectiveness and efficiency.

- **H1:** Task characteristics are positively related to level of fit in apps mobile banking.

According to task-technology fit theory, when the task fits customer needs and improves performance, then customers will adopt the information system (Gebauer *et al.*, 2010). Technology characteristics are the attributes of the tools users use when carrying out specific tasks and they include software, hardware and support services (Goodhue and Thompson, 1995). When technology is utilised, the chances are that it has a good fit (Schrier *et al.*, 2010). However, it is likely that this scenario applies in apps channels as well.

- **H2:** Technology characteristic is positively related to level of fit in apps mobile banking.

Customer satisfaction is the "fit" between the advantage of using a system and the need of customers (Goodhue, 1998). According to Goodhue (1998), satisfaction is the most appropriate way to measure the usefulness of systems. Furthermore, the most appropriate way to measure "task-technology fit" would be the feeling of users about the systems and how the system satisfaction meets the task needs (Goodhue, 1998).

Financial institutions are growing fast nowadays and have evolved from traditional systems to a more digital approach this is important as the nature of a relationship between customers, products and services is a significant element of the banking industry (Mohsan *et al.*, 2011).

- **H3:** There is a positive relationship between task characteristics and user satisfaction in apps mobile banking.
- **H4:** There is a positive relationship between technology characteristics and user satisfaction in apps mobile banking.
- **H5:** There is a positive relationship between fit and user satisfaction in apps mobile banking.

The evaluation of quality perceptions and services can determine the continuous use of the Internet by customers (Ribbink *et al.*, 2004). The success of IT products and services depends on the continuous intention of individuals (Parthasarathy and Bhattacherjee, 1998, Karahanna *et al.*, 1999). Bhattacherjee (2001) indicates that when the expectations of the information system are satisfied, then customers will continue using the information system. Reddick and Zheng (2017) find that satisfaction with government mobile apps is the strongest predictor of future use. However, once customers develop loyalty towards an app then they will continue to use it. Figure 1 schematically depicts all the research hypotheses.

- **H6:** There is a positive relationship between task characteristics and continuance intention of using apps in mobile banking.
- **H7:** There is a positive relationship between technology characteristics and continuance intention of using apps in mobile banking.

Figure 1. Research model

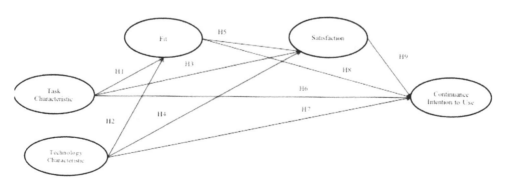

- **H8:** There is a positive relationship between fit and continuance intention of using apps in mobile banking.
- **H9:** There is a positive relationship between satisfaction and continuance intention of using apps in mobile banking.

Methodology and Sample Selection

This study uses convenience sampling approach and to measure the variables, measurement items are adopted from prior established researches as a methodological norm in measuring latent variables (Westland, 2015, Valaei *et al.*, 2017). The measurement items of task characteristics, technology characteristics, and fit constructs are adopted from Schrier *et al.* (2010). The measurement items of user satisfaction and continuance intention were adopted from (Rezaei and Valaei, 2017, Valaei and Baroto, 2017). Prior to data analysis, we took several steps to ensure that any possible bias is avoided. For instance, Harman's one factor test (Podsakoff *et al.*, 2003) shows that there is no common method bias, as no single factor accounts for more than 50% of the total variance (the results of principal component analysis with no rotation showed a total variance of 45.3%).

258 responses were received. We addressed the missing values through an expectation-maximization algorithm (EMA) (Little, 1988) applying SPSS software (Version 20). Eight cases were deleted from the collected data and a sample size of 250 acceptable responses was used for data analysis. Finally, to check the sample size efficiency to detect effect, a-priori sample size calculator for structural equation models (Soper, 2015) showed that sample size of 250 is adequate, as the recommended minimum sample size for an anticipated effect size of 0.3 and desired statistical power of 0.95 is 223.

A seven level Likert scale was used within where 1 denotes "strongly disagree" and 7 denotes "strongly agree". Table 1 shows the sample information. To analyse the models, SmartPLS software version 3.2.4 (Ringle *et al.*, 2015) is used. To test the measurement and structural models using partial least squares (PLS), a variance-based structural equation modelling approach (Valaei and Jiroudi, 2016). PLS approach is one of the proper methods to test SEM mode of analysis and it has an appropriate way of analysing conceptual frameworks with more than one dependent variable (Hair *et al.*, 2017, Hair *et al.*, 2011, Rezaei *et al.*, 2016, Valaei, 2017). In addition, PLS is a fully-fledged SEM (Valaei and Jiroudi, 2016) and is a well-established technique for estimating path coefficients in causal models (Birkinshaw *et al.*, 1995).

Table 1. Sample information (N= 250)

		Frequency	Percentage
Gender	Male	113	45.2
	Female	137	54.8
Age	18 – 24 years old	205	82.0
	25 – 34 years old	38	15.2
	35 – 44 years old	5	2.0
	45 – 54 years old	1	0.4
	55 – 64 years old	1	0.4
Race	Chinese	221	88.4
	Malay	8	3.2
	Indian	9	3.6
	Others	12	4.8
Monthly Expenses	Below 2000	187	74.8
	2001 - 4000	47	18.8
	4001 – 6000	9	3.6
	More than 6001	7	2.8

Results

Measurement Model Assessment

Before assessing the structural model, the researcher needs to ensure the validity and reliability of measurement model. To assess the measurement model, Cronbach's alpha, rho_A values, composite reliability, AVE (average variance extracted) and discriminant validity are examined. As tabulated in Table 2, all factor loadings are higher than the threshold of 0.7 and the AVEs are higher than 0.5. All values of rho_A (as a new measure of construct reliability), composite reliability, and Cronbach's alpha are acceptable (more than 0.7). Figure 2 schematically shows the measurement model within which the Task characteristic→ Continuance intention to use apps has the lowest path coefficient.

To assess the discriminant validity, Table 3 shows the Fornell-Larcker criterion (Fornell and Larcker, 1981). The results show that this criterion is met and the square roots of AVEs (diagonals in Table 3) are higher than the correlations between the constructs.

Another measure of discriminant validity is assessing the cross loading criterion. According to Table 4, all loadings of each construct (bold values in Table 4) are

Table 2. Reliability and validity

Research Construct	Item	Loading	Rho_A	AVE	Composite Reliability	Cronbach Alpha
Task characteristics	TaskCh1	0.856	0.852	0.767	0.908	0.848
	TaskCh2	0.891				
	TaskCh3	0.880				
Technology characteristics	TechCh1	0.780	0.854	0.575	0.890	0.852
	TechCh2	0. 803				
	TechCh3	0.733				
	TechCh4	0.737				
	TechCh5	0.775				
	TechCh6	0.720				
Fit	Fit1	0.841	0.896	0.698	0.920	0.891
	Fit2	0.869				
	Fit3	0.771				
	Fit4	0.854				
	Fit5	0.838				
User satisfaction	Sat1	0.916	0.899	0.831	0.937	0.898
	Sat2	0.898				
	Sat3	0.921				
Continuance intention to use apps	CI1	0.914	0.900	0.831	0.936	0.898
	CI2	0.902				
	CI3	0.917				

Figure 2. Results of measurement model

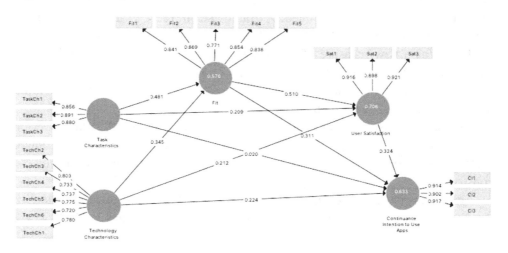

Table 3. Fornell-Larcker criterion

Constructs	Continuance Intention to Use Apps	Fit	Task Character-istics	Technology Character-istics	User Satisfaction
Continuance Intention to Use Apps	**0.911**				
Fit	0.736	**0.835**			
Task Characteristics	0.627	0.716	**0.876**		
Technology Characteristics	0.672	0.672	0.680	**0.759**	
User Satisfaction	0.744	0.802	0.718	0.696	**0.912**

Note: The diagonals represents the square root of AVE values and off-diagonals are the correlations between variables.

Table 4. Cross loadings criterion

Items	Continuance Intention to Use Apps	Fit	Task Characteristics	Technology Characteristics	User Satisfaction
CI1	**0.914**	0.629	0.522	0.577	0.658
CI2	**0.902**	0.688	0.595	0.615	0.673
CI3	**0.917**	0.691	0.595	0.642	0.701
Fit1	0.620	**0.841**	0.640	0.636	0.689
Fit2	0.642	**0.869**	0.651	0.588	0.705
Fit3	0.504	**0.771**	0.499	0.456	0.560
Fit4	0.653	**0.854**	0.587	0.551	0.695
Fit5	0.638	**0.838**	0.598	0.559	0.685
Sat1	0.708	0.754	0.659	0.683	**0.916**
Sat2	0.654	0.745	0.671	0.582	**0.898**
Sat3	0.670	0.692	0.632	0.637	**0.921**
TaskCh1	0.517	0.568	**0.856**	0.554	0.581
TaskCh2	0.563	0.649	**0.891**	0.588	0.661
TaskCh3	0.566	0.658	**0.880**	0.641	0.639
TechCh2	0.550	0.538	0.554	**0.803**	0.552
TechCh3	0.475	0.488	0.524	**0.733**	0.486
TechCh4	0.514	0.488	0.464	**0.737**	0.468
TechCh5	0.545	0.554	0.541	**0.775**	0.577
TechCh6	0.484	0.480	0.434	**0.720**	0.502
TechCh1	0.486	0.504	0.570	**0.780**	0.574

higher than the cross loadings of other measurement items of other constructs. However, this criterion is met.

The last discriminant validity criterion is Heterotrait-monotrait ratio . Shown in Table 5, all values are lower than the threshold of 0.9. Therefore, the discriminant validity of the constructs is met and the measurement model is reliable and valid.

Structural Model Assessment

The results of Table 6 show that the model has high predictive relevancy and the R^2 and Q^2 values have large effect size. The results of hypothesis testing (tabulated in Table 7 and schematically depicted in Figure 3) show that all hypotheses are supported except H6 (Task Characteristics → Continuance Intention to Use Apps with a weak path coefficient of 0.02 and insignificant T-value of 0.277). The highest significant path coefficients are received for the Fit → User Satisfaction and Task Characteristics → Fit relationships with value of 0.51 and 0.481 respectively.

DISCUSSION AND CONCLUSION

The ubiquity of apps in today's business environment is clear. Apps are used not only for fun, entertainment, and games, but also for facilitating access to government

Table 5. Heterotrait-monotrait ratio

Constructs	Continuance Intention to Use Apps	Fit	Task Characteristics	Technology Characteristics
Fit	0.817			
Task Characteristics	0.716	0.817		
Technology Characteristics	0.766	0.766	0.797	
User Satisfaction	0.826	0.892	0.820	0.793

Note: The threshold value for Heterotrait-monotrait ratio is 0.9 (Teo *et al.*, 2008).

Table 6. R^2 and Q^2 values

	R^2	Q^2	**Effect Size**
User satisfaction	0.706	0.551	Large
Continuance intention to use apps	0.633	0.492	Large

Table 7. Results of hypothesis testing

Hypothesis	Path	Path coefficient	Standard Error	T-Statistics	Decision
H1	Task Characteristics -> Fit	0.481	0.066	7.345*	Supported
H2	Technology Characteristics -> Fit	0.345	0.074	4.633*	Supported
H3	Task Characteristics -> User Satisfaction	0.209	0.052	4.019*	Supported
H4	Technology Characteristics -> User Satisfaction	0.212	0.061	3.45*	Supported
H5	Fit -> User Satisfaction	0.51	0.064	8.03*	Supported
H6	Task Characteristics -> Continuance Intention to Use Apps	0.02	0.073	0.277	Not Supported
H7	Technology Characteristics -> Continuance Intention to Use Apps	0.224	0.062	3.611*	Supported
H8	Fit -> Continuance Intention to Use Apps	0.311	0.075	4.169*	Supported
H9	User Satisfaction -> Continuance Intention to Use Apps	0.324	0.074	4.405*	Supported

Note: *p<0.01

Figure 3. Bootstrapping results

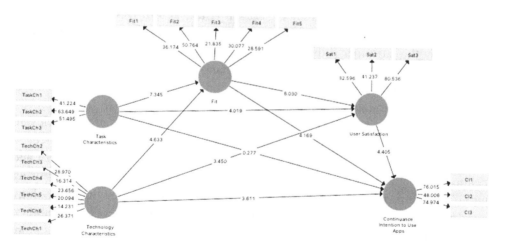

services (Reddick and Zheng, 2017) and simplifying methods of citizen participation (Wilson *et al.*, 2017). Due to their mobility and convenience, banks started to utilise apps for improving their services. Previous research on the user adoption of banking apps for performing transactions is very limited. This study applied task-technology fit theory to broaden our understanding towards the aspects of task-technology fit in satisfaction and continuance intention of using banking apps.

Previous research shows that task characteristics are closely related to the fit (Hollingsworth, 2015). An appropriate fit for the technology device-specific activity could be achieved by the combination of the relevant task characteristics. The findings of this study imply that task characteristic of transaction-based apps (path coefficient of 0.481) is more relevant than technology characteristic.

Task-technology fit can be affected by the functionality of technology. The performance of an app can be influenced by the fit between technologies (Trice and Treacy, 1988). Due to the convenience mobile devices provide, the degree of fit becomes important. The findings suggest that degree of fit is highly associated with mobile apps' user satisfaction (path coefficient of 0.51). According to Goodhue (1998), satisfaction is the most appropriate way to measure the usefulness of systems.

A poor fit decreases the intention to adopt a new technology (Lee *et al.*, 2005, Liang *et al.*, 2007). The results show that the higher the degree of fit, the higher is the continuance intention to use apps for online transactions (path coefficient of 0.311). Furthermore, continuous intention of information systems is dependant on the satisfaction of the consumers (Larsen *et al.*, 2009). Delone and McLean (2003) indicate that the determination of nett benefit and customer loyalty can be assumed by the customer satisfaction in IS success model. In line with previous researches (Zeithaml *et al.*, 1996, Szymanski and Henard, 2001, Heitmann *et al.*, 2007, Reddick and Zheng, 2017), this study finds a positive relationship between customer satisfaction and continuous intention to use apps.

Surprisingly, the results indicate that the task characteristics are not relevant to continuous intention to use apps for online transactions (path coefficient = 0.02 and T-value = 0.277). However, banks should note that the degree of fit and technology characteristics of apps are conducive to continuance intention of using apps. Therefore, policy makers and managers need to consider the technology characteristics of banking apps in terms of reliability, ease of control, usability, enjoyment experience, convenience, time saving ability, low risk, and customisation. Further research is required to examine other factors associated with the fit and the extent to which they may impact user satisfaction and continuous intention to use apps for online banking transactions.

REFERENCES

Alcaide–Muñoz, L., Rodríguez–Bolívar, M. P., Cobo, M. J., & Herrera–Viedma, E. (2017). Analysing the scientific evolution of e-Government using a science mapping approach. *Government Information Quarterly*, *34*(3), 545–555. doi:10.1016/j.giq.2017.05.002

Bhattacherjee, A. (2001). Understanding information systems continuance: An expectation-confirmation model. *Management Information Systems Quarterly*, *25*(3), 351–370. doi:10.2307/3250921

Birkinshaw, J., Morrison, A., & Hulland, J. (1995). Structural and competitive determinants of a global integration strategy. *Strategic Management Journal*, *16*(8), 637–655. doi:10.1002/smj.4250160805

Delone, W. H., & McLean, E. R. (2003). The DeLone and McLean model of information systems success: A ten-year update. *Journal of Management Information Systems*, *19*(4), 9–30. doi:10.1080/07421222.2003.11045748

Fornell, C., & Larcker, D. F. (1981). Evaluating structural equation models with unobservable variables and measurement error. *JMR, Journal of Marketing Research*, *18*(1), 39–50. doi:10.2307/3151312

Gebauer, J., Shaw, M. J., & Gribbins, M. L. (2010). Task-technology fit for mobile information systems. *Journal of Information Technology*, *25*(3), 259–272. doi:10.1057/jit.2010.10

Goodhue, D. L. (1998). Development and measurement validity of a task-technology fit instrument for user evaluations of information system. *Decision Sciences*, *29*(1), 105–138. doi:10.1111/j.1540-5915.1998.tb01346.x

Goodhue, D. L., & Thompson, R. L. (1995). Task-technology fit and individual performance. *Management Information Systems Quarterly*, *19*(2), 213–236. doi:10.2307/249689

Hair, J. F., Hult, G. T. M., Ringle, C., & Sarstedt, M. (2017). *A primer on partial least squares structural equation modeling (PLS-SEM)*. London, UK: Sage Publications Ltd.

Hair, J. F., Ringle, C. M., & Sarstedt, M. (2011). PLS-SEM: Indeed a silver bullet. *Journal of Marketing Theory and Practice*, *19*(2), 139–152. doi:10.2753/MTP1069-6679190202

Heitmann, M., Lehmann, D. R., & Herrmann, A. (2007). Choice goal attainment and decision and consumption satisfaction. *JMR, Journal of Marketing Research, 44*(2), 234–250. doi:10.1509/jmkr.44.2.234

Hollingsworth, C. L. (2015). *An Examination of Fit and the Use of Mobile Devices for Performing Tasks*. Academic Press.

Karahanna, E., Straub, D. W., & Chervany, N. L. (1999). Information technology adoption across time: A cross-sectional comparison of pre-adoption and post-adoption beliefs. *Management Information Systems Quarterly, 23*(2), 183–213. doi:10.2307/249751

Larsen, T. J., Sørebø, A. M., & Sørebø, Ø. (2009). The role of task-technology fit as users' motivation to continue information system use. *Computers in Human Behavior, 25*(3), 778–784. doi:10.1016/j.chb.2009.02.006

Laukkanen, P., Sinkkonen, S., & Laukkanen, T. (2008). Consumer resistance to internet banking: Postponers, opponents and rejectors. *International Journal of Bank Marketing, 26*(6), 440–455. doi:10.1108/02652320810902451

Lee, K. C., Lee, S., & Kim, J. S. (2005). Analysis of mobile commerce performance by using the task-technology fit. In *Mobile Information Systems* (pp. 135–153). Springer. doi:10.1007/0-387-22874-8_10

Liang, T.-P., Huang, C.-W., Yeh, Y.-H., & Lin, B. (2007). Adoption of mobile technology in business: A fit-viability model. *Industrial Management & Data Systems, 107*(8), 1154–1169. doi:10.1108/02635570710822796

Lin, H.-H., & Wang, Y.-S. (2006). An examination of the determinants of customer loyalty in mobile commerce contexts. *Information & Management, 43*(3), 271–282. doi:10.1016/j.im.2005.08.001

Little, R. J. A. (1988). Missing-Data Adjustments in Large Surveys. *Journal of Business & Economic Statistics, 6*(3), 287–296.

Mohsan, F., Nawaz, M. M., Khan, M. S., Shaukat, Z., & Aslam, N. (2011). Impact of customer satisfaction on customer loyalty and intentions to switch: Evidence from banking sector of Pakistan. *International Journal of Business and Social Science, 2*(16).

Nikhashemi, S. R., Valaei, N., & Tarofder, A. K. (2017). Does Brand Personality and Perceived Product Quality Play a Major Role in Mobile Phone Consumers' Switching Behaviour? *Global Business Review, 18*(3), 108–127. doi:10.1177/0972150917693155

Parthasarathy, M., & Bhattacherjee, A. (1998). Understanding post-adoption behavior in the context of online services. *Information Systems Research, 9*(4), 362–379. doi:10.1287/isre.9.4.362

Podsakoff, P. M., MacKenzie, S. B., Jeong-Yeon, L., & Podsakoff, N. P. (2003). Common Method Biases in Behavioral Research: A Critical Review of the Literature and Recommended Remedies. *The Journal of Applied Psychology, 88*(5), 879–903. doi:10.1037/0021-9010.88.5.879 PMID:14516251

Rahmani, Z., Tahvildari, A., Honarmand, H., Yousefi, H., & Daghighi, M. S. (2012). Mobile Banking and its Benefits. *Oman Chapter of Arabian Journal of Business and Management Review, 2*(5), 38–41. doi:10.12816/0002266

Reddick, C. G., & Zheng, Y. (2017). Determinants of citizens' mobile apps future use in Chinese local governments: An analysis of survey data. *Transforming Government: People, Process and Policy, 11*(2), 213–235. doi:10.1108/TG-11-2016-0078

Rezaei, S., Shahijan, M. K., Valaei, N., Rahimi, R., & Ismail, W. K. W. (2016). Experienced international business traveller's behaviour in Iran: A partial least squares path modelling analysis. *Tourism and Hospitality Research*. doi:10.1177/1467358416636930

Rezaei, S., & Valaei, N. (2017). Branding in a multichannel retail environment: Online stores vs app stores and the effect of product type. *Information Technology & People, 30*(4), 853–886.

Rezaei, S., & Valaei, N. (2017). Crafting experiential value via smartphone apps channel. *Marketing Intelligence & Planning, 35*(5), 688–702. doi:10.1108/MIP-08-2016-0141

Rezaei, S., Wee, C. H., & Valaei, N. (2017). Essential of Apps Marketing Implementation and E-Commerce Strategies: Apps Users' Decision-Making Process. In *Apps Management and E-Commerce Transactions in Real-Time* (pp. 141–158). IGI Global. doi:10.4018/978-1-5225-2449-6.ch006

Ribbink, D., Van Riel, A. C., Liljander, V., & Streukens, S. (2004). Comfort your online customer: Quality, trust and loyalty on the internet. *Managing Service Quality: An International Journal, 14*(6), 446–456. doi:10.1108/09604520410569784

Ringle, C. M., Wende, S., & Becker, J.-M. (2015). *SmartPLS 3*. Boenningstedt: SmartPLS GmbH. Retrieved from http://www.smartpls.com

Sangle, P. S., & Awasthi, P. (2011). Consumer's expectations from mobile CRM services: A banking context. *Business Process Management Journal*, *17*(6), 898–918. doi:10.1108/14637151111182684

Schrier, T., Erdem, M., & Brewer, P. (2010). Merging task-technology fit and technology acceptance models to assess guest empowerment technology usage in hotels. *Journal of Hospitality and Tourism Technology*, *1*(3), 201–217. doi:10.1108/17579881011078340

Soper, D. (2015). A-priori sample size calculator for Structural Equation Models [Software].

Szymanski, D. M., & Henard, D. H. (2001). Customer satisfaction: A meta-analysis of the empirical evidence. *Journal of the Academy of Marketing Science*, *29*(1), 16–35. doi:10.1177/0092070301291002

Taghavi-Fard, M., & Torabi, M. (2010). The Factors Affecting the Adoption of Mobile Banking Services by Customers and Rank Them (Case Study: Bank Tejarat In Tehran, Iran). *Journal Excavations Business Management*, *3*, 136–162.

Trice, A. W., & Treacy, M. E. (1988). Utilization as a dependent variable in MIS research. *ACM SIGMIS Database*, *19*(3-4), 33–41. doi:10.1145/65766.65771

Valaei, N. (2017). Organizational structure, sense making activities and SMEs' competitiveness: An application of confirmatory tetrad analysis-partial least squares (CTA-PLS). *VINE Journal of Information and Knowledge Management Systems*, *47*(1), 16–41. doi:10.1108/VJIKMS-04-2016-0015

Valaei, N., & Baroto, M. B. (2017). Modelling continuance intention of citizens in government Facebook page: A complementary PLS approach. *Computers in Human Behavior*, *73*, 224–237. doi:10.1016/j.chb.2017.03.047

Valaei, N., & Jiroudi, S. (2016). Job satisfaction and job performance in the media industry: A synergistic application of partial least squares path modelling. *Asia Pacific Journal of Marketing and Logistics*, *28*(5), 984–1014. doi:10.1108/APJML-10-2015-0160

Valaei, N., & Rezaei, S. (2017). Does Web 2.0 utilisation lead to knowledge quality, improvisational creativity, compositional creativity, and innovation in small and medium-sized enterprises? A sense-making perspective. *Technology Analysis and Strategic Management*, *29*(4), 381–394. doi:10.1080/09537325.2016.1213806

Valaei, N., Rezaei, S., & Ismail, W. K. W. (2017). Examining learning strategies, creativity, and innovation at SMEs using fuzzy set Qualitative Comparative Analysis and PLS path modeling. *Journal of Business Research*, *70*, 224–233. doi:10.1016/j. jbusres.2016.08.016

Wannemacher, P., & L'Hostis, A. (2015). *Global Mobile Banking Functionality Benchmark*. Cambridge.

Westland, J. C. (2015). Data Collection, Control, and Sample Size. In *Structural Equation Models* (pp. 83–115). Springer International Publishing.

Wilson, A., Tewdwr-Jones, M., & Comber, R. (2017). Urban planning, public participation and digital technology: App development as a method of generating citizen involvement in local planning processes. *Environment and Planning B. Urban Analytics and City Science*.

Zeithaml, V. A., Berry, L. L., & Parasuraman, A. (1996). The behavioral consequences of service quality. *The Journal of Marketing*, 31-46.

Conclusion

ACHIEVEMENTS IN THE USE OF SOCIAL MEDIA IN CITIZENS' PARTICIPATION AND FUTURE CHALLENGES

Introduction

The generalization of the access to general public to internet, together with the evolution of information and communication technology (ICT) technologies have increased the popularity of technology-based self-services. In this sense self-service technologies have changed both the way of interaction between different stakeholders with public sector, and the provision by different level of government of several services. So, the implementation in the public sphere of e-government implies the adoption of services of provision of public information, and the new offer of online services provides via web. The use of e-government stimulates and support good governance.

In the field of transparency, the increasing use of by public sector Internet has become an important tool in increasing public transparency and accountability. The new applications developed under web 2.0 scene, in general, and social media, in particular, can be understand as the new challenge in the use of Internet by government. In general, social media tools provide new and innovative methods that could help the immediate interaction between citizens and governments, and as Bertot et al. (2012) affirm, are "a central component of e-government in a very short period of time".

Around the world many government agencies have initiated electronic government (e-government) development, starting a new phase in the evolution of citizen participation in public administration decision making. Public sector agencies take advantage of Internet-based applications to facilitate community development and communication with constituents and to provide online application services.

Is in this context, where citizens increasingly demand an active role in public affairs and decision-making process. So, the relationship between citizens and governments has changed, and e-government represented the new alternative, extending and promoting its participatory opportunities to citizens.

Recently, scholars and researches has produced a growing body of literature focuses on government efforts in the use of new technologies in order to achieve a greater citizen participation and to create greater information exchange between citizens and government. Therefore, social media research topic, and particularly e-participation, is a key theme in the field of e-Government knowledge. In this sense, there is a gradual increase in the number of studies published in international journal in the last years. While the field of e-government has progressed significantly in the literature, there still have significant gaps in our understanding of the relationships among the management of e-participation applications, and citizens' experiences of e-participation (Kim & Lee, 2012).

In this context, the present book pretend to solved some question related with e-participation. In particular, questions about incentives, strategies, and technological tools used for implementing e-participation; the successful experiences in e-participation around the world; and the challenges and risks that can enhance e-Participation using social media technologies.

Theoretical Framework

E-Government is evolving over time and becoming increasingly mature as a discipline. The theories about development of e-Government are diverse, and adding and combining existing theories from different disciplines such as Politics, Sociology, Computing, Information System, Economics, Public Management and others.

Nowadays, new forms of citizen participation in political activity has emerged through information and communication technologies (ICT) under the umbrella of e-government, attracting, not only the attention from researchers, but also by practitioner communities. The government initiatives of e-Participation projects at all levels have suffered an incredible mushrooming, and the contributions in the scientific literature have grown exponentially (Medaglia, 2012).

As a part of e-Government, e-Participation tries to make the government's decisions more legitimate and publicly supported, aiming at encouraging public participation through technology. In the same line, e-Participation has a central role in the education of people about the complex process of policy making. Therefore the citizen has an understanding and better awareness about the rationale of the produced policy. As Park & Cho (2009) affirm, social media has a potential to shape a positive opinion about governments, providing mechanism for mutual cooperation between citizens and government. We can include in social media tools several categories: from sharing webs, as Youtube or Instagram; following by microblogs, as Twitter or wikis; to social networks as Facebook or Google+. In this sense, as an integral part of Web 2.0 technologies Social media characterized by user content, the creation of online profile and relative network (Magro, 2012).

Through participation in public affairs, citizens can produce social reforms in order to share the benefits to society. E-Participation empowers people and represents an innovative redistribution in order to consider citizens' opinion into the economic and political decisions.

Nowadays, e-Participation is an emerging research, and consequently, has different disciplines fields and research areas. There are limited present theories of e-Participation. In fact, the area does not have its own well-developed theories and methods. In the field of forms of participation, the majority used are the democratic models, relating the type of democracy established in the country (e.g. participatory democracy) with the manner than the citizens participate in public affairs. By the other hand, the e-participation is studied under theories related with the account in public sector.

Other theories have been used for a minority amount of researches. In this sense, primarily on institutional and governance theories, innovation diffusion theory, actor network theory, and finally, account of citizen associations.

So, with the exception of democratic models and political account, there is no evidence of shared theoretical background in the e-Participation sphere. In general, every research adopts the particular theory ad hoc in base to the particular research task (Saebo et al., 2008).

In this sense, following Medaglia (2012) the categories used by researches in order to analyze the development of e-Participation, could classify in:

- **e-Participation Actors:** Including citizens, politicians, government institutions, and voluntary organizations.
- **e-Participation Activities:** Actions taken by citizens and governments as e-Voting, online political discourse, online decision making, e-Activism, e-Consultation, or e-Petitioning.
- **Contextual Factors:** Inherent to living place. Between others: Information availability, infrastructure, underlying technologies, accessibility, policy and legal issues, and governmental organization.
- **e-Participation Effects:** Derivatives of implementation of e-Participation as civic engagements effects, deliberative effects, and democratic effects.
- **e-Participation Evaluation:** The assets and measurement the effects of e-Participation in order of quantity of e-Participation, demographic of participants, and tone and style in online activities.

Nevertheless, e-Participation has become an integral part of e-government initiatives worldwide, and the economic, cultural and other contextual differences between developed and developing countries could established some barriers in order to adapt the country context to social media participation. In this sense, it´s interesting the determination of gaps in organizational capacity between developed and developing countries in order to assets the implementation agenda and the advances in policy-making.

Conclusion

The rapid development of ICT influences the lifestyle of people, their interaction and communication significantly. The development of e-Participation has produced a rapidly growing research in this field. The number of contributions and the great dynamism shows in the field of e-Participation research area encompasses a wide range of perspectives. The findings summarized in the previous chapters can be read as a basis for grounded on the gaps, trends, and potentials of current e-Participation research, including the measures taken in developing countries.

In a first block, we analyzed the relation between social media, e-Government and e-Participation. The first chapter tries to identify research gaps and possibilities for improvement in social media and its use in citizens' e-Participation. Authors conclude that the future research should focus on specific projects in developing countries to better understand strategic objectives, gaps in innovation, challenges and risk on the adoption of social media. In addition, international organizations should lead political and social changes in these countries so that their citizenry can freely express their ideas and fight their rights, given that the adoption of technological advances improves economic, democratic and social development of these countries.

In the sphere of public administration, the adoption of e-government and the development of e-Participation have a large influence in the improvement of public administration. Consequently, a large number of governments put their effort in the promotion its positions of social media. Although, the governments are using social media for obtaining feedbacks on their activities.

Additionally, there are many benefits of social networks consists of increasing citizen's trust on the government and to improving the face of government. But there are risks, the politicians fear losing control over information, and facing to the destructive behaviour of haters.

So, analysing the political and economical behaviour of the country, as Niewiadomski and Anderson affirm, populism is the child of the paradoxical nature of representative democracy. In this sense, populism provides an opportunity for leaders to gain political control by using a variety of deceptive techniques and emotional manipulations. But that's not a real scene; the assault on the notion of truth is a major technique of such manipulation. E-participation could strengthen democracy and create a common environment to build common goals. The strategy of populism will change the society in a tyrannical form of government.

In a second block, we are going to study the different forms of implementation and development of e-Participation and social media in developing countries. In general, the provision of a stable and reliable net of ITC is the most measure demanded. But, every country has its own idiosyncratic environment.

Starting by Turkey, the access to ITCs is still scarce, existing severe legal regulation, bureaucratic resistance and significant disruptions in civilian intervention. The use of Facebook by the municipalities has no mutual interaction with citizens, with the exception of shares and liking. The information provides by municipal webs is scarce, and some departments don´t disclose any information. The Facebook usage by municipalities can be considered as a one-way information transmission tool that is far from interactive.

The following developed country analyzed is Mexico. Valle-Cruz and Sandoval-Almazan studies the differences between two municipalities in this developing country. In the one hand, very few have been done in updating laws and regulations that imply the use of technology in government. But in the other hand, websites or Apps are the media to participatory budget through technology. The information flows into two different ways, from government to citizens (G2C) and in the opposite, from citizens to government (C2G). In this context, the governments should focus their efforts on avoiding corruption, making governments transparent, opening data, and properly managing the privacy of information. Even more, municipalities should encourage the use of social media and generate strategies for citizens' participation and collaboration. Public policies for society could be improved increasing the information provided by citizens in social networks.

In the particular case of Cameroon, reinforce the perception than it´s clear that e-participation initiatives using Web 2.0 and social media tools provides new opportunities for meaningful participation in good governance in developing countries, showing than Facebook, YouTube and Twitter are the most used platforms in order to be transparent and reduce the corruption. But the development of ITCs is in their tender youth and it is necessary more investments in infrastructures and human capital.

Freitas and Everton study the cyberactivism in Brazil, and concluding that, while the cyberactivism could increase the legitimacy of democratic processes via increasing the outputs provides by social media, there are still possibilities to improve these practices. The expansion of cyberactivist networks –as well as the consolidation of other mechanisms of political participation– is the result of decades of democracy in the country. The continuity of the process encouraging those mechanisms will depend on the future political scenario. If the Brazil politicians are able to continue with the expansion of cyberactivism, the trend is to consolidate and strengthen democratic inclusive practices and encourage citizens towards a more effective participation in policymaking processes.

The last country analyzed is Philippines. So, at local governments level, is necessary taken some measures in order to stablish and advance in the field of Open Government. In this sense, the construction, provision and maintenance of infrastructures of ICTs and Internet is the first step. In the political sphere, the Open government could be improved with the establishment of policy frameworks. In third place, the provision of free information through the creation of data standards and the dissemination of information retrieved. Together this, local managers and staff with high capacitation and education in ITCs, could improve the development of Open Government. Finally, the establishment of a private and public system of leadership and sponsorship could facilitate the advance of Open Government.

Finally, the use of social media tolls in classroom and the use of apps in banking transactions are the last issues of study. In the first case, the students like to be participants of their learning environment and the design process. While student thinks than teachers are in a step under them, only with the help of teachers, social media could become in a usual way to collected proposal and provided feedback of results obtained.

In the second case, nowadays, the use of apps in generalized, not only for games, fun and communication, but also as a mean to interact easily with governments, retrieving information and facilitating the provision of public services. In this sense, banks are the one of the business that utilizes the apps to inform, connect, and provide services to their customers. As Valaei et al. affirm, the intention to use banking apps continually time by time is positively related with the satisfaction of customer. Moreover, the degree of fit and technology characteristics of apps conduces to a continuance intention of using banking apps. The characteristics of apps in terms of reliability, ease of control, usability, and convenience could be consider in order to improve the apps and increase the use of banking apps.

Future Challenge

Future research is necessary to deepen the analyses related to e-Participation. In this sense, these researches could focus on specific projects in developing countries to better understand strategic objectives, gaps in innovation, challenges and risk on the adoption of social media. In the specific case of Turkey, futures researches could evaluate other social media accounts, different of Facebook, in order to know if the situation of Facebook accounts is a general tendency of institutions in Turkey in all social net. Finally, its necessary the study of other factors associated with the fit in order to improve and increase the use of banking apps.

Francisco José Alcaraz-Quiles
University of Granada, Spain

Laura Alcaide-Muñoz
University of Granada, Spain

REFERENCES

Bertot, J. C., Jaeger, P. T., & Hansen, D. (2012). The impact of polices on government social media usage: Issues, challenges, and recommendations. *Government Information Quarterly*, *29*(1), 30–40. doi:10.1016/j.giq.2011.04.004

Kim, S., & Lee, J. (2012). E-Participation, Transparency, and Trust in Local Government. *Public Administration Review*, *72*(6), 819–828. doi:10.1111/j.1540-6210.2012.02593.x

Magro, M. J. (2012). A Review of Social Media Use in E-Government. *Adm. Sci.*, *2*, 148-161. Retrieved June 5, from www.mdpi.com/journal/admsci

Medaglia, R. (2012). E-Participation research: Moving characterization forward (2006-2011). *Government Information Quarterly*, *29*(3), 346–360. doi:10.1016/j.giq.2012.02.010

Park, J., & Cho, K. (2009). Declining relational trust between government and publics, and potential prospects of social media in the government public relations. In *Proceedings of EGPA Conference 2009*. The Public Service: Service Delivery in the Information Age.

Saebo, O., Rose, J., & Flak, L. S. (2008). The shape of e-Participation: Characterizing an emerging research area. *Government Information Quarterly*, *25*(3), 400–428. doi:10.1016/j.giq.2007.04.007

Compilation of References

Abdelsalam, H. M., Reddick, C. G., Gamal, S., & Al-Shaar, A. (2013). Social media in Egyptian government websites: Presence, usage, and effectiveness. *Government Information Quarterly*, *30*(4), 406–416. doi:10.1016/j.giq.2013.05.020

Abu-Shanab, E. (2012). Digital Government Adoption in Jordan: An Environmental Model. *The International Arab Journal of e-Technology*, *2*(3), 129-135.

Accenture. (2001). *Accenture Public Service Value Governance Framework*. Retrieved June 13, from www.accenture.com

Adweek. (2016). *Here's How Many People Are on Facebook, Instagram, Twitter and Other Big Social Networks*. Retrieved from http://www.adweek.com/digital/heres-how-many-people-are-on-facebook-instagram-twitter-other-big-social-networks/

Ae Chun, S., Luna-Reyes, L. F., Sandoval-Almazán, R., Carlo Bertot, J., Jaeger, P. T., & Grimes, J. M. (2012). Promoting transparency and accountability through ICTs, social media, and collaborative e-government. *Transforming Government: People, Process and Policy*, *6*(1), 78–91.

Ahmed, N. (2006). *An Anthology of E-Participation Models*. Paper presented at the E-Participation and E-Government: Understanding the Present and Creating the Future. Report of the Ad Hoc Expert Group Meeting, Budapest, Hungary.

Aitamurto, T. (2012). Crowdsourcing for Democracy: A New Era in Policy-Making. *Publications of the Committee for the Future, Parliament of Finland*. Available at: https://papers.ssrn.com/sol3/papers.cfm?abstract_id=2716771

Aitamurto, T., Landemore, H., Lee, D., & Goel, A. (2014). *Crowdsourced Off-Road Traffic Law in Finland*. Retrieved from https://www.eduskunta.fi/FI/tietoaeduskunnasta/julkaisut/Documents/tuvj_1+2014.pdf

Aksoy, L., van Riel, A., Kandampully, J., Bolton, R. N., Parasuraman, A., Hoefnagels, A., ... Komarova Loureiro, Y. (2013). Understanding Generation Y and their use of social media: A review and research agenda. *Journal of Service Management*, *24*(3), 245–267. doi:10.1108/09564231311326987

Al-Aama, A. Y. (2015). The use of Twitter to promote e-participation: Connecting government and people. *International Journal of Web Based Communities*, *11*(1), 73–96. doi:10.1504/IJWBC.2015.067082

Alcaide-Muñoz, L., & Rodríguez-Bolívar, M. P. (Eds.). (2018). International e-Government Development: Policy, Implementation and Best Practices. Palgrave McMillan. doi:10.1007/978-3-319-63284-1

Alcaide-Muñoz, C., & Gutierrez-Guiterrez, L. J. (2017). Six Sigma and organizational ambidexterity: A systematic review and conceptual framework. *International Journal of Lean Six Sigma*, *8*(4), 436–356. doi:10.1108/IJLSS-08-2016-0040

Alcaide-Muñoz, L., & Rodríguez-Bolívar, M. P. (2015). Understanding e-government Research. *Internet Research*, *25*(4), 633–673. doi:10.1108/IntR-12-2013-0259

Alcaide-Muñoz, L., Rodríguez-Bolívar, M. P., Cobo, M. J., & Herrera-Viedma, E. (2017). Analyzing the scientific evolution of e-Government using a science mapping approach. *Government Information Quarterly*, *34*(3), 545–555. doi:10.1016/j.giq.2017.05.002

Alcaide-Muñoz, L., Rodríguez-Bolívar, M. P., & Garde-Sánchez, R. (2014). Estudio cienciométrico de la investigación en transparencia informativa, participación ciudadana y prestación de servicios públicos mediante la implementación del e-Gobierno. *Revista de Contabilidad*, *17*(2), 130–142. doi:10.1016/j.rcsar.2014.05.001

Alcaid-Muñoz, L., & Garde-Sánchez, R. (2014). Implementation of e-Government and reforms in Public Administration in crisis periods: A Scientometric Approach. *International Journal of Public Administration in the Digital Age*, *2*(1), 1–23. doi:10.4018/ijpada.2015010101

Al-Dalou, R., & Abu-Shanab, E. (2013). *E-participation levels and technologies*. Paper presented at the 6th International Conference on Information Technology (ICIT 2013).

Al-Khamayseh, S., Hujran, O., Aloudat, A., & Lawrence, E. (2006). *Intelligent M-Government: Application of Personalisation and Location Awareness Techniques*. Mobile Government Consortium International LLC.

Almarabeh, T., & AbuAli, A. (2010). A general framework for e-government: Definition maturity challenges, opportunities, and success. *European Journal of Scientific Research, 39*(1), 29–42.

Almarabeh, T., & AbuAli, A. A. (2010). General Framework for E-Government: Definition Maturity Challenges, Opportunities, and Success. *European Journal of Scientific Research, 39*(1), 29–42.

Alsaif, F. (2011). *Intelligence-friendly environments: A study of New Zealand primary school classroom design in relation to multiple intelligences theory* (Master's thesis). Victoria University of Wellington.

Alsaif, F. (2015). *New Zealand learning environments: The role of design and the design process* (PhD thesis). Victoria University of Wellington.

Andersen, T. B. (2009). E-Government as an anti-corruption strategy. *Information Economics and Policy, 21*(3), 201–210. doi:10.1016/j.infoecopol.2008.11.003

Anderson, D. (2013). *E-participation: Innovative Strategies, Emerging Trends and Services for the Empowerment of People*. Retrieved from http://www.un.org/esa/socdev/egms/docs//2013/ict/DennisAnderson.pdf

Antovski, L., & Gusev, M. (2005). *M-Government Framework*. Mobile Government Consortium International LLC.

Araújo, R., Penteado, C., & Santos, M. (2015, December). Democracia Digital e Experiências de e-Participação: Webativismo e políticas públicas. *Historia, Ciencias, Saude--Manguinhos, 22*(supl.), 1597–1619. doi:10.1590/S0104-59702015000500004 PMID:26785869

Arendt, H. (1963). *Eichmann in Jerusalem: A Report on the Banality of Evil*. Penguin Classics.

Armano, D. (2010). Six Social Media Trends for 2010, 2009. *Harvard Business Review*. Retrieved June 18, from http://blogs.hbr.org/cs/2009/11/six_social_media_trends.html

Armstrong, D., & Gilson, J. (2011). Introduction: Civil Society and International Governance. In D. Armstrong, V. Bello, J. Gilson, & D. Spini (Eds.), *Civil Society and International Governance* (pp. 1–13). New York: Routhledge.

Armstrong, T. (2009). *Multiple intelligences in the classroom*. Alexandria, VA: ASCD.

Arstein, R. (1969). A ladder of citizen participation. *Journal of the American Institute of Planners, 35*(4), 216–224. doi:10.1080/01944366908977225

Au, M., Lam, J., & Chan, R. (2015). Social Media Education: Barriers and Critical Issues. Springer Berlin Heidelberg. doi:10.1007/978-3-662-46158-7_20

Babaoglu, C., Akıllı, S., & Demircioglu, M. A. (2012). E-Government Education at the Public Administration Departments in Turkey. In R. Gil-Garcia, N. Helbig, & A. Ojo (Eds.), *ICEGOV-Open Innovation of Global Change* (pp. 71–85). New York: ACM. doi:10.1145/2463728.2463745

Banday, M.T., & Mattoo, M.M. (2013). Social Media in e-Governance. *Scientific Research Journal*, 47-56.

Bannister, F., & Connolly, R. (2014). ICT, public values and transformative government: A framework and programme for research. *Government Information Quarterly*, *31*(1), 119–128. doi:10.1016/j.giq.2013.06.002

Basu, S. (2004). E-government and developing countries: An overview. *International Review of Law Computers & Technology*, *18*(1), 109–132. doi:10.1080/13600860 410001674779

Bauer, F., & Kaltenböck, M. (2011). Linked open data: The essentials. Edition mono/monochrom.

Bauman, Z. (1989). *Modernity and the Holocaust*. Cornell University Press.

Bediang, G., Stoll, B., Geissbuhler, A., Klohn, A. M., Stuckelberger, A., Nko'o, S., & Chastonay, P. (2013). Computer literacy and E-learning perception in Cameroon: The case of Yaounde Faculty of Medicine and Biomedical Sciences. *BMC Medical Education*, *13*(1), 57. doi:10.1186/1472-6920-13-57 PMID:23601853

Belachew, M. (2010). E-government initiatives in Ethiopia. *Proceedings of the 4th International Conference on Theory and Practice of Electronic Governance*.

Bélanger, F., & Carter, L. (2008). Trust and risk in e-Government adoption. *The Journal of Strategic Information Systems*, *17*(2), 165–176. doi:10.1016/j.jsis.2007.12.002

Bennett, W., & Segerberg, A. (2013). *The logic of Connective Action: Digital Media and the Personalization of Contentious Politics*. Cambridge, UK: Cambridge University Press. doi:10.1017/CBO9781139198752

Bensghir, K. T. (2002). Web'deki Belediyelerimiz: Eskişehir Büyükşehir Belediyesi [Our municipalities on the Web: Eskisehir Metropolitan Municipality]. *Çağdaş Yerel Yönetimler Dergisi*, *11*(1), 107–124.

Bershadskaya, L., Chugunov, A., & Trutnev, D. (2014). *Evaluation of E-Participation in Social Networks: Russian E-Petitions Portal* (Vol. 21). Retrieved from http://www.medra.org/servlet/aliasResolver?alias=iospressISSNISBN&issn=1871-1073&volume=21&spage=76

Bershadskaya, L., Chugunov, A., & Trutnev, D. (2014). Evaluation of E-Participation in Social Networks: Russian E-Petitions Portal. In M. W. A. Janssen, F. Bannister, O. Glassey, H. J. Scholl, E. Tambouris, M. A. Wimmer, & A. Macintosh (Eds.), *Electronic Government and Electronic Participation* (pp. 76–83). Amsterdam: IOS Press.

Bertot, J. C., Jaeger, P. T., & Grimes, J. M. (2010). *Crowd-sourcing transparency: ICTs, social media, and government transparency initiatives.* Digital Government Society of North America. Retrieved from http://dl.acm.org/citation.cfm?id=1809874.1809887

Bertot, J. C., Jaeger, P. T., & Grimes, J. M. (2010). Using ICTs to create a culture of transparency: E-government and social media as openness and anti-corruption tools for societies. *Government Information Quarterly, 27*(3), 264–271. doi:10.1016/j.giq.2010.03.001

Bertot, J. C., Jaeger, P. T., & Hansen, D. (2012). The impact of polices on government social media usage: Issues, challenges, and recommendations. *Government Information Quarterly, 29*(1), 30–40. doi:10.1016/j.giq.2011.04.004

Bhattacherjee, A. (2001). Understanding information systems continuance: An expectation-confirmation model. *Management Information Systems Quarterly, 25*(3), 351–370. doi:10.2307/3250921

Bill, D. (2014, August). *8 Tips and Tricks to Redesign Your Classroom*. Retrieved October 3, 2014 from: http://www.edutopia.org/blog/8-tips-and-tricksredesign-your-classroom

Birkinshaw, J., Morrison, A., & Hulland, J. (1995). Structural and competitive determinants of a global integration strategy. *Strategic Management Journal, 16*(8), 637–655. doi:10.1002/smj.4250160805

Bista, S. K., Nepal, S., & Paris, C. (2013). The human touch of government services. In *Proceedings of the Late-Breaking Results, Project Papers and Workshop Proceedings of the 21ˢᵗ Conference on User Modeling, Adaptation, and Personalization (UMAP'13)*. Rome, Italy: Springer International Publishing.

Bland, D. C. (2009). Re-imagining school through young people's drawings. *Proceedings of the 1st International Visual Methods Conference University of Leeds.*

Bonsón, E., Royo, S., & Ratkai, M. (2015). Citizens' engagement on local governments' Facebook sites. An empirical analysis: The impact of different media and content types. *Western Europe Government Information Quarterly, 32*(1), 52-62.

Bonsón, E., Royo, S., & Ratkai, M. (2015). Citizens' engagement on local governments' Facebook sites. An empirical analysis: The impact of different media and content types in Western Europe. *Government Information Quarterly, 32*(1), 57–62. doi:10.1016/j.giq.2014.11.001

Bonsón, E., Royo, S., & Ratkai, M. (2017). Facebook Practices in Western European Municipalities. An Empirical Analysis of Activity and Citizens' Engagement. *Administration & Society, 49*(3), 320–347. doi:10.1177/0095399714544945

Bonsón, E., Torres, L., Royo, S., & Flores, F. (2012). Local e-Government 2.0: Social Media and Corporate Transparency in Municipalities. *Government Information Quarterly, 29*(2), 123–132. doi:10.1016/j.giq.2011.10.001

Bossio, J. (2012). Using Web 2.0 to Influence PERU's ICT Sector. *IMPACT 2.0*, 63.

Boulianne, S. (2015). Social media use and participation: A meta-analysis of current research. *Information Communication and Society, 18*(5), 524–538. doi:10.1080/1369118X.2015.1008542

Bourdieu, P. (2011). O campo político. *Revista Brasileira de Ciência Política, Brasília, 2011*(5). 10.1590/S0103-33522011000100008

Bowler, S., Donovan, T., & Karp, J. A. (2007). Enraged or engaged? Preferences for direct citizen participation in affluent democracies. *Political Research Quarterly, 60*(3), 351–362. doi:10.1177/1065912907304108

Brandt, E. (2006, August). Designing exploratory design games: A framework for participation in participatory design? In *Proceedings of the ninth conference on Participatory design: Expanding boundaries in design* (vol. 1, pp. 57-66). Trento, Italy: Academic Press. doi:10.1145/1147261.1147271

Breind, Y., & Francq, P. (2008). Can Web 2.0 applications save e-democracy? A study of how new internet applications may enhance citizen participation in the political process online. *Int. J. Electron. Democr, 1*(1), 14–31. doi:10.1504/IJED.2008.021276

E. Brousseau, M. Marzouki, & C. Méadel (Eds.). (2012). *Governance, regulations, and powers on the Internet.* Cambridge, UK: Cambridge University Press. doi:10.1017/CBO9781139004145

Bullock, K. (2014). *Citizen Participation and Democracy. In Citizens, Community and Crime Control* (pp. 25–49). Springer.

Bwalya, K. J. (2009). Factors affecting adoption of e-government in Zambia. *The Electronic Journal on Information Systems in Developing Countries*, 38.

Cadwalladr, C. (2017). Daniel Dennett: 'I begrudge every hour I have to spend worrying about politics'. *The Guardian*. Retrieved from https://www.theguardian. com/science/2017/feb/12/daniel-dennett-politics-bacteria-bach-back-dawkins-trump-interview

Campbell, S., & Flagg, R. (2010). *Examples of Agencies Using Online Content and Technology to Achieve Mission and Goals*. Retrieved June 10, from www.usa.gov

Canares, M., de Guia, J., Narca, M., & Arawiran, J. (2014). *Opening the Gates: Will Open Data Initiatives Make Local Governments in the Philippines More Transparent?* Retrieved from http://opendataresearch.org/sites/default/files/publications/Opening the Gates - Will Open Data Initatives Make Local Government in the Philippines More Transparent.pdf

Castells, M. (1996). *The Rise of the Network Society, The Information Age: Economy, Society and Culture* (Vol. I). Malden, MA: Blackwell.

Castells, M. (2013). *Redes de Indignação e Esperança: Movimentos sociais na era da Internet*. Rio de Janeiro: Zahar.

Cepik, M., & Canabarro, D. (Eds.). (2010). *Governança de TI: transformando a Administração Pública no Brasil Rio Grande do Sul: CEGOV/UFRGS*. Retrieved from http://www.lume.ufrgs.br/bitstream/handle/10183/78940/000764826. pdf?sequence=1

Cercel, D.-C., & Trausan-Matu, S. (2014). Opinion Propagation in Online Social Networks: A Survey. New York: ACM. doi:10.1145/2611040.2611088

Cha, M., Haddadi, H., Benevenuto, F., & Gummadi, P. K. (2010). Measuring user influence in twitter: The million follower fallacy. *4th Int'l AAAI Conference on Weblogs and Social Media, 10*(10-17), 30.

Chan, C. M. L. (2013). From Open Data to Open Innovation Strategies: Creating E-Services Using Open Government Data. *Proceedings of the 46th Hawaii International Conference on System Sciences (HICSS-46)*, 1890–1899. doi:10.1109/HICSS.2013.236

Chang, A., & Kannon, P. K. (2008). *Leveraging Web 2.0 in government. E-Government Technology Series*. IBM Center for the Business of E-Government. Retrieved June 10, from www.businessofgovernment.org

Chan, H. S., & Chow, K. W. (2007). Public Management Policy and Practice in Western China: Metapolicy, Tacit Knowledge, and implications for Management Innovation Transfer. *American Review of Public Administration, 37*(4), 479–497. doi:10.1177/0275074006297552

Charalabis, Y., & Loukis, E. (2012). Transforming government agencies' approach to e-participation through efficient exploitation of social media. *Proceedings of the 2011 European Conference on Information Systems*, 1–12.

Chatfield, A. T., & Brajawidagda, U. (2013). *Political will and strategic use of YouTube to advancing government transparency: An analysis of Jakarta government-generated YouTube videos.* Paper presented at the International Conference on Electronic Government. doi:10.1007/978-3-642-40358-3_3

Chen, Y., Chen, H., Huang, W., & Ching, R. K. (2006). E-government strategies in developed and developing countries: An implementation framework and case study. *Journal of Global Information Management, 14*(1), 23–46. doi:10.4018/jgim.2006010102

Chesnevar, C. I., Maguitman, A. G., González, M. P., & Estevez, E. (2016). *Opinion Aggregation and Conflict Resolution in E-Government Platforms: Contrasting Social Media Information through Argumentation* (P. Novais & D. Carneiro, Eds.). IGI Global. doi:10.4018/978-1-5225-0245-6.ch011

Chomsky, N. (2017). *Requiem for the American Dream: The 10 Principles of Concentration of Wealth & Power.* Seven Stories Press.

Chun, S. A., Shulman, S., Sandoval, R., & Hovy, E. (2010). Government 2.0: Making connections between citizens, data and government. *Information Polity, 15*(1), 1.

Chun, S. A., & Cho, J.-S. (2012). E-participation and Transparent Policy Decision Making. *Information Polity, 17*, 129–145.

CIA. (2017). *The World Factbook - Africa: Cameroon.* Retrieved 01-07-2017, 2017, from https://www.cia.gov/library/publications/resources/the-world-factbook/geos/cm.html

Clancy, G., Fröling, M., & Peters, G. (2015). Ecolabels as drivers of clothing design. *Journal of Cleaner Production, 99*, 345–353. doi:10.1016/j.jclepro.2015.02.086

Classroom Architect. (2008). Retrieved October 3, 2014 from: http://classroom.4teachers.org/index.html

CNPS. (2008). *General information on social security in Cameroon.* Retrieved from http://www.cnps.cm/index.php?view=article&id=78:immobilier&format=pdf

CNPS. (2015). *Reserved for Employers*. Retrieved from http://www.cnps.cm/index. php?option=com_content&view=article&id=83&Itemid=105

CNPS. (2016). *Disclosure of false news about CNPS: The General Manager reassures and invites vigilance 2017*. Retrieved from http://www.cnps.cm/index. php?option=com_content&view=article&id=585%3Adivulgation-de-fausses-nouvelles-sur-la-cnps--le-dg-rassure-et-invite-a-la-vigilance&catid=4%3Aarticles-actualites&lang=en

CNPS. (2017). *History of CNPS*. Retrieved from http://www.cnps.cm/index. php?option=com_content&view=article&id=78&Itemid=97&lang=en

Coleman, S. (2017). *Can the Internet Strengthen Democracy?* Cambridge, UK: Polity Press.

Coleman, S., & Sampaio, R. (2016). Sustaining a democratic innovation: A study of three e-participatory budgets in Belo Horizonte. *Information Communication and Society, 20,* 1–16.

Colicchia, C., & Strozzi, F. (2012). Supply chain risk management: A new methodology for a systematic literature review. *Supply Chain Management, 17*(4), 403–418. doi:10.1108/13598541211246558

Cooke, J., Ariss, S., Smith, C., & Read, J. (2015). On-going collaborative priority-setting for research activity: A method of capacity building to reduce the research-practice translational gap. *Health Research Policy and Systems, 13*(1), 25. doi:10.1186/s12961-015-0014-y PMID:25948236

Couldry, N. (2007). New media for global citizens? The future of the digital divide debate. *The Brown Journal of World Affairs, 14,* 249–261.

Criado, J. I., Sandoval-Almazan, R., & Gil-Garcia, J. R. (2013). Government innovation through social media. *Government Information Quarterly, 30*(4), 319–326. doi:10.1016/j.giq.2013.10.003

Cropf, R. A., Benmamoun, M., & Kalliny, M. (2012). The Role of Web 2.0 in the Arab Spring. *Cases on Web 2.0 in Developing Countries: Studies on Implementation, Application, and Use: Studies on Implementation, Application, and Use,* 76.

Cuillier, D., & Piotrowski, S. J. (2009). Internet information-seeking and its relation to support for access to government records. *Government Information Quarterly, 26*(3), 441–449. doi:10.1016/j.giq.2009.03.001

Dadashzadeh, M. (2010). Social media in government: From eGovernment to eGovernance. *Journal of Business & Economics Research*, *8*(11), 81–86. doi:10.19030/jber.v8i11.51

Damanpour, F., & Schneider, M. (2008). Characteristics of Innovation and Innovation Adoption in Public Organizations: Assessing the Role of Managers. *Journal of Public Administration: Research and Theory*, *19*(3), 495–522. doi:10.1093/jopart/mun021

Davies, T. (2014). The construction of open government data. *64th Annual Meeting of the International Communication Association*.

Davies, T. G., & Bawa, Z. A. (2012). The Promises and Perils of Open Government Data (OGD). *The Journal of Community Informatics*, *8*(2), 1–6. Retrieved from http://ci-journal.net/index.php/ciej/article/view/929/926

Dawes, S. S. (2010). Stewardship and usefulness: Policy principles for information-based transparency. *Government Information Quarterly*, *27*(4), 377–383. doi:10.1016/j.giq.2010.07.001

Dawes, S. S., & Helbig, N. (2010). Information strategies for open government: Challenges and prospects for deriving public value from government transparency. *International Conference on Electronic Government*, 50–60. doi:10.1007/978-3-642-14799-9_5

Dawkins, R. (1990). *The Selfish Gene*. Oxford University Press.

De Winter, M., Baerveldt, C., & Kooistra, J. (1999). Enabling children: Participation as a new perspective on child health promotion. *Child: Care, Health and Development*, *25*(1), 15–23. doi:10.1046/j.1365-2214.1999.00073.x PMID:9921418

Debatin, B., Lovejoy, J. P., Horn, A. K., & Hughes, B. N. (2009). Facebook and online privacy: Attitudes, behaviors, and unintended consequences. *Journal of Computer-Mediated Communication*, *15*(1), 83–108. doi:10.1111/j.1083-6101.2009.01494.x

DeiwiksC. (2009). *Populism*. Retrieved from https://www.ethz.ch/content/dam/ethz/special-interest/gess/cis/cis-dam/CIS_DAM_2015/WorkingPapers/Living_Reviews_Democracy/Deiwiks.PDF

Delbufalo, E. (2012). Outcomes of inter-organizational trust in supply chain relationships: A systematic literature review and a meta-analysis of the empirical evidence. *Supply Chain Management*, *17*(4), 377–402. doi:10.1108/13598541211246549

Delone, W. H., & McLean, E. R. (2003). The DeLone and McLean model of information systems success: A ten-year update. *Journal of Management Information Systems*, *19*(4), 9–30. doi:10.1080/07421222.2003.11045748

Denyer, D., & Tranfield, D. (2009). Producing a systematic review. In D. Buchanan & A. Brymand (Eds.), *The Sage Handbook of Organizational Research Methods* (pp. 671–689). London: Sage Publications.

DeVaujany, F. X., Carton, S., Mitev, N., & Romeyer, C. (2014). Applying and theorizing institutions frameworks in ISI research: A systematic analysis from 1999 to 2009. *Information Technology & People, 27*(3), 280–317. doi:10.1108/ITP-10-2013-0185

Dini, A. A., & Sæbø, Ø. (2016). *The current state of social media research for eParticipation in developing countries: a literature review.* Paper presented at the System Sciences (HICSS), 2016 49th Hawaii International Conference on. doi:10.1109/HICSS.2016.339

DiSalvo, B., Yip, J., Bonsignore, E., & DiSalvo, C. (2017). *Participatory Design for Learning.* New York: Routledge.

Dominguez-Torres, C. F. (2011). *Cameroon's Infrastructure: A Continental Perspective.* Academic Press.

Ebrahim, Z., & Irani, Z. (2005). E-government adoption: Architecture and barriers. *Business Process Management Journal, 11*(5), 589–611. doi:10.1108/14637150510619902

Edwards, A., Bekkers, V., & de Kool, D. (2013). Social media monitoring: Responsive governance in the shadow of surveillance? *Government Information Quarterly, 30*(4), 335–342. doi:10.1016/j.giq.2013.05.024

Eisenstadt, M., & Vincent, T. (1998). *The Knowledge Web.* Stylus Publishing Inc.

Ellis, K., & Kent, M. (2011). *Disability and New Media.* New York: Routledge.

Ellison, N., & Hardey, M. (2014). Social Media and Local Government: Citizenship, Consumption and Democracy. *Local Government Studies, 40*(1), 21–40. doi:10.1080/03003930.2013.799066

Emmanouilidou, M., & Kreps, D. (2010). A framework for accessible m-government implementation. *Electronic Government, an International Journal, 7*(3), 252–269.

Engresser, S., Ernst, N., Esser, F., & Büchel, F. (2017). Populism and social media: how politicians spread a fragmented ideology. *Information, Communication & Society, 20*, 1109-1126.

Epstein, D.; Katzenbach, C. & Musiani, F. (2016). Editorial – Doing internet governance: how science and technology studies inform the study of internet governance. *Internet Policy Review.*

Evans, A. M., & Campos, A. (2013). Open government initiatives: Challenges of citizen participation. *Journal of Policy Analysis and Management, 32*(1), 172–185. doi:10.1002/pam.21651

Ferro, E. & Molinari, F. (2010). Making sense of Gov 2.0 strategies: "No citizens, no party". *JeDEM-eJournal of eDemocracy and Open Government, 2*(1), 56-68.

Fidel, R., Scholl, H. J., Liu, S., & Unsworth, K. (2007). Mobile government fieldwork: A preliminary study of technological, organizational, and social challenges (Vol. 228). Digital Government Research Center.

Figueiredo, F., Almeida, J. M., Gonçalves, M. A., & Benevenuto, F. (2014). On the Dynamics of Social Media Popularity: A YouTube Case Study. *ACM Trans. Internet Technol., 14*(4), 24:1–24:23. 10.1145/2665065

Fornell, C., & Larcker, D. F. (1981). Evaluating structural equation models with unobservable variables and measurement error. *JMR, Journal of Marketing Research, 18*(1), 39–50. doi:10.2307/3151312

Freitas, C. (2016). Sociotechnical and Political Processes shaping Digital Democracy in Brazil: the case of the project e-Democracia In Inovação, Governança Digital e Políticas Públicas: conquistas e desafios para a democracia. Belo Horizonte: Arraes Editores.

Freitas, C., & Aranha, M. (2017). Commons como Motor de Inovação nas Sociedades Contemporâneas. In *Proceedings of Communication and Policy Research Latin America Conference*. CPRLatam.

Freitas, C., Fiuza, F., & Queiroz, F. (2015). Os Desafios ao Desenvolvimento de um Ambiente para Participação Política Digital: O Caso de uma Comunidade Virtual Legislativa do Projeto e-Democracia no Brasil. *Organizações & Sociedade, 22*(75), 639–657. doi:10.1590/1984-9230759

Fukuyama, F. (1992). *The End of History and the Last Man*. New York: Free Press.

Furuholt, B., & Wahid, F. (2008). *E-government Challenges and the Role of Political Leadership in Indonesia: The Case of Sragen*. Paper presented at the Hawaii International Conference on System Sciences. doi:10.1109/HICSS.2008.134

Ganapati, S., & Reddick, C. (2014). The use of ICT for Open Government in U.S. Municipalities. *Public Performance & Management Review, 37*(3), 365–387. doi:10.2753/PMR1530-9576370302

Gao, X., & Lee, J. (2017). E-government services and social media adoption: Experience of small local governments in Nebraska state. *Government Information Quarterly*, *34*(4), 627–634. doi:10.1016/j.giq.2017.09.005

Garson, D. G. (2006). *Public Information Technology and E-Governance: Managing the Virtual State*. London: Jones and Bartlett Pub.

Gebauer, J., Shaw, M. J., & Gribbins, M. L. (2010). Task-technology fit for mobile information systems. *Journal of Information Technology*, *25*(3), 259–272. doi:10.1057/jit.2010.10

GEM. (2015). *Producto Interno Bruto Municipal*. Toluca, México. Retrieved from http://igecem.edomex.gob.mx/sites/igecem.edomex.gob.mx/files/files/Archivos PDF/Productos Estadisticos/Índole Económica/PIB/PIB_municipal2015.pdf

GGAP. (2012). *Good Governance Action Plan*. Retrieved from http://www.gov.ph/governance/wp-content/uploads/2015/04/good-governance-cluster-plan-2012-2016.pdf

Gokce, O., & Orselli, E. (2012). E-Demokrasi Vatandaşların Siyasete İlgilerinin ve Katılımlarının Arttırılmasının Bir Aracı Mı? [Is e-Democracy a Tool to Arise the Interest of Citizen to Politics and for Participation]. in. E-Devlet. Ankara: Nobel.

Gomes, W. (2011). *90 anos de Comunicação e Política* (Vol. 9). Salvador: Contemporânea.

Goodhue, D. L. (1998). Development and measurement validity of a task-technology fit instrument for user evaluations of information system. *Decision Sciences*, *29*(1), 105–138. doi:10.1111/j.1540-5915.1998.tb01346.x

Goodhue, D. L., & Thompson, R. L. (1995). Task-technology fit and individual performance. *Management Information Systems Quarterly*, *19*(2), 213–236. doi:10.2307/249689

Groat, L., & Wang, D. (2002). *Architectural research methods*. New York: John Wiley &Sons, Inc.

Guillamón, M. D., Rios, A. M., Gesuele, B., & Metallo, C. (2016). Factors influencing social media use in local governments: The case of Italy and Spain. *Government Information Quarterly*, *33*(3), 460–471. doi:10.1016/j.giq.2016.06.005

Gurstein, M. B. (2011). Open data: Empowering the empowered or effective data use for everyone? *First Monday*, *16*(2). doi:10.5210/fm.v16i2.3316

Hagen, P., & Robertson, T. (2010). Social technologies: challenges and opportunities for participation. In *Proceedings of the 11th Biennial Participatory Design Conference* (pp. 31-40). ACM. doi:10.1145/1900441.1900447

Hair, J. F., Hult, G. T. M., Ringle, C., & Sarstedt, M. (2017). *A primer on partial least squares structural equation modeling (PLS-SEM)*. London, UK: Sage Publications Ltd.

Hair, J. F., Ringle, C. M., & Sarstedt, M. (2011). PLS-SEM: Indeed a silver bullet. *Journal of Marketing Theory and Practice, 19*(2), 139–152. doi:10.2753/MTP1069-6679190202

Halonen, A. (2012). *Being open about data. Analysis of the UK Open Data Policies and applicability of open data.* London: The Finnish Institute in London.

Hanington, B., & Martin, B. (2012). *Universal Methods of Design: 100 Ways to Research Complex Problems, Develop Innovative Ideas, and Design Effective Solutions.* Beverly, MA: Rockport Publishers.

Hao, X., Zheng, D., Zeng, Q., & Fan, W. (2016). How to strengthen the social media interactivity of e-government: Evidence from China. *Online Information Review, 40*(1), 79–96. doi:10.1108/OIR-03-2015-0084

Harder, C. T., & Jordan, M. M. (2013). The transparency of county websites: A content analysis. *Public Administration Quarterly, 37*(1), 103–128.

Harris, A., & Rea, A. (2009). Web 2.0 and Virtual World technologies: A Growing impact on IS Education. *Journal of Information Systems Education, 20*(2).

Hartley, J., & Kostoff, R. N. (2003). How useful are key words' in scientific journals? *Journal of Information Science, 29*(5), 433–438. doi:10.1177/01655515030295008

Heckmann, D. (2011). Open government - Retooling democracy for the 21st century. *Proceedings of the Annual Hawaii International Conference on System Sciences,* 1–11. doi:10.1109/HICSS.2011.334

Heeks, R. (2002). e-Government in Africa: Promise and practice. *Information Polity, 7*(2-3), 97-114.

Heeks, R. (2003). *Success and failure rates of eGovernment in developing/transitional countries: Overview.* IDPM, University of Manchester. Retrieved from http://www.egov4dev.org/sfoverview.htm

Heeks, R. (2001). *Understanding e-governance for development.* Institute for Development Policy and Management Manchester.

Heeks, R., & Bailur, S. (2007). Analyzing e-government research: Perspectives, philosophies, theories, methods, and practice. *Government Information Quarterly, 24*(2), 243–265. doi:10.1016/j.giq.2006.06.005

Heitmann, M., Lehmann, D. R., & Herrmann, A. (2007). Choice goal attainment and decision and consumption satisfaction. *JMR, Journal of Marketing Research, 44*(2), 234–250. doi:10.1509/jmkr.44.2.234

Hellman, R. (2011). The Cloverleaves of Social Media Challenges for e-Governments. *Proceedings of eChallenges e-2011 Conference*, 1–8.

Hine, C. (2000). *Virtual Ethnography*. London: Sage Publications. doi:10.4135/9780857020277

Hofmann, J., Katzenbach, C., & Gollatz, K. (2014) *Between Coordination and Regulation: Conceptualizing Governance in Internet Governance*. HIIG Discussion Paper Series, Berlim, n. 2014-04.

Hofmann, S., Beverungen, D., Michael, R., & Becker, J. (2013). What Makes Local Governments' Online Communications Successful? Insights From A Multi-Method Analysis Of Facebook. *Government Information Quarterly, 30*(4), 387–396. doi:10.1016/j.giq.2013.05.013

Holgersson, J., & Karlsson, F. (2014). Public e-service development: Understanding citizens' conditions for participation. *Government Information Quarterly, 31*(3), 396–410. doi:10.1016/j.giq.2014.02.006

Hollingsworth, C. L. (2015). *An Examination of Fit and the Use of Mobile Devices for Performing Tasks*. Academic Press.

Holzer, M., & Manoharan, A. (2016). Digital Governance in Municipalities Worldwide ~ A Longitudinal Assessment of Municipal Websites Throughout the World. E-Governance Institute National Center for Public Performance, Rutgers University.

Holzer, M., You, M.-B., & Manoharan, A. (2010). Digital Governance in Municipalities Worldwide ~ A Longitudinal Assessment of Municipal Websites Throughout the World. E-Governance Institute National Center for Public Performance, Rutgers University.

Hood, C. (2008). The Tools Of The Government. In *The Information Age. In The Oxford Handbook of Public Policy*. Oxford, UK: Oxford University Press.

Hooghe, M., Marien, S., & Quintelier, E. (2010). Inequalities in non-institutionalized forms of political participation: A multi-level analysis of 25 countries. *Political Studies, 58*(1), 187–213. doi:10.1111/j.1467-9248.2009.00801.x

Huang, W.-L., & Feeney, M. K. (2016). Citizen Participation in Local Government Decision Making: The Role of Manager Motivation. *Review of Public Personnel Administration, 36*(2), 188–209. doi:10.1177/0734371X15576410

Hu, G., Pan, W., Lin, H., Kang, K., & Best, M. L. (2014). Study on the Framework of e-Government Services Capability. An empirical investigation. *Social Science Computer Review, 32*(1), 56–73. doi:10.1177/0894439313501614

Hughes, D. J., Rowe, M., Batey, M., & Lee, A. (2012). A tale of two sites: Twitter vs. Facebook and the personality predictors of social media usage. *Computers in Human Behavior, 28*(2), 561–569. doi:10.1016/j.chb.2011.11.001

Hui, G., & Hayllar, M. R. (2010). Creating public value in e-Government: A public-private-citizen collaboration framework in Web 2.0. *Australian Journal of Public Administration, 69*(1), 120–131. doi:10.1111/j.1467-8500.2009.00662.x

Hussain, Y. (2014). *Social Media as a Tool for Transparency and Good Governance in the Government of Gilgit-Baltistan.* Crossroads Asia Working Paper Series, 22.

INEGI. (2015). *Encuesta Intercensal 2015.* INEGI. Retrieved from http://www.beta.inegi.org.mx/proyectos/enchogares/especiales/intercensal/

Inglehart, R., & Norris, P. (2016). *Trump, Brexit, and the Rise of Populism: Economic Have-Nots and Cultural Backlash.* HKS Working Paper No. RWP16-026. Retrieved from https://ssrn.com/abstract=2818659

International Labor Organization. (2001). *Facts on Social Security.* Retrieved from http://www.ilo.org/wcmsp5/groups/public/---dgreports/---dcomm/documents/publication/wcms_067588.pdf

Ionescu, G., & Gellner, E. (1969). Introduction. In G. Ionescu & E. Gellner (Eds.), *In Populism - Its Meanings and National Characteristics.* London: Weidenfeld & Nicolson.

Islam, M. S. (2008). Towards a sustainable e-Participation implementation model. *European Journal of ePractice, 5*(10).

Jaeger, P. T., & Bertot, J. C. (2010). Transparency and technological change: Ensuring equal and sustained public access to government information. *Government Information Quarterly, 27*(4), 371–376. doi:10.1016/j.giq.2010.05.003

Jamieson, K. H. (2017). New name for fake news: 'viral deception'/Interviewer: B. Stelter. *Reliable Sources, CNN, CNN.com.* Retrieved from http://www.cnn.com/videos/tv/2017/03/05/new-name-for-fake-news-viral-deception.cnn

Janssen, M., Charalabidis, Y., & Zuiderwijk, A. (2012). Benefits, Adoption Barriers and Myths of Open Data and Open Government. *Information Systems Management*, *29*(4), 258–268. doi:10.1080/10580530.2012.716740

Jho, W., & Song, K. J. (2015). Institutional and technological determinants of civil e-Participation: Solo or duet? *Government Information Quarterly*, *32*(4), 488–495. doi:10.1016/j.giq.2015.09.003

Johnson, M. (2013). *How social media changes user-centred design: Cumulative and strategic user involvement with respect to developer–user social distance.* Aalto University Publication Series. Retrieved September 17, 2014 from: http://inuse.fi/2013/03/15/johnson-2013-how-social-media-changes-user-centred-design/

Joseph, R. C. (2013). A structured analysis of e-Government studies: Trends and opportunities. *Government Information Quarterly*, *30*(4), 435–440. doi:10.1016/j.giq.2013.05.006

Justino, P. (2007). Social security in developing countries: Myth or necessity? Evidence from India. *Journal of International Development*, *19*(3), 367–382. doi:10.1002/jid.1298

Kaasinen, E., Koskela-Huotari, K., Ikonen, V., & Niemeléi, M. (2013). Three approaches to co-creating services with users. In J. C. Spohrer & L. E. Freund (Eds.), Advances in the Human Side of Service Engineering (pp. 286–295). Academic Press.

Kacem, A, Belkaroui R., & Jemal D. (2016). Towards Improving e-Government Services Using Social Media-Based Citizen's Profile Investigation. *ICEGOV '15-16.*

Kaltwasser, C. R. (2013). *Populism, its opposites, and its contentious relationship with democracy.* Retrieved from https://www.opendemocracy.net/can-europe-make-it/crist%C3%B3bal-rovira-kaltwasser/populism-its-opposites-and-its-contentious-relationsh

Kamal, N., Fels, S., Fergusson, M., Preece, J., Cosley, D., & Munson, S. (2013). *Designing Social Media for Change.* New York: ACM. doi:10.1145/2468356.2479642

Kamel, S. H. (2013). The Value of Social Media in Egypt's Uprising and Beyond. *The Electronic Journal on Information Systems in Developing Countries*, 60.

Kant, I. (1784). *Answering the Question: What is Enlightenment?* Retrieved from http://library.standrews-de.org/lists/CourseGuides/religion/rs-vi/oppressed/kant_what_is_enlightenment.pdf

Karahanna, E., Straub, D. W., & Chervany, N. L. (1999). Information technology adoption across time: A cross-sectional comparison of pre-adoption and post-adoption beliefs. *Management Information Systems Quarterly, 23*(2), 183–213. doi:10.2307/249751

Karakiza, M. (2014). The impact of Social Media in the Public Sector. *Proceedings of the International Conference on Strategic Innovative Marketing*, 384-392.

Karamagioli, E., Staiou, E., & Goucos, D. (2014). Can open government models contribute to more collaborative ways of governance? an assessment of the Greek opengov initiative. In Open Government: Opportunities and challenges for public governance. Springer Publications.

Karkin, N. (2011). The Critical Analysis of Civic Engagement in Public Policy Formation in the Light of the Stakeholder Theory. *Bulletinul, 2011*(1), 9-18.

Karkin, N. (2012). e-Katılım Kavramı ve Süreci: Kamu Siyasa Oluşum Sürecine Vatandaş Katkısının Olabilirliği [e-Participation Concept and Practice: The Feasibility of Citizen Engagement in Public Policy Formulation]. *Sosyo-Ekonomi Dergisi, 2012*(1), 41-62.

Karkin, N., & Çalhan, H. S. (2011). Vilayet ve İl Özel İdare Web Sitelerinde E-Katılım Olgusu [The E-Participation Concept in the Web Sites of Turkish Governorships and Special Provincial Administrations]. *Süleyman Demirel Üniversitesi Sosyal Bilimler Enstitüsü Dergisi, 13*(1), 55-80.

Karkin, N., & Çalhan, H. S. (2012). An Interactive e-Participation Model for the Public Administration System in Turkey: SIBIYO. *Ege Akademik Bakış, 12*(1), 107-125.

Kavanaugh, A. L., Fox, E. A., Sheetz, S. D., Yang, S., Li, L. T., Shoemaker, D. J., ... Xie, L. (2012). Social Media Use by Government: From The Routine To The Critical. *Government Information Quarterly, 29*(4), 480–491. doi:10.1016/j.giq.2012.06.002

Keck, M., & Sikkink, K. (1998). *Activists beyond Borders: Advocacy Networks in International Politics*. New York: Cornell University Press.

Kenyon, G. (2016). *The Man Who Studies the Spread of Ignorance*. Retrieved from http://www.bbc.com/future/story/20160105-the-man-who-studies-the-spread-of-ignorance

Kesavarapu, S., & Choi, M. (2012). M-government - A framework to investigate killer applications for developing countries: An Indian case study. *Electronic Government: An International Journal, 9*(2), 200–219. doi:10.1504/EG.2012.046269

Khan, G. F. (2017). Social-Media-Based Government. In Social Media for Government (pp. 7–20). Springer. doi:10.1007/978-981-10-2942-4_2

Khasawneh, R. T., & Abu-Shanab, E. A. (2013). E-Government and Social Media Sites: The Role and Impact. *World Journal of Computer Application and Technology*, *1*(1), 10–17.

Kietzmann, J. H., Hermkens, K., McCarthy, I. P., & Silvestre, B. S. (2011). Social media? Get serious! Understanding the functional building blocks of social media. *Business Horizons*, *54*(3), 241–251. doi:10.1016/j.bushor.2011.01.005

Kim, S., & Lee, J. (2011). *E-Participation, Transparency, and Trust in Local Government*. Retrieved from https://spaa.newark.rutgers.edu/sites/default/files/files/Transparency_Research_Conference/Papers/Kim_Soonhee.pdf

Kim, G.-H., Trimi, S., & Chung, J.-H. (2015). Big-Data Applications in the Government Sector. *Communications of the ACM*, *57*(3), 78–85. doi:10.1145/2500873

Kim, S., & Lee, J. (2012). E-Participation, Transparency and Trust in Local Government. *Public Administration Review*, *72*(6), 819–828. doi:10.1111/j.1540-6210.2012.02593.x

Kochhar, R. (2017). *Middle Class Fortunes in Western Europe*. Retrieved from http://www.pewglobal.org/2017/04/24/middle-class-fortunes-in-western-europe/

Kolstad, I., & Wiig, A. (2009). Is transparency the key to reducing corruption in resource-rich countries? *World Development*, *37*(3), 521–532. doi:10.1016/j.worlddev.2008.07.002

Kolstad, I., Wiig, A., & Williams, A. (2009). Mission improbable: Does petroleum-related aid address the resource curse? *Energy Policy*, *37*(3), 954–965. doi:10.1016/j.enpol.2008.09.092

Komito, L. (2005). e-Participation and Governance: Widening the net. *The Electronic. Journal of E-Government*, *3*(1), 39–48.

Korac-Kakabadse, A., & Korac-Kakabadse, N. (1999). Information Technology's Impact on the Quality of Democracy: Reinventing the 'Democratic Vassel.' In Reinventing Government In The Digital Age. London: Routledge.

Koten, E., & Erdoğan, B. (2014). Sanaldan Gerçeğe Ağlara Tutunmak: Engelli Gençlerin Facebook'ta Sosyalleşme Deneyimleri [Transition from Sticking to Virtual to Real Networks: The Socilisation Experiences of Disabled Young People]. *Alternatif Politika*, *6*(3), 333-358.

Kumar, R., & Best, M. L. (2006). Impact and sustainability of e-government services in developing countries: Lessons learned from Tamil Nadu, India. *The Information Society*, 22(1), 1–12. doi:10.1080/01972240500388149

Kumar, R., & Sharma, M. K. (2012). Impact of ICT For Women Literacy In Indian Rural Areas Of e-Governance. *Journal of Information and Operations Management*, 3(1), 194–195.

Kushchu, I. (2007). *Mobile Government: An Emerging Direction in E-government* (1st ed.). Hershey, PA: IGI Publishing. doi:10.4018/978-1-59140-884-0

Kuzma, J. (2010). Asian government usage of Web 2.0 social media. *European Journal of ePractice*, (9), 1-13.

Lakoff, G. (2017). *Two Questions About Trump and Republicans that Stump Progressives*. Retrieved from https://georgelakoff.com/2017/07/01/two-questions-about-trump-and-republicans-that-stump-progressives/

Lakoff, G. (1995). Metaphor, Morality, and Politics, Or, Why Conservatives Have Left Liberals in the Dust. *Social Research*, 62(2).

Lakoff, G. (2016). *Moral Politics: How Liberals and Conservatives Think*. University Of Chicago Press. doi:10.7208/chicago/9780226411323.001.0001

Lakoff, G., & Johnson, M. (2003). *Metaphors We Live By*. University Of Chicago Press. doi:10.7208/chicago/9780226470993.001.0001

Lam, D. (2006). The demography of youth in developing countries and its economic implications. Ann Arbor, 1001, 48106.

Landsbergen, D. (2010). Government as part of the revolution: using social media to achieve public goals. *Electron J e-Govern*, 8(2), 135–147.

Larsen, T. J., Sørebø, A. M., & Sørebø, Ø. (2009). The role of task-technology fit as users' motivation to continue information system use. *Computers in Human Behavior*, 25(3), 778–784. doi:10.1016/j.chb.2009.02.006

Lathrop, D., & Ruma, L. (2010). *Open government: Collaboration, transparency, and participation in practice*. O'Reilly Media.

Laukkanen, P., Sinkkonen, S., & Laukkanen, T. (2008). Consumer resistance to internet banking: Postponers, opponents and rejectors. *International Journal of Bank Marketing*, 26(6), 440–455. doi:10.1108/02652320810902451

Lee, K. C., Lee, S., & Kim, J. S. (2005). Analysis of mobile commerce performance by using the task-technology fit. In *Mobile Information Systems* (pp. 135–153). Springer. doi:10.1007/0-387-22874-8_10

Legge, J. S. Jr, & Devore, J. (1987). Measuring productivity in US public administration and public affairs programs 1981-1985. *Administration & Society*, *19*(2), 147–156. doi:10.1177/009539978701900201

Lev-On, A., & Steinfeld, N. (2015). Local engagement online: Municipal Facebook pages as hub of interaction. *Government Information Quarterly*, *32*(3), 299–307. doi:10.1016/j.giq.2015.05.007

Liang, T.-P., Huang, C.-W., Yeh, Y.-H., & Lin, B. (2007). Adoption of mobile technology in business: A fit-viability model. *Industrial Management & Data Systems*, *107*(8), 1154–1169. doi:10.1108/02635570710822796

Lindblom, C. (1980). *The policy making process*. Prentice-Hall Foundations of Modem Political Science Series.

Linders, D. (2012). From e-government to we-government: Defining a typology for citizen e-participation in the age of social media. *Government Information Quarterly*, *29*(4), 446–454. doi:10.1016/j.giq.2012.06.003

Lindgren, I., & Jansson, G. (2013). Electronic services in the public sector: A conceptual framework. *Government Information Quarterly*, *30*(2), 163–172. doi:10.1016/j.giq.2012.10.005

Lin, H.-H., & Wang, Y.-S. (2006). An examination of the determinants of customer loyalty in mobile commerce contexts. *Information & Management*, *43*(3), 271–282. doi:10.1016/j.im.2005.08.001

Lironi, E. (2016). *Potential and Challenges of E-Participation in the European Union*. Retrieved from http://www.europarl.europa.eu/RegData/etudes/STUD/2016/556949/IPOL_STU(2016)556949_EN.pdf

Little, R. J. A. (1988). Missing-Data Adjustments in Large Surveys. *Journal of Business & Economic Statistics*, *6*(3), 287–296.

Lukyanenko, R., Parsons, J., Wiersma, Y. F., Sieber, R., & Maddah, M. (2016). Participatory design for user-generated content; Understanding the challenges and moving forward. *Scandinavian Journal of Information Systems*, *28*(1), 37–70.

Luna-Reyes, L. F., & Gil-García, J. R. (2011). Using institutional theory and dynamic simulation to understand complex e-Government phenomena. *Government Information Quarterly*, *28*(2), 329–345. doi:10.1016/j.giq.2010.08.007

Luna-Reyes, L. F., Picazo-Vela, S., & Fernandez-Haddad, M. (2016). Opening the black box: Developing strategies to use social media in government. *Government Information Quarterly, 33*(4), 693–704. doi:10.1016/j.giq.2016.08.004

Maciel, C., Roque, L., & Garcia, A. C. B. (2010). Interaction and communication resources in collaborative e-democratic environments: The democratic citizenship community. *Information Polity, 15*(1-2), 73-88.

Macintosh, A. (2004). Characterizing E-Participation in Policy-Making. In *Proceedings of the 37th Annual Hawaii International Conference on System Science.* Computer Society Press. Retrieved from http://csdl2.computer.org/persagen/DLAbsToc.jsp?resourcePath=/dl/proceedings/hicss/&toc=comp/proceedings/hicss/2004/2056/05/2056toc.xml&DOI=10.1109/HICSS.2004.1265300

Magnusson, M., Bellström, P., & Thoren, C. (2012). *Facebook usage in government – a case study of information content.* Retrieved from http://aisel.aisnet.org/amcis2012/proceedings/EGovernment/11

Magro, M. J. (2012). A Review of Social Media Use in E-Government. *Adm. Sci., 2*, 148-161. Retrieved June 5, from www.mdpi.com/journal/admsci

Maia, R. (2011). Internet e esfera civil: limites e alcances da participação política. In R. Maia (Ed.), *Internet e Participação Política no Brasil*. Porto Alegre: Editora Sulina.

Mainka, A., Hartmann, S., Stock, W. G., & Peters, I. (2014). *Government and Social Media: A Case Study of 31 Informational World Cities.* Academic Press.

Marković, A. M., Labus, A., Vulić, M., & Radenković, B. (2013). *Using social networks for improving egovernment services.* Academic Press.

Mathiason, J. (2013). *Information and Communication Technologies and eParticipation for the Empowerment of People and eGovernance.* Retrieved from http://www.un.org/esa/socdev/egms/docs//2013/ict/BackgroundPaper.pdf

Maumbe, B. M., & Owei, V. (2006). *Bringing M-government to South African Citizens: Policy Framework, Delivery Challenges and Opportunities.* Mobile Government Consortium International LLC.

Mbu Daniel, T. (2015). Economic Growth, Crisis, and Recovery in Cameroon: A Literature Review. *Journal of Industrial Distribution & Business, 6*(1), 5–15. doi:10.13106/ijidb.2015.vol6.no1.5.

Mcnamara, J. (2011). *Social Media Strategy and Governance: Gaps, Risks and Opportunities.* Sydney, Australia: University of Technology Sydney.

Medaglia, R. (2012). eParticiatpion research: Moving characterization forward (2006-2011). *Government Information Quarterly*, *29*(3), 346–360. doi:10.1016/j.giq.2012.02.010

Meijer, A., & Thaens, M. (2013). Social media strategies: Understanding the differences between North American police departments. *Government Information Quarterly*, *30*(4), 343–350. doi:10.1016/j.giq.2013.05.023

Mejabi, O. V., Azeez, A. L., Adedoyin, A., & Oloyede, M. O. (2015). Challenges to Open Data Institutionalisation : Insights from stakeholder groups in Nigeria. *2015 Open Data Research Symposium*.

Merchant, G. (2012). Unravelling the social network: Theory and research. *Learning, Media and Technology*, *37*(1), 4–19. doi:10.1080/17439884.2011.567992

Mergel, I. (2013). A framework for interpreting social media interactions in the public sector. *Government Information Quarterly*, *30*(4), 327–334. doi:10.1016/j.giq.2013.05.015

Mergel, I. (2016). Social media institutionalization in the US federal government. *Government Information Quarterly*, *33*(1), 142–148. doi:10.1016/j.giq.2015.09.002

Mergel, I., & Bretschneider, S. I. (2013). A three-stage adoption process for social media use in government. *Public Administration Review*, *73*(3), 390–400. doi:10.1111/puar.12021

Meso, P., Musa, P., Straub, D., & Mbarika, V. (2009). Information infrastructure, governance, and socio-economic development in developing countries. *European Journal of Information Systems*, *18*(1), 52–65. doi:10.1057/ejis.2008.56

Metzas, G., Apostolou, D., Bothos, E., & Magoutas, B. (2011). Information Markets For Social Participation in Public Policy Design and Implementation. *Proceedings of Fifth International AAAI Conference on Weblogs and Social Media*. Retrieved from https://www.aaai.org/ocs/index.php/ICWSM/ICWSM11/paper/view/3862

Michels, A. (2017). Participation in citizens' summits and public engagement. *International Review of Administrative Sciences*. doi:10.1177/0020852317691117

Mitrovic, Z. (2015, March). Strengthening the evidence-base for open government in developing countries. *Building Open Data Capacity through e-Skills Acquisition*, 1–38.

Mkude, C. G., & Wimmer, M. A. (2013). Strategic Framework for Designing E-Government in Developing Countries. In M. A. Wimmer, M. Janssen, & H. J. Scholl (Eds.), *Electronic Government: 12th IFIP WG 8.5 International Conference, EGOV 2013, Koblenz, Germany, September 16-19, 2013. Proceedings* (pp. 148-162). Berlin: Springer Berlin Heidelberg.

Mohsan, F., Nawaz, M. M., Khan, M. S., Shaukat, Z., & Aslam, N. (2011). Impact of customer satisfaction on customer loyalty and intentions to switch: Evidence from banking sector of Pakistan. *International Journal of Business and Social Science*, 2(16).

Moon, K. L., Ngai, E. W. T., & Tao, S. S. C. (2015). Social media research: Theories, constructs, and conceptual framework. *International Journal of Information Management*, 35(1), 33–44. doi:10.1016/j.ijinfomgt.2014.09.004

Moore, K., & McElroy, J. C. (2012). The influence of personality on Facebook usage, wall postings, and regret. *Computers in Human Behavior*, 28(1), 267–274. doi:10.1016/j.chb.2011.09.009

Moreno, M. A., Kota, R., Schoohs, S., & Whitehill, J. M. (2013). The Facebook influence model: A concept mapping approach. *Cyberpsychology, Behavior, and Social Networking*, 16(7), 504–511. doi:10.1089/cyber.2013.0025 PMID:23621717

Mudde, C. (2004). The Populist Zeitgeist. *Government and Opposition*, 39(4), 541–563. doi:10.1111/j.1477-7053.2004.00135.x

Mudde, C., & Kaltwasser, C. R. (2013). Populism. In M. Freeden, L. T. Sargent, & M. Stears (Eds.), *The Oxford Handbook of Political Ideologies* (pp. 493–512). Oxford, UK: Oxford University Press.

Mueller, M. (2013). *Networks and States: the global politics of internet governance*. MIT Press.

Murti, D. C. W. (2013). Keyboard Action End up Political Party: Understanding the Intertwining Relations of Social Media Activism, Citizenship, and the Dynamics of Democracy in Indonesia. *Online Journal of Communication and Media Technologies*, 3(2), 32.

Musiani, F. (2015). *Nais sans géants: architecture décentralisée et services Internet* (2nd ed.). Paris: Presses des Mines. doi:10.4000/books.pressesmines.1853

Musso, J., Weare, C., & Hale, M. (2000). Designing Web Technologies for Local Governance Reform: Good Management or Good Democracy? *Political Communication*, 17(1), 1–19. doi:10.1080/105846000198486

Nair, P., & Fielding, R. (2007). *The language of school design: Design patterns for 21st century schools*. Minneapolis, MN: Design Share.

Näkki, P., & Antikainen, M. (2008). Online tools for codesign: User involvement through the innovation process. *New Approaches to Requirements Elicitation, (96)*, 92–97.

Nam, T. (2012). Suggesting frameworks of citizen-sourcing via Government 2.0. *Government Information Quarterly, 29*(1), 12–20. doi:10.1016/j.giq.2011.07.005

Nam, T., Pardo, T. A., & Burke, G. B. (2012). e-Government interoperability: Interaction of policy, management, and technology dimensions. *Social Science Computer Review, 30*(1), 7–23. doi:10.1177/0894439310392184

Ndou, V. (2004). E-government for developing countries: Opportunities and challenges. *The Electronic Journal on Information Systems in Developing Countries, 18*.

Nesset, V., & Large, A. (2004). Children in the information technology design process: A review of theories and their applications. *Library & Information Science Research, 26*(2), 140–161. doi:10.1016/j.lisr.2003.12.002

Newbert, S. L. (2007). Empirical research on the resource-based view of the firm: An assessment and suggestions for future research. *Strategic Management Journal, 28*(2), 121–146. doi:10.1002/smj.573

Ngulube, P. (2007). The nature and accessibility of e-government in Sub Saharan Africa. *International Review of Information Ethics, 7*(9), 1–13.

Nica, M., & Grayson. (2011). M. Effects of Teaching Business Web 2.0 Style. *International Journal of Business and Social Science, 2*(18).

Nikhashemi, S. R., Valaei, N., & Tarofder, A. K. (2017). Does Brand Personality and Perceived Product Quality Play a Major Role in Mobile Phone Consumers' Switching Behaviour? *Global Business Review, 18*(3), 108–127. doi:10.1177/0972150917693155

Nkwe, N. (2012). E-government: Challenges and opportunities in Botswana. *International Journal of Humanities and Social Science, 2*(17), 39–48.

Nord, J. H., & Nord, G. D. (1995). MIS research: Journal status assessment and analysis. *Information & Management, 29*(1), 29–42. doi:10.1016/0378-7206(95)00010-T

Norris, D., & Reddick, C. G. (2013). Local E-Government In The United States: Transformation or Incremental Change? *Public Administration Review, 73*(1), 165–175. doi:10.1111/j.1540-6210.2012.02647.x

O'Hara, K. (2012). Transparency, open data and trust in government: shaping the infosphere. *Proceedings of the 4th Annual ACM Web Science Conference*, 223–232. doi:10.1145/2380718.2380747

O'Rain, S., Curry, E., & Harth, A. (2012). XBRL and open data for global financial ecosystems: A linked data approach. *International Journal of Accounting Information Systems*, *13*(2), 141–162. doi:10.1016/j.accinf.2012.02.002

O'Reilly, T. (2005). *What Is Web 2.0 Design patterns and business models for the next generation of software*. Retrieved June 30, from http://oreilly.com

Ona, S., Hecita, I. J., & Ulit, E. (2014). *Exploring the Role of Open Government Data & New Technologies the Case of the Philippines: Opportunities in Maternal Health and Child Care (MHCC) & Micro, Small, and Medium Enterprises (MSMEs)*. Open Data Research Network. Retrieved from http://www.opendataresearch.org/sites/default/files/publications/Open Data Opportunities in Maternal Health and Child Care and MSMEs-print.pdf

Organisation of Economic Cooperation and Development (OECD). (2001). Engaging Citizens in Policy Making: Information, Consultation and Participation. *OECD Public Management Brief*. Retrieved from http://www.oecd.org/dataoecd/24/34/2384040.pdf

Organisation of Economic Cooperation and Development (OECD). (2007). *Participative Web and User-Created Content: Web 2.0, Wikis and Social Networking*. Paris: OECD. Retrieved from http://www.oecd.org/sti/ieconomy/participativewebandusercreatedcontentweb20wikisandsocialnetworking.htm

Ornager, S., & Verma, N. (2005). *E-Government Tool-Kit for Developing Countries*. UNESCO.

Osborne, S. P., & Strokosch, K. (2013). It takes two to Tango? Understanding the Co-production of Public Services by Integrating the Services Management and Public Administration Perspectives. *British Journal of Management*, *24*(S1), S31–S47. doi:10.1111/1467-8551.12010

Ostling, A. (2010). ICT in politics: From peaks of inflated expectations to voids of disillusionment. *Eur. J. ePractice, 9*, 49–56.

Ozdesim, Sobaci, Yavuz, & Karkin. (2014). Political Use of Twitter: The Case of Metropolitan Mayor Candidates in 2014 Local Elections in Turkey. *ICEGOV '14 Proceedings of the 8th International Conference on Theory and Practice of Electronic Governance*, 41-50.

Panopoulou, E., Tambouris, E., & Tarabanis, K. (2014). Success factors in designing e-Participation initiatives. *Information and Organization, 14*(4), 195–213. doi:10.1016/j.infoandorg.2014.08.001

Papaloi, A., Staiou, E. R., & Gouscos, D. (2012). *Blending Social Media with Parliamentary Websites: Just a Trend, or a Promising Approach to e-Participation? In Web 2.0 Technologies and Democratic Governance* (pp. 259–275). Springer.

Park, J., & Cho, K. (2009). Declining relational trust between government and publics, and potential prospects of social media in the government public relations. In *Proceedings of EGPA Conference 2009*. The Public Service: Service Delivery in the Information Age.

Park, M. J., Dulambazar, T., & Rho, J. J. (2015). The effect of organizational social factors on employee performance and the mediating role of knowledge sharing: Focus on e-Government utilization in Mongolia. *Information Development, 31*(1), 53–68. doi:10.1177/0266666913494908

Park, M. J., Kang, D., Rho, J. J., & Lee, D. H. (2016). Policy Role of Social Media in Developing Public Trust: Twitter communication with government leaders. *Public Management Review, 18*(9), 1265–1288. doi:10.1080/14719037.2015.1066418

Parthasarathy, M., & Bhattacherjee, A. (1998). Understanding post-adoption behavior in the context of online services. *Information Systems Research, 9*(4), 362–379. doi:10.1287/isre.9.4.362

Parvcek, P., & Sachs, M. (2010). Open Government—Information Flow in Web 2.0. *Eur. J. ePractice, 9*, 57–68.

Pawlak, E. J., Way, I. F., & Thompson, D. H. (1982). *Assessing factors that influence skills training in organizations*. Academic Press.

Picazo-Vela, S., Gutiérrez-Martínez, I., & Luna-Reyes, L. F. (2012). Understanding risks, benefits, and strategic alternatives of social media applications in the public sector. *Government Information Quarterly, 29*(4), 504–511.

Pinho, J. A. G. (2008). Investigando portais de governo eletrônico de estados no Brasil: Muita tecnologia, pouca democracia. *RAP – Revista de Administração Pública, 42*(03), 471–493. doi:10.1590/S0034-76122008000300003

Plato, . (2008). *The Republic* (B. Jowett, Trans.). United States: Simon & Brown.

Podsakoff, P. M., MacKenzie, S. B., Jeong-Yeon, L., & Podsakoff, N. P. (2003). Common Method Biases in Behavioral Research: A Critical Review of the Literature and Recommended Remedies. *The Journal of Applied Psychology*, *88*(5), 879–903. doi:10.1037/0021-9010.88.5.879 PMID:14516251

Polat, B., Bakıroğlu, C. T., & Sayın, M. E. D. (2013). E-Transformation of Municipalities and Social Media's Role on e-Participation in European e-Municipalities. *Academic Journal of Interdisciplinary Studies*, *2*(9), 386.

Porumbescu, G. A. (2016). Linking public sector social media and e-government website use to trust in government. *Government Information Quarterly*, *33*(2), 291–304. doi:10.1016/j.giq.2016.04.006

Prajapati, M., & Sharma A. (2014). *Role of Web 2.0 in E-Governance*. Academic Press.

Rahmani, Z., Tahvildari, A., Honarmand, H., Yousefi, H., & Daghighi, M. S. (2012). Mobile Banking and its Benefits. *Oman Chapter of Arabian Journal of Business and Management Review*, *2*(5), 38–41. doi:10.12816/0002266

Rashid, N., & Rahman, S. (2010). *An investigation into critical determinants of e-government implementation in the context of a developing nation*. Paper presented at the International Conference on Electronic Government and the Information Systems Perspective. doi:10.1007/978-3-642-15172-9_2

Reddick, C. G. (2010). *Citizens and E-government: Evaluating Policy and Management*. IGI Global. doi:10.4018/978-1-61520-931-6

Reddick, C. G., & Zheng, Y. (2017). Determinants of citizens' mobile apps future use in Chinese local governments: An analysis of survey data. *Transforming Government: People, Process and Policy*, *11*(2), 213–235. doi:10.1108/TG-11-2016-0078

Reggi, L., & Ricci, C. A. (2011). Information strategies for open government in Europe: EU regions opening up the data on structural funds. *International Conference on Electronic Government*, 173–184. doi:10.1007/978-3-642-22878-0_15

Reilly, K. M. A., & Smith, M. L. (2013). The emergence of open development in a network society. *Open development: Networked innovations in international development*.

Relly, J. E., & Sabharwal, M. (2009). Perceptions of transparency of government policymaking: A cross-national study. *Government Information Quarterly*, *26*(1), 148–157. doi:10.1016/j.giq.2008.04.002

Remenyi, D. (2013). *Case Study Research (2nd ed.)*. Academic Conferences and Publishing International Limited.

Reyes, L. F. M., & Finken, S. (2012, August). Social media as a platform for participatory design. In *Proceedings of the 12th Participatory Design Conference: Exploratory Papers, Workshop Descriptions, Industry Cases* (vol. 2, pp. 89-92). ACM. doi:10.1145/2348144.2348173

Rezaei, S., Shahijan, M. K., Valaei, N., Rahimi, R., & Ismail, W. K. W. (2016). Experienced international business traveller's behaviour in Iran: A partial least squares path modelling analysis. *Tourism and Hospitality Research*. doi:10.1177/1467358416636930

Rezaei, S., & Valaei, N. (2017). Branding in a multichannel retail environment: Online stores vs app stores and the effect of product type. *Information Technology & People*, *30*(4), 853–886.

Rezaei, S., & Valaei, N. (2017). Crafting experiential value via smartphone apps channel. *Marketing Intelligence & Planning*, *35*(5), 688–702. doi:10.1108/MIP-08-2016-0141

Rezaei, S., Wee, C. H., & Valaei, N. (2017). Essential of Apps Marketing Implementation and E-Commerce Strategies: Apps Users' Decision-Making Process. In *Apps Management and E-Commerce Transactions in Real-Time* (pp. 141–158). IGI Global. doi:10.4018/978-1-5225-2449-6.ch006

Ribbink, D., Van Riel, A. C., Liljander, V., & Streukens, S. (2004). Comfort your online customer: Quality, trust and loyalty on the internet. *Managing Service Quality: An International Journal*, *14*(6), 446–456. doi:10.1108/09604520410569784

Ringle, C. M., Wende, S., & Becker, J.-M. (2015). *SmartPLS 3*. Boenningstedt: SmartPLS GmbH. Retrieved from http://www.smartpls.com

Robertson, S. P., Vatrapu, R. K., & Medina, R. (2009). The social life of social networks: Facebook linkage patterns in the 2008 US presidential election. *Proceedings of the 10th Annual International Conference on Digital Government Research: Social Networks: Making Connections between Citizens, Data and Government*.

Rodríguez-Bolívar, M. P., Alcaide-Muñoz, L., & López-Hernández, A. M. (2015). Research and experiences in implementing e-Government endeavors in emerging countries: A literature review. In Digital Solution for Contemporary Democracy and Government. IGI Global.

Rodríguez-Bolivar, M. P. (2017). Governance Models for the Delivery of Public services Through the Web 2.0 technologies: A political view in large Spanish Municipalities. *Social Science Computer Review, 35*(2), 203–225. doi:10.1177/0894439315609919

Rodríguez-Bolívar, M. P., & Alcaide-Muñoz, L. (2018). Political Ideology and Municipal Size as Incentives for the Implementation and Governance Model of Web 2.0 in Providing Public Services. *International Journal of Public Administration in the Digital Age, 5*(1), 36–62. doi:10.4018/IJPADA.2018010103

Rodríguez-Bolívar, M. P., Alcaide-Muñoz, L., & López-Hernández, A. M. (2010). Trends of e-government research: Contextualization and research opportunities. *International Journal of Digital Accounting Research, 10*, 87–111. doi:10.4192/1577-8517-v10_4

Rodríguez-Bolívar, M. P., Alcaide-Muñoz, L., & López-Hernández, A. M. (2012). Studying e-government: Research methodologies, data compilation techniques and future outlook. *Academia (Caracas), 51*, 79–95.

Rodríguez-Bolívar, M. P., Alcaide-Muñoz, L., & López-Hernández, A. M. (2016). Scientometric Study of the Progress and Development of e-Government Research During the Period 2000-2012. *Information Technology for Development, 22*(1), 36–74. doi:10.1080/02681102.2014.927340

Rossel, P., Finger, M., & Misuraca, G. (2006). "Mobile" e-Government Options: Between Technology-driven and User-centric. *Electronic Journal of E-Government, 4*(2), 79–86. Retrieved from http://www.ejeg.com/volume-4/vol4-iss2/v4-i2-art5.htm

Rothwell, W. J., Graber, J. M., & Graber, J. M. (2010). *Competency-based training basics*. American Society for Training and Development.

Sabo, O., Rose, J., & Skiftenesflak, L. (2008). The shape of eParticipation: Characterizing an emerging research area. *Government Information Quarterly, 25*(3), 400–428. doi:10.1016/j.giq.2007.04.007

Sæbø, Ø. (2012). *E-government in Tanzania: current status and future challenges.* Paper presented at the International Conference on Electronic Government. doi:10.1007/978-3-642-33489-4_17

Said, I. (2007). Architecture for Children: Understanding Children [sic] Perception towards Built Environment. In *Proceedings of International Conference Challenges and Experiences in Developing Architectural education in Asia.* Islamic University of Indonesia. Retrieved March 1, 2012, from http://eprints.utm.my/3575/

Sandoval-Almazan, R., & Gil-Garcia, J. R. (2013). *Cyberactivism through Social Media: Twitter, YouTube, and the Mexican Political Movement" I'm Number 132".* Paper presented at the System Sciences (HICSS), 2013 46th Hawaii International Conference on.

Sandoval-Almazan, R., & Gil-Garcia, J. R. R. (2012). Social Media In State Governments: Preliminary Results About The Use Of Twitter In Mexico. Trauner Verlag.

Sandoval-Almazán, R., & Valle-Cruz, D. (2016). Understanding Network Links in Twitter: A Mexican Case Study. *Proceedings of the 17th International Digital Government Research Conference on Digital Government Research - Dg.o '16,* 122–128. doi:10.1145/2912160.2912204

Sandoval-Almazan, R. (2015). Using Twitter in political campaigns: The case of the PRI candidate in Mexico. *International Journal of E-Politics, 6*(1), 1–15. doi:10.4018/IJEP.2015010101

Sandoval-Almazan, R., Cruz, D. V., & Armas, J. C. N. (2015). Social Media in Smart Cities: An Exploratory Research in Mexican Municipalities. *Proceedings of the 48th Hawaii International Conference on System Sciences (HICSS-48).* doi:10.1109/HICSS.2015.284

Sandoval-Almazan, R., & Gil-Garcia, J. R. (2012). Are government internet portals evolving towards more interaction, participation, and collaboration? Revisiting the rhetoric of e-government among municipalities. *Government Information Quarterly, 29,* 72–S81. doi:10.1016/j.giq.2011.09.004

Sandoval-Almazan, R., & Gil-Garcia, J. R. (2013). *Cyberactivism through Social Media: Twitter, YouTube, and the Mexican Political Movement.* IEEE Computer Society.

Sandoval-Almazan, R., Gil-Garcia, J. R., Luna-Reyes, L. F., & Diaz-Murillo, D. E. L. G. (2011). The use of Web 2.0 on Mexican State Websites: A Three-Year Assessment. *Electronic Journal of E-Government, 9*(2), 107–121.

Sandoval-Almazan, R., Gil-Garcia, J. R., Luna-Reyes, L. F., Luna, D. E., & Rojas-Romero, Y. (2012). *Open Government 2.0: Citizen Empowerment Through Open Data, Web and Mobile Apps.* New York: ACM; doi:10.1145/2463728.2463735

Sandoval-Almazan, R., & Ramon Gil-Garcia, J. (2014). Towards cyberactivism 2.0? Understanding the use of social media and other information technologies for political activism and social movements. *Government Information Quarterly, 31*(3), 365–378. doi:10.1016/j.giq.2013.10.016

Sandoval-Almazan, R., Ramon Gil-Garcia, J., & Valle-Cruz, D. (2017). Going Beyond Bureaucracy Through Gamification: Innovation Labs and Citizen Engagement in the Case of "Mapaton" in Mexico City. In A. A. Paulin, L. G. Anthopoulos, & C. G. Reddick (Eds.), *Beyond Bureaucracy. Public Administration and Information Technology* (pp. 133–149). Cham: Springer International Publishing; doi:10.1007/978-3-319-54142-6_9

Sandy, G. A., & McMillan, S. (2005). *A Success Factors Model For M-Government.* Mobile Government Consortium International LLC.

Sanghi, S. (2007). *The Handbook of Competency Mapping.* Vasa. doi:10.4135/9788132108481

Sangle, P. S., & Awasthi, P. (2011). Consumer's expectations from mobile CRM services: A banking context. *Business Process Management Journal, 17*(6), 898–918. doi:10.1108/14637151111182684

Schellong, A. (2007). *Extending the Technology Enactment Framework.* PNG Working Paper No PNG07-003, Program on Networked Governance, 3.

Scholl, H. J., & Dwivedi, Y. K. (2014). Forums for electronic government scholars: Insight from a 2012/2013 study. *Government Information Quarterly, 31*(2), 229–242. doi:10.1016/j.giq.2013.10.008

Schrier, T., Erdem, M., & Brewer, P. (2010). Merging task-technology fit and technology acceptance models to assess guest empowerment technology usage in hotels. *Journal of Hospitality and Tourism Technology, 1*(3), 201–217. doi:10.1108/17579881011078340

Schuppan, T. (2009). E-Government in developing countries: Experiences from sub-Saharan Africa. *Government Information Quarterly, 26*(1), 118–127. doi:10.1016/j.giq.2008.01.006

SEDESOL. (2015a). *Informe anual sobre la situación de pobreza y rezago social 2015: Lerma, México.* Retrieved from http://www.gob.mx/cms/uploads/attachment/file/42816/Mexico_051.pdf

SEDESOL. (2015b). *Informe anual sobre la situación de pobreza y rezago social 2015: Metepec, México.* Retrieved from http://www.gob.mx/cms/uploads/attachment/file/42819/Mexico_054.pdf

SEDESOL. (2015c). *Informe anual sobre la situación de pobreza y rezago social 2015: Toluca, México.* Retrieved from http://www.gob.mx/cms/uploads/attachment/file/42871/Mexico_106.pdf

Segata, J. O. (2015). Ciberespaço, a etnografia e algumas caixas pretas. *Revista Z Cultural, 1*, 5–12.

Serrat, O. (2017). Social Media and the Public Sector. In Knowledge Solutions. Springer.

Shirazi, F. (2012). Measuring the Efficiency of Digital Communities: A Case Study. *Measuring the Efficiency of Digital Communities: A Case Study*, 95-101.

Sidorova, A., Evangelopoulos, N., Valacich, J. S., & Ramakrishnan, T. (2008). Uncovering the intellectual core of the information systems discipline. *Management Information Systems Quarterly, 32*(3), 467–482. doi:10.2307/25148852

Silva, S. (2011). Exigências Democráticas e dimensões analíticas para a interface digital do Estado. In *Internet e Participação Política no Brasil*. Porto Alegre: Editora Sulina.

Silveira, S. A. (2017). Tudo sobre tod@s. Redes digitais, privacidade e venda de dados pessoais.

Smith, M. L., & Reilly, K. M. A. (2014). *Open development: Networked innovations in international development*. MIT Press.

Snead, J. T., & Wright, E. (2014). e-Government research in the United State. *Government Information Quarterly, 31*(1), 129–136. doi:10.1016/j.giq.2013.07.005

Snyder, T. D. (2017). *On Tyranny: Twenty Lessons from the Twentieth Century*. Tim Duggan Books.

Sobaci, M. Z., & Altınok, R. (2011). Türkiye'de Büyükşehir Belediyelerinin E-Katılım Uygulamaları: Website İçerik Analizi [E-Participation Applications of Metropolitan Municipality in Turkey: A Webside Content Analysis]. Kamu Yönetimi Forumu, Ankara, Turkey.

Sobaci, Z. (2010). What the Turkish parliamentary web site offers to citizens in terms of e-participation: A content analysis. *Information Polity, 15*(3), 227-241.

Sobaci, M. Z., & Eryigit, K. Y. (2015). Determinants of E-Democracy Adoption in Turkish Municipalities: An Analysis for Spatial Diffusion Effect. *Local Government Studies, 41*(3), 1–25. doi:10.1080/03003930.2014.995296

Sobacı, M. Z., & Karkın, N. (2013). The Use of Twitter by Mayors in Turkey: Tweets for Better Public Services? *Government Information Quarterly, 30*(4), 417–425. doi:10.1016/j.giq.2013.05.014

Song, C., & Lee, J. (2016). Citizens' Use of Social Media in Government, Perceived Transparency, and Trust in Government. *Public Performance & Management Review*, *39*(2), 430–453. doi:10.1080/15309576.2015.1108798

Song, Ch., & Lee, J. (2013). *Can Social Media Restore Citizen Trust in Government*. Omaha, NE: School of Public Administration.

Soper, D. (2015). A-priori sample size calculator for Structural Equation Models [Software].

Stake, R. E. (1998). *Investigación con estudio de casos*. Ediciones Morata.

Stamati, T., Papadopoulos, T., & Anagnostopoulos, D. (2015). Social media for openness and accountability in the public sector: Cases in the Greek context. *Government Information Quarterly*, *32*(1), 12–29. doi:10.1016/j.giq.2014.11.004

Stiglitz, J. E. (2002). Information and the Change in the Paradigm in Economics. *The American Economic Review*, *92*(3), 460–501. doi:10.1257/00028280260136363

Stiglitz, J. E. (2003). On Liberty, the Right to Know, and Public Discourse: The Role. *Globalizing Rights: The Oxford Amnesty Lectures*, *1999*, 115.

Sundar, D. K., & Garg, S. (2005). *M-Governance: A Framework for Indian Urban Local Bodies*. Mobile Government Consortium International LLC.

Surel, P., & Muller, Y. (2002). *A Análise das Políticas Públicas*. Pelotas: Editora da Universidade Católica de Pelotas.

Susha, I., & Grönlund, A. (2014). 'Context clues for the stall of the Citizens' Initiative: Lessons for opening up e-participation development practice. *Government Information Quarterly*, *31*(3), 454–465. doi:10.1016/j.giq.2014.02.005

Szymanski, D. M., & Henard, D. H. (2001). Customer satisfaction: A meta-analysis of the empirical evidence. *Journal of the Academy of Marketing Science*, *29*(1), 16–35. doi:10.1177/0092070301291002

Taghavi-Fard, M., & Torabi, M. (2010). The Factors Affecting the Adoption of Mobile Banking Services by Customers and Rank Them (Case Study: Bank Tejarat In Tehran, Iran). *Journal Excavations Business Management*, *3*, 136–162.

Tapscott, D., Williams, A. D., & Herman, D. (2008). Government 2.0: Transforming government and governance for the twenty-first century. *New Paradigm, 1*.

Tauberer, J. (2014). Open Government Data: The Book (2nd ed.). Academic Press.

The Global Economy. (2016). *Cameroon: Political stability*. Retrieved 02-07-2017, 2017, from http://www.theglobaleconomy.com/Cameroon/wb_political_stability/

The Scottish Government. (2011). *Scotland's Digital Future: A Strategy for Scotland*. Retrieved from http://www.gov.scot/Resource/Doc/343733/0114331.pdf

Thompson, M. (2008). ICT and development studies: Towards development 2.0. *Journal of International Development*, 20(6), 821–835. doi:10.1002/jid.1498

Thomson, P. (2008). *Doing visual research with children and young people*. London: Routledge.

Tranfield, D., Denyer, D., & Smart, P. (2003). Towards a Methodology for Developing Evidence-Informed Management Knowledge by Means of Systematic Review. *British Journal of Management*, 14(3), 207–222. doi:10.1111/1467-8551.00375

Transparency International. (2016). *Corruption Perceptions Index 2016*. Retrieved from https://www.transparency.org/country/CMR#

Trice, A. W., & Treacy, M. E. (1988). Utilization as a dependent variable in MIS research. *ACM SIGMIS Database*, 19(3-4), 33–41. doi:10.1145/65766.65771

Trivellato, B., Boselli, R., & Cavenago, D. (2014). Design and implementation of open government initiatives at the sub-national level: Lessons from Italian cases. In Open Government: Opportunities and challenges for public governance. Springer Publications. doi:10.1007/978-1-4614-9563-5_5

Turhan, D. G. (2016). *Digital Natives and Digital Activism in the Framework of Information Society Context* (Unpublished PhD thesis). Suleyman Demirel University, Social Sciences Institute, Department of International Relations.

Turkish Statistical Institute (TURKSTAT). (2016) *Household Informatics Technology Usage Research*. Retrieved from http://www.tuik.gov.tr/PreHaberBultenleri.do?id=21779

Tuten, T., Wetsch, L., & Munoz, C. (2015). Conversation Beyond the Classroom: Social Media and Marketing Education. Springer International Publishing. doi:10.1007/978-3-319-11797-3_182

Ubaldi, B. (2013). Open Government Data: Towards Empirical Analysis of Open Government Data Initiatives. *OECD Working Papers on Public Governance*, 22, 15-35.

UNDESA. (2016). *United Nations E-Government Survey 2016: E-Government in support of sustainable development*. Retrieved from https://publicadministration.un.org/egovkb/Portals/egovkb/Documents/un/2016-Survey/Executive%20Summary.pdf

United Nations Department of Economic and Social Affairs. (2012). *Report of the Expert Group Meeting on "Promoting People's Empowerment in Achieving Poverty Eradication, Social Integration and Decent Work for All"*. Retrieved from http://www.un.org/esa/socdev/csocd/2013/egm-empowerment-final.pdf

United Nations Department of Economic and Social Affairs. (2016). *United Nations E-government Survey 2016*. Retrieved from http://workspace.unpan.org/sites/Internet/Documents/UNPAN96407.pdf

United Nations Department of Economic and Social Affairs. (2017). *E-Participation Index*. Retrieved from https://publicadministration.un.org/egovkb/en-us/About/Overview/E-Participation

United Nations. (2016). *United nations e-government survey 2016: E-government in support of sustainable development*. Retrieved from https://publicadministration.un.org/egovkb/en-us/reports/un-e-government-survey-2016

Valaei, N. (2017). Organizational structure, sense making activities and SMEs' competitiveness: An application of confirmatory tetrad analysis-partial least squares (CTA-PLS). *VINE Journal of Information and Knowledge Management Systems*, *47*(1), 16–41. doi:10.1108/VJIKMS-04-2016-0015

Valaei, N., & Baroto, M. B. (2017). Modelling continuance intention of citizens in government Facebook page: A complementary PLS approach. *Computers in Human Behavior*, *73*, 224–237. doi:10.1016/j.chb.2017.03.047

Valaei, N., & Jiroudi, S. (2016). Job satisfaction and job performance in the media industry: A synergistic application of partial least squares path modelling. *Asia Pacific Journal of Marketing and Logistics*, *28*(5), 984–1014. doi:10.1108/APJML-10-2015-0160

Valaei, N., & Rezaei, S. (2017). Does Web 2.0 utilisation lead to knowledge quality, improvisational creativity, compositional creativity, and innovation in small and medium-sized enterprises? A sense-making perspective. *Technology Analysis and Strategic Management*, *29*(4), 381–394. doi:10.1080/09537325.2016.1213806

Valaei, N., Rezaei, S., & Ismail, W. K. W. (2017). Examining learning strategies, creativity, and innovation at SMEs using fuzzy set Qualitative Comparative Analysis and PLS path modeling. *Journal of Business Research*, *70*, 224–233. doi:10.1016/j.jbusres.2016.08.016

Valle-Cruz, D., Sandoval-Almazan, R., & Gil-Garcia, J. R. (2016). Citizens' perceptions of the impact of information technology use on transparency, efficiency and corruption in local governments. *Information Polity*, *21*(3), 1–14.

Valle-Cruz, D., Sandoval-Almazan, R., & Gil-Garcia, J. R. (2016). Citizens' perceptions of the impact of information technology use on transparency, efficiency and corruption in local governments. *Information Polity*, *21*(3), 1–14. doi:10.3233/IP-160393

Van Deursen, A. J. A. M., & van Dijk, J. A. G. M. (2009). Improving digital skills for the use of online public information and services. *Government Information Quarterly*, *26*(2), 333–340. doi:10.1016/j.giq.2008.11.002

Van Veenstra, A. F., Janssen, M., & Boon, A. (2011). Measure to improve: A study of eParticipation in frontrunner Dutch municipalities. Lecture Notes in Computer Science, 6847, 157–168. doi:10.1007/978-3-642-23333-3_14

Vaterlaus, J. M., Barnett, K., Roche, C., & Young, J. A. (2016). "Snapchat is more personal": An exploratory study on Snapchat behaviors and young adult interpersonal relationships. *Computers in Human Behavior*, *62*, 594–601. doi:10.1016/j.chb.2016.04.029

Verma, N., & Gupta, M. P. (2012). *Open government data: More than eighty formats.* Paper presented at the 9th International Conference on E-Governance (ICEG 2012), Cochin, Kerala, India.

Viana, A. (1996). Abordagens metodológicas em Políticas Públicas. *Revista de Administração Pública.*

Wang, C., Medaglia, R., & Saebo, O. (2016). *Learning form e-Government: An agenda for social media research in IS. In PACIS 2016 Proceeding* (p. 190). Association for Information Systems.

Wannemacher, P., & L'Hostis, A. (2015). *Global Mobile Banking Functionality Benchmark.* Cambridge.

Warren, A. M., Sulaiman, A., & Jaafar, N. I. (2014). Social media effects on fostering online civic engagement and building citizen trust and trust in institutions. *Government Information Quarterly*, *31*(2), 291–301. doi:10.1016/j.giq.2013.11.007

Watson, D. (2017). The seat of learning (quest for the ideal school chair) (Talking Point). *Times Educational Supplement,* (5232), 44-45.

We Are Social. (2017). *The Digital in 2017 Global Overview.* Retrieved from https://wearesocial.com/special-reports/digital-in-2017-global-overview

Weber, L., Loumakis, A., & Bergman, J. (2003). Who Participates and Why? An Analysis of Citizens on the Internet and the Mass Public. *Social Science Computer Review*, *21*(1), 26–42. doi:10.1177/0894439302238969

Weller, K. (2015). Accepting the challenges of social media research. *Online Information Review*, *39*(3), 281–289. doi:10.1108/OIR-03-2015-0069

B. Wellman, & S. Berkowitz (Eds.). (1998). *Social structures: A network approach.* Cambridge, UK: Cambridge University Press.

Wellman, B., Salaff, J., & Gulia, M. (1996). Computer Networks as Social Networks. *Annual Review of Sociology*, (22), 211–238.

Welp, Y., & Breuer, A. (2014). *ICTs and democratic governance: The Latin American experience.* Academic Press. 10.1109/ICEDEG.2014.6819946

Westland, J. C. (2015). Data Collection, Control, and Sample Size. In *Structural Equation Models* (pp. 83–115). Springer International Publishing.

White, S. (1996). Depoliticising development: The uses and abuses of participation. *Development in Practice*, *6*(1), 6–15. doi:10.1080/0961452961000157564

Wijnhoven, F., Ehrenhard, M., & Kuhn, J. (2015). Open government objectives and participation innovations. *Government Information Quarterly*, *32*(1), 30–42. doi:10.1016/j.giq.2014.10.002

Wilson, A., Tewdwr-Jones, M., & Comber, R. (2017). Urban planning, public participation and digital technology: App development as a method of generating citizen involvement in local planning processes. *Environment and Planning B. Urban Analytics and City Science.*

Wirtz, B. W., Daiser, P., & Binkowska, B. (2016). E-Participation: A strategic framework. *International Journal of Public Administration*, *39*, 1–12.

Wolfswinkel, J. F., Furtmueller, E., & Wilderon, C. P. M. (2013). Using grounded theory as a method for rigorously reviewing literature. *European Journal of Information Systems*, *22*(1), 45–55. doi:10.1057/ejis.2011.51

Wukich, C., & Mergel, I. (2016). Reusing social media information in government. *Government Information Quarterly*, *33*(2), 305–312. doi:10.1016/j.giq.2016.01.011

Yang, T.-M., Lo, J., Wang, H.-J., & Shiang, J. (2013). Open data development and value-added government information. *Proceedings of the 7th International Conference on Theory and Practice of Electronic Governance - ICEGOV '13*, 238–241. doi:10.1145/2591888.2591932

Yildiz, M., Ocak, N., Yildirim, C., Cagiltay, K., & Babaoglu, C. (2016). Usability in Local E-Government: Analysis of Turkish Metropolitan Municipality Facebook Pages. *International Journal of Public Administration in the Digital Age*, *3*(1), 53–69. doi:10.4018/IJPADA.2016010104

Yin, R. K. (2009). *Case study research: Design and methods (Rev.)*. Newbury Park, CA: Sage Publications.

Yusifov, F. (2016). Big Data in E-Government: Issues, Opportunities and Prospects. *16th European Conference on e-Government*, 352-355.

Zeithaml, V. A., Berry, L. L., & Parasuraman, A. (1996). The behavioral consequences of service quality. *The Journal of Marketing*, 31-46.

Zhang, J., & Zhang, Z. (2010). The Knowledge Management of Furniture Product Design and Development. *Proceedings 3rd International Conference on Information Management, Innovation Management and Industrial Engineering, 1*, 464-467.

Zhao, F., Scavarda, A. J., & Waxin, M. F. (2012). Key issues and challenges in e-government development. An integrative case study of the number one eCity in the Arab World. *Information Technology for Development, 25*(4), 395–422.

Zheng, L., & Medaglia, R. (2017). Mapping government social media research and moving it forward: A framework and a research agenda. *Government Information Quarterly*. doi:10.1016/j.giq.2017.06.001

Zheng, L., & Zheng, T. (2014). Innovation Through Social Media in the Public Sector: Information and Interactions. *Government Information Quarterly, 31*(1), S106–S117. doi:10.1016/j.giq.2014.01.011

Zheng, Y., Schachter, H. L., & Holzer, M. (2014). The impact of government form on e-participation: A study of New Jersey municipalities. *Government Information Quarterly, 31*(4), 653–659. doi:10.1016/j.giq.2014.06.004

Zuiderwijk, A., Janssen, M., Choenni, S., Meijer, R., & Alibaks, R. S. (2012). Socio-technical Impediments of Open Data. *Electronic Journal of E-Government, 10*(2), 156–172. Retrieved from http://www.ejeg.com/issue/download.html?idArticle=255

Zukang, S. (2012). *E-Government Survey 2012: E-Government for the People*. United Nations Report.

About the Contributors

Laura Alcaide-Muñoz is Associate Professor in Accounting and Finance in the Department of Financial Economy and Accounting at the University of Granada. She is interested in E-government, E-Participation and Smart Cities. She has been author of numerous articles in leading SSCI journals (Business, Economics, Information Science and Public Administration) and has written book chapters in prestigious editorials like IGI Global, Springer and Routledge-Taylor & Francis. Also, she has edited books in editorial like Springer and Palgrave McMillan.

Francisco José Alcaraz-Quiles is an Associate Professor in Accounting in the Financial Economic and Accounting Department of the University of Granada in Spain. He is member of the Spanish Association of Accounting University Teachers and of European Accounting Association. He has diverse publications in national and international journal as RC-Spanish Accounting Review, Journal of Cleaner Production, Lex Localis- Journal of Local self-government, or International Review of Administrative Sciences. His research interests include public administration, sustainability, accountability, and transparency by the public sector.

* * *

Elvettin Akman completed his education till bachelor's degree in Ankara. He completed his bachelor degree at the Department of Public Administration of Süleyman Demirel University and then got a master degree from Sakarya University, Institute of Social Sciences, Public Administration Department with his thesis entitled "Social Responsibility in Local Government Management: Çankaya Municipality Example". He completed his doctorate with the thesis entitled "Analysis of public policy and law - making process in Turkey" at Süleyman Demirel University Social Sciences Institute Public Administration Department. He works as an Assistant Professor in Süleyman Demirel University, Faculty of Economics and Administrative Sciences, Department of Political Science and Public Administration. He has three edited books titled "Social Responsibility with Different Viewpoints", "Social Work with Social Policy and Public Administration Composition" and "Public Administration Education" and many academic articles.

Cristina Alcaide-Muñoz is a Ph.D. student in Business Administration Department of Public University of Navarre (Spain). She holds a research grant in the Department of Business Administration, focusing on High-Performance manufacturing organizations. Her research encompasses information technologies and operations management, particularly, quality management and strategic planning. Moreover, she is teaching operations management and human resources management at Public University of Navarre.

Rasim Alguliyev is director of the Institute of Information Technology of Azerbaijan National Academy of Sciences (ANAS) and academician-secretary of ANAS. He is full member of ANAS and full professor. He received BSc and MSc in electronic computing machines from Azerbaijan Technical University in 1979. He received his PhD and Doctor of Science (higher degree after PhD) in Computer Science in 1995 and 2003, respectively. His research interests include: Information Security, Information Society, E-Government; Online Social Network Analysis, Cloud Computing, Evolutionary and Swarm Computation, Data Mining, Big Data Analytics, and Scientometrics. He is author of more than 580 papers, 4 monographs, 4 patents, and several books. He is the Editor-in-Chief of the journals Problems of Information Technologies and Problems of Information Society.

Fatimah Alsaif is an interior architect and researcher. She has PhD in Architecture from Victoria university of Wellington. She is passionate about designing and renovating learning environments. She is also keen in using participatory design in her work.

Cenay Babaoglu received his Ph. D. degree in public administration from the Department of Political Science and Public Administration at Hacettepe University. He works in the Department of Public Administration at Nigde Omer Halisdemir University as assistant professor. His research topics are public policy, Turkish administrative history, the relationship between information and communication technologies and public administration.

Ransome Epie Bawack is a research assistant with the Artificial Intelligence and Management Sciences Research Group (GRIAGES) at the Catholic University of Central Africa (CUCA), Cameroon. He obtained a Master's degree in Management and Information Systems from CUCA in 2017, and a Bachelor's degree in

Computer engineering from the University of Buea, Cameroon in 2013. His has published in the International Journal of Medical Informatics (IJMI). His current research focuses on the big data, cloud computing, health information systems, financial technology, ERP, and the business value of IT.

Ma. Beth S. Concepcion is currently pursuing her doctoral degree in information technology at De La Salle University (DLSU) - Manila, Philippines. She obtained her master's degree in information management at University of St. La Salle - Bacolod last 2009. She received her bachelor's degree in information management at West Visayas State University – Iloilo in 2002, Cum Laude. She is an Associate Professor of the College of Information and Communications Technology, West Visayas State University. She also served as College Secretary (2010-2014) and Chairperson of the Department of Information Systems (2004-2010). She worked as a research assistant at DLSU - Jesse Robredo Institute of Governance for a research project in Open Government Open Government Data under the International Development Research Centre (IDRC) and the World Wide Web Foundation (2014-2016). Ms. Concepcion presented and published research papers on open data, information systems, decision support systems, data analytics, technopreneurship, and innovation.

Samuel Fosso Wamba, Ph.D., HDR, is a Full Professor at the Toulouse Business School, France. He earned an MSc in Mathematics from the University of Sherbrooke in Canada, an MSc in e-commerce from HEC Montreal, Canada, and a PhD in industrial engineering for his work on RFID-enabled supply chain transformation from the Polytechnic School of Montreal, Canada. His current research focuses on business value of IT, business analytics, big data, inter-organizational system (e.g. RFID technology) adoption and use, e-government, IT-enabled social inclusion, IT and talent management, supply chain management, electronic commerce and mobile commerce. He has published papers in the proceedings of a number of international conferences (IEEE, AMCIS, HICSS, ICIS, and PACIS) and in renowned international journals, including the Academy of Management Journal, European Journal of Information Systems, Production Planning and Control, the International Journal of Production Economics, Information Systems Frontiers, the International Journal of Production Research, the Business Process Management Journal, etc. He has been organizing special issues on IT-related topics for top IS and OM journals. He is CompTIA-RFID+ certified. More information at: http://fossowambasamuel.com.

Christiana Soares de Freitas has a PhD in Sociology of Science and Technology at the University of Brasilia (UnB/Brazil). She has been a faculty member at the University of Brasilia since then. She is currently Professor Adjunct IV. She teaches undergraduate courses at the Public Policy Department and graduate and post-graduate courses at the Law School of the same university. She is a founding member of the National Institute of Digital Democracy (INCT.DD) in Brazil. She coordinates the Research Group on State, Regulation, Internet and Society (GERIS/ UnB) since 2015. Her areas of expertise include innovation in the public sector; digital democracy; crowdsourcing and crowdlaw; internet and governance regulation; public policy studies.

Hwang Ha Jin received MBA (1986) and Doctor of Business Administration (1990) from Mississippi State University, USA. He taught at Minnesota State University (Associate Professor of MIS, 1989-1991), Mankato, Minnesota, USA., Australian Catholic University (ACU, Visiting Professor, 2009, Visiting Senior Lecturer, 1999), North Sydney, Australia, Catholic University of Daegu (1991-2010), Korea, and KIMEP University, Kazakhstan (2010-2016). He is currently Head and Professor of Information Systems at Department of Business Analytics, Sunway University Business School, Sunway University (SU), Malaysia. Before joining SU in August 2016, He had worked at KIMEP University, Kazakhstan for six years, where he served as Dean of Bang College of Business (2014-2016) and Professor of Operations Management and Information Systems. He also served as Vice President of External Relations and Cooperation (2005-2009) and Associate Vice President of Academic Affairs (1997-1999) for Catholic University of Daegu, Korea. He has been serving as Editor-In-Chief for International Journal of Hybrid Information Technology since August 2011. He served as President of Korea Association of Information Systems (2005) and President of Korea Internet Electronic Commerce Association (2008). He also served as Publicity Chair for IEEE/ACIS International Conference (2008), Portland, U.S.A., and Conference Chair for KAIS International Conference (2005), Daegu, Korea. He has published articles in numerous journals such as International Journal of Multimedia and Ubiquitous Engineering, International Journal of Software Engineering and Its Applications, International Journal of Computer and Information Science, and many top-tier Korean journals. He has also published books including Electronic Commerce/Electronic Business (coauthor, 4th edition, 2012), Ubiquitous Computing and u-Business(2006), Management Information Systems (2005), 21st Century Digital Business (2004).

Jean Robert Kala Kamdjoug received his BSc Degree and MSc in Mathematics and Computer science from the University of Yaoundé 1, Cameroon, MSc in Decision System from LILLE 1 University - Science and Technology and obtained his Ph.D. in Mathematics and Computer Science from the EHESS and Telecom Bretagne. Dr. Kala Kamdjoug is currently an Associate Professor of Information System, Operational research, Computer Science and Head of Management Department at the FSSM (Faculty of Social Science and Management) of CUCA (Catholic

University of Central Africa). His current research interests are business value of IT, Information System, Decision Support System, e-government, IT-enabled social inclusion and electronic commerce, mobile commerce, and Social Commerce. To date, He has published papers in the proceedings of a number of international conferences (AMCIS, WorldCIST, ICTO and AIM) and in renowned international journals, including International Journal of Medical Informatics, Computational Economics, Savings and development, African Review of Money Finance and Banking, Revue Sciences de Gestion, International Journal of Technology Diffusion, Advances in Economics and Business, Revue des Sciences de Gestion.

Isabela Nascimento is currently a student at the Department of Public Policy Studies at the University of Brasilia, Brazil. Participates in the Research Group on State, Regulation, Internet and Society (GERIS) and works with Transparency and Information Access Law in Ministry of Social Development. Her area of research and fields of interest are: Social Participation, Human Rights, Gender and Sexuality, Political and Digital Activism, Transparency.

S. R. Nikhashemi is a Senior Lecturer at the Department of Marketing, Sunway University Business School, Malaysia. He received his Ph.D. Degree from the University Putra Malaysia and holds a Master Degree in Business Administration in Marketing and Bachelor in Accounting. He has published in several high-ranking journals such as Journal of Management Development, Asia Pacific Journal of Marketing and Logistics, Journal of Fashion Marketing and Management, Global Business Review, International Journal of Quality and Service Sciences, among others.

Aime Noutsa Fobang, after his Master's degree, decided to go further in his education contributing on Scientific Research. He is a Young researcher at GRIAGES-UCAC (Cameroon). Interested in various topics related to Information Systems mainly HRIS, ICT adoption, E-participation, or data science. He has published some articles in some journals and books.

Sherwin E. Ona is Associate professor of Political Science and Development Studies at De La Salle University (DLSU). He is also a senior researcher of the Jesse M. Robredo Institute of Governance. Dr. Ona was the former research director of the College of Computer Studies, DLSU where he served as faculty member until his transfer to the political science department of the College of Liberal Arts in 2013. As part of his research endeavors, Dr. Ona was one of the proponents of the e-Participation in local communities project funded by the International Development Research Corporation (IDRC), a crown company of Canada. In 2012, he was also part of IDRC's "Open Data for Developing Countries" initiative, a network of research teams from Africa, Latin America, and Asia that examined the challenges and opportunities of Open government data in developing countries. In 2013, the ODDC engagement was further continued with a research grant from the IDRC on the development of a competency-based training program for Open Government. At present, Dr. Ona is one of the senior team leads for the project entitled, "Uncovering ICT-enabled Innovation spaces in DRRM" under the Newton-Agham project of the British Council and CHED.

Rodrigo Sandoval-Almazan received his Ph. D. in Administrative Sciences from the Tecnológico de Monterrey. He is a full professor and researcher at Autonomous University of the State of México. He writes and presents widely on issues of E-Government, Open Government, and Social Media areas. Additionally, he is level 2 of the National System of Researchers in Mexico, member of the Digital Government Society, Director of NOVAGOB Lab Mexico.

Naser Valaei is a PostDoc researcher at Department of Marketing, KEDGE Business School, Talence, France. His research has been published in Journal of Business Research, Computers in Human Behaviour, Information Technology & People, Marketing Intelligence & Planning, VINE, Technology Analysis & Strategic Management, Management Research Review, Journal of Marketing Channels, International Review of Retail, Distribution, and Consumer Research, Asia Pacific Journal of Marketing and Logistics, Hospitality and Tourism Research, among others. He serves as a reviewer to various international refereed journals.

Brenda Vale wrote her first book on sustainable design in 1975. Following their design of award winning commercial buildings in the UK, by 1998 they built the award winning first autonomous house and the first zero-emissions settlement there. They developed the Australian government's National Australian Built Environment Rating System (NABERS), now in operation. Their current research is in the field of ecological footprints, resilience and behaviour, with four published books in this area.

David Valle-Cruz received his Ph. D. in Economic and Administrative Sciences from the Autonomous University of the State of Mexico in 2017. He has a Master Degree in Informatics and is a Computer Engineer. His research is related to E-Government, Open Government, Social Media, Emerging Technologies and Artificial Intelligence issues. Nowadays, he is professor in informatics at Autonomous University of the State of Mexico. He has been awarded as the best paper and poster in the Annual International Conference on Digital Government Research.

Farhad Yusifov received his Master's degree in data processing and automation control systems from Azerbaijan State Oil Academy in Baku, Azerbaijan. He received his PhD degree in 2010 from Institute of Information Technology of ANAS. His primary research interests include various areas in e-government, public administration, e-governance, e-voting, social media, particularly in the area of Web usage mining. Since 2010, he is a member of editorial board of journals Problems of Information Technologies and Problems of Information Society. He is the head of department of Institute of Information Technology of ANAS. He is the author of more than 40 papers.

Index

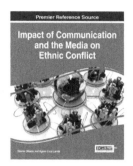

Stay Current on the Latest Emerging Research Developments

Become an IGI Global Reviewer for Authored Book Projects

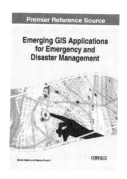

Premier Reference Source

Emerging GIS Applications for Emergency and Disaster Management

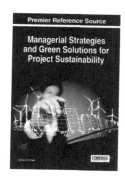

Premier Reference Source

Managerial Strategies and Green Solutions for Project Sustainability

Premier Reference Source

Comparative Approaches to Using R and Python for Statistical Data Analysis

Premier Reference Source

Solutions for High-Touch Communications in a High-Tech World

The overall success of an authored book project is dependent on quality and timely reviews.

In this competitive age of scholarly publishing, constructive and timely feedback significantly decreases the turnaround time of manuscripts from submission to acceptance, allowing the publication and discovery of progressive research at a much more expeditious rate. Several IGI Global authored book projects are currently seeking highly qualified experts in the field to fill vacancies on their respective editorial review boards:

Applications may be sent to:
development@igi-global.com

Applicants must have a doctorate (or an equivalent degree) as well as publishing and reviewing experience. Reviewers are asked to write reviews in a timely, collegial, and constructive manner. All reviewers will begin their role on an ad-hoc basis for a period of one year, and upon successful completion of this term can be considered for full editorial review board status, with the potential for a subsequent promotion to Associate Editor.

If you have a colleague that may be interested in this opportunity,
we encourage you to share this information with them.

Printed in the United States
By Bookmasters